ENGAGING
with
Barth

ENGAGING
with *Barth*

Contemporary evangelical critiques

Edited by David Gibson *and* Daniel Strange

APOLLOS

APOLLOS (an imprint of Inter-Varsity Press)
Norton Street, Nottingham NG7 3HR, England
Email: ivp@ivpbooks.com
Website: www.ivpbooks.com

First published 2008

British Library Cataloguing in Publication Data
A catalogue record for this book is available from the British Library.
ISBN: 978-1-84474-245-5

Set in Monotype Garamond 11/13pt
Typeset in Great Britain by Servis Filmsetting Limited, Manchester
Printed and bound in Great Britain by Ashford Colour Press Ltd, Gosport, Hampshire

Inter-Varsity Press publishes Christian books that are true to the Bible and that communicate the gospel, develop discipleship and strengthen the church for its mission in the world.

Inter-Varsity Press is closely linked with the Universities and Colleges Christian Fellowship, a student movement connecting Christian Unions in universities and colleges throughout Great Britain, and a member movement of the International Fellowship of Evangelical Students. Website: www.uccf.org.uk.

CONTENTS

CONTRIBUTORS

Henri Blocher is Gunter H. Knoedler Professor of Systematic Theology, Wheaton College Graduate School of Biblical and Theological Studies, Illinois, and is *doyen honoraire* at the Faculté Libre de Théologie Évangélique in Vaux-sur-Seine, where he was formerly Professor of Systematic Theology. He is President of the Fellowship of European Evangelical Theologians. His books include *In the Beginning* (IVP, 1984), *Evil and the Cross* (Apollos, 1994) and *Original Sin: Illuminating the Riddle* (Apollos, 2004).

Oliver D. Crisp is Lecturer in Theology, University of Bristol, UK. Previously, he taught at the University of St Andrews (2002–4) and was the Frederick J. Crosson Research Fellow at the Center for Philosophy of Religion, University of Notre Dame, USA (2004–5). He is the author of *Jonathan Edwards and the Metaphysics of Sin* (Ashgate, 2005), *Divinity and Humanity: The Incarnation Reconsidered* (Cambridge University Press, 2007) and *An American Augustinian: Sin and Salvation in the Dogmatic Theology of William G. T. Shedd* (Paternoster, 2007). He also co-edited *Jonathan Edwards: Philosophical Theologian* (Ashgate, 2003) with Paul Helm.

David Gibson is Associate Minister at High Church, Hilton, Aberdeen. He studied theology at Nottingham University and King's College London, and has worked as a Staff Worker for the Religious and Theological Studies Fellowship, part of UCCF. He has published a number of articles and was a contributor to *Encountering God's Word: Beginning Biblical Studies* (Apollos, 2003). He is a doctoral candidate at the University of Aberdeen, where his thesis examines the exegesis of election in Calvin and Barth.

Ryan Glomsrud is a DPhil candidate at the University of Oxford. He holds a BA from Wheaton College, Illinois, and an MA from Westminster Seminary California. His research interests include nineteenth-century German intellectual and cultural history as well as the history of the Reformed theological tradition. His dissertation explores Karl Barth's relationship to the Protestant Reformation, early Reformed orthodoxy, and nineteenth-century historiography of the tradition. He is a visiting doctoral student (Graduate in Residence) at Harvard Divinity School.

Paul Helm was Professor of the History and Philosophy of Religion, King's College London, 1993–2000, and previously a Reader in Philosophy at the University of Liverpool. He held the J. I. Packer Chair of Philosophical Theology at Regent College, Vancouver, 2001–5, where he is a Teaching Fellow. His books include *Eternal God* (Clarendon, 1988), *The Providence of God* (IVP, 1993) and *John Calvin's Ideas* (Oxford University Press, 2004).

Michael S. Horton is J. Gresham Machen Professor of Systematic Theology at Westminster Seminary California, and editor of *Modern Reformation* magazine. To date three volumes of his four-part project have appeared: *Covenant and Eschatology: The Divine Drama* (Westminster John Knox, 2002), *Lord and Servant: A Covenant Christology* (Westminster John Knox, 2005) and *Covenant and Salvation: Union with Christ* (Westminster John Knox, 2007). He has also authored *God of Promise: Introducing Covenant Theology* (Baker, 2006).

A. T. B. McGowan is Principal of the Highland Theological College, Dingwall, Scotland. He holds an Honorary Professorship in Reformed Doctrine at the University of Aberdeen, is an Adjunct Professor of Theology at Reformed Theological Seminary and a Visiting Professor of Theology at Westminster Theological Seminary, Philadelphia. His most recent publications are (ed.), *Always Reforming: Explorations in Systematic Theology* (Apollos, 2006), 'Justification and the *Ordo Salutis*', in Bruce L. McCormack (ed.), *Justification in Perspective: Historical Developments and Contemporary Challenges* (Baker, 2006) and *The Divine Spiration of Scripture* (Apollos, 2007).

Donald Macleod has been Professor of Systematic Theology at the Free Church of Scotland College, Edinburgh, since 1978, and Principal since

1999. Prior to his appointment to the college he served in two pastoral charges, first, in Kilmallie (Inverness-shire) and then in Partick (Glasgow). His books include *The Person of Christ* (IVP, 1998) and *Jesus Is Lord: Christology Yesterday and Today* (Mentor, 2001).

Michael J. Ovey is Principal of Oak Hill Theological College, London, where he also teaches doctrine and apologetics. He read law at Oxford and worked as a lawyer drafting Government legislation. Theological study at Cambridge was followed by serving as a curate at All Saints Crowborough, and a doctoral thesis in patristic trinitarian theology from King's College London. He has also taught at Moore Theological College, Sydney, where he completed an MTh on John's Gospel. He is the co-author of *Pierced for our Transgressions* (IVP, 2007).

Sebastian Rehnman (BA, MPhil, Gothenburg University; DPhil, University of Oxford) is Professor of Philosophy of Religion at Misjonshøgskolen, Stavanger, Head of the Department of Systematic Theology, Johannelunds teologiska högskola, Uppsala, and Docent of Philosophy of Religion at Uppsala University. He has been a visiting scholar to the University of Oxford and Yale University. His publications include *Divine Discourse: The Theological Methodology of John Owen* (Baker Academic, 2002).

Daniel Strange is Lecturer in Culture, Religion and Public Theology at Oak Hill Theological College, London. Previously, he was Co-ordinator of the Religious and Theological Studies Fellowship. His doctoral dissertation, undertaken at the University of Bristol and entitled *The Possibility of Salvation among the Unevangelised: An Analysis of Inclusivism in Recent Evangelical Theology*, was published by Paternoster in 2002. He has published a number of other articles and chapters in the area of the theology of religions and systematic theology.

Mark D. Thompson is Academic Dean and Head of Theology at Moore Theological College, Sydney. His doctoral research was at the University of Oxford, where he studied the doctrine of Scripture in the theology of Martin Luther. He is the author of numerous articles and *A Sure Ground on Which to Stand* (Paternoster, 2004), *A Clear and Present Word: The Clarity of Scripture* (Apollos, 2006), *Too Big for Words? The Transcendent God and Finite Human Language* (Latimer House, 2006). He was joint editor of *The Gospel to the Nations* (Apollos, 2000).

Garry J. Williams is Academic Dean of Oak Hill Theological College, London, where he teaches church history and doctrine. He read theology at

Oxford where he later completed a doctorate on Hugo Grotius' understanding of the atonement. Since 2005 he has been Visiting Professor of Historical
Theology at Westminster Theological Seminary, Philadelphia. He has published on subjects including the history of evangelicalism and the atonement,
and is writing a biblical, historical and systematic exposition of penal substitutionary atonement.

ABBREVIATIONS

BDAG W. Bauer, W. F. Arndt, F. W. Gingrich and F. W. Danker, *A Greek-English Lexicon of the New Testament and Other Early Christian Literature*, 3rd ed. (Chicago: University of Chicago Press, 1999)

BECNT Baker Exegetical Commentary on the New Testament

CD Karl Barth, *Church Dogmatics*, ed. G. W. Bromiley and T. F. Torrance (Edinburgh: T. & T. Clark, 1956–75)

CSEL Corpus scriptorum ecclesiasticorum latinorum

CTJ *Calvin Theological Journal*

ET English translation

EQ *Evangelical Quarterly*

ESV English Standard Version

EuroJTh *European Journal of Theology*

EvT *Evangelische Theologie*

ExAud *Ex auditu*

GD Karl Barth, *The Göttingen Dogmatics: Instruction in the Christian Religion*, vol. 1, trans. G. W. Bromiley, ed. H. Reiffen (Grand Rapids: Eerdmans, 1991)

ICC International Critical Commentary

IJST *International Journal of Systematic Theology*

JETS *Journal of the Evangelical Theological Society*

JSNT *Journal for the Study of the New Testament*

JTS	*Journal of Theological Studies*
KD	Karl Barth, *Die kirchliche Dogmatik* (Munich: C. Kaiser, 1932; Zurich: Evangelischer Verlag, 1938–67)
LXX	The Septuagint
MT	The Masoretic Text
NICNT	New International Commentary on the New Testament
NIGTC	New International Greek Testament Commentary
NIV	New International Version
NKJV	New King James Version
NT	New Testament
OT	Old Testament
ProEccl	*Pro ecclesia*
RelS	*Religious Studies*
RSV	Revised Standard Version
SBET	*Scottish Bulletin of Evangelical Theology*
SJT	*Scottish Journal of Theology*
Them	*Themelios*
TNIV	Today's New International Version
TrinJ	*Trinity Journal*
TS	*Theological Studies*
WBC	Word Biblical Commentary
WTJ	*Westminster Theological Journal*

FOREWORD

The Anglo-American evangelical infatuation with the thought of Karl Barth is not a recent phenomenon. Indeed, while the reception of Barth in places such as Switzerland, Germany, the Netherlands and South Africa was far from creedally orthodox, there has been a tradition in Britain and the United States of reading him in as evangelical and orthodox a way as possible. For example, the Torrance brothers, T. F. and James, and Colin Gunton, while not self-identifying as evangelicals in terms of, say, the UCCF Doctrinal Basis, nevertheless offered readings of Barth that addressed topics of central evangelical concern, such as incarnation and atonement, and also brought to the fore certain areas of classic orthodoxy to which evangelicalism pays lip service but often in practice neglects, such as the Trinity.

Such appropriation of Barth was, perhaps, not surprising. It is true that the reception of Barth's works in other countries has tended to be in a manner theologically and ecclesiastically antithetical to traditions of evangelical orthodoxy; but in the English-speaking world a tradition developed where he was generally presented as a figure who offered a profound critique of liberalism and a means whereby evangelicalism could respond to, or perhaps better 'sidestep', the criticism of some of its most cherished positions (most obviously the inspiration and authority of Scripture), without abandoning orthodoxy. There were, of course, strident voices that opposed such a reception, most notably Cornelius Van Til and his followers; but Van Til's critique failed to carry the day in Anglo-American evangelical circles.

Yet for all of the positive appropriation of Barth, broader concerns remained with his theology. In addition to Barth's own disdain for conservative evangelicalism, there was also the apparent incipient universalism; the positive appropriation of the slippery *Historie* (that which is reported as fact) and *Geschichte* (the interpretation of that fact) distinction; the radical Christological reconstruction of the concept of revelation; and, perhaps above all, the sheer vastness and complexity of the *Church Dogmatics*, which militated against a unified and coherent account of his thought, something that should surely be basic to any positive interaction. Indeed, there sometimes seem as many Barths as there are Barthians. To all this, one might also add the practical, ecclesiastical point: the failure of Barthianism to stem the collapse of Europe's churches, both numerically and doctrinally. This last observation is, perhaps, the greatest elephant in the room when it comes to discussing how Barth's thought impacts preaching and the Christian life.

In the early nineties, it appeared to me that Barth had probably had his day. His theological writings, while always stimulating, had a very dated, 1950s feel about them; and, while beloved by a few theological intellectuals, his ideas made no impact on the grass roots of the church. In addition, the one major mainstream comprehensive Protestant systematic theology to emerge at that time, the one that sought to carry theological discussion forward, was that of Wolfhart Pannenberg; and his work marked a return to precisely the questions of history that Barth had dismissed as theologically wrong-headed. I well remember a debate at about this time over a cup of coffee with colleagues on faculty in the Theology Department at the University of Nottingham. We were discussing the resurrection of Christ: both myself and an atheist colleague agreed that whether the tomb was empty or not was absolutely crucial for the validity of the Christian faith; my Barthian colleague, with whom I shared a common orthodox vocabulary, thought that the historicity of the resurrection was irrelevant. The discussion seemed to me to capture how the same old questions that divide liberals and evangelicals keep coming back to haunt us: the Barthian bomb had detonated in the playground of the theologians, but now the noise and dust had died down and the children had returned to playing their traditional games.

Yet over a decade after that conversation, it seems that positive reception of Barth by evangelicals continues apace. Why is this? Four reasons come to mind (though this is by no means an exhaustive list). First, Barth's view of Scripture is both aesthetically appealing (all the talk of a *dynamic* view of Scripture over the alleged *static* conceptions of traditional evangelical orthodoxy), and apparently allows for a form of scriptural authority that is not destroyed by the hard critical questions about the Bible text and about historicity. Indeed, the emphasis on hermeneutics in contemporary evangelical theology is obviously more conducive to positive Barth reception than the concern of an earlier generation for inspiration. Second, the provisionality of Barth's theology is, again, aesthetically appealing to a world where claims to truth have a distasteful ring of arrogance about them. Third, the *Historie–Geschichte* distinction is attractive to a form of evangelicalism that has picked up on certain currents in linguistic philosophy, with its implications for the perceived relevance of questions about extratextual referentiality. Finally, and positively connected to all the above, the current obsession in some quarters with story and narrative makes aspects of Barth's project most seductive.

Of course, these are not insubstantial or irrelevant issues, and we ignore them at our peril. But is Barth the answer? On one level, I would most definitely say no. For myself, I believe Herman Bavinck, the great Dutch theologian, offers a more helpful resource on each of these points; but, on another level, interacting with Barth as a great mind wrestling with serious issues is surely of tremendous value. I often tell my students that great theologians are most helpful at precisely those points where I disagree with them, for it is there I am forced to wrestle most passionately, and there that my own thought is clarified and strengthened.

Given all these issues, and the fact that Barth looks set to remain a polarizing factor in evangelical thought and politics, it is a pleasure to commend the following chapters. The authors have all resisted the temptation to become infatuated with Barth, but have also avoided the kind of caricaturing that serves to do nothing other than break the Ninth Commandment. For those looking for a way to appreciate Barth and to remain really evangelical, this collection will prove a stimulating and thought-provoking read. I hope that it not only opens up new vistas of non-infatuated evangelical discussion of Barth, but also helps to carry forward the discussion of central elements of Christian orthodoxy.

Carl R. Trueman
Professor of Historical Theology and Church History
Westminster Theological Seminary (Pennsylvania)

INTRODUCTION

David Gibson and Daniel Strange

In *Karl Barth: His Life from Letters and Autobiographical Texts*, in the preface 'To the English Reader', Eberhard Busch observes:

> More than perhaps any other theologian in the twentieth century, Karl Barth has dominated the subject-matter of theology and posed the questions with which the theologians of the different churches have been, and are, occupied, although they may want to 'go beyond' him, go back behind him or even protest against his answers.[1]

This volume aims to engage with Karl Barth's questions and answers on a range of topics vital to Christian theology. Specifically, whether by going beyond, behind or against Barth, the chapters presented here attempt to provide a contemporary orientation to certain aspects of Barth's theology that can be deemed problematic from the standpoint of historic, confessional evangelicalism. Why engage with Barth? And why the particular approach of this book?

The answer to the first question is that Barth's significance as arguably the greatest theologian of the twentieth century – increasingly being recognized

---

1. *Karl Barth: His Life from Letters and Autobiographical Texts*, trans. J. Bowden (Grand Rapids: Eerdmans, 1994), p. xiii.

in an ongoing renaissance of international Barth scholarship – means that Barth provides both opportunity and challenge for evangelicalism. There is renewed interest in the question of how evangelicals should or should not appropriate Barth. Given the sheer diversity within worldwide evangelicalism, a consensus is unlikely to be reached. Be that as it may, in a range of areas, evangelical theology stands to gain from careful and critical listening to what Barth has to say.

As undergraduate students studying in British departments of theology and religious studies, encountering Karl Barth in our lecture room for the first time was a welcome breath of fresh air rather than a devastating bombshell. Here was a theologian who appeared to speak the language of historic confessional orthodoxy with both passion and verve; someone who sought to relocate and refocus the theological task within and towards its proper place – the believing community of faith; someone whose contribution to theology in the last hundred years had been so gargantuan that it could span what we were beginning to think were the incommensurable worlds of evangelical theology and the theology of the modern university. Barth's life (1886–1968) and theological development is the story of a passionate revolt against Protestant liberalism, and the setting of an entirely new agenda for theology in Barth's turn to the Bible as divine address to humanity. Indeed, the significance of Barth as a reader of Holy Scripture from the earliest days of his academic career is only just beginning to be appreciated. As well as awakening a new interest in the Bible, Barth provided a massive recovery of the Reformed tradition within academic theology, and on page after page of the *Church Dogmatics* creates stunning depth and breadth for Christian doctrine in a way unparalleled in the modern era. The reader will find that these aspects of Barth's project – and many more besides – are well appreciated in this book. In the light of such factors, we suggest that an evangelicalism that engages with Barth thoughtfully and meditates carefully on his corpus with critical discernment will be an evangelicalism enriched in its basic confession. Barth offers too much simply to ignore and the gateway he provides to the tradition too absorbingly rich and imaginative, too multifaceted to be simplistically rejected. Evangelical theology has no future in this kind of obscurantism, itself often born out of the worst kind of insecurity.

The answer to the second question is that, rightly or wrongly, we perceive there to be an imbalance in the current literature. While there are numerous excellent studies highlighting the richness of Barth's thinking and delineating his theology in a range of areas, more cautionary voices about certain aspects of his project are thin on the ground. One could make a case that in many quarters Barth's theology is increasingly received with ringing endorsement (the odd critical adjustment notwithstanding) as the most compelling account of orthodox, and indeed Reformed, post-Kantian Christianity. This book is an attempt to engage critically with this emerging status quo by suggesting that in key places Barth has not seen further and higher than those on whose shoulders he stands. Barth's theology contains not only a restatement of orthodoxy but also substantial revisions to it, and there is little by way of contemporary analysis and critique of those revisions. Where Barth is wrong, the consequences may be extremely serious for a variety of theological and pastoral issues, and these concerns need to be highlighted. An evangelicalism that appropriates aspects of Barth's theology without substantial criticism will be an evangelicalism that is impoverished in central aspects of its witness and confession of the gospel.

Our aim, then, in this book is to model courteous and critical engagement with Barth in some of the places where we suggest he does not offer a satisfactory way of interpreting Scripture, reading church history and confessing Christian doctrine. We realize that such comments may seem incongruous, even embarrassing, in a work of academic theology. However we would argue that Barth himself has given us the confessional platform, context, language and even tone to make such comments. For outside the often sterile feel of the academy and within the life of the body of Christ, we wish passionately to affirm that theology really matters; that the healthy up-building of disciples really matters; and that our discernment as to whether or not the content of thinking presented as Christian theology keeps 'the pattern of sound teaching' (2 Tim. 1:13) really matters.

We hope this book contributes clearly and constructively to further debate about Barth's theology in general and its relation to evangelical theology in particular. Indeed, the aim of the book is not negative but rather renders engagement with Barth as a subservient task to the wider programme of constructive theological thinking that seeks to articulate the gospel for the contemporary world. In this sense, this book is simply one movement in a range of interpretive ventures that must be carried out by constructive Christian dogmatics. We hope that where others are involved in this more fundamental task, the contents of this volume will help highlight avenues of faithfulness to the gospel that need to be explored on a deeper and broader scale.

It is important to stress that each chapter aims to model what critical comment might look like in individual instances: they are in no way offered as definitive statements on all of Barth's exegesis, or all of his historical or systematic theology! Given that Barth's most comprehensive theological undertaking was his *Church Dogmatics*, it is right that the weight of the book focuses on this dogmatic enterprise. We have deliberately kept an overall theological emphasis and have not treated a range of issues that may be discussed in the light of Barth's theology (e.g. politics or postmodernity).

We are grateful to the contributors and to others who gave invaluable advice along the way. In particular, we wish to thank Suzanne McDonald, Andrew Sach, Edwin Tay and Mark Thompson. Each of them offered constructive comments in the early stages that helped shape the project towards the final result. We are also grateful to Carl Trueman for writing the foreword, and to Phil Duce, Theological Books Editor at IVP, for his attentive help at every point and for his encouragement and support with the initial proposal.

We owe a special debt of thanks to our wives, Angela and Elly respectively. With immeasurable patience and grace they bore with husbands working out of hours during a time in which both our families welcomed new arrivals. We are grateful to them beyond words.

Soli Deo gloria.

1. KARL BARTH'S CHRISTOCENTRIC METHOD

Henri Blocher

Forty years after their demise (the time of trial in Scripture!), most theologians, even famous ones, are remembered by only a few. Karl Barth remains present on the scene and one can observe a new wave of interest in his contribution, one that brings forth a plethora of Barth studies. This lease of posthumous life may lend credibility to Thomas F. Torrance's appreciation: 'Karl Barth is the greatest theological genius that has appeared on the scene for centuries.'[1] But, soberly, it is still too early to tell. If the analysis is right, that Barth appealed, after the Second World War, to liberals because he enabled them to recover the themes of Christian tradition without renouncing biblical criticism, and to conservatives because they felt they could remain faithful to the gospel and yet escape the rigidity and isolation of their training,[2] the current

---

1. 'Introduction', *Barth, Theology and Church: Shorter Writings, 1920–1928*, trans. L. Pettibone Smith (New York: Harper & Row, 1962), p. 7.
2. R. A. Muller, 'The Place and Importance of Karl Barth in the Twentieth Century: A Review Essay', *WTJ* 50 (1988), p. 152; R. H. Roberts, 'The Reception of the Theology of Karl Barth in the Anglo-Saxon World: History, Typology and Prospect', in S. W. Sykes (ed.), *Karl Barth: Centenary Essays* (Cambridge: Cambridge University Press, 1989), esp. p. 131; G. Dorrien, *The Barthian Revolt in Modern Theology: Theology Without Weapons* (Louisville: Westminster John Knox, 2000), pp. 10–11, 80, 163.

Barthian 'revival' among a younger generation may raise interesting questions.[3]
In any case, it shows how relevant a new scrutiny of Barth's legacy should
appear today.

One conspicuous feature of Barth's theology has attracted many readers:
the role Jesus Christ plays, not only as a topic, but as the determinative reference and model for the construction of Barth's whole discourse. His *method* is
Christological, if one does not give too technical a sense to the word. The
focus of the present investigation will be the role of Jesus Christ and the way
it shapes Barth's theology as it unfolds.

Preliminary remarks are in order on what may be called 'Barth hermeneutics': how should one read Barth? Hunsinger complains that 'even his most
sympathetic interpreters (to say nothing of determined opponents) often end
up distorting him, offering little more than a caricature to be either embraced
or dismissed'.[4] One must warn against the temptation to tame what sounds
most daring in Barth's expression. Jacques Maritain observes that every strong,
revolutionary thinker finds commentators 'who *tone down* or who *drain off* the
meaning'[5] – who tame the tiger. Many readers, when they come upon statements that overthrow their beliefs, that offend common sense, that seem to
involve contradiction, cannot believe the author really meant such a thing –
especially if the author has impressed them with his science and subtlety, and
even more if the author is prestigious! They automatically 'correct' what they
read. Such statements abound under Barth's pen, for example that demons are
real but have no being; that eternal life is no life continuing after death; that an
event that happens once for all happens, *for that reason*, 'on several occasions'.[6]
The combination of Barth's commanding tone with a style 'full of reversals,
upsets, conundrums and surprises'[7] tends to paralyse further inquiry. He

---

3. George Hunsinger comments on the interest shown by 'younger scholars' for what
    he calls 'the postliberalism of Barth and Balthasar' in two representative
    institutions. See *Disruptive Grace: Studies in the Theology of Karl Barth* (Grand Rapids:
    Eerdmans, 2000), p. 16.
4. *Disruptive Grace*, p. 253. Hunsinger comments, 'With his uniquely innovative blend
    of modernism and traditionalism, he has continually baffled modernists and
    traditionalists alike' (ibid.).
5. *La Philosophie morale: Examen historique et critique des grands systèmes* (Paris: Gallimard
    NRF, 1960), p. 219, n. 1 (I have translated all quotations from works not published
    in English.)
6. Respectively, *CD* III/3, p. 523; *CD* III/2, p. 632; IV/4, p. 39.
7. Hunsinger, *Disruptive Grace*, p. 9.

tempts his interpreters to a flattering reading by using traditional language – with a different meaning.[8] Yet, the failure to integrate shocking utterances and, in Berkouwer's words, 'to interpret Barth as "harmless" . . . is to misunderstand the fundamental structure of his thinking and to do him a gross injustice'.[9]

Two issues of substance bear upon interpretation of Barth: to what extent should one presume Barth to be consistent with himself? And this, also, through the various stages of his career? Most writers stress his aversion to system, and Jean-Louis Leuba charged J. Hamer with gross error because he had 'systematized' the target of his critique.[10] Barth bluntly claimed that, on many points, 'dogmatics must be inconsistent from a logical point of view'.[11] Yet, while still recoiling from the ambition of building a system, he came to recognize that theology ought to reflect the coherence of truth, to look 'somewhat like a system' (*etwas wie ein System*).[12] He is reported to have said, 'Under God's humour, one can also have, after all, a system.'[13] In the *Church Dogmatics*, Barth even uses the word 'system' for the divine decision to elect Jesus Christ and humankind in Jesus Christ, for the all-determinative Model *or System* according to which everything that happens 'in Jesus Christ'.[14] Even if Barth had avoided such statements, the estimate of able interpreters would carry much weight: Berkouwer discerns 'a remarkable consistency in Barth's thinking';[15] in Denis Müller's eyes, 'the *Church Dogmatics*, Barth's *magnum opus*' offers

---

8. As G. C. Berkouwer analyses (concerning death being the absolute end) in idem, *The Triumph of Grace in the Theology of Karl Barth*, trans. H. R. Boer (London: Paternoster, 1956), p. 340, n. 37.

9. Ibid., p. 340.

10. 'Karl Barth systématisé. Etude critique de Jérôme Hamer, Karl Barth. L'occasionalisme théologique de Karl Barth. Etude sur sa méthode dogmatique, Paris, 1949', in J.-L. Leuba, *Etudes barthiennes* (Geneva: Labor & Fides, 1986), pp. 37–46.

11. *Credo*, trans. P. Jundt and J. Jundt (Paris: Je Sers, 1936), p. 52.

12. *CD* I/2, pp. 868–869.

13. W. Schneemelcher, 'Theologische Arbeitstagung', *EvT* 10 (1950–1), p. 570, as quoted by A. Moda, 'La dottrina barthiana dell'elezione: verso una soluzione delle aporie?', in S. Rostagno (ed.), *Barth contemporaneo* (Turin: Claudiana, 1990), p. 100, n. 103.

14. *CD* II/2, p. 7.

15. *Triumph of Grace*, p. 258 (precisely on our topic, as it governs the whole of Barth's theology).

'all the features of a system'.[16] Henri Bouillard sees Barth growing 'more and more systematic' as he adds volume to volume.[17] The language of necessity, which he often uses for inferences he draws, witnesses to the place of logic in the development of his teaching – though an idiosyncratic kind of logic, both fearless and paradoxical.

Should one characterize Barth's logic as dialectical? This question is bound up with the second issue: that of continuity through successive decades. No-one doubts the discontinuity at the time of the First World War, between lib-eralism and the 'crisis' theology of the Wholly Other. When he 'changed gear' a second time,[18] around 1930, the magnitude of the change is not measured in identical ways. Hans Urs von Balthasar established, in his influential 1951 study, the pattern that prevailed for decades: Barth's first post-liberal theology was *dialectical*, but, under the pressure of his exchanges with Erich Przywara, in response to Erik Peterson's comments,[19] and as a result of his Anselm studies, he moved to an *analogical* type, which dominates the *Church Dogmatics*.[20] Barth emphasized the break: of his *Römerbrief* he wrote in 1932, 'When, however, I look back at the book, it seems to have been written by another man to meet a situation belonging to a past epoch.'[21] Yet, mainly since Bruce L. McCormack's magisterial *Karl Barth's Critically Realistic Dialectical Theology: Its Genesis and Development 1909–1936*,[22] most scholars concur, in Webster's words, that '"dialectic" is a permanent feature of Barth's theology, not a temporary

---

16. *Karl Barth* (Paris: Cerf, 2005), p. 12.

17. *Karl Barth I. Genèse et évolution de la théologie dialectique* (Paris: Aubier-Montaigne, 1957), p. 231.

18. John Webster's metaphor, 'Introducing Barth', in J. Webster (ed.), *The Cambridge Companion to Karl Barth* (Cambridge: Cambridge University Press, 2000), p. 12.

19. Story told by P. Corset, 'Premières Rencontres de la théologie catholique avec l'oeuvre de Barth (1922–1932)', in P. Gisel (ed.), *Karl Barth: genèse et réception de sa théologie* (Geneva: Labor & Fides, 1987), pp. 154–190. 'Quoting from St Ambrose, [Peterson] sharpens his protest: "Non in dialectica complacuit Deo salvum facere populum suum" [It did not please God to save his people through dialectics]' (ibid., p. 171).

20. Balthasar added that one could 'see [Barth] holding on to the same basic insight throughout his career'; see H. U. von Balthasar, *The Theology of Karl Barth*, trans. J. Drury (New York: Holt, Rinehart & Winston, 1971), p. 32.

21. Foreword for the English translation of the Romans commentary, *The Epistle to the Romans*, trans. E. C. Hoskyns (London: Oxford University Press, 1933), p. vi.

22. Oxford: Clarendon, 1995.

phase left behind in the 1930s'.[23] Dorrien explains that 'Barth's recollections of his early career were often faulty and he had a lifelong tendency to exaggerate the degree of his various shifts of position'; his 'later theology contained crucial dialectical elements . . . yet at the same time he claimed to have no interest in dialectical reasoning and lamented that he was "the originator of this unfortunate term"'.[24]

This introduction is no place to settle the issue. 'Dialectic' and 'analogy' are slippery words. The very 'early' Barth could speak of 'analogies' (though at the same time denying any continuity with the divine reality!)[25] As to the former term, Bouillard distinguishes three main uses.[26] At first, Barth delighted in the theme, commenting about the 'No' of judgment, '*This* No is really yes. *This* judgment is grace. *This* condemnation is forgiveness. *This* death is life. *This* hell is heaven,'[27] and exhorting theologians to keep walking on the narrow ridge 'looking *from one side to the other*, from positive to negative and from negative to positive. Our task is to interpret the Yes by the No and the No by the Yes without delaying more than a moment in either a fixed Yes or a fixed No.'[28] After 1930, he avoids the term or uses it for views he repudiates,[29] but still moves back and forth between the equivalents of Yes and No. As he grows stronger on affirmation, he proclaims, 'The second is no longer closed up and concealed and kept from us in the first, the life of Jesus Christ in His death, the grace of God in His judgment, His Yes in His No.'[30] However, as soon as one inquires about *our* participation, one is sent oscillating from one pole to the other: all this is true in Jesus Christ, *not* in ourselves. But in ourselves, we are nothing, a mere illusion: 'The critical vigilance of dialectical theology, as it insists on God's impossible possibility . . . never disappeared from Barth's thought.'[31] 'Dialectical' may not be the most apt word, as Sung Wook Chung

---

23. 'Introducing Barth', p. 13.

24. *Barthian Revolt*, p. 70, quoting from J. D. Godsey (ed.), *Karl Barth's Table Talk* (Edinburgh: Oliver & Boyd, 1963), p. 24.

25. *The Word of God and the Word of Man*, trans. D. Horton (New York: Harpers, 1957), p. 321 (p. 305 affirms 'in the worldly the analogy of the heavenly').

26. *Karl Barth I*, p. 73.

27. 'The Need and Promise of Christian Preaching' (1922), in idem, *Word of God*, p. 120.

28. 'The Word of God and the Task of the Ministry' (1922), in ibid., p. 207.

29. Bouillard, *Karl Barth I*, p.137, who gives two references for a pejorative use in *KD* I/2, p. 23, and II/1, p. 660. I noticed *CD* II/2, p. 13; IV/1, pp. 80, 483.

30. *CD* IV/1, p. 344. Endlessly balancing between Yes and No is the way of myth!

31. Müller, *Karl Barth*, p. 66.

argues,[32] but the permanence of the typical 'gesture', intellectual and spiritual, of the dialectical period may be acknowledged.[33]

The foregoing considerations are enough to clear the way for our exploration. This inquiry will attempt to reconnoitre the contours of the theme, the role of Jesus Christ, mainly in the *Church Dogmatics*; it will observe its influence in parts of the dogmatic field and note tensions; it will sound Barth's motives and glance at his arguments; it will, finally, try to weigh them and reach some evaluation from the standpoint of evangelical theology.

Jesus Christ: Alpha and Omega

'Christocentrism' is the term most commonly found to describe the role of Jesus Christ in Barth's theology. He himself used it.[34] The composition of the word does not signal the properly Barthian sense: that Christ is in the 'centre' is hardly an original feature; it could be found in all orthodox theologies and even in many liberal ones. For Barth, he is in the centre *and* the beginning *and* the end – he fills the whole theological space.[35] In Richard A. Muller's typology, it is called 'principial christocentrism': it 'is characterized by the understanding of Christ (rather than Scripture and God) as both *principium essendi* [principle of being] and *principium cognoscendi theologiae* [principle of the knowledge of theology]'.[36] By tacit convention, 'Christocentrism' and its cognates are used with such an import in Barthian studies. Critics, not lightweights in the scholarly world, have complained that this amounts to 'Christomonism': A. Moda lists Paul Althaus (first in print), Reinhold Niebuhr, Helmut Thielicke, K. Okayama,[37] to whom we may add Richard Muller[38] and even,

---

32. *Admiration and Challenge: Karl Barth's Theological Relationship with John Calvin* (New York: Peter Lang, 2002), p. 9 (critical of McCormack).

33. To illustrate: Bouillard, *Karl Barth I*, p. 238, dealing with time in *CD* III, exclaims, 'How could one not be struck by the parallelism between this conception and that of the *Römerbrief* which it is intended to supersede?'

34. E.g. *CD* IV/1, p. 683.

35. As Berkouwer, *Triumph of Grace*, p. 123, observes.

36. 'A Note on "Christocentrism" and the Imprudent Use of Such Terminology', *WTJ* 68 (2006), p. 256.

37. 'La dottrina barthiana', p. 89, n. 36.

38. 'Place and Importance', pp. 147, 150–151. In his recent 'Note on "Christocentrism"', p. 257, he maintains that the word provides a 'convenient and quite accurate label'.

though with a limiting 'perhaps', the faithful translator Geoffrey Bromiley.[39] Barth resented the charge, and his imperial anger flared up: 'fools (*die Toren*) would say: Christomonist'.[40] Later he warned against a Christomonistic danger.[41] If the word implies disregarding Barth's *intentions* of maintaining a trinitarian framework, a consistent partnership in the covenant and concrete methodology, it is inappropriate – but of course, intentions are not what count in the end. Berkouwer introduced 'panchristism'[42] and 'Jesucentric' to characterize Barth's thinking.[43] The latter term, despite unpleasant overtones, highlights the fact that the *man* Jesus of Nazareth stands at the beginning of the ways of God. Webster notes that Barth, in his later writings, was alert to the danger of 'Christological totalitarianism'.[44] The phrase, finally, that many Barthians prefer was coined by Barth to define his 1930 turn: 'christological concentration'.[45] This comparatively neutral expression is unobjectionable.[46]

Statements are not wanting that express Barth's conviction: '[A] church dogmatics must, of course, be christologically determined as a whole and in all its parts'; Christology must govern the very foundations, or else, it is nothing.[47] 'Therefore, dogmatics must actually be Christology and only Christology.'[48] Since the doctrine of election determines all the dealings of God with humans,[49] the identification of election with Jesus Christ as the

---

39. 'Karl Barth', in P. E. Hughes (ed.), *Creative Minds in Contemporary Theology* (Grand Rapids: Eerdmans, 1966), p. 52: 'Christomonism is perhaps a more valid description.' Bromiley then hastens to put it aside.

40. *CD* IV/1, p. 683.

41. *CD* IV/4 (fragment), p. 19: a Christomonistic swallowing of anthropology is precisely ruled out by right 'Christocentrism'.

42. *Karl Barth en de kinderdoop* (Kampen: J. H. Kok, 1947), p. 125.

43. *Triumph of Grace*, p. 258.

44. *Barth's Ethics of Reconciliation* (Cambridge: Cambridge University Press, 1995), p. 137.

45. '*Parergon*: Karl Barth über sich selbst', *EvT* 8 (Dec. 1948), pp. 268–282; cf. esp. p. 272. This includes two notes, the first one written in 1938 (1928–38 period).

46. Jacques de Senarclens, 'La Concentration christologique', in E. Wolf, C. von Kirschbaum and R. Frey (eds.), *Antwort. Karl Barth zum siebzigsten Geburtstag am 10. Mai 1956* (Zollikon-Zurich: Evangelischer Verlag, 1956), p. 191, recommends 'christological' rather than 'christocentric' (H. U. von Balthasar's word).

47. *CD* I/2, p. 123.

48. Ibid., p. 872.

49. *CD* II/2, p. 148; see n. 14 above.

Electing God and the Elect Man (and vicariously Reprobate) is another form of Christological concentration: 'Not only does the *decretum absolutum* [absolute decree] take the name of Christ but it is identical [*s'identifica*] with the very Christ event.'[50] In *Church Dogmatics* IV/1: 'Jesus Christ, very God and very man, born and living and acting and suffering and conquering in time, is as such the one eternal Word of God at the beginning of all things.'[51] In the fragment on *The Christian Life*, which he did not publish himself: in Jesus' history 'we have to do with the centre, core and origin of the totality as such'.[52]

To Brunero Gherardini Barth wrote (24 May 1952), 'Myself, I needed much time to realize that the verse John 1:14 was the centre and the theme of all theology, even better: that it was, itself, the whole of theology *in nuce* [in a nutshell].'[53] Actually, he had said in a 1922 address, 'All my thoughts circle about the one point which in the New Testament is called Jesus Christ.'[54] 'This extraordinary "christological concentration," as it has been called,' Denis Müller writes, 'is the signature of the whole theology of Barth, already in the "Commentary on the Epistle to the Romans," and, in repetitive and systematic fashion, of his immense *Dogmatics*.'[55]

Under the various names, commentators roughly agree that questions are to be handled and decided in the exclusive and all-inclusive light of the Christ event. '[F]or Barth all God's dealings with men are effected in and through the person of Jesus Christ'.[56] As he stresses the resurrection as the essential Christ event, Ingolf U. Dalferth summarizes:

> [There is] one grammer [*sic*]; and this is Christology. It is the task of dogmatic
> discourse proper to work out the world of meaning that the presence of Christ

---

50. Brunero Gherardini, 'Riflettando sulla dottrina dell'elezione in Karl Barth', in Rostagno, *Barth contemporaneo*, p. 109.

51. *CD* IV/1, p. 49

52. *The Christian Life* (*Das christlichen Leben*), p. 10, quoted by Webster, *Barth's Ethics*, p. 102.

53. As quoted by E. Busch, 'Un Magnificat perpétuel: remarques sur la Dogmatique de Karl Barth', trans. D. Seydoux and P. Gisel, *Index Volume of the French Dogmatique* (Geneva: Labor & Fides, 1980), p. 22.

54. Barth, *Word of God*, p. 216.

55. *Karl Barth*, p. 43.

56. Colin Brown's wording, *Karl Barth and the Christian Message* (London: Tyndale, 1967), p. 150.

carries with it; and because of the centrality of the resurrection, everything it states is
to be determined christologically. This amounts to nothing less than . . . redefining
virtually every dogmatic concept in christological terms: 'God,' 'power,' 'freedom,'
'person,' 'man and woman,' 'predestination,' 'history,' 'time,' 'law,' 'being,' and
everything else is – in sometimes quite complicated and twisted ways – derived from
the central eschatological reality of the risen Christ.[57]

One must highlight two innovative features of Barth's thought. The central,
original and final Jesus Christ on whom he 'concentrates' is God the Son *and
identically* the man Jesus of Nazareth. Affirming Jesus Christ as eternally pre-
existent, the Mediator of the work of creation: this is plain orthodoxy – but
with the explanation that he is so in his divine nature only, as the Logos not
yet 'incarnate' (*asarkos*). Though, at times, he seems to endorse it, this doctrine
is deeply distasteful to Barth. He denounces it as an abstract speculation that
negates the heart of the gospel, God's choice and self-determination.[58] He
sees in it the root of grievous errors:

> Do not ever think of the second person of the Trinity as only *Logos*. That is the
> mistake of Emil Brunner. There is no *Logos asarkos*, but only *ensarkos* [enfleshed].
> Brunner thinks of a *Logos asarkos*, and I think this is the reason for his natural
> theology. The *Logos* becomes an abstract principle. Since there is only and always a
> *Logos ensarkos*, there is no change in the Trinity, as if a fourth member comes in after
> the incarnation.[59]

'The man Jesus is in [the] genuine and real yesterday of God's eternity.'[60]
He speaks in Revelation 1:8, not the Son of God only.[61] A shadow of

---

57. 'Karl Barth's Eschatological Realism', in S. W. Sykes (ed.), *Karl Barth: Centenary
    Essays* (Cambridge: Cambridge University Press, 1989), p. 38.

58. E.g. *CD* III/1, p. 54: the *Logos asarkos*, an abstraction, would leave us with a
    'formless Christ'; cf. III/2, pp. 483–484; IV/1, p. 52; against the *extra Calvinisticum*,
    p. 181; IV/2, pp. 100–101, gods forged by humankind are *logoi asarkoi*.

59. *Karl Barth's Table Talk*, p. 49, quoted by Brown, *Karl Barth and the Christian Message*, p.
    109. The last clause is odd.

60. *CD* III/2, p. 484, II/2, p. 104, affirm a difference between the man Jesus and all
    others in this respect: Jesus was in the beginning as all creation in God's plan: 'But
    He was so not merely in that way.'

61. Cf. *CD* III/2, pp. 463, 465, 516, and Bouillard's (negative) comment, *Karl Barth I*,
    pp. 271–272.

equivocation hovers over the proposition: sometimes, the man Jesus is said to pre-exist *in the divine counsel*, as predestined;[62] the Logos is not *incarnatus* (incarnate) before the Annunciation but *incarnandus* (who must become incarnate, is going to be so).[63] However, these precautions are inconstant, the difference between the man Jesus and us, as regards pre-existence, is emphasized,[64] and *incarnandus* counts as *incarnatus*. McCormack summarizes Barth's logic in many passages: Barth

> must deny to the Logos a mode or a state of being above and prior to the decision to be incarnate in time. He must . . . say that there is no Logos in and for himself in distinction from God's act of turning toward the world and humanity in predestination.[65]

The forbidden thought is that which separates between the divine Son and the man Jesus, who are *one* from all eternity.[66]

The second feature is no less noteworthy: the role of Jesus Christ is not only *noetic*, for our knowledge, but *ontic* (or *ontological*), in the order of *being*. As Runia observed, many writers have missed the point.[67] Since Barth started, with most German theologians since Kant, with the problem of *revelation*, one could mistakenly assume that he was concerned only with the noetic dimension: against natural theology, only the Word incarnate (echoing the Barmen declaration!). But he forcefully said the opposite, using the words 'noetic' and 'ontic'.[68] Already in 1935, not without a touch of humour, he claimed the right to use them![69] Webster sums up the matter:

> Noetically, 'creation' and 'history' are not 'natural' categories, nor are they the fruit of

---

62. *CD* III/2, p. 477.

63. I remember receiving this answer from my doctoral mentor, Prof. Jean Bosc (1910–69).

64. See n. 60 above.

65. 'Grace and Being: The Role of God's Gracious Election in Karl Barth's Theological Ontology', in J. Webster (ed.), *Cambridge Companion to Karl Barth*, p. 95 (cf. p. 100). More below on the controversy among Barth's interpreters.

66. *CD* II/2, p. 103.

67. *De Theologische Tijd bij Karl Barth, met name in zijn anthropologie* (Franeker: T. Wever, 1955), pp. 94–96 (referring to H. Vogel and even H. U. von Balthasar).

68. *CD* II/2, p. 63; III/1, p. 28.

69. *Credo*, p. 229.

human consciousness of contingency or temporal passage. Ontologically, the content of such terms is Christologically determined.[70]

And he adds the comment, since Jesus' life is the *ratio essendi* (principle of being) of all the rest: of this point the 'sheer enormity as a claim is not to be under-estimated. For so much hangs on so little: an entire ontology of created being rests upon a mere fragment.'

The ontological cast of the Christological concentration reflects Karl Barth's preoccupation with being, which may have escaped the eye of some readers because of his use of the traditional language of revelation and, later, of condemnation and judgment, but which should be discerned as underlying such a use.[71] He defines salvation as the fulfilment of being, even ventures the thought that reconciliation would have taken place without sin.[72] His doctrine of sin, it has been observed, 'bears an explicit metaphysical-ontological character'.[73] His choice of the word 'Nothingness' (*das Nichtige*) for evil 'is symptomatic of the whole undertaking',[74] at least of its ontological slant. The work of Jüngel and of McCormack has raised the awareness of this orientation. They have shown how different Barth's ontology is. Usually, it is described as 'actualistic', and sometimes 'dynamic'.[75] The key reference is event. One could adduce much evidence of this emphasis: for example, the error of natural theology, on analogy, 'is that it makes out of the "He" an "it," out of becoming a being . . . This static instead of dynamic understanding of the analogy must be expressly repudiated.'[76] Yet, Alan Torrance draws attention to a passage that

---

70. *Barth's Ethics*, p. 65.

71. He criticizes Roman Catholic theology for reducing theology to ontology – but, precisely, Roman Catholic ontology is not the same as his, *CD* II/1, p. 583. In K. Barth, *The Humanity of God*, trans. T. Wieser and J. Newton Thomas (Richmond, Va.: John Knox, 1960), p. 93, the theologian after his heart 'has his ontology "as though he had it not"'.

72. *CD* IV/1, pp. 8, 47 and 90–91 respectively.

73. Van Oyen, 'De Categorie der recognitio en de theologische anthropologie', in idem, *Pro Regno, pro Sanctuario* (1950), p. 345, as quoted by Runia, *Theologische Tijd*, p. 137, who adds that Barth operates with the Greek concept of the *meōn* (relative non-being).

74. Brown, *Karl Barth and the Christian Message*, p. 123.

75. I confess dissatisfaction with this association of words: for Aristotle, the 'act'/'actual' (*energeia*) is the term opposed to *dynamis* (power)!

76. *CD* II/1, p. 231.

should temper a neat categorization of Barth as an 'actualist': Barth, indeed, writes that 'God is who He is in His works', but adds, 'He is the same even in Himself, even before and after and over His works, and without them. They are bound to Him, but He is not bound to them.'[77] Inner tensions may lie beneath the surface of Barthian ontology.

Effects of Christological concentration

To expound Jesus' central role more fully, one has to sketch how Barth decides to 'concentrate' theology upon Christology. How does he proceed, and with what results? Only a brief account can be offered here, with the hope that the *link* with Christocentrism will come to light.

The Christological derivation of Barth's *anthropology* first meets the eye.[78] Paul D. Molnar writes, 'Anthropology is . . . irreversibly grounded in Christology. This is the hallmark of Barth's theology.'[79] Aware of departing from traditional procedures,[80] Barth endeavoured 'to infer [*schliessen*] from His [Jesus'] human nature the character of our own'.[81] And this is no merely noetic necessity. The man Jesus is 'the real basis' of creation.[82] As the Archetype and Model, Christ first is human and we participate in humanity only as we participate in him.[83] He is 'the original'; we are 'the copy'.[84] Jesus is the 'true' (*wahr*) and 'real' (*wirklich*) man, and we are real only in him; 'the sinful man as such is not the real man',[85] only a *Schattenmensch* (shadow person).[86] This entails that,

---

77. Ibid., p. 260, quoted by A. J. Torrance, 'The Trinity', in Webster, *Cambridge Companion to Karl Barth*, p. 90, n. 28.

78. For a more detailed treatment, see my 'Karl Barth's Anthropology', in Sung Wook Chung (ed.), *Karl Barth and Evangelical Theology* (Carlisle: Paternoster, 2007), pp. 96–135.

79. 'Barth, Karl (1886–1968)', in T. H. Hart (ed.), *The Dictionary of Historical Theology* (Grand Rapids: Eerdmans; Carlisle: Paternoster, 2000), p. 53b.

80. *CD* III/2, p. ix: 'None of the old or more recent fathers known to me was ready to take the way to a theological knowledge of man which I regard as the only possible one.'

81. Ibid., p. 54, 'the character of' is added in the English translation.

82. Ibid., p. 483.

83. Ibid., p. 59.

84. Ibid.

85. Ibid., p. 32.

86. Ibid., p. 198; cf. pp. 121–128.

contrary to superficial chronology, Jesus is the First Adam, ontologically *prius* (first), whereas Adam was really *posterius* (afterwards), Adam the mere 'type' who foreshadowed *the man* Jesus.[87]

The priority of the man Jesus is of one piece with Barth's thesis affirming that the covenant (of grace and reconciliation) is the *inner foundation* of creation; what some readers fail to notice is that the priority extends to human *sinfulness* as well. Not only does Barth boldly draw the whole of his hamartiology from Christolology: sin is *pride*, as contrary to the humiliation of deity in incarnation; sin is *inertia* (*Trägheit*), as contrary to the exaltation of humanity in incarnation; sin is the *lie*, as contrary to the warrant offered by the union of the two natures;[88] but, again, he goes far beyond a mere noetic role. Adam is second also *as sinner*. Not that Jesus sinned before history began, but his condemnation/reprobation for human sin preceded in the order of being, and is to be considered as the determinative ground of Adam's and our disobedience.[89] With no fear of paradox, Barth can write:

> He is the man whom God in His eternal counsel, giving Him the command, treated as its transgressor, thus rejecting Him in His righteous wrath, and actually threatening Him with final dereliction. That this was true of Adam, and is true of us, is the case *only because* in God's counsel, and in the event of Golgotha, it became true *first of all in Jesus Christ*.[90]

How is such a statement to be understood? Negatively, it amounts to the rejection of the usual scheme: first, the divine–human relation established by creation; then, humanity's disobedience, which entails guilt and incurs wrath; and third, God's new work of reconciliation through the Word incarnate (and application through the Holy Spirit who creates faith, the means of reception). Barth's concentration rules this out, since it implies that the man Jesus appears only at the third stage.[91] Positively, Barth's proposition means that the foundation of everything resides in God's decision to be the God of grace, a decision identical with Jesus Christ himself, in whom God and man

---

87. *CD* II/2, p. 740; III/2, p. 205, and *Christ and Adam: Man and Humanity in Romans 5*, trans. T. A. Smail (Edinburgh: Oliver & Boyd, 1965).

88. *CD* IV/1, pp. 139–144; cf. IV/3.1, pp. 369–372.

89. *CD* IV/3.1, pp. 500–501, 509–510.

90. *CD* II/2, p. 739 (italics mine).

91. In orthodoxy, all three stages are defined in God's counsel; but this is no preexistence: it expresses God's intention to cause to exist later.

are united. In order to be *grace*, it has to overcome wrath, to reverse con-demnation. Therefore, in the event that is the decision itself in history, the divine No must be heard, and Jesus must be treated *as if* he had deserved God's No. This, in turn, entails that the correlate of that No must stamp human life considered in itself (that unreality) and humans cannot but be sinners in themselves.[92] Already in the *Göttingen Dogmatics*, Barth dealt with the Covenant of grace (§24) before the doctrine of sin (§§25–26). His view of the Law as 'the form of the Gospel', as theologically posterior to Reconciliation,[93] also leads to the priority of Jesus as regards sinfulness. It flows from the same concentration, since, otherwise, the legal relationship would not depend on the *Logos ensarkos*. Human sin, the breaking of the Law, necessarily comes after Christ.

The doctrine of sin is bound with that of *Nothingness*.[94] Nothingness is the preferred name for evil ('chaos' is also used), and to sin is to be overcome by Nothingness. Barth agrees with Origen and Augustine (and, I believe, Scripture) that evil can have no *being*, for only what God creates has being, and what God creates is good (1 Tim. 4:4). Yet he will not drift into the optimistic conclusion that evil, then, is a mere appearance: evil is not mere non-being, and Barth chooses a word (*das Nichtige*) that suggests 'aggressive force', 'destructiveness'. Barth discerns that evil is not explained as a possibility of freedom, a conception that gives evil an ontological footing *within* creation.[95] Created freedom (as we see in Christ) is freedom to say *yes* to God, only yes. Barth's solution, again a novel one, makes evil, under the name Nothingness, a reality *produced by God's rejection of it*. As God says Yes to his creation, he impli-citly says No to what is not this creation, and Nothingness arises as the corre-late of that No: 'Nothingness is that which God does not will. It lives only by the fact that it is that which God does not will. But it does live by this fact. For not only what God wills, but what He does not will, is potent, and must have a real correspondence.'[96]

Barth's Christological concentration is involved here: since it grounds cre-ation on reconciliation, and since reconciliation means victory over the foe,

92. This logic (with words intimating necessity) can be found, e.g., in *CD* II/1, p. 141.
93. *CD* II/2, §37; and K. Barth, 'Gospel and Law', in idem, *God, Grace and Gospel*, trans. J. S. McNab (Edinburgh: Oliver & Boyd, 1959 [1936]).
94. I dealt with this Barthian doctrine in my book *Evil and the Cross*, trans. D. G. Preston (Vancouver: Regent College Publishing, 2003 repr.), pp. 76–83.
95. *CD* IV/1, pp. 409–410.
96. *CD* III/3, p. 352.

creation had to exhibit the same structure. A hostile reference had to be posited: the Nothingness that God wills not, and creation itself had to take the form of a victorious Yes (Barth finds an echo of the conflict in Gen. 1:2). 'Jesus is Victor!'[97] The next consequence is that Nothingness is no longer to be feared. 'Has not God come between man and the chaos and "beforehand" *separated* the one from the other?'[98] Nothingness defeated from the origin (since Jesus Christ is the origin) has no more power than a 'fleeting shadow',[99] an 'epiphenomenon',[100] while sin is excluded as the 'ontological impossibility'.[101] Barth's rhetoric swings back and forth from the warning about the deadly danger of Nothingness for us and the proclamation of its powerlessness in Christ.

To an original hamartiology probably corresponds an original soteriology (including both 'objective' reconciliation and 'subjective' participation: Barth insists that the objective contains the subjective).[102] The briefest of accounts must mention first that Barth refuses the distinction between Christ's person and work.[103] His actualistic ontology interprets the person as 'event'; more decisively, a separate consideration of the work presupposes a framework that would not simply derive from the Christological centre. Despite the use of 'judicial' language that sounds familiar to evangelical readers, Barth expressly distances himself from the orthodox doctrine of atonement (with punishment 'satisfying' the demands of justice).[104] Rather than undergoing our punishment as such (that we may be spared), Jesus Christ on the cross annihilated both sin and sinner.[105] This real suppression opens the way for a resurrection or new creation of the 'true' and 'real' man in Jesus Christ (really righteous, *not* justified through the imputation of a *justitia aliena* [alien righteousness, not

---

97. Johann Christoph Blumhardt's motto, by which Barth summarized his own message.

98. *CD* III/2, p. 175. Berkouwer, *Triumph of Grace*, p. 227, underlines the frequent use of 'beforehand'.

99. *CD* III/3, p. 361.

100. *CD* IV/3.1, p. 328.

101. *CD* III/2, p. 174 and *passim*.

102. *CD* IV/1, pp. 87–88.

103. Ibid., pp. 127–128.

104. Ibid., p. 253. Berkouwer, *Triumph of Grace*, p. 138, n. 79, observes 'the hesitation in the whole of this paragraph' (in fine print!); cf. *CD* IV/1, p. 257, for further criticism.

105. Ibid., p. 254.

one's own]). Barth's objection to a 'theory of satisfaction' is that satisfaction would be required by some reality above the event.[106]

When reconciliation is concerned, 'there cannot be an exclusive but only an inclusive Christology'.[107] Barth stresses that 'whether he knows and believes it or not . . . [man] belongs to the Head, Jesus Christ, of whose body he is or is to become a member'.[108] 'God has given it to all men in Jesus Christ', though many are not aware of the fact.[109] '[O]bjectively, all are justified, sanctified and called'.[110] Of all it must be said, 'They are no longer sinners, but righteous. They are no longer lost, but saved.'[111] This fact 'is the ground on which [as humans] we stand, the horizon by which we are bounded, the atmosphere in which we breathe',[112] 'it is like the fixed star which shines unchanged above all the clouds created by [man]'.[113] In Christ 'the conversion of the world to God' has taken place.[114] A few times, Barth qualifies this reality, for unbelievers, with the words 'virtual' or 'potential', or the phrase *de jure*,[115] but the context shows that an 'Amyraldian' (hypothetical universalism) reading would be a total misreading: every time Barth explains what difference being a Christian makes, he restricts the privilege to the *knowledge* of the fact, which enables one to behave accordingly.[116]

Shall, therefore, everyone be saved in the end? The issue has been debated among commentators, generally under the technical name *apokatastasis* (restoration). Nearly all agree that Barth's thought tends towards such a view, a corollary of Christological concentration. Undoubtedly, Barth refrained from affirming it clearly.[117] His zeal for divine freedom and his wrath against any 'bourgeois' possession of grace prevented him from doing so. However, Barth hastens to add that we may hope for it – sometimes with the unpleasant *innuendo* that those who reject *apokatastasis* are happy to imagine other humans being tormented in

---

106. Ibid., p. 276.
107. Ibid., p. 354.
108. *CD* II/2, p. 539.
109. *CD* IV/1, p. 92.
110. Ibid., p. 148.
111. Ibid., p. 316.
112. *CD* II/2, p. 777.
113. *CD* IV/3.1, p. 475.
114. *CD* IV/1, p. 77; the original does not use *Welt* (world) but *Geschöpf* (creature).
115. E.g. *CD* IV/3.1, p. 278.
116. E.g. *CD* IV/1, pp. 77, 92, 661–662, 758.
117. Still *CD* IV/3.1, p. 477.

hell.[118] What of that dam of unbelief that many set up against the tide of grace? He answers, 'The stream is too strong and the dam too weak for us to be able reasonably to expect anything but the collapse of the dam, and the onrush of the waters.'[119] Barth's position, tongue in cheek, is summarized by what he told Jüngel: 'I don't teach it [*apokatastasis*], but I don't say, either, that I don't teach it.'[120]

Universal salvation in the end would also seem to follow from Barth's doctrine of election, inasmuch as all are elect in Christ, who took upon himself, exclusively, reprobation. The man who behaves as if he were rejected 'does it all in vain, because the choice he thus makes is eternally denied and annulled in Jesus Christ'.[121] This embodies Christocentrism. 'The christological orientation', Jüngel writes, 'set forth *materialiter* [in substance] *in nuce* in the *Church Dogmatics* I/2, §15, fully unfolded itself later in the doctrine of election, which recasts completely traditional conceptions of predestination.'[122] Concentration in the Only Real Man makes it impossible to keep a separate category of people who would not be 'in him'. Double predestination must be reinterpreted no longer to draw a dividing line through humankind, but as affecting all; 'in themselves' all humans are rejected, the objects of divine wrath. But God in Christ has taken rejection for himself; in him, in whom we have our real being, they are no longer rejected but God's elect.[123] Concentration compresses classical dualities into one event with two aspects.

Jesus' eternal election means that God binds *himself* to this man. This implies that the divine decision is a divine *self-determination* in the strongest sense: 'It is part of the doctrine of God because originally God's election of man is a predestination not merely of man but of Himself.'[124] 'All that can be predicated of the true God must be filled and interpreted in terms of . . . the act of His self-abasement.'[125] Even stronger: God's elective determination 'belongs no

---

118. *Die Botschaft von der freien Gnade Gottes* (1947), p. 7, as quoted and rightly noticed by Berkouwer, *Triumph of Grace*, pp. 115, 118.

119. *CD* IV/3.1, pp. 355–356.

120. E. Jüngel, 'La Vie et l'oeuvre de Karl Barth', in Gisel, *Karl Barth: genèse et réception*, p. 56.

121. *CD* II/2, p. 317.

122. 'La Vie et l'oeuvre de Karl Barth', p. 55.

123. E.g. *CD* II/2, pp. 162–163. See pp. 44, 453 on the reprobate, a shadow, who exists only in the person of Jesus Christ, and the whole treatise, §§32–35.

124. *CD* II/2, p. 3.

125. *CD* IV/1, p. 142. Berkouwer, *Triumph of Grace*, p. 307, observes, 'In this connection it is eminently noteworthy that Barth frequently speaks about the "passion of God" but in not so unqualified terms of the "death of God".'

less to Him than all that He is in and for Himself'.[126] Godhead is 'grounded in
and to be unfolded from Christology' and 'includes his humanity':[127] just as
man outside Jesus Christ is a mere 'abstraction', so also would be any God
outside Jesus Christ (making the *Logos asarkos* a forbidden thought). This truth
may be translated in the trinitarian idiom 'There is no such thing as Godhead
in itself. Godhead is always the Godhead of the Father, the Son and the Holy
Spirit.'[128] Barth interprets the Trinity as self-determination: 'In His own
freedom, God above all willed and determined Himself to be the Father of the
Son in the unity of the Spirit.'[129] Such Trinity means history: 'in correspondence with His triune being . . . God is historical even in Himself';[130] and
again, 'The true and living God is the One whose Godhead consists in this
history, who is in these three modes of being the one God';[131] his action 'is the
strangely logical final continuation of the history in which He is God'.[132]

The logical consequence? God thus becomes (from all eternity) *ontologically
dependent* on created being. However, Barth's (Reformed?) attachment to divine
transcendence leads him to deny such a conclusion (he also maintains the
Chalcedonian distinction of the two natures). Paul D. Molnar, on the strength
of numerous statements in the *Church Dogmatics*, and seeing the fateful consequence of the other view, has maintained, against McCormack, that Barth
maintains the difference between the immanent and economic Trinity, the *Logos
asarkos* and him *incarnandus* (respectively 'eternally necessary' and 'eternally contingent').[133] McCormack has replied that Molnar does not take into account

126. *CD* II/2, p. 7. Cf. E. Jüngel, '"Pas de Dieu sans l'homme . . ." La théologie de Karl
      Barth entre le théisme et l'athéisme', in Gisel, *Karl Barth: genèse et réception*, p. 204:
      'God is totally defined by the event of his identity with that man in favour of all
      men.'
127. *Humanity of God*, p. 46. On p. 72 ('The Gift of Freedom: Foundation of Evangelical
      Ethics', trans. T. Wieser), Barth claims, 'The concept of God without man is
      indeed as anomalous as wooden iron.'
128. *CD* II/2, p. 115.
129. *Humanity of God* ('Gift of Freedom'), p. 71.
130. *CD* IV/1, p. 112.
131. Ibid., p. 203.
132. Ibid.
133. P. D. Molnar, *Divine Freedom and the Doctrine of the Immanent Trinity* (London: T. & T.
      Clark, 2002), and 'The Trinity, Election and God's Ontological Freedom: A
      Response to Kevin W. Hector', *IJST* 8.3 (2006), pp. 294–306. On the latter phrases,
      cf. p. 298, n. 8, and p. 302; on the consequence, cf. pp. 297–299, 302, 304.

'Jesus Christ the *Subject* of election'; he adduces quotations that Molnar cannot fit into his interpretation; he explains that Barth's views changed around 1936–9 and that passages inconsistent with the change represent 'residual elements of classical theism'.[134] Barth's wording betrays some awareness of tensions: '*Indeed*, we dare not encroach on God's freedom . . . *But* . . .'[135]

A similar tension may be felt between a desire to protect a minimal distinction between the works of creation, reconciliation and redemption and, on the other hand, the powerful tendency to let the central one absorb the two others. While 'redemption' (eschatological liberation) could not be dealt with at length, since volume V was never written, creation looks more like an anticipatory reflection of reconciliation than like *another* work. The covenant of (reconciling) grace as the inner ground, Jesus as the really First Adam, the allegorical interpretation of Genesis 1 – 2, the victory pattern, all point in this direction. Creation and reconciliation, Berkouwer writes, 'are constantly . . . woven through each other'.[136] Barth expressly deprives succession of any ultimate significance. Not only is eternity characterized by the perfect unity and coincidence of past (beginning), present (succession) and future (end),[137] but the Christ event as revealed in the forty days confers to its time the attributes of eternity.[138] For theological meaning, Barth rejects the sequence of history, the 'coming after' through successive stages,[139] including that of cross and resurrection.[140] It is a constant theme that 'fulfilled time', which means for Barth,

---

134. B. L. McCormack, 'Seek God where he May Be Found: A Response to Edwin Chr. van Driel', *SJT* 60.1 (2007), p. 64; cf. p. 71, n. 23: 'a good bit of residual metaphysics'; p. 62 on Molnar's ignoring Jesus as subject of election. The article replies to van Driel, 'Karl Barth on the Eternal Existence of Jesus Christ', *SJT* 60.1 (2007), pp. 45–61. Though differently from Molnar, van Driel criticizes McCormack, while adding, 'In the end, the problem lies, I think, not so much in McCormack's reading, but in an ambiguity in the formulations of Barth' (p. 56).

135. *CD* II/2, p. 509 (my italics). J. Moltmann, *The Crucified God: The Cross of Christ as the Foundation and Criticism of Christian Theology*, trans. R. A. Wilson and J. Bowden (New York: Harper & Row, 1974), p. 79, n. 60, perceives the same tension in Barth, and he would do away with the distinction that cannot be drawn from the Christological event itself.

136. *Triumph of Grace*, p. 250; R. Prenter criticized this point 'not unjustly'.

137. *CD* II/1, p. 608.

138. *CD* III/2, p. 464 and *passim*.

139. *CD* III/1, p. 333 ('step-like succession').

140. *CD* I/2, p. 111 ('the resurrection is not a second and further stage').

'the suspension, the total relativising of all other time and of its apparently moved and moving content'.[141] Berkouwer observes that, though Catholic theologians also bind together creation and redemption,

> Barth differs from the Roman Catholic conception in that he emphasizes even more than it does the unity of creation and redemption. He does so especially by denying the validity of the 'step-wise' conception of the before and after of creation and redemption which *continues* to function in Roman Catholic theology.[142]

Concentrating diversity in the one Christological event is the hallmark of Barth's theology.

The motives and arguments supporting the concentration

A theologian's motives, whether rooted in biography or in the substance of doctrine, may be more complex than meets the eye, and never capable of any sure elucidation. Yet some attention to what observers perceive helps understanding and adds fairness to judgment. Barth's motives (in the larger sense) for pursuing the Christocentric program deserve a moment of consideration.

Barth associated his Christological turn with his rejection of *natural theology*, and this, in the same fateful years, with his fight against the *deutsche Christen* (German Christians), the Protestants who greeted Adolf Hitler as a God-given saviour and prophet of the German *Geist* (spirit). Berkouwer highlights the warning Barth caught in Hitler's 'intoxicating' chant of Might: he saw that the notion of 'power' had to be radically revised in the light of the Christ event.[143] The 'German Christians' were predominantly liberals, whose custom of listening to voices other than the voice of Jesus Christ made them vulnerable to Nazi 'seduction' (*Verführung!*). The experience reinforced Barth's eye-opening disappointment with his former teachers in 1914, when these university professors gave their support to the Kaiser's war politics: a sign of the *worldliness* of their theology.[144] He also linked his aversion for natural theology with his

---

141. *CD* I/1, p. 116; cf. IV/4, p. 24.
142. *Triumph of Grace*, p. 251.
143. Ibid., p. 312.
144. Dorrien, *Barthian Revolt*, pp. 37–38, dispels the confusion about the precise dates: the manifesto, which ninety-three professors signed, was issued on 3 October; but on 1 August, Wilhelm II had called the nation to war in a speech Adolph Harnack wrote!

socialist commitment: natural theology makes Christianity a comfortable
'bourgeois possession' (*Verbürgerlichung*).[145] Apart from his disgust at the *beati
possidentes*' (happy owners') assurance, Barth's socialism probably undergirded
one of the constant traits in his reactions: his almost angry refusal to admit any
ultimate division among human beings. The older Barth still entertained the
thought that the Holy Spirit might prefer *un*converted people and that the
knowledge of Christ might reside in some when nobody perceives its presence, not even the persons involved![146] Concern for solidarity made it intoler-
able to maintain in election the *alios/alios* (others/others) of Calvin's definition
and he could only find peace in the concentrated election/reprobation of *all*
in Jesus Christ.

Barth's critique of liberalism,[147] or 'neo-Protestantism' as he would say, he
turned against Roman Catholicism, as a twin target:[148] neo-Protestants were
doing in a rough and weak manner what Roman Catholics had been doing for
centuries with more subtlety and depth. His Christological concentration,
therefore, was to protect the heirs of the Reformation from the 'dissipation'
or even 'dismemberment' of grace that plagues Roman Catholic theology;[149]
it fights back that invention of Antichrist, the *analogia entis* (analogy of
being).[150] When Barth pointed to the influence of his Anselm studies on his
Christological turn (in his *Parergon* note of 1938), he suggested another form
of struggle against the *subtler* forms of natural theology: he realized that his
proclamation of the Wholly Other, of the infinite qualitative distinction
between time and eternity, was a remnant of a *negative*, nevertheless natural,

---

145. *CD* II/1, p. 141 (K. Barth, *Die kirchliche Dogmatik* [Munich: C. Kaiser, 1932; Zurich:
    Evangelischer Verlag Zürich, 1938–67] II/1, p. 157). The English translation
    renders 'respectability', losing the political connotation of the German word.
146. *CD* IV/3.1, p. 365.
147. Calling on psychoanalysis, one could (recklessly) envisage that Karl Barth's
    relationship with his father played a part! Fritz Barth was considered conservative:
    he tried to counter the young Karl's preference for liberal masters; yet, Fritz Barth
    disappointed his orthodox supporters, no longer believing the virgin birth (Müller,
    Karl Barth, pp. 16–17); finally, it was Karl who restored orthodoxy regarding the
    virgin birth!
148. E.g. *CD* I/2, §20.
149. *CD* IV/1, pp. 84–88.
150. *CD* I/1, p. xiii. The Antichrist replaces Christ (*anti* = 'instead of') – the analogy of
    being replaces the Christ of the Barthian Christocentric model as the way to think
    of God and creature together.

theology; it implied that he was imposing upon God's freedom a preconceived dialectical antithesis. He then tried to free himself from that preconception and to draw everything from God's free act of judgment and grace in Jesus Christ.[151] And there is a further extension: Protestant orthodoxy did not fare much better. The doctrine of verbal inspiration paved the way for the *Aufklärung* (Enlightenment) natural theology,[152] for it amounted to an obvious profanation of the 'mystery' of revelation (according to which mystery form contradicts content!).[153] Much later, Barth confronts his own view of the covenant (the Christologically concentrated one) with the rival 'covenant theology' (Cocceius', implying two covenants). Barth traces back the disagreement to the doctrine of Scripture: Cocceius' mistake, he claims, was that of reading 'the Bible as a divinely inspired source-book'.[154] An *analogia entis* creational relationship, a corpus of sacred texts, detract from the exclusive fullness of the Christ event. Hence, likely, Barth's harsh comments on pietists (evangelicals) at some stages of his career.[155] He scented that the human subject was given too much attention with the stress on experience[156] and loathed the separation between church and world, saved and unsaved.

Barth's strictures do not belie his effort to appropriate the heritage of the church. Among his motives, one must make room for his conviction that he was faithful to the purest elements of tradition. Apart from the dogmas he did confess, Nicaea and Chalcedon (disregarding possible shifts in mean-

---

151. Instead of defining beforehand God's Word on human lips as the 'impossible possibility', one should start from the Word God uttered once for all in the flesh, by becoming flesh.

152. *CD* I/2, pp. 522–525.

153. Ibid., p. 522.

154. *CD* IV/1, p. 55. This implies, Barth says, 'historicizing' the action and revelation of God, and no longer acknowledging the character of Scripture as a witness.

155. Famously, his quip 'I would rather be in hell with the world church than in heaven with Pietism, be it of a lower or a higher order, of an older or more modern observance', quoted by E. Busch, *Karl Barth and the Pietists: The Young Karl Barth's Critique of Pietism and Its Response*, trans. D. W. Bloesch (Downers Grove: IVP, 2004), p. 43. Barth's attitude shifted later in life (ibid., pp. 291–302; Busch distinguishes six stages).

156. De Senarclens, 'La Concentration christologique', in Wolf, Kirschbaum and Frey, *Antwort*, p. 196, notices that Augustin Gretillat and Frédéric Godet in French-speaking Switzerland, though labelled orthodox, were not immune to liberal influence.

ing), Barth, who never tired of quoting Fathers, Scholastics, Reformers and their successors, might have pointed to forerunners. The Scotist tradition of an eternal Christ (not only Son), a minority one until recently, comes to mind. Though Reformed in affiliation and despite severe criticisms of Lutheranism,[157] Barth may have felt a congeniality with Luther, as Hunsinger argues.[158] Although it applies differently, the word 'dialectic' may be used for both, with the same taste for hyperboles; Barth claims to follow a 'theology of the cross'. Hans-Joachim Iwand quotes a Christocentric statement by Luther: 'This one article reigns in my heart: faith in Christ, from whom, through whom and in whom all my theological reflections flow back and forth day and night.'[159] Osiander (whom Calvin considered such a nuisance!) offers interpretations that sound pre-Barthian in some ways: Jesus Christ as man the Model of creation, justification not by strict imputation of an 'alien' righteousness but by the gift of actual, divine, righteousness.[160] Among the Reformed, Barth expresses some affinity with the supralapsarian position, though his is a 'purified' supralapsarianism.[161] A Frenchman cannot but think of Pascal and his Christocentric statements. Finally, the influence of Barth's beloved master, Wilhelm Herrmann, cannot be ignored. After McCormack, Dorrien sheds light on the striking continuities between the emphases of the Ritschlian theologian, especially his 'Jesuscentrism', and Barthian accents:[162] though he took a critical stance towards Herrmann's theology in the mid-twenties, Barth, who had 'absorbed Herrmann through every pore', did not eliminate many of the seeds that had fallen on the fertile ground of his mind. In Dorrien's opinion,

---

157. Already in K. Barth, 'The Doctrinal Task of the Reformed Churches' (1923), in idem, *Word of God*, pp. 218–271. In Barth, *Humanity of God*, p. 50, he disavows 'the fatal Lutheran doctrine of the two natures and their properties'.

158. *Disruptive Grace*, pp. 279–304, the chapter entitled 'What Karl Barth Learned from Martin Luther'.

159. 'Von Primat der Christologie', in Wolf, Kirschbaum and Frey, *Antwort*, p. 186, quoting *D. Martin Luthers Werke. Kritische Gesamtausgabe* (Weimar: Böhlau, 1833–), vol. XL/3, p. 33.

160. Berkouwer, *Karl Barth en de kinderdoop*, pp. 129–132 (nuanced); Philip Bachmann, according to Busch, *Karl Barth and the Pietists*, pp. 67–68, 85–86 (where Barth thinks he moves away from Osiander).

161. *CD* II/2, p. 143. Berkouwer stresses differences; cf. *Karl Barth en de kinderdoop*, pp. 118–119 (with reference to the work of Hendricus Berkhof).

162. *Barthian Revolt*, pp. 14–36.

[though] he replaced Herrmann's anthropocentric hand pump with the giant waterfall of the biblical Word and orthodox dogma [Barth's own image], it was precisely the Herrmannian elements in Barth's theology that saved it from degenerating into a sterile orthodox dogmatism.[163]

Firmer than any church tradition, Barth's Christocentric assurance rests on the witness of Scripture, as he hears it. He never subjected his theological work to the verdict of scientific exegesis (whether liberal or conservative), as Trutz Rendtorff stressed,[164] and it looks unlikely that he attributed, *historically*, his view of election to the man Paul; in the case of Jesus Christ, however, God and Man, ontologically the beginning of all the ways of God, he was convinced that the text could not be read otherwise. The foundation of certainty was laid for him in the passages that ascribe creation to Jesus Christ, the Christological hymn of Colossians 1 and the Prologue of the Fourth Gospel (he also claimed Rev. 1:8).[165] It seemed clearer than daylight that the subject in such *sedes doctrinae* (seats, i.e. basic passages, to ground the doctrine) was not the 'abstract' *Logos asarkos*, but the concrete, incarnate, Jesus Christ.[166] Obviously, Karl Barth could also take comfort from the fullness ascribed to Christ the Redeemer throughout Scripture and that Calvin's Christocentrism wished to reflect.[167]

Last but not least, Barth's architectonic love for *symmetry* should be mentioned. He delighted in building grand structures, displaying logical geometry – which partially accounts for the appeal of his dogmatics. The doctrine of sin and reconciliation reaches unmatched heights in this respect. To the Christological triad of deity, humanity and their union corresponds the triad of the basic forms of sin, then the triad of justification, sanctification and vocation, then the triad of faith, love and hope, and then the triad of the Christic offices![168] One remembers also the symmetry of Israel and the church

---

163. Ibid., pp. 174–175.

164. 'L'Autonomie absolue de Dieu: pour comprendre la théologie de Karl Barth et ses conséquences', in Gisel, *Karl Barth: genèse et réception*, p. 244.

165. *CD* III/2, p. 465.

166. Ibid., pp. 483–484, and already the discussion in *CD* II/2, pp. 95–99. Runia, *Theologische Tijd*, p. 112, n. 104, observes that the role of John 1 is 'remarkable' (*opvallend*).

167. On Barth's Calvinian correspondences, see Sung Wook Chung, *Admiration and Challenge*, 2002), esp. pp. 66–67; cf. p. 84, nn. 95–96 on Christocentrism, and p. 225.

168. *CD* IV/1, §58.4.

in the doctrine of election. The Christological concentration makes it possible (unlike traditional orthodoxy) to arrange the whole of the divine work in a beautiful symmetrical fashion:

> Even as His command, the Word of God is the Word of His truth and reality in the act of creation, in the act of reconciliation and the act of redemption. Or we might put it in this way, that it reveals the kingdom of the Lord Jesus Christ as the kingdom of nature, the kingdom of grace and the kingdom of glory. Or we might say that it manifests the pre-temporal, co-temporal and post-temporal eternity of God . . . Of course, there can be no question of three parts or even three stages of the one Christian truth and knowledge. The position is as in the doctrine of the Trinity. Three times in these three concepts we have to say the one whole, in which Jesus Christ is the presupposition and the epitome of creation and redemption from the dominating centre of reconciliation as it has taken place in Him.[169]

Who spoke of a doctrinal cathedral? Most noteworthy is the attempt to safe-guard some diversity while the last sentence tends to absorb ultimate diversity into the one all-determinative centre, in loyal service to Christological con-centration.[170]

Moving cautiously towards appraisal

If hanging in the air, even grandiose cathedrals are not safe enough as places of worship. The majestic proportions of Barth's Christocentric theology are not sufficient to establish its viability; some attempt must be made to sound the strength of its foundations and to probe the durability of its cement and linkages.

---

169. *CD* II/2, p. 549.
170. One finds the same wrestling with the need to preserve some plurality and the same ultimate subsumption under the unity defined by reconciliation, the same parallel with the Trinity in H.-A. Drewes and E. Jüngel (eds.), *Das christlichen Leben. Die kirchliche Dogmatik IV.4: Fragmente aus dem Nachlass Vorlesungen 1959–1961* (Zurich: Theologischer Verlag, 1976), pp. 9–10: though in our pilgrim-theology we cannot but think of creation, reconciliation and redemption as a 'step by step' sequence, we are to see them as one. Barth, apparently (and surprisingly), calls them 'three modes of divine being' (*drei Seinswesen Gottes*) and applies to them the rule *opera Trinitatis ad extra sunt indivisa* (the external works of the Trinity are undivided).

Dwelling on the magnitude of Barth's achievement would border on the ridiculous: so obvious! Less trite would be the appreciation for his exegetical efforts (fine print), moved by a true love of the Scriptures, and for his attitude towards orthodox tradition, which contrasts with the scornful ignorance of (most) liberals. As he concentrated on Christology, his intention to exalt the freedom of divine grace and to glorify the one Mediator finds an echo in evangelical hearts. During the short-lived Barthian era, preachers in mainline churches had again substance to preach.

Yet one may not gloss over ambiguities that affected even such strengths (and partly explain that the effect did not last).[171] The twofold meaning of the word *Aufhebung* (suppression, taking up) applies to Barth's relationship to Scripture and tradition: he took over the legacy, he lifted up the themes of Bible, creeds and Reformation; at the same time, he so radically reinterpreted them that he came close to abrogating them in their previous understanding. Had it not been for prestige and rhetorical power, the unceasing shifts between what we are in Christ, the only reality, and what we are in ourselves, though a fleeting shadow; between the threat of the *Nichtige* and the victory won, already and beforehand; between God's independence from created being and his involvement as determining his very essence – these and others would have been considered unsatisfactory by most readers. When one compares Molnar's and McCormack's sets of quotations, it is difficult not to acknowledge with the latter 'an inconsistency in Barth's thought'.[172]

---

171. As I have observed in French Protestantism.

172. 'Grace and Being', p. 102. Consider, on the one hand, 'the immanent Trinity is said to be wholly identical in content with the economic Trinity' (ibid., p. 100, referring to *CD* I/1, p. 479), and yet the distinction is a necessary one, and Barth rejects the idea that revelation is the basis of the Trinity (ibid., p. 101, referring to *CD* I/1, p. 312). In Barth's later work, one still meets 'a triune being of God which is independent of the covenant of grace' (McCormack, 'Grace and Being', p. 102), in this statement of *CD* IV/1, p. 52: 'The second "person" of the Godhead in Himself and as such is not God the Reconciler. In Himself and as such He is not revealed to us. In Himself and as such He is not *Deus pro nobis* [God for us], either ontologically or epistemologically.' This sounds like the doctrine Barth rejects elsewhere – yet it is 'the content of a necessary and important concept in Trinitarian doctrine when we have to understand the revelation and dealings of God in the light of their free basis in the inner being and essence of God'. Barth moves on to say that, as he is going to deal with the atonement, it would be 'pointless' and 'impermissible' to go back to this *Logos asarkos*; but the concept is

Leaving aside the problem of dialectical logic as such, the frustration lies in the outcome: the two sets of statements tend to neutralize each other, and the brightness of fiery oratory results in uncertain ashes. The account of the *Nichtige* as necessarily produced by God's No of rejection, and this No necessarily implied by God's Yes to his creation, resembles a piece of speculative legerdemain. Barth is not to be held responsible for the ultimate consequences of his choices that he did not draw himself[173] (for if such were counted against us theologians, O Lord, who could stand?), yet, the features that were just mentioned arouse legitimate preoccupations.

Barth's Christological concentration appears to agree with the Bible inasmuch as two basic truths of faith are affirmed: the Agent and Mediator of creation was this Person whom we now call Jesus (who had been predestined to be our Reconciler, the Head of redeemed Humanity); his reconciling work implied a 'recapitulation' (*anakephalaiōsis*, Eph. 1:10) of created reality so that Christ is the Man, in whom we contemplate the perfection of manhood as originally designed. This does not entail, however, that Jesus' manhood *existed* in the beginning, with the consequence that all human beings, by virtue of (the first) creation, must be said to be 'in Christ'. Here Barth's language conflicts with that of the New Testament: for Paul, being in Christ means sharing in the *new* creation (2 Cor. 5:17, 'if anyone', not the ontological status of all). Paul speaks of Andronicus and Junia as *having been in Christ before he was* (Rom. 16:7). C. E. B. Cranfield summarizes, 'The last words of the verse indicate that Andronicus and Junia were converted before Paul and are senior to him as

---

valid and necessary to honour the freedom of God. In the Molnar–McCormack debate, (1) I would (provisionally) lean towards McCormack's side as regards Barth's deeper and more original concern and contribution; (2) consider Barth's inconsistency as a more serious matter, not to be minimized as residual metaphysics (McCormack, 'Seek God', p. 77, acknowledges that 'statements can be found later' than 1939), but as required by the defence of God's freedom; (3) differ in value judgment. I consider McCormack's strictures on the *extra Calvinisticum* and traditional theism (ibid., p. 68) to be unfounded and an 'actualistic ontology' insufficient to honour God's sovereign freedom. Barth comes close to the idea of self-constitution (*CD* IV/1, p. 209, 'self-positing', *sich selbst setzende*), and I share van Driel's misgivings on the notion ('Barth on the Eternal Existence', p. 56: 'the notion of divine self-constitution is incoherent').

173. This is the procedure of Cornelius Van Til's critique, which was so repellent to many readers, as they could not perceive the depth of Van Til's penetration.

Christians.'[174] Human beings, though they were created by the Logos, are not 'in Christ' before they come to distinct faith in him. This was also Calvin's teaching, with which Barth's statement clashes.[175]

On the vexed issue of *apokatastasis*: while one may be grateful that Barth refrained from affirming it, he came close to it. The distance from the New Testament is significant. Brunero Gherardini warns:

> [A] conception likely to sweep aside also the remnants of personal responsibility, everything being decided in advance in Christ's destiny, not taking into account that the perspective of that salvation, in spite of all, can hardly be reconciled with the Word of the Lord, especially with the word he pronounces in his terrible 'vae': 'Woe to you, Chorazim' . . . The threat of the 'everlasting fire' (Mk. 9:7), of the 'gehenna' (Matt. 5:22), of the 'weeping and gnashing of teeth' (Matt. 8:12f.), however one wishes to interpret it, seems to lose all meaning . . . On this rocky ground, the very originality, which all acknowledge, of Barth's doctrine of Election seems to suffer shipwreck.[176]

Barth's view of Scripture allowed him such a departure from textual meanings; however, it causes a serious tension with his love and respect for the Bible.

What about the support Barth thought he could find in key Bible passages? Revelation 1:8 is hardly relevant: if the words were uttered by the Son, Jesus Christ, they would not ascribe pre-existence to the *man* Jesus as such. Even without the *communicatio idiomatum* (communication of properties, understood in Luther's sense as being from one nature of the incarnate Son of God to the other), it is a perfectly acceptable way of speaking to refer to someone by a name he acquired later and to ascribe to that person something that belongs to a previous stage: 'President Wilson was born in this house.' If it were said of Christ (not so in Rev. 1:8), 'This man pre-existed,' it would not necessarily be *as man*. The three other texts, John 1, Colossians 1 and Hebrews 1 deal with creation and incorporate reminiscences of wisdom traditions (particularly Wisdom 7). Hebrews 1:1–3, which accurately revises the wording of Wisdom 7.25–26 to rule out any inferiority for the Son's deity, makes no mention of the incarnation (the epistle deals with Christ's humanity in 2:5ff., and stresses the

---

174. *Romans*, vol. 2, ICC (Edinburgh: T. & T. Clark, 1979), p. 790.

175. *Institutio religionis christianae* 3.22.2: 'not all are members of Christ'; equivalent statement in the French text of 3.21.7, 'those who belong to the body of Jesus Christ' are the remnant (Rom. 11:5), not all.

176. 'Riffletando sulla dottrina dell'elezione', in Rostagno, *Barth contemporaneo*, p. 117.

order: *we* share in blood and flesh; in order to help us, the Son *also* came to participate in them, 2:14 – not Barth's order). Runia vigorously challenges Barth's reading of John's Prologue.[177] The gist of his reply is the reminder that 'one cannot lose sight of the historical perspective here. The Prologue *begins not* with verse 14.'[178] He claims, 'Nowhere has the work of creation been interpreted soteriologically, but in all texts the caesura of the incarnation has been considered, whether *expressis verbis* [in explicit terms] (John 1:14) or not.'[179] Though the structure of John 1:1–18 is not simply linear (the coming and rejection of vv. 10–11 are probably already those of the incarnate one), there is no reason to project the 'becoming flesh' into the opening statements of the passage.

The Christ hymn in Colossians 1 offers what could be points of contact with the Barthian interpretation: 'image of the invisible God' in 1:15 may recall the Adamic privilege of Genesis 1:26–27, and 'firstborn' the messianic title of Psalm 89:27, and therefore direct the reader's thought to Jesus Christ's *human* nature when creation 'in him' is affirmed. Even so, however, the connection is not explicit, and there is no hint, in the Old Testament, of a *creative* role attributed to Adam or to the psalm's (new) David. Sharing in God's creation, on the contrary, is the personified Wisdom of Proverbs 8:22–31. The Proverbs poem sowed seeds that germinated in the sapiential tradition of Judaism – harvested in the New Testament! Interpreters have recognized Wisdom Christology in Colossians 1:15 ff.[180] This insight opens an alternative explanation: 'firstborn' follows from the emphasis on the divine begetting of Wisdom in Proverbs 8 as the beloved child of YHWH (vv. 24, 25, 30; Wisdom 7.22 uses *monogenēs* (only begotten) for the spirit of Wisdom); 'image' (of the divine goodness) is said of her in Wisdom 7.26. Without going as far as C. F. Burney in a famous article,[181] who suggested our hymn unfolds the possible meanings of *rē'šît*

---

177. *Theologische Tijd*, pp. 82–83, 100–102, 112–114.

178. Ibid., p. 83, n. 182.

179. Ibid., p. 114. He also argues that the *houtos* (he) of John 1:2 refers to the first verse.

180. Ibid., p. 114, n. 115, mentions already G. Sevenster. A most convincing treatment is A. Feuillet's 'L'Hymne christologique de l'Epître aux Colossiens (I, 15–20)', in idem, *Le Christ, sagesse de Dieu d'après les épîtres pauliniennes* (Paris: J. Gabalda, 1966), pp. 163–273.

181. 'Christ as the APXH of Creation (Prov. viii 22, Col. i 15–18, Rev. iii 14)', *JTS* 27 (1926), pp. 160–177, 173–176, on Col. 1:15; the four meanings are 'beginning', 'sum-total', 'head' and 'firstfruits'. He quotes, p. 174, a passage from Epiphanius (*Refutation of All Heresies* 2.73.7) showing that he perfectly perceived the reference to Proverbs 8.

(beginning) in Proverbs 8:22 (and Gen. 1:1), a sapiential reference is likely enough[182] to neutralize any ascription of creation to the man Jesus as such: if Christ, in the text, can be the image and the firstborn *as* Wisdom uncreated and creative, Barth's reading is no longer necessary. The construction of the hymn, with two panels that answer each other,[183] also provides an exegetical argument: the first panel is devoted to creation (1:15–17), the second to reconciliation (1:18–20), which *adds* a new 'prime rank' to Christ's glory. They are distinct, without any hint of a 'Barthian' reversal of order. A fair correspondence may be established among the three 'sapiential' texts: the image of Colossians 1 corresponds to the effulgence of God's glory and to the stamp of his being in Hebrews 1, and, in John's Gospel, to the Logos, who was with God and who was God *en archē* (in the beginning).[184]

Was Barth entitled to talk disparagingly of an 'abstract' *Logos asarkos*? Klaas Runia's protest is loud and clear: 'Indeed, it is no abstract logos that John is speaking of. But it is certainly the logos *asarkos*!!'[185] God the Son is *concretissimus* (most concrete): both as God *a se*, in the absolute oneness of the divine essence, and as the distinct second *hypostasis* (the word suggested 'concrete' reality). He is the original and final Reality, more real than any that can be conceived. Actually, Barth's use of 'abstract' offers a symptom of his own method: since, for him, everything must be drawn from the Christ event, whatever may be said of God in himself is *abs-tracted* (drawn from) the only concrete refer-

---

182. The LXX word in Prov. 8:30 *harmozousa* (holding together in harmony) may be related to the role of Christ in Col. 1:17: '[I]n him all things hold together'.

183. He who is the image (15a) / He who is the principle (18b); firstborn of every creature (15b) / firstborn of the dead (18b); everything in heaven and on earth (16a) / everything . . . either on earth or in heaven (20a, b); 'hinge' part, 'and he himself is' repeated (17a, 18a).

184. Does it correspond to the 'form' (*morphē*) of God in Phil. 2:6? The same preexistence stage is in view: the structure of the passage and the strong likelihood that 'having become in the likeness of human beings' explains (appositionally) 'he divested himself', so that the *kenōsis* (emptying) includes the incarnation itself, show that the hymn's 'storyline' starts in heaven. Yet *morphē* remains far in usage from 'image' and rather means 'essential condition'. Cf. P. T. O'Brien, *The Epistle to the Philippians*, NIGTC (Grand Rapids: Eerdmans; Carlisle: Paternoster, 1991), pp. 186–271 (appendix, pp. 263–268, 'The Adam–Christ Parallel and Christ's Preexistence'); G. D. Fee, *Paul's Letter to the Philippians*, NICNT (Grand Rapids: Eerdmans, 1995), pp. 191–229.

185. *Theologische Tijd*, p. 83, n. 182.

ence. But a serious problem then emerges: how can one draw plurality from the *one* event? How does Barth know, *if there is no other source*, that the event is the union of these *two*, God and man? De facto, Barth relies on the witness of Scripture (and probably church tradition) to discern the duality in the Person/event; the problem is whether he may do so as a rigorous procedure, given his doctrine of Scripture as defined in §19 of *Church Dogmatics* I/2. If the fallible human witness of the writers only becomes the Word of God when and where *visum est Deo* (it pleases God), a 'happening' that ever eludes our grasp, Scripture as a permanent resource, as a corpus that can be objectively exegeted, is 'too human' to be a reliable guide in theology. Barth in practice disregards this difficulty, and offers no solution. Yet the difficulty is entailed by radical 'concentration'.

A similar situation obtains with the concentration of all 'times' into the one 'Eternal Time' of the Christ event (more precisely the forty days of the Risen One) and with the consequent reversal of the creation–reconciliation order. Barth wishes to safeguard some minimal plurality, and the very notion of *event* seems to require some 'before' against which newness arises, and yet, Barth goes farther than anyone else, compressing all into one – farther than Scotists and supralapsarians.[186] He affirms, as was seen, the coincidence of past, present and future; he denies, in deeper truth, succession. The contrast with Scripture is glaring. Berkouwer writes:

> The remarkable thing about the Bible is precisely this, that while it speaks clearly about the dimension of 'from eternity' and in terms of this dimension of the *unity* and the *omnipotence* of God's works – also with respect to sin – it never devaluates the decisive significance of the historical and the 'step-wise' character of creation and redemption but honors them and fully takes them into account.[187]

Althaus complained about the 'epochlessness' of God's action according to Barth.[188] The biblical meaning of saving grace includes that it intervenes as a new factor, which overthrows a situation that did not proceed from that grace: Good *News* because previously people *were* lost! The affirmation of a creational covenant in Eden, 'in Adam' as the Head, distinct from the covenant of redemptive grace 'in Christ', besides exegetical support, finds its warrant in that newness so hard to maintain (as Barth tries to) if nothing precedes. The

---

186. Ibid., p. 116.
187. *Triumph of Grace*, p. 252. Similar emphasis in Runia, *Theologische Tijd*, p. 44.
188. Berkouwer, *Triumph of Grace*, p. 254.

newness, further, is that of *grace* inasmuch as it implies the lifting of condemnation, a well-deserved condemnation under Law (the logic of Rom. 7:7 – 8:4): impossible to maintain if the Law is 'the form of the Gospel', not a prior stage! Runia objects to the thesis that Jesus' time (the forty days) takes on the attributes of eternity (contemporaneous with all times and the real content of all): it violates the Chalcedonian rule, *atreptōs* (without change).[189] He asks pointedly, 'Is it still *real time*? Is it a mere play on words if this time is still called time?'[190] In the *Römerbrief* eternity sounded like the annihilation of time. Barth tried to correct this trait and brought changes; 'yet, the tingling question remains whether, in the end, they make so much of a difference'.[191] The classical notion of eternity as pure present, *nunc aeternum*, without before and after, seems to favour Barth's speculation (this prompted me to re-examine that notion), but orthodoxy, though adhering to the notion, humbly preserved the Bible's historical sequence and emphasis;[192] Barth's bolder recasting of tradition, which suits the 'pure present' ultimacy and combines it with Christology, entangled him in serious problems.

Underlying the issue of historical sequence, one should discern that of evil or sin. Orthodoxy accepts, indeed orthodoxy affirms, that the dispensation of grace under the Old Testament was grounded in the later work of reconciliation. What makes the order of creation and reconciliation impossible to reverse is the intervening event of disobedience, the entrance of sin and, through sin, of death into the world (Rom. 5:12). Creation proceeds from God 'superlatively good' (Gen. 1:31). The misuse of the good gift of freedom places creation under condemnation, in an alienated state. 'But Christ has appeared once for all at the culmination of the ages to do away with sin' (Heb. 9:26, TNIV): redemption presupposes previous evil. 'If man had not been perishing, the Son of man would not have come': Augustine's saying faithfully summarizes the import of countless New Testament state-

---

189. *Theologische Tijd*, p. 55.

190. Ibid., p. 54.

191. Ibid., p. 47. Berkouwer, *Triumph of Grace*, p. 165, n. 81, notices that between *Credo* (1935) and *CD* III/2 (1948), the option 'endless time' was dropped.

192. Barth's option, again, differs from Calvin's. Muller, 'Note on "Christocentrism"', p. 258, highlights the contrast and refers to Calvin's Commentary on Jer. 31:31 and to the *Institutes* 2.9.4. I point to the *Institutes* 1.2.1, where the order in the twofold knowledge of God is stressed; 1.6.1 (last part), where Calvin sounds quite apologetic, explaining how he can use New Testament passages when dealing with creation.

ments.[193] This logic Barth will not accept: he replaces it by an ontological interpretation of evil as 'Nothingness' that proceeds necessarily, though indirectly and paradoxically, from God's grace; for Berkouwer, the Reformers replaced the scholastic motive 'Nature vs. Grace' by the biblical 'sin vs. Grace' and Barth by the 'Chaos vs. Grace' antithesis.[194] Even sympathetic commentators have expressed some concerns over Barth's doctrine of evil.[195]

The majestic symmetry of Barth's construction requires such a doctrine of evil: the latter is the price to be paid for the former. The groundless (and therefore inexcusable) intrusion of sin, this 'opaque mystery', ruins the beautiful structure where everything falls into place: it is *atopos* (out of place). We cannot master rationally its presence within God's creation, under God's sovereignty, without starting to neutralize the evilness of evil. That our theology is unable to go beyond the sequence Creation–Sin–Redemption, and must therefore renounce symmetry, is a sign of the scandal of evil. In this light, Barth's achievement looks suspiciously like an extraordinary (and paradoxical) attempt at *comprehending* the message – and its mysteries.[196] Overcoming historical sequence has typified idealism, and the temptation to rationalize evil besets every thinker (including the orthodox, despite biblical discipline's restraint): Barth's Christological concentration offers a case for study.

While many have thought of comparing Barth with Hegel, Balthasar may not be far off the mark in placing him alongside Origen, jointly praised.[197] Two powerful thinkers who wanted to be faithful to the gospel, and whose bent for speculative constructions led them far from usual understandings . . . Barth himself loudly protested against the suggestion that his theology obeyed a pre-

---

193. *Sermon 174,2*, Patrologia latina, ed. J.-P. Migne (Paris: Migne, 1844–64), vol. 38, col. 940.

194. *Triumph of Grace*, p. 381; cf. pp. 377–380 on Barth's flawed demonology.

195. So even O. Weber, 'Kirche und Welt', in Wolf, Kirschbaum and Frey, *Antwort*, p. 234 ('BARTHS Lehre vom Bösen, vom "Nichtigen", wie er sich ausdrückt, bereitet gewiss ernste Fragen' [Barth's doctrine of evil, of 'Nothingness', as he expresses himself, raises serious questions indeed].

196. Berkouwer, *Triumph of Grace*, p. 307, uses the word for the incarnation that Barth, in effect, tries to 'comprehend'.

197. 'Christlicher Universalismus', in Wolf, Kirschbaum and Frey, *Antwort*, pp. 240–244, esp. p. 240: 'We owe to Origen and to Karl Barth the two most thorough-going sketches of a theology of the Word, of the Word who is the eternal Son of the Father, yet not the *Logos nudus* ['naked' Logos] but *incarnandus* and *incarnatus*, who as such bears and justifies the creation.'

conceived idea: he wrote to Gherardini, 'I have no Christological principle . . .
I rather seek to orient myself, for each theological question, and somehow *ab
ovo* [from the start], not from some Christological dogma, but from Jesus
Christ himself.'[198] Are these, however, viable alternatives? Can the Object be
referred to in theological discourse without a concept as the tool of reference?
One cannot doubt Barth's *intention* to honour the object (who remains the
subject) through 'concentration', but common human frailty dictates that
intentions sometimes fail to reach their goal.

© Henri Blocher, 2008

---

198. Letter dated 24 May 1952, as quoted by Busch, 'Un Magnificat perpétuel', p. 21.
     A similar claim appears in *CD* IV/3.I, p. 174.1; cf. also 'Introduction', *Theology and
     Church*, p. 7. *Shorter Writings, 1920–1928*, trans. L. Pettibone Smith (New York: Harper
     & Row, 1962), p. 7.

2. DOES IT MATTER IF CHRISTIAN DOCTRINE IS CONTRADICTORY? BARTH ON LOGIC AND THEOLOGY

Sebastian Rehnman

Introduction

The catholic or ecumenical creeds of the Christian religion claim a lot of things. For instance, that God exists, that God is triune, that God created everything except himself, that God became incarnate in Jesus Christ the resurrected one, and that there is one, holy, catholic and apostolic church. That these claims are true is crucial for Christianity.[1] Christian theologians have therefore always been concerned with maintaining and defending the truth of Christianity. So they have given grounds for belief in God and the historical claims of the Christian religion. But a precondition for such grounds is that it makes sense to suppose that the claims of the catholic creeds are true. If creedal claims are contradictory, it does not even make sense to suppose that they could possibly be true. So the traditional defence of creedal claims has included a rebuttal of a charge of contradiction.

---

1. In this chapter I take it for granted that the creeds do express claims and not just emotions or exhortations. Barth also holds to some kind of realism. For a brief argument that non-realism is subversive of Christian faith, see W. Alston, 'Realism and the Christian Faith', *International Journal for Philosophy of Religion* 38 (1995), pp. 37–60.

This concern with maintaining and defending the truth of Christianity is found in Karl Barth. In his 'swan song', *Introduction to Evangelical Theology*, he claimed that Christianity stands or falls in relation to truth. He therefore made a valiant appeal to Christians to take objections seriously and to stand for revelation in order to glorify God and benefit the world.[2]

In this chapter I shall first present how Barth understood the charge that Christian claims are contradictory and how he suggested that that charge could be solved. I shall then analyse the solution he suggests and defend an alternative solution to the charge of contradiction.

The problem of contradiction

This section will present how, according to Barth, the charge of contradiction poses a problem for the Christian religion.

The significance of the problem of contradiction comes through already in Barth's methodological introduction to *Church Dogmatics*. In the very first section he discusses the criteria of Christian theology and specifically the law of non-contradiction, that something cannot be so and not so at the same time. There he writes:

> Even the minimum postulate of non-contradiction is acceptable to theology only in a very specific interpretation . . . theology does not claim that the 'contradictions' which it asserts are in principle insolvable. But the sentences in which it claims their removal will be sentences about the free agency of God and thus not sentences that 'dismiss the contradictions out of the world.'[3]

This passage focuses on the implications of the law of non-contradiction for theology. The law of non-contradiction is, according to Barth, inapplicable to theology unrestrictedly, since theology occasionally states what is contradictory. He does not here make clear what those occasions are, because this formulation is one of principle. But the specific theological statements he has in mind will, of course, be on the periphery or at the centre of the Christian religion or somewhere in between. Since the problem of contradiction will be really significant only if it pertains to central Christian doctrines, we need to

---

2. *Einführung in die evangelische Theologie*, 3rd ed. (Zurich: Theologischer Verlag, 1985), pp. 91, 107–108, 110, 133–134.
3. *KD* I/1, p. 7; *CD* I/1, p. 9.

turn to such places to find what 'contradictions' Barth may believe that theology 'asserts'. Let us turn to the doctrines of the triunity and incarnation of God,[4] since these are undoubtedly central Christian doctrines.

The first central instance in which the law of non-contradiction poses a problem for Barth is precisely with reference to the triunity of God:

> The great central difficulties which of old forthrightly beset the doctrine of the Triunity at this point, beset us too . . . . We, too, cannot state how in this case 3 can really be 1 and 1 can really be 3 . . . . None of the terms used, . . . can adequately say what they ought to say and we like to say with them. If someone only paid attention to what these terms as such can say in their immanent possibility of meaning, and did not accept what they can refer to here, he would only be endlessly annoyed . . . On all sides good care is thus taken to see that the *mysterium trinitatis* [mystery of the Trinity] remains a mystery.[5]

The doctrine of God's triunity means, according to Barth, that three really is one and one really is three. But the very meaning of those words shows that three cannot be one and one cannot be three, as that is contradictory. So, 'When we have said what' divine triunity is, 'we have said nothing'.[6] Thus, divine triunity is real, but can be stated only in a contradictory way. This is precisely why the doctrine is a mystery according to Barth.

The second central instance in which the law of non-contradiction poses a problem for Barth is with reference to the incarnation of God:

> The incompatibility of divine and human essences as the essence of one and the same subject is intuitive. The repugnance at the sentence, that Jesus Christ is the one who is of divine and human essences, in whom both these are united, is inevitable. However one may define divine and human essence, unless one will do violence to

---

4. In this chapter I use the term 'triunity' for the property of being one in three, since it more clearly conveys the meaning than 'trinity' (*trinitas*). This is also Barth's view and his English translators therefore use 'triunity' (*CD* I/1, p. 369). The more literal idiom of Barth's German and my native Swedish customizes, but I hope that this usage is not awkward to English readers. According to W. G. T. Shedd, *Dogmatic Theology*, 3 vols. (New York: Scribners, 1888–94), 1.267, the English term 'Trinity' is an abbreviation of 'Triunity', but he provides no evidence for this.
5. *KD* I/1, pp. 387–388; *CD* I/1, pp. 367–368.
6. Ibid., pp. 387, 367.

the one or the other, . . . one can only define them in sharp distinction, yea, opposition. The sentence about Jesus Christ as the one who is of divine and human essences, dares thus the union of that which by definition is incompatible.[7]

So the doctrine of the incarnation means, according to Barth, that 'divine and human essences' are united 'as the essence of one and the same subject'.[8] But this does not make sense, because from the very meaning of the words ('by definition') it follows that divine and human natures are incompatible. Thus, the doctrine of the incarnation is true but contradictory. This is precisely why the doctrine is a mystery according to Barth.

Let me make clear what the charge of contradiction involves. The issue is not whether or not someone has been or is speaking against the doctrines of triunity and incarnation. For Barth uses the terms 'contradiction', 'incompatibility' and 'repugnance' in the context of the 'immanent possibility of meaning' and 'definition', and since those terms refer to what is conceivable or supposable, they indicate that those doctrines contain words whose meaning cannot be supposed to agree. The charge is that buried within those doctrines is the claim that God is *p* and *not-p* eternally, and the claim that Christ is *p* and *not-p* simultaneously. So the issue is that the truth of divine triunity and incarnation can only, according to Barth, be expressed in a logically inconsistent way.[9]

---

7. *KD* IV/2, p. 65; *CD* IV/2, p. 61.
8. It is unclear to me why Barth here uses the abstract 'essence' rather than the concrete 'nature', which is more common in this context. In the following I have revised his usage and employ 'nature'. I shall henceforth use 'Jesus Christ is the one in whom divine and human natures are united' as synonymous with Barth's Christological point in this passage. If anyone does not like this substitution, it will be easy for him or her to stay with 'essence' in such a way that the main points of this chapter remain.
9. It appears that Barth assumes Kant's definition of the law of non-contradiction and his related concept of analyticity. According to this view the concept of the predicate is already contained in the subject in analytic statements, and contradictions arise when the predicate contains incompatible concepts: I. Kant, *Kritik der reinen Vernunft*, vol. 4: *Gesammelte Schriften* (Berlin: Georg Reimer, 1900–1983 [1787]) B10, 15–18, 190–193. On Barth's generally Kantian framework see, for instance, J. C. McLelland, 'Philosophy and Theology – A Family Affair (Karl and Heinrich Barth)', in H. M. Rumscheidt (ed.), *Footnotes to a Theology: The Karl Barth Colloquium* (Waterloo, Ont.: Corporation for the Publication of

But (someone may ask) why is it problematic for Christianity or for anything else to claim what is contradictory? Briefly, a contradictory claim is problematic because it says that something is true that cannot be supposed to be true. Let us see why some sentences are not contradictory and why some are.

Some sentences are not contradictory. For instance, 'Karl wears glasses,' 'A triangle is a figure with three angles and three sides' and 'If God exists, then the chief human end is to glorify and enjoy him.' These sentences are grammatically well formed in that they follow the rules of putting words together. They are also meaningful sentences because the words (arguably) have meaning; that is, they purport to describe what may be the case. Words have meaning either if they are everyday words with everyday meaning or technical words with technical meaning defined by everyday words. Now, grammatically well-formed and meaningful indicative sentences usually express statements or propositions that make claims: something that can be supposed to be true. Thus, one can make sense out of the above sentences. In such sentences the meaning of the words agree and therefore those sentences can also be called 'non-contradictory'. Now, a claim does not stand alone. For one claim entails other claims. The claim expressed in 'Karl wears glasses' entails 'Someone wears glasses,' and what is stated in 'A widow is running' entails 'A woman is running.' So a claim p entails another claim q, if and only if p and not-q are contradictory. When one can ultimately understand what it would be like for a claim and any claim it entails to be true, then they are not contradictory. But a non-contradictory claim and any other claim it entails may actually be false. For instance, 'Barth died in 1986' and its entailment 'Barth lived in 1985' are non-contradictory but false. We know though what it would be like for Barth to live to be one hundred years old.

Some sentences are contradictory. These *appear* to be indicative sentences that describe something that can be supposed to be true. Contradictory sentences are initially meaningful but ultimately meaningless. For instance, 'Greed is three foot long,' 'Some triangles have four sides' or 'God pulled the hair of

---

Academic Studies in Religion in Canada, 1974), pp. 30–52; S. Fischer, *Revelatory Positivism? Barth's Earliest Theology and the Marburg School* (Oxford: Oxford University Press, 1988); B. L. McCormack, *Karl Barth's Critically Realistic Dialectical Theology: Its Genesis and Development 1909–1936* (Oxford: Clarendon, 1995).

Kant's view of contradiction is commonly regarded as too narrow, but nothing much would seem to turn on this issue for present purposes. This chapter has profited from the rigorous analysis of the related concept of coherence in R. Swinburne, *The Coherence of Theism*, rev. ed. (Oxford: Clarendon, 1993), pp. 11–50.

bald-headed Sam.' The first sentence is grammatically well formed, but ultimately has no meaning. For a vice is not the kind of thing that can have length, and so it claims the contradictory that greed is something that cannot have length and can have length. Similarly, the second sentence cannot be supposed to be true, since 'triangle' entails 'a figure with three sides'. The third sentence is grammatically well formed but ultimately meaningless, since it entails the contradictory. For, 'a completely bald-headed person' entails 'a hairless person'. The denial of 'All bald-headed persons are hairless' is 'Not all bald-headed persons are hairless.' This denial entails 'Some hairless persons are not hairless,' which in turn entails 'There are certain persons, such that these persons are hairless and these persons are not hairless.' When one cannot ultimately understand what it would be like for a claim and any claim it entails to be true, then they are contradictory. Contradictory sentences do not claim anything that can be supposed to be the case, since what is claimed to be the case cannot conceivably be the case: the claim cannot under any circumstances be supposed to be true.

Note, however, that contradiction is not about lack of imagination. For sometimes we cannot picture the non-contradictory. We cannot form a mental image of every cello that has ever existed, now exists and will exist on this planet due to our lack of time and energy. However, that does not make the sentence 'Every cello that has ever existed, now exists and will exist on this planet is brown' contradictory. For there are recognized ways of showing whether or not what the sentence expresses is true.

This is what the law of non-contradiction is all about.[10] It says that something cannot be *p* and *not-p* simultaneously. It is a law in the sense that nothing can be correctly thought and nothing can really exist without conformity to it. One cannot make sense of a sentence that is claimed to be both true and false simultaneously. This possibility of ultimately understanding what it would be like for a claim and any other claim it entails to be true presupposes the truth of the law of non-contradiction. For instance, 'Karl Barth died in 1968' and 'Karl Barth did not die in 1968' do not ultimately make sense together, because something cannot be *p* and *not-p* simultaneously. However, if it is asked why

---

10. Traditionally, the law of non-contradiction is one of three first principles: (1) the law of *identity*, (2) the law of *non-contradiction*, and (3) the law of the *excluded middle*. The law of non-contradiction has been analysed since antiquity. E.g. Aristotle, *Metaphysica*, Loeb Classical Library (London: Heinemann, 1933), 1005b20–1012b30, 1062a35–1063b35; *De interpretatione*, Loeb Classical Library (Cambridge, Mass.: Harvard University Press, 1938), 17a25–19b4.

something cannot be this, then the meaning of 'die in 1968' has not been understood. And if the law of non-contradiction is assumed to be false, then every claim will make sense with everything. So the demand for proof of logical laws has since Aristotle been regarded as a sign of deficient education. 'It is widely taken as axiomatic that if the description of a putative phenomenon entails a violation of a logical law, then that phenomenon cannot exist. [. . . Thus] The implications for philosophy, science, and theology are wide.'[11]

The law of non-contradiction concerns claims about divine triunity and incarnation. The sentences 'God is triune' and 'Jesus Christ is the one in whom divine and human natures are united' may be true only if what they claim is not contradictory. But if it does not ultimately make sense to suppose what those sentences claim, then it cannot be true that God is triune and became incarnate in Jesus Christ. Perhaps it first seems to make sense to suppose 'God is triune' or 'Jesus Christ is the one in whom divine and human natures are united,' but ultimately it does not, according to the charge of contradiction. For the first sentence entails, according to Barth, that three is one and one is three, which cannot be conceived to be true. The second sentence entails, according to Barth, that two natures are one nature and one nature is two natures, which cannot be supposed to be true. This is not an issue about natural languages (such as German and English), but about what is expressed, stated or claimed with the words having the meaning they do in such languages. Those statements are, according to Barth, contradictory merely from what they ultimately say. For buried within these claims is something that cannot be supposed to be true, which can be shown by drawing out what is involved in those doctrines.

Barth's suggested solution to the problem of contradiction

The last section showed that, according to Barth, the central Christian doctrines of God's triunity and incarnation entail contradictions. But since the contradictory cannot be supposed to be true, those doctrines pose a genuine problem for Barth. This section will present and analyse Barth's suggested solution to this problem.

In the passage quoted above from the methodological introduction to *Church Dogmatics*, Barth places the word 'contradiction' within quotation

---

11. S. Priest, 'Logical Laws', in T. Honderich (ed.), *The Oxford Companion to Philosophy*, 2nd ed. (Oxford: Oxford University Press, 2005), p. 540.

marks. It is possible that he did so to signal apparent, as opposed to genuine, contradictions. For if contradictions can be solved, then they were only apparent contradictions. Still, the contradictory poses a problem for Barth, and that fundamental passage suggests a solution to it.

Barth introduces his solution with the assertion that only a 'very specific interpretation' of the law of non-contradiction 'is acceptable'.[12] For apparently 'any concession' to the principle that no genuine contradiction is true 'involves abandoning the theme of theology'.[13] To uphold 'the theme of theology' some contradictions have, according to Barth, to be made (e.g. divine triunity and incarnation), and thus a 'very specific interpretation' of the law of non-contradiction is required. But what such 'interpretation' is 'acceptable'? Barth appears to define it thus: 'theology does not really claim that the "contradictions" which it asserts are in principle insolvable'. This does not, however, modify or restrict the applicability of the law of non-contradiction. For Barth asserts that he does not claim that apparent contradictions are insolvable; that is, he asserts that all apparent contradictions can be solved. This is in full agreement with the law of non-contradiction. If all apparent theological contradictions can be solved, then ultimately all theological statements make sense. This agrees with the view that no true theory – about God or whatever – can contain a contradiction, and thus Barth fully accepts the law of non-contradiction. So he has not offered a 'very specific interpretation' of the law of non-contradiction.[14]

However, Barth's main point seems rather to be that some (apparent) contradictions cannot be solved in accordance with (the standard 'interpretation' of) the law of non-contradiction. This would seem to be a reason for accepting only a 'very specific interpretation' of the law of non-contradiction. It is

---

12. Barth is in this context rejecting Heinrich Scholz's formulation of his first *wissenschaftliche* criteria: 'freedom from contradiction in all the sentences to be constructed into so-called science' (*KD* I/1, p. 7; *CD* I/1, p. 8). This formulation would seem to be the standard view that a description of a putative thing that entails a contradiction cannot be true, for such a thing cannot exist. Likewise, every theory that contains such descriptions is necessarily false.

13. Ibid.

14. Perhaps Barth desired, but failed, to express a weaker view, namely that generally or ultimately there are solutions, although we may not yet have come up with one for a particular instance. There is, however, no support for this in the (German and English) text and the solution he suggests points (as we shall see) in an entirely different direction.

here that Barth's solution to the charge of contradiction comes to the fore. For he claims that contradictions can be solved with reference to 'sentences about the free agency of God'. Although the contradictions are genuine, God is free to do the contradictory, as divine action is not subject to logical laws. So Barth suggests that the law of non-contradiction should be modified as holding only for some reality (the creation) and not for all reality (the Creator). That is why sentences about the free agency of God do not 'dismiss the contradictions out of the world'; they are part of the world but God is free to be and do the contradictory. So (purported) theological contradictions are solved, according to Barth, not by showing that they are only apparently contradictory and so free from contradiction, but by statements about divine freedom. There is 'freedom from contradiction' because there is divine freedom from contradiction. God is here free from contradiction not in the sense of free from believing and saying what is contradictory, but free to know, say and do the contradictory. For 'God is a free Lord, not only over the law of non-contradiction, but over his own deity.'[15]

Barth thus suggests that (purported) theological contradictions can be solved with reference to statements about divine freedom. But can puzzling statements be shown not to be contradictory by adding other statements? Yes, that is the only way to proceed. For evidence that a statement is not contradictory makes it possible for us to suppose the truth of it and of any other entailed statement. Additional statements aim to prove this by providing a more detailed account that makes the implicit explicit. Such proofs or arguments that a statement is not contradictory are either deductive or inductive. But since there is (arguably) just one instance of triunity and one instance of incarnation, an inductive argument is not possible. So the status of statements about triunity and incarnation can only be established by entailment of other presumably non-contradictory statements. But usually we need not show that it makes sense to suppose that what a statement claims to be the case is the case. For we know innumerable statements that are not contradictory and

---

15. *Christliche Dogmatik im Entwurf* (Munich: C. Kaiser, 1927), p. 217. I am indebted to Axel Karlsson for calling my attention to this passage. According to Barth, the law of non-contradiction and sentences such that 'two and two are four . . . do not have their value, truth and validity in themselves or in something which is as such "absolute", i.e. a humanly settled metaphysical, logical or mathematical system independent of God's freedom, will and decision, but only in the freedom, will and decision of God as the Creator of all creaturely power' (*KD* II/1, p. 602; *CD* II/1, p. 535; cf. *Einführung*, p. 102).

innumerable statements that are contradictory. It is only when there is a charge that a given statement is contradictory that we need to examine whether or not it actually is contradictory. But since statements usually are non-contradictory, the burden of proof lies on the one who claims that a particular statement is contradictory. Barth takes it for granted that statements about divine triunity and incarnation are contradictory and therefore proceeds by adding statements.

However, adding statements in order to show the status of another statement needs to be done in a particular way. One attempt would be simply to point out that the controversial 'God is triune' entails 'there is a God' and, since it is assumed that the latter statement is not contradictory, neither is the former. Similarly, one may attempt to show that the puzzling 'Jesus Christ is the one in whom divine and human natures are united' is not contradictory by one of its non-contradictory entailments: 'There is a human nature.' This attempt will not do. For even contradictory statements may entail non-contradictory statements; the contradictory 'Some triangles have four sides' entails the non-contradictory 'Some triangles have sides.' This vain attempt shows, however, that in investigating a purported contradiction we assume and have to assume both that there are non-contradictory statements and that those presumably non-contradictory statements can establish whether or not another statement is contradictory. For every statement cannot be supposed to be simultaneously contradictory. So, if the additional statements are non-contradictory and the puzzling one is entailed by them, then the puzzling claim is shown to be non-contradictory. Hence the proof that a statement is not contradictory cannot move from the purportedly contradictory to the presumably non-contradictory, but must move from the presumably non-contradictory to the purportedly contradictory. Whether or not a statement is contradictory cannot be established by other statements it entails, but by whether or not it is entailed by statements that are assumed to be non-contradictory.

Now Barth seeks to show that God can be triune and incarnate by adding statements about divine freedom. His solution does not need to be interpreted as claiming that 'God is triune' and 'Jesus Christ is the one in whom divine and human natures are united' entail 'God is free.' Rather, it can be interpreted in the opposite way, namely that 'God is free' entails 'God is triune' and 'Jesus Christ is the one in whom divine and human natures are united.' In other words, his suggestion is that God's triunity and incarnation are entailed by God's freedom.

Barth's principal point about divine freedom of contradiction can again be traced to his doctrines of God and Christ. For instance, 'No logical necessity need prevent us from establishing this simple recognition' that the numerical unity of God 'lacks' the 'limitations necessarily connected with the concept of numerical unity in general . . . Rather, in him these limits of what we otherwise understand as unity are abolished.'[16] Similarly, the section on the incarnation quoted above continues:

> 'Inevitable' is the repugnance to the sentence about the union of the two 'natures' in Jesus Christ, only for a thinking that is unconditionally bound by some general presuppositions. But such unconditional binding – whether by church dogma or general logic and metaphysics – is not appropriate to *recta ratio* [right reason], a basically free thinking. *Recta ratio* is ready for the objectivity demanded of it towards this object, and thus is free reason: free towards this object.[17]

So, according to Barth, God really is triune and incarnate, but that can be expressed only in contradictory sentences. But as logical laws do not hold for God, they do not hold for theology. Although it is impossible from the 'immanent possibility of meaning' that '3 can really be 1 and 1 can really be 3', and 'the incompatibility of divine and human essences as the essence of one and the same subject is intuitive', God is free to be and do the contradictory. For divine freedom allows for the predication of contradictory properties to God and Christ. On this account of divine freedom, God is able to be and do the non-contradictory as well as the contradictory. Just as there are non-contradictory actions (e.g. creating the world, calling Abraham etc.) so there are contradictory actions (e.g. becoming incarnate), and that just as there are non-contradictory beings (e.g. plants, humans, God etc.) so there are contradictory beings (e.g. squared triangles, a triune God etc.) on a par with one another.[18]

However, this account of divine freedom cannot solve the charge against divine triunity and incarnation, since God cannot be free in the sense that Barth supposes. First, the contradictory is not anything God can be or do. Recall that a contradictory sentence claims something to be the case that does not make sense and so it does not claim anything. For the claim cannot under any circumstances be supposed to be true. So, if claims of divine triunity and incarnation are contradictory, they do not succeed in describing a being or an action, and therefore do not really claim anything God is or does. Secondly, it

---

16. *KD* I/1, pp. 373–374; *CD* I/1, p. 354.

17. *KD* IV/2, pp. 66–67; *CD* IV/2, p. 62.

18. '[T]hat which within creation signifies the absurd is also the object of God's omnipotence' (*KD* II/1, p. 601; *CD* II/1, p. 534).

cannot be supposed to be true that divine freedom means that God can eternally be the non-contradictory and the contradictory, and that Jesus Christ can
simultaneously be the non-contradictory and the contradictory, since that
cannot both be true of God or Christ under any circumstances. Hence this
account of divine freedom rather intensifies than solves the charge of contradiction with respect to triunity and incarnation by increasing rather than
decreasing what cannot be supposed to be true. It would seem even on Barth's
account that we should not assume more contradictions than necessary. It is
of course then very confused to say that God is free to be and do the contradictory, since that is not anything that can be or be done. But if 'God is free'
is non-contradictory, it cannot entail sentences that do not make sense. Thus,
Barth's solution to the charge of contradiction fails because there is absolutely
nothing that would count as God being or doing the contradictory.[19]

Notice that the last paragraph does not limit God to our power of imagination or lack thereof. The limitation really lies with us, who use expressions
that may appear to be indicative sentences and so deceive some of us into
thinking that something is claimed. Moreover, granted that triunity and incarnation are contradictory, it should not on Barth's view be regarded as more of
a limitation on God's freedom that he cannot be triune and incarnate, than that
he cannot be corporeal or cannot pull the hair of a bald-headed person. Given
that God is an indivisible, infinite and omnipresent spirit as well as the first
cause of everything that is material, God is not free to be essentially corporeal.
Corporeality is denied to God not because it predicates something God is not
free to be, but because it does not really ascribe anything at all to God. Or
imagine that Sam is completely bald-headed and that someone claimed, 'God
pulled Sam's hair.' That indicative sentence purports to state a fact. But since
someone who is bald-headed has no hair to be pulled, the sentence does not
describe nor claim anything. It is contradictory to suppose that God pulled
something that cannot be pulled. So denying that God can pull Sam's hair does
not restrict God's freedom.

---

19. If Barth were consistent in claiming that God is free to be and do the
    contradictory, theology 'would be outside the realm of rational enquiry and
    discussion'. For then Barth 'need never be disturbed by any reasoning or any
    evidence, for if his omnipotent [or omnilibertarian] being could do what is logically
    impossible, he could certainly exist, and have any desired attributes, in defiance of
    every sort of contrary consideration' (J. L. Mackie, 'Omnipotence', *Sophia* 1 (1962),
    p. 16). But Barth clearly thinks that God can be discussed and does take account of
    differing considerations. So he is inconsistent in affirming the contradictory.

However, this revised account of divine freedom will not do as it stands. For there are non-contradictory claims about being and doing for which God is not free. For example, God (as God) is not free to go to bed, eat strawberries or stop at the traffic lights, since God is not the kind of being that can do these things. So divine freedom is not power to do any non-contradictory action. Nor can divine freedom be power to be or bring about any non-contradictory state of affairs. For God cannot be said to be free to bring about necessary states of affairs such as that he is an infinite, eternal and immutable spirit, or that all bodies tomorrow are spatial. For God simply is an infinite, eternal and immutable spirit, and bodies are spatial tomorrow irrespective of what anyone does. Nor is God free to bring about every contingent non-contradictory state of affairs, since then God could change the past. But God is not now free to have the apostle Paul escape out of Damascus in a cart instead of a basket in (about) AD 35. For then Paul escaped in a basket and did not escape in a basket. Lastly, God is not free to sin. For he is supposed to be essentially good, and divine freedom thus means ability to perform all those actions that are known to be good and ability not to do all those actions that are known to be evil. Again, all this cannot sensibly be said to restrict God's freedom, since what is denied does not really claim anything at all.[20]

At this stage it could, however, be objected that the doctrines of the triunity and the incarnation of God are mysteries, and therefore we cannot understand what it would be like for those doctrines to be true. 'On all sides good care is'

---

20. Even given Barth's 'theology of the Word', there should be some hesitation on his part about his conception of divine freedom. For according to Scripture, God cannot repent, lie, break a promise, swear by anything greater than himself, and so forth. Moreover, genuine church dogmatics does not claim that God is free to be and do the contradictory. See e.g. Augustine, *Contra Faustum*, vol. 25, CSEL (Vienna: Tempsky, 1866–), 26.5; Anselm, *Proslogion*, ed. F. S. Schmitt, 6 vols., vol. 1: *Anselmi opera omnia* (Edinburgh: Thomas Nelson, 1946–61 [1078–9]) 7; T. Aquinas, *Summa contra gentiles*, ed. A. Leone (Rome: Forzanii et socii, 1894 [1259–65]), 2.25.20; *Summa theologiae*, 22nd ed., 6 vols. (Taurini: Marietti, 1940 [1266–73]), 1.25.3; F. Turretin, *Institutio theologicae elencticae* (Geneva: Samuel de Tournes, 1679–85), 3.21. René Descartes is generally held to be the exception that confirms the rule that Christians do not suppose that God is free to undo the laws of logic and do not suppose that God is limited by them. For two careful contemporary analyses of the concept of omnipotence, see G. van den Brink, *Almighty God: A Study of the Doctrine of Divine Omnipotence* (Kampen: Kok Pharos, 1993); Swinburne, *Coherence*, pp. 153–166.

to be taken, according to Barth, 'to see that the *mysterium trinitatis* remains a mystery', because nothing 'can adequately say what we ought to say and like to say'. The doctrines of the triunity and incarnation of God are contradictory because they are mysteries.

However, we cannot believe the contradictory. No-one can believe something without believing that the grounds make it likely to be true. If someone believes that God is triune, then that is believed because it seems more likely for him or her than that God is not triune. If someone believes that God became incarnate, then that is believed because it seems more likely for him or her than that God did not become incarnate. For no sense can be made of 'Karl believes that God became incarnate, but believes that there are no grounds whatsoever for God being incarnate.' But, if God is believed to be triune or incarnate, then there is sufficient ground to believe this. Conversely, if it does not make sense to suppose that what the sentence 'God is triune' or 'Jesus Christ is the one in whom divine and human natures are united' claims to be true is true, then there cannot be any grounds to believe that God is triune or incarnate. If Barth replies that the contradiction of divine triunity and incarnation is ground for believing that God is triune and became incarnate in Jesus Christ, then that will have to be denied. First, because contradiction is no ground for believing anything, since something that does not make sense to suppose to be true cannot be supposed to be likely to be true. Secondly, and as a consequence, no-one can believe anything on the ground that it is contradictory, since claiming that something cannot be supposed to be true entails that everything counts against it being true. If Barth believes that everything counts against divine triunity and incarnation, he must believe that divine triunity and incarnation are unlikely and then cannot believe divine triunity and incarnation to be true. He may wish or hope that those mysteries are true, but in the strict sense he cannot believe that they are more likely than not.[21]

But perhaps Barth would counter by stating that the triunity and incarnation of God are known only by revelation and are therefore mysteries. A

---

21. Faith's 'only limit being proven contradictions in the propositions themselves, for then no evidence can justify belief or render it possible'. '[W]e can believe in mysteries however profound, but we cannot believe in palpable contradictions'. For 'In such a case, instead of believing both statements, [the mind] will believe neither' (J. Buchanan, *Analogy Considered as a Guide to Truth and Applied as an Aid to Faith* [Edinburgh: Johnstone, Hunter, 1864], pp. 558, 538–539). Similar points are developed in R. Swinburne, *Faith and Reason*, 2nd ed. (Oxford: Clarendon, 2005), pp. 23–26; and S. Wolfram, *Philosophical Logic* (London: Routledge, 1989), p. 182.

mystery revealed is, no doubt, still a mystery. For from the nature of things, the infinite can be only partly and not fully revealed to the finite. But a (putative) revelation cannot be contradictory. For if so, then it cannot be supposed to be true under any circumstances, and thus cannot be supposed to be a revelation. Although revelatory mysteries are inaccessible to human discovery, humans can determine whether or not purported revelations are contradictory. But if the mysteries of triunity and incarnation are not contradictory, it does not follow that we know everything that can be known of God. It does only follow that the partially revealed is intelligible, and that that which has not been revealed is (at least now) unintelligible. This also implies that mysteries must be believed in just this way, namely believed as not fully but partially revealed truths. For this reason, mysteries are traditionally said to be above but not against reason, apprehensible but not comprehensible, and known-that but not known-why or known-how.

A creedal solution

The law of non-contradiction has implications for anything that can be supposed to be true. According to Barth the central Christian doctrines of the triunity and incarnation of God contain genuine contradictions. His attempt to solve this problem by means of adding statements about divine freedom makes things even worse. For there is absolutely nothing that would count as God being or doing the contradictory. So on his account Christianity cannot be supposed to be true.

If those doctrines are still to be confessed, then a counter-argument is needed. In order to show whether or not these statements are contradictory, one needs to present an argument in the form of a more detailed account. For the only way to prove that a statement is not contradictory is a detailed explication of it. The status of statements about triunity and incarnation will have to be established through other presumably non-contradictory statements by which they are entailed. However, if such a proof is to settle the question, then the statements also need to be authoritative (or entailed by authoritative statements). The Athanasian Creed is commonly taken as the foremost orthodox formulation of the triunity and incarnation of God.[22] Here is its passage on the triunity of God:

---

22. For a solid work on this creed, see J. N. D. Kelly, *The Athanasian Creed: The Paddock Lectures for 1962–3* (London: A. & C. Black, 1964). I have used Kelly's edition of the Latin text for my own translation below.

This is the catholic faith: that we worship one God in trinality and trinality in unity, not confusing the persons or dividing the substance. For the Father's person is one, the Son's another, and the Holy Spirit's another; but the divinity of the Father, the Son and the Holy Spirit is one: of equal glory and coequal majesty. Such as the Father is, such is the Son, and such is the Holy Spirit. The Father is increate, the Son is increate, and the Holy Spirit is increate. The Father is infinite, the Son is infinite, and the Holy Spirit is infinite. The Father is eternal, the Son is eternal, and the Holy Spirit is eternal. Yet there are not three eternals, but one eternal; just as there are not three increates or three infinites, but one increate and one infinite. Likewise the Father is omnipotent, the Son is omnipotent, and the Holy Spirit is omnipotent. Yet there are not three omnipotents, but one omnipotent. So the Father is God, the Son is God, and the Holy Spirit is God; and yet there are not three Gods, but there is one God. Thus the Father is Lord, the Son Lord, and the Holy Spirit Lord; and yet there are not three Lords, but there is one Lord. For just as we are obliged by Christian truth to acknowledge each person singly both God and Lord, so we are forbidden by the catholic religion to speak of three Gods or Lords. The Father is of none, not made nor begotten. The Son is of the Father alone, not made nor created but begotten. The Holy Spirit is of the Father and the Son, not made nor created nor begotten, but proceeding. Thus there is one Father, not three Fathers; one Son, not three Sons; and one Holy Spirit, not three Holy Spirits. In this triunity there is nothing earlier or later, nothing greater or lesser, but all three persons are coeternal and coequal with each other. So in all things (as was said above) both trinality in unity and unity in trinality must be worshipped.

Here is the relevant passage on the incarnation of God:

Thus the right faith is that we should believe and confess that our Lord Jesus Christ, the Son of God, is equally both God and man. He is God from the Father's substance, begotten before time; and he is man from his mother's substance, born in time. Perfect God and perfect man, subsisting of a rational soul and human flesh; equal to the Father according to his divinity and less than the Father according to his humanity. Although he is God and man, he is nevertheless not two but one Christ. He is one not by the transformation of his divinity into flesh, but by the assumption of humanity into God; one entirely not by confusion of substance, but by unity of person. For just as the rational soul and flesh is one man, so God and man is one Christ.

So whether or not triunity and incarnation are contradictions will have to be established from such authoritative and precise statements as these. For such terms as 'triune' and 'unity of person' are of course technical terms, and in order to discern whether or not they ultimately have meaning, we need to adhere to the rules whereby their meaning was introduced. The paradigmatic use of those terms is found in the creed.

However, from the Athanasian Creed it is clear that Barth does not correctly apply the meaning of those terms.

There occurs first an error in Barth's formulation of triunity. He claims that according to 'the doctrine of the Triunity . . . 3 can really be 1 and 1 can really be 3'. However, the orthodox doctrine does not claim that, but that God is three in one way and that God is one in another way. This is obvious from the key distinction the Athanasian Creed infers between 'person' (*persona*) and 'divinity' (*divinitas*) in verses 5–6. These terms do not have the same meaning. First the word *divinitas* can be used either in the abstract for divine nature or in the concrete for a supreme being. In verses 6 and 33 the meaning is abstract, since it is used attributively and not denominatively. This divinity is all those attributes or properties without which something would not be divine.[23] The creed lists some such attributes: increatedness, infinity, eternity and omnipotence (vv. 8–14). So traditional synonyms of 'divinity' are 'the divine essence', 'the divine nature', 'deity', 'godhead' and so forth. But in verses 4 and 31 this divinity is considered as existing and is therefore called 'substance' (*substantia*); that is, something that exists of itself and not in another as subject. The verb 'subsist' (*subsistere*; cf. v. 32) is traditionally used for the particular way in which a substance exists.[24] The creed throughout names this substance 'God' (*Deus*). Secondly, there is the meaning of *persona*: 'each person singly [is] both God

---

23. For writers contemporaneous with the Athanasian Creed who used 'divinity' for 'divine nature', see ibid., p. 92. For an analysis of 'nature' (*natura*) contemporaneous with the creed, see Boëthius, *Contra Eutychen et Nestorius*, in H. F. Stewart, E. K. Rand and S. J. Tester (eds.), *The Theological Tractates: The Consolation of Philosophy* (Cambridge, Mass.: Harvard University Press, 1918 [512]), 1. Boëthius defines 'nature' as 'the specific difference that informs one and the same thing' (I) or as 'the specific property of any substance' (IV). Augustine (*De moribus ecclesiae Catholicae et de moribus Manichaeorum*) defines 'nature' (*natura*) as 'all that something is in its kind', quoted in R. Goclenius, *Lexicon philosophicum* (Frankfurt: Mathias Becker, 1613), p. 739.

24. '[W]hereas Augustine, although prepared on occasion to use *substantia* of divine being, felt distinctly uneasy about it, and considered *essentia* more suitable, the Quicunque shows no such compunction' (Kelly, *Athanasian Creed*, p. 81). For more on *substantia* and *subsistere* in this context, cf. Boëthius, *Contra Eutychen et Nestorius* 2–3; Turretin, *Institutio* 3.23.4–5.

and Lord' (v. 19). A *persona* is of course a particular kind of substance, namely something that exists of itself in a rational or intellectual way.[25] In other words, the property *personalitas* (personality) is a mode of subsistence. In verses 21–27 the creed maintains that the one divinity subsists in three modes distinguished by the properties paternity, filiation and procession, and the relations paternity, filiation and spiration. So God is not in the orthodox formulation supposed to be three in the same sense as he is supposed to be one. If God is three in one way and God is one in another way, then it is not contradictory to claim that God is three and one. It is of utmost relevance then that 'God is triune' is entailed by 'God is three in the way of persons and one in the way of divinity'.

There occurs a second error in Barth's formulation of the incarnation. He claims that according to the doctrine of the incarnation, 'divine and human natures' are united 'as the nature of one and the same subject'. However, according to the Athanasian Creed, Christ 'is one not by the transformation of his divinity into flesh, but by the assumption of humanity into God; one entirely not by confusion of substance, but by unity of person' (vv. 35–36). So, according to orthodoxy, the divine nature and the human nature are united not in a third nature but in the person of the Son.[26] But the kind of unity that is supposed in Barth's charge of contradiction is that of monophysitism, namely that there is in Christ only one nature.[27] Such a view of course con-

---

25. The Augsburg Confession 1.1: 'the term "person" is used with the signification which ecclesiastical writers have used in this matter', namely 'not a part or a quality in something else, but that which properly subsists' (my trans. of the Latin text found in vol. 3 of P. Schaff, *The Creeds of Christendom: With a History and Critical Notes*, ed. D. S. Schaff, 6th ed., 3 vols. [New York: Harpers, 1931]). For a contemporaneous explanation of the meaning of *persona*, see Boëthius, *Contra Eutychen et Nestorius* 3. According to Kelly, there is in the creed a 'real distinction of the persons', but in relation to the divinity the persons are 'forms' or 'modes'; that is, 'the one and only respect in which' they differ is 'in the relation they bear to each other as a result of their different modes of origin within the divine substance which they are' (*Athanasian Creed*, pp. 73–75).

26. Here I use the more common term 'nature' instead of the creed's 'substance' (*substantia*). These terms were synonymous in ecclesiastical Latin at that time; cf. Kelly, *Athanasian Creed*, pp. 92, 81.

27. Barth's formulation here does not agree with his orthodox formulations in what follows (cf. *KD* IV/2, pp. 65ff.; *CD* IV/2, pp. 61ff.). But my subsequent argument addresses only whether or not orthodox Christology is contradictory.

tradicts the creed. For the latter claims that there is a *unitas personae* (unity of persons) consisting of both *divinitas* and *humanitas*, that is, one intellectual mode of subsistence that contains both all those properties without which something would not be divine, and all those properties without which something would not be human. So Christ is not in the orthodox formulation supposed to be the transformation of two natures into one, but is claimed to be God according to his divine nature and man according to his human nature. That is not obviously contradictory. So it is of utmost relevance that 'Jesus Christ is the one in whom divine and human natures are united' is entailed by 'Jesus Christ is God according to his divine nature and man according to his human nature.'

The Athanasian Creed thus shows that Barth does not correctly apply the meaning of key terms and that the paradigmatic use of the terms does not entail his purported contradictions. The creed's more detailed statements show that the less detailed statements are not contradictory. For it gives 'divinity', 'humanity' and 'person' distinct meanings, and in a valid distinction the terms have separate meanings. So, given the validity of the distinction between 'person', 'humanity' and 'divinity', it is not contradictory to claim that there is one indivisible divinity common with three persons or that there is one person with divinity and humanity. However, Barth may regard this more detailed account insufficient and demand descriptions of circumstances that would make those statements true. He is after all objecting to words such as 'person', and the above argument assumes that that term is non-contradictory. Perhaps then these orthodox formulations entail contradictions after all. Yet, the terms are much less vague than Barth allows for and so, if the orthodox formulations do entail contradictions, they are buried much more deeply than his erroneous formulations purport. The only way to investigate this is by considering a still more detailed account; to see whether or not the orthodox formulations are entailed by statements that Barth and the Athanasian Creed assume are not contradictory. What is needed is non-contradictory descriptions of states of affairs, in which the divinity can be predicated of each person but in which one person cannot be predicated of another person; and in which human properties and divine properties can be predicated to the person but not to the opposite nature. Let us turn to more detailed descriptions of triunity and incarnation.

A more detailed description of the orthodox understanding of triunity will have to start from the doctrine of 'modes of subsistence' (*tropos hyparcheos* or *modus subsistendi*). For the orthodox formulation supposes that triunity is entailed by that doctrine. In metaphysics a 'mode' is a particular way something is.[28] For instance, a mode is how something is coloured or shaped. So the identity of modes depends on the identity of the substance that possesses them. Modes 'lack the fully determinate identity-conditions characteristic of objects proper' because they 'are *existentially* dependent ones, depending for their existence upon the objects (often substances) which "possess" them'.[29] Hence we need to distinguish between the modes of being that a material and temporal substance can possess, and the modes of being that an immaterial and atemporal substance can possess.[30] A triangular-shaped rock is a substance possessing a mode, and the spatial extension is the attribute of which the mode is an instance. A material thing or substance cannot simultaneously have several modes. Three modes or forms of a rock imply three different things or three successive events. But material and temporal limitations are obviously not imposed on an immaterial and atemporal substance; infinity with respect to space is omnipresence and infinity with respect to time is eternity. Further, knowledge is existentially dependent (at least) partly upon the person knowing. In the case of self-knowledge the person knowing modifies himself rather than brings about another by knowing himself as object, and modifies himself further by understanding the identity of knowing himself as object and his own knowing. In other words, there are three modes of self-knowledge in a person. We need once again to distinguish between modes of finite self-knowledge and modes of infinite self-knowledge. For that a self-knowledge is the particular self-knowledge it is, is (at least) partly determined by whose self-knowledge it is. An infinite spirit would possess self-knowledge in a way that differs from that of human beings or angels. So infinity with respect to self-knowledge is three modes of subsistence. For God's knowing actualization of himself actualizes all that is divine as well as the actualization that the knowing actualization of himself is identical to himself. Thus, all the essential properties of the divine essence subsist in three modes.[31]

---

28. For a contemporary argument for ontological modes, see E. J. Lowe, *The Possibility of Metaphysics: Substance, Identity, and Time* (Oxford: Clarendon, 1998), pp. 38, 78–83. For a summary of this ancient doctrine, see Goclenius, *Lexicon philosophicum*, pp. 694–703.

29. Lowe, *Possibility of Metaphysics*, pp. 156–157, 181–182.

30. Sabellianism or modalism seems to entail a denial of either modes in metaphysics *tout court* or kinds of substances. The movement appears not to have used the terms for 'mode of subsistence' (*tropos hyparcheos* and *modus subsistendi*); cf. J. N. D. Kelly, *Early Christian Doctrines*, 5th ed. (London: A. & C. Black, 1977), pp. 121–123.

31. Perhaps there can be only one person in a finite substance, but there appear to be no a priori grounds that there cannot be more than one person in an infinite and

The orthodox doctrine of God's triunity is thus entailed by the ontology of modes.[32] Not that the doctrine was discovered by human reason, but the revelation of God as Father, Son and Spirit was seen to agree with the doctrine of modes of subsistence. On the basis of the revealed nouns 'Father', 'Son' and 'Spirit', and the predicates 'beget' and 'proceed', the church inferred the doctrine of the triunity of God. The Athanasian Creed claims that the implicitly revealed properties paternity, filiation and procession modify one existing divine substance and do not create three divine substances: 'there are not three Gods, but there is one God'. For a divine person is the divinity with a personal property and the three personal properties modify the divinity. The divinity as generating is the Father, the divinity as generated is the Son, and the divinity as proceeding is the Spirit. These are the internal, necessary and eternal personal acts of God that modify the divinity trinally. Each person is what he is in relation to the other persons and without one person there would not be any other person. The second person does not emanate from the first person as person but as mode of the essence, and the third person does not emanate from the first and second persons as persons but as modes of the essence. So God is not one in the way that finite personal substances are one, but one in the way that an infinite personal substance is one with modal relations.[33]

---

immaterial substance: 'That in one essence there can be but one person, may be true where the substance is finite and limited, but hath no place in that which is infinite' (J. Owen, *A Brief Declaration and Vindication of the Doctrine of the Trinity: As Also of the Person and Satisfaction of Christ*, ed. W. H. Goold, 24 vols., vol. 2: *The Works of John Owen* [London: Johnstone & Hunter, 1850–55 (1669)], p. 388).

32. 'Ita persona differre dicetur ab essentia, non realiter, id est essentialiter, ut res et res; sed modaliter, ut modus a re' (Thus the persons are said to differ from the essence not really, that is, essentially, as thing and thing; but modally, as mode from thing) (Turretin, *Institutio* 3.27.3). This would seem to be an improvement of the persons being really distinct from each other and rationally distinct from the deity (Aquinas, *Summa theologiae* 1.28–30), which in turn was an improvement of the classical definition of *persona*: 'naturae rationabilis individua substantia' (individual substance of rational nature) (Boëthius, *Contra Eutychen et Nestorius* 3.). For defence of modes of subsistence in this context, see Turretin, *Institutio* 3.27; Shedd, *Dogmatic Theology*, esp. 1.273–285.

33. Cf. the precise definition: 'a divine person is nothing but the divine essence, upon the account of an especial property, subsisting in a special manner . . . [A]ll the essential properties of that [divine] nature are in that person . . ., not as that person, but as the person is God' (Owen, *Brief Declaration and Vindication*, vol. 2, p. 407).

Therefore 'God is triune' is entailed by the more detailed description of the (presumably) non-contradictory state of affairs of modes of the infinite spirit. If it is granted that those descriptions are not contradictory, and it is granted that they entail the statement Barth called into question, then the charge of contradiction must be withdrawn. There is no evidence that he called the secondary claims about God as infinite spirit into question, but only evidence that he did not understand modes of subsistence. So, given that Barth and the Athanasian Creed equally assume that the additional statements are non-contradictory and that those statements entail the puzzling one, the argument should be persuasive – that is, getting Barth justified in believing what he would not otherwise be justified in believing.

But what is to be said of the personal union? A more detailed account of the orthodox doctrine of incarnation is needed to prove whether it is contradictory or not. For Barth may uphold his view by pointing out that both the property of being eternal ('begotten before time') and the property of being temporal ('born in time') are predicated by the Athanasian Creed to the 'one Christ', and it cannot be supposed to be true that Christ both is eternal and temporal. So, as the orthodox doctrine of the incarnation attributes incompatible properties to the same thing in the same respect, it cannot be supposed to be true. For no real thing can instantiate such properties at the same time and in the same respect.

However, that the orthodox doctrine is not contradictory can be defended by a more detailed account of the incarnation as a part–whole relation. For in becoming incarnate, the Son of God brought about a whole consisting of two parts, namely the whole consisting of his person and a human body and soul. Such an analysis is taken from the Athanasian Creed in two ways. First, the complex preposition 'according to' (*secundum*) in the Athanasian Creed can naturally be read as indicating which part gives the whole a particular property. For 'according to' modifies or specifies 'equal' (*aequalis*) and 'lesser' (*minor*), and so Christ is equal to the Father according to the divine part and lesser than the Father according to the human part. Equality with God the Father is therefore only predicated of Christ to the extent that he is divine: 'of equal glory and coequal majesty. Such as the Father is, such is the Son,' that is, increate, infinite, eternal and omnipotent. Likewise, equality with his mother Mary is predicated only of Christ to the extent that he is human: 'from his mother's substance' with 'rational soul and human flesh'. With this in mind we should read 'begotten before time . . . according to divinity' and 'born in time . . . according to humanity'. Secondly, a part–whole analysis of the incarnation is taken from the creed's famous soul–flesh analogy: 'For just as rational soul and flesh is one man, so

God and man is one Christ.'[34] Just as the soul immaterially but temporally, and the body materially and temporally, has the attribute of being part of a whole human being, so the human nature materially and temporally, and the divine nature immaterially and atemporally has the attribute of being part of the whole Christ.

However, if the predicative strategy and the anthropological analogy are to establish that the doctrine of the incarnation is not contradictory, they need to be entailed by a general theory of how two things or substances (e.g. 'God and man') can compose one thing or substance (e.g. 'one Christ'). Now, mereology is the formal analysis of parts and their wholes, where a whole is a composite substance that can persist identically through changes in (at least) one of its proper parts.[35] For instance, our cornel bushes are red according to the bark, but green according to the leaves and whitish according to the cortex. Such wholes do not depend for their identity upon the identity of their parts, but they commonly have their attributes according to their parts. For instance, verdure can be predicated of the bush on account of the leaves. But from the fact that one part of the bush is green and another is not green, it does not follow that the whole bush is green and not green, or that the bush is green and red all over. Rather the parts depend for their identity upon the identity of the whole. So wholes have some of their properties in themselves and some of their properties in their parts. All properties depend on causal interrelations that unify parts into wholes. Cortex, bark, leaves, and so forth causally interact to form a shrub with stem of moderate length.

Such a metaphysics of the incarnation in terms of the part–whole relation is traditional and can be applied to the Athanasian Creed.[36] For it claims that

---

34. It is central to this analogy that human beings are wholes consisting of the parts *body* and *soul*. 'The one and only point to which attention is drawn [by the analogy] is the way in which, without losing their separate identity, two distinct substances are united in man so as to form one individual, a single person' (Kelly, *Athanasian Creed*, p. 99). There is an interesting parallel in J. Calvin, *Institutio religionis christianae*, ed. P. Barth and W. Niesel, vols. 3–5: *Ioannis Calvini opera selecta* (Munich: C. Kaiser, 1926–62 [1559]), 2.14.1.

35. Aristotle analyses the part–whole relation in many places. See e.g. Aristotle, *Metaphysica* 1034b32, 1023b12–1024a28. A summary of the scholastic discussion is found in Goclenius, *Lexicon philosophicum*, pp. 788–798, 1132–1135. For one contemporary formulation, see Lowe, *Possibility of Metaphysics*, pp. 118–121, 164–167.

36. 'It is one thing to speak of the whole Christ; another to speak of the whole of Christ. The whole Christ is God and man, but not the whole of Christ. The whole

the 'one entirely' (*unus omnino*) or whole Christ 'suffered for our salvation, descended to hell, rose from the dead, ascended to heaven, sits at the Father's right hand, whence he will come to judge living and dead' (vv. 38–39). These properties are attributed to the whole Christ. But God cannot (arguably) suffer, rise from the dead and ascend from earth to heaven, since God is impassible, immortal and omnipresent. Human beings can, though, suffer, die and move to different places. Thus, suffering, resurrection and ascension can truly be predicated of Christ if and only if one part of him, the human nature, has power in itself to do these things. Equally, the Athanasian Creed claims that the whole Christ derives some of his properties from his constituent natures. For instance, Christ is eternal ('begotten before time') and temporal ('born in time'). The property of being eternal is derived from his divine nature and the property of being temporal is derived from his human nature. Thus, Christ is eternal by having a part that in itself has the property of being eternal, and Christ is temporal by having a part that in itself has the property of being temporal. The whole Christ has these properties according to his parts and, since they belong to divinity and humanity respectively, he does not have them in the same respect and therefore not in an incompatible way: 'not by transformation of his divinity into flesh' and 'not by confusion of substance, but by unity of person'.

There is, of course, in the case of Christ not a literal but an analogical part–whole relation as this whole consists of parts of different natures.[37] Incomplete parts constitute a proper whole, but neither the Son of God nor the human nature is an incomplete part. (A rational soul and a human body are [arguably] incomplete parts for the constitution of a whole human being.) But as causal relations unify physical parts into a composite physical substance, so

---

Footnote 36 (*continued*)

[Christ] denotes a person in the concrete, but the whole [of Christ] a nature in the abstract. Therefore it is rightly said that the whole Christ is God or man, since this denotes the person; but not the whole of Christ, since this denotes each nature that is in him' (Turretin, *Institutio* 13.7.17, 13.6.6, 8). For a medieval formulation, see Aquinas, *Summa theologiae*, e.g. 3a.2.4. For two contemporary defences along these lines: E. Stump, 'Aquinas' Metaphysics of the Incarnation', in S. Davis, D. Kendall and G. O'Collins (eds.), *The Incarnation: An Interdisciplinary Symposium on the Incarnation of the Son of God* (Oxford: Oxford University Press, 2002), pp. 197–218; B. Leftow, 'A Timeless God Incarnate', in Davis, Kendall and O'Collins, *Incarnation*, pp. 203–249.

37. Cf. Turretin, *Institutio* 13.6.5, 3.23.5.

God the Son entered special causal relations with a true human body and a reasonable soul such as to form one substance. 'He is one . . . by the assumption of humanity into God'; that is, his human part is so causally related from conception to the Son that it exists only in so far as he exists (and thus the human part is no person). Given that (a timeless) Son of God can enter into causal relations with temporal things (and the doctrine of creation certainly implies this), he can enter into 'a special and personal sustentation' with a human body and soul.[38] A simple being cannot literally have parts, but the Son can be related to something with parts and so by analogy have parts. Thus, the term 'part–whole relation' is used in similar senses of physical substances and of Christ.

So the incarnation is entailed by a more detailed description of the (presumably) non-contradictory state of affairs of part–whole relations. If it is granted that those descriptions are not contradictory, and it is granted that they entail the statement Barth called into question, then the charge of contradiction must be withdrawn. There is no evidence that he called the secondary claims about part–whole relations and the possibility of God entering into causal relations with the creation into question. So, given that Barth and the Athanasian Creed equally assume that the additional statements are non-contradictory and that those statements entail the puzzling one, the argument should be persuasive.

Barth may of course continue to bring the charge of contradiction to the doctrine of the incarnation and to the doctrine of triunity. The way to proceed, then, is to spell out still more detailed accounts with tertiary claims. If the secondary claims would be called into question, then those claims will need to be defended by tertiary claims and the argument would go on until final agreement is (hopefully) reached. There could also be a disagreement over what entails what and a secondary argument about that. But since sentences usually express non-contradictory statements, and non-contradictory statements are needed to show whether or not a doubtful statement is contradictory, it is Barth or a disciple of him who has the burden of proof to develop further a positive argument in favour of contradiction.

Nevertheless, the more detailed accounts above do not claim to make everything known about the triunity and incarnation of God. They only claim that divine triunity and incarnation are non-contradictory and therefore intelligible in so far as they are revealed (and, implicitly, not comprehensible in so far as they are not revealed). That is why those doctrines are

---

38. Ibid., 13.6.5.

mysteries. For this is just what a 'mystery' means in the traditional sense, namely 'partially, but not fully, revealed' truths.[39] Traditionally, the term points primarily to the source and, secondarily, to the content. So, thankfully, Barth's sense of 'mystery' is not that of the catholic church.[40] For 'unless a man believes [the catholic faith of the triunity and incarnation of God] faithfully and firmly, he will not be saved'.[41] But since mysteries are intelligible in so far as they are revealed, we are not demanded to believe what cannot, but what can, be supposed to be true. This reflects in turn an evidence-sensitive and thus a cognitive view of faith, namely sensitive to evidence in favour of

---

39. Buchanan, *Analogy*, p. 529. There are judicious analyses of 'mystery' in ibid., pp. 526–556, 569–570; and D. S. Boyer, 'The Logic of Mystery', *RelS* 43 (2007), pp. 89–102. The traditional concept of 'mystery' clearly goes back to the New Testament idea of a humanly undiscoverable truth made manifest by God (e.g. Mark 4:11; Rom. 16:25). This traditional sense of 'mystery' even has confessional status. E.g. the usage at the end of one of the longer and more technical articles of the Westminster Confession of Faith (4.8) presupposes partial intelligibility: 'The doctrine of this high mystery of predestination is to be handled with special prudence' (S. W. Caruthers [ed.], *The Westminster Confession of Faith: The Preparation and Printing of its Seven Leading Editions and a Critical Text* [Manchester: R. Aikman, 1937]). Similarly, the Belgic Confession states, 'although this doctrine [of triunity] far surpasses all human understanding, nevertheless we now believe it by means of the word of God, but expect hereafter to enjoy perfect knowledge and benefit thereof in heaven' (art. 9 in vol. 3 of Schaff, *Creeds*). Notice also the use of 'mystery' in e.g. Aquinas, *Summa contra gentiles* 4.1; Calvin, *Institutio* 2.14.1; Turretin, *Institutio* 1.10.2, 3.23.1, 3.25.4–6, 13.3.1, 13.4.1; Shedd, *Dogmatic Theology*, 1.249–250.

40. That sense appears rather to be a post-Kantian trajectory. There is e.g. (to my mind) a terrible expression of it in Herman Bavinck, who maintained that Christian dogmatics is 'all mystery' in so far as it deals with revelation: 'welke God van zichzelven . . . heft geopenbaard . . . In zooverre is het alles mysterie, waar de dogmatiek over handelt' (which God himself . . . has revealed . . . In so far as is it all mystery, which dogmatics deals with) (H. Bavinck, *Gereformeerde Dogmatiek*, 2nd ed. [Kampen: J. H. Bos, 1906–11], 2.1). Bavinck maintains that that which has been revealed is incomprehensible, not that that which has not been revealed is incomprehensible. For a brief analysis of the accentuated or conceptual divine transcendence in theology since Kant, see e.g. Alston, 'Realism and the Christian Faith', esp. pp. 51–53.

41. Athanasian Creed, v. 42.

the truth of (purported) revelation.[42] Now, since the contradictory cannot be believed, the traditional view of faith and mystery endorses the laws of logic in theology:

> The logical laws of identity, non-contradiction and excluded middle are applicable to every part of our knowledge, and we should incur the peril of being involved in utter absurdity or in sheer scepticism, did we disown their authority either in philosophy or in religion.[43]

So, in order to show that the triunity and incarnation are indeed mysteries and not contradictions, the church has developed rather elaborate statements. The most rigorous formulations state and defend the doctrine both exegetically and metaphysically, and only those parts of the church that have adhered to such formulations have been able to maintain those doctrines. But those formulations are not an expression of rationalism, if that 'signifies an appeal . . .

---

42. 'In much of the mainstream of the tradition . . . personal faith involves belief, and for faith to be reasonable it must be well grounded. So faith is sensitive to evidence, and to the status of that evidence. If evidence is called into question, then faith will, other things being equal, be weakened, unless a rebuttal can be found' (P. Helm, 'Introduction', in idem [ed.], *Faith and Reason* [Oxford: Oxford University Press, 1999], pp. 8–9). On this view, faith is well grounded only if it is based on reason and/or revelation. In contrast, the non-cognitive account of faith follows Kant in disregarding or even opposing well-groundedness.

43. Buchanan, *Analogy*, p. 540. (I have revised capitalization in this quotation to contemporary standards.) 'It becomes us to remember that these [religious] truths are presented to the same mind which takes cognizance of all other truth, – that to be of any practical use they must be known, and to be known, they must be dealt with by the same faculties, and according to the same laws, which regulate our knowledge in other cases, – that these faculties and laws come into spontaneous and active operation as soon as any object is presented to our thoughts so as to engage our attention, insomuch that it is not with us a matter of option, but of necessity, that we should be governed by them, – and that it is not only unreasonable, but impossible to believe two contradictory propositions, when they are clearly seen to be contradictory' (ibid., pp. 246–247). For the applicability of logical laws to the doctrines of triunity and incarnation, see e.g. Calvin, *Institutio* 4.17.24; Turretin, *Institutio* 1.10.2, 3.25.14, 13.6.23; Shedd, *Dogmatic Theology*, 1.250–251, 268, 298, 2.265. For a classic and general discussion of the law of non-contradiction in theology, see Turretin, *Institutio* 1.10.

to limit religion to those grounds, whether a priori or experiential, which are available to all people, at all times, and in all places'.[44] For church dogmatics emphatically endorses revelational mysteries to particular people, at particular times and in particular places. The doctrines of divine triunity and incarnation are rather an expression of rational belief, in the minimalist sense of intelligible belief. For in the traditional sense, 'right reason' is faith seeking understanding of revelation by means of metaphysics and logic; not Barth's sense of presuming to think at the expense of logic and metaphysics.[45]

It is precisely here I believe that Barth's theology fails. Church dogmaticians traditionally present highly precise and detailed accounts of divine triunity and incarnation. Theologians like Athanasius, Augustine, Anselm, Thomas Aquinas, John Duns Scotus, Francis Turretin, John Owen and William Shedd analyse and argue extensively for Christian doctrines. But contrary to real church dogmatics, Barth refused seriously to engage with metaphysics, that is in integrating all human sources of the knowledge of God.[46] In his own words:

> '[N]ot only the most important but also the most interesting and beautiful problems
> in dogmatics start where one thinks one must stop, because of the fable
> "unprofitable scholasticism" and the slogan "the Greek thinking of the church
> fathers"'.[47]

Although we generally should not believe in fables and slogans, Barth thought on such grounds that he must not integrate revelation and reason in the development of the doctrines of divine triunity and incarnation. Instead of developing those doctrines in sufficient detail and connecting secondary claims with primary claims, Barth charges them with contradiction. He failed to profit from the thinking of the fathers and the scholastics in maintaining and defending the truth of Christianity.

---

44. M. Westphal, 'Modern Philosophy of Religion', in P. L. Quinn and C. Taliaferro (eds.), *A Companion to Philosophy of Religion* (Oxford: Blackwell, 1997), p. 112.

45. For a traditional definition and defence of *recta ratio*, see Turretin, *Institutio* 1.10.3–16. For a survey of the faith-seeking-understanding programme, see P. Helm, *Faith and Understanding* (Edinburgh: Edinburgh University Press, 1997).

46. For an excellent analysis of Barth's confused views on natural theology, see B. Leftow, 'Can Philosophy Argue God's Existence?', in T. Senor (ed.), *The Rationality of Belief and the Plurality of Faith: Essays in Honor of William P. Alston* (Ithaca: Cornell University Press, 1995), pp. 40–70.

47. *KD* I/1, p. ix; *CD* I/1, p. xiv.

Conclusion

Christian theologians have always been concerned with maintaining and defending the truth of Christianity. They have given grounds for belief in God incarnate and grounds to suppose that those grounds make sense. In this chapter I have not given grounds for the truth of Christianity, but given grounds for supposing that the triunity and the incarnation of God are not contradictory and therefore possibly true. For the only reply that is needed in the face of the charge of contradiction is one that establishes that the puzzling statements ultimately make sense.

Karl Barth claims, however, that the central Christian doctrines of the triunity and incarnation of God are contradictory. For they purportedly entail terms whose meaning is logically inconsistent. Barth attempts to solve this by claiming that God is free to be and do the contradictory. I have argued that that solution fails, since the contradictory is absolutely nothing. I have also shown that the paradigmatic case of the Athanasian Creed does not entail Barth's purported contradictions, which are rather factually erroneous. An alternative solution to the charge of contradiction was defended by accounts of modes of subsistence and part–whole relations. I have also argued that Barth's sense of mystery is not only untraditional but also invalid. For the church claims that mysteries are comprehensible in so far as they are revealed, but incomprehensible in so far as they are not revealed.

Barth clearly wants to confess the triunity and incarnation of God with the church, but when he claims that those doctrines are contradictory, he fails in his intention of maintaining and defending them. For then Christianity cannot possibly be supposed to be true. But great confusion about logical laws would seem to be the only reason why a Christian theologian would claim that central doctrines are contradictory. As Barth does not want to say that the triunity and incarnation of God are necessarily false, he was presumably unaware of the implications of his charges of contradiction. So, since it would seem partly to be the dogmatician's calling to deal with the meaning and consistency of Christian doctrines, this chapter has aimed to clear up some of the confusion.[48]

© Sebastian Rehnman, 2008

---

48. Thanks to Henri Blocher, Oliver Crisp, David Gibson, Paul Helm, Axel Karlsson, Anders Kraal, Donald and Elizabeth Ritter, Mark Sluys, for comments on the penultimate version of this chapter.

3. KARL BARTH AS HISTORICAL THEOLOGIAN: THE RECOVERY OF REFORMED THEOLOGY IN BARTH'S EARLY DOGMATICS

Ryan Glomsrud

Introduction: Barth's 'Reformed' identity

The renaissance in Karl Barth scholarship today is a result of the diversity of approaches taken in recent years to the Swiss theologian's life and thought. Setting aside long-running debates about the best model for understanding Barth's theological development from the early to later years, scholars have turned their attention to areas of Barth's oeuvre that have previously been ignored. The topic before us in this chapter, Karl Barth as historical theologian, emerges out of the recent exposure to historical-theological topics treated by Barth during the course of his career, his lectures and writings on the theologies of Martin Luther, Ulrich Zwingli, John Calvin and Friedrich Schleiermacher, as well as the theologies of the Reformed Confessions and the nineteenth century.[1]

---

1. K. Barth, *Die Theologie Zwinglis: Vorlesung, Göttingen, Wintersemester 1922/1923*, ed. Matthias Freudenberg (Zurich: Theologischer Verlag, 2004); *The Theology of John Calvin*, trans. G. W. Bromiley (Grand Rapids: Eerdmans, 1995); *The Theology of Schleiermacher: Lectures at Göttingen, Winter Semester of 1923/24*, trans. G. W. Bromiley, ed. D. Ritschl (Grand Rapids: Eerdmans, 1982); *The Theology of the Reformed Confessions, 1923*, trans. D. L. Guder and J. J. Guder (Louisville: Westminster John

Barth's historical interests, especially in the Protestant Reformation and theology of the Reformed tradition, have given rise to reflection on his recovery of a uniquely Reformed identity in the wake of nineteenth-century liberalism. It is now commonplace to associate Barth's 1920s lectures in Göttingen with his discovery of classical Protestant theology, his first interest in John Calvin and use of Reformed orthodox theology, and an emerging post-liberal and yet 'Reformed' perspective.[2] One scholar has proclaimed that in reaction to nineteenth-century Protestantism, the early Barth developed 'a profound sympathy for the great theologians of the sixteenth and seventeenth centuries, and acquired a masterly knowledge of Reformed and Lutheran scholasticism'.[3] John Webster astutely notes that this became one of the 'principal features' of Barth's early development, namely that he was 'instructed by the traditions of Reformed Christianity'.[4] More recently, Kurt Anders Richardson insists that while never a 'traditionalist', Barth was nonetheless a uniquely 'Reformed Protestant theologian', one whose entire theological existence was characterized by 'loyalty to Reformation doctrines', with 'constant reference to Luther and Calvin and to the traditions that emerged out of them'.[5] There is today, in other words, a trajectory of scholarship keenly aware of Barth's project to rehabilitate to some extent the classical Protestant theology of the Reformation and post-Reformation eras as a viable alternative to the religious thought patterns of the nineteenth century.[6] John Webster provides the conclusion that Barth's period of discovery of the classical Reformed

---

Knox, 2002); *Protestant Theology in the Nineteenth Century: Its Background and History*, trans. B. Cozens and J. Bowden, new ed. (London: SCM, 2001).

2. See e.g. T. F. Torrance, *Karl Barth, Biblical and Evangelical Theologian* (Edinburgh: T. & T. Clark, 1990), p. 28.

3. T. F. Torrance, *Karl Barth: An Introduction to his Early Theology 1910–1931* (Edinburgh: T. & T. Clark, 1962), p. 54.

4. 'The Theology of Zwingli', in idem, *Barth's Earlier Theology* (Edinburgh: T. & T. Clark, 2005), p. 15.

5. *Reading Karl Barth: New Directions for North American Theology* (Grand Rapids: Baker Academic, 2004), p. 10.

6. See also J. R. Franke, 'Karl Barth, the Postmodern Turn, and Evangelical Theology', in Sung Wook Chung (ed.), *Karl Barth and Evangelical Theology* (Grand Rapids: Baker Academic, 2006), p. 281; Sung Wook Chung, *Admiration and Challenge: Karl Barth's Theological Relationship with John Calvin* (New York: Peter Lang, 2002).

tradition proved to be 'perhaps *the* . . . crucial phase of his development'.[7]

As part of a collection of critical perspectives, this chapter aims to make a general cautionary point about Barth's 'recovery' of the Reformed tradition in the light of this trend in scholarship. The intention here is not to challenge the reality of Barth's significant engagement with classical Reformed theology, but merely to issue an interpretative reminder or suggest a hermeneutical principle that will be important for considering the question of Barth's relationship to the tradition. His attention throughout his career to the all-but-forgotten orthodox theology of the post-Reformation era, including theologians such as Theodore Beza, Johannes Wollebius, Amandus Polanus and Johann Heinrich Heidegger certainly does deserve careful scholarly attention, for these thinkers featured heavily in the bulk of Barth's historical and dogmatic efforts during the Göttingen period as well as later in the fine-print sections of the *Church Dogmatics*. But in taking up the study of Barth's reclamation of Calvin and Reformed theology, the crucial interpretative reminder points in a different, perhaps surprising, direction: *never forget the nineteenth century*. For in fact, Barth's recovery of Reformed theology was intertwined with the inheritance of nineteenth-century conceptions of that tradition. In other words, the historians and theologians of the nineteenth century must always be figured into the equation of Barth and the classical Reformed tradition, whether as general background for his life and thought or, as in the case of this study, as the *vehicle* for his engagement with pre-critical theology. It was not simply the case that Barth discovered Reformed orthodoxy and then proceeded throughout his career to reformulate and revise the tradition in ways he deemed necessary. Rather, the burden of this chapter is to demonstrate that in the *Göttingen Dogmatics* at least, Barth encountered Reformed orthodoxy almost exclusively in the texts of the nineteenth-century historiographers of the tradition and not in the primary sources themselves. Barth himself recognized this to some degree, acknowledging that the collections of Reformed and Lutheran confessions and symbols on which he lectured were the unique bequest of nineteenth-century theologians and the phenomenon of 'flourishing academic historicism'.[8] As a consequence, what Barth engaged was a stylized and edited representation of post-Reformation theology, a particular reading and summary of the tradition that, while common to the nineteenth century, has in subsequent years come up

---

7. 'The Theology of the Reformed Confessions', in idem, *Barth's Earlier Theology*, p. 41 (italics original).

8. *Theology of the Reformed Confessions*, p. 16.

for substantial critique.[9] Barth's 'recovery' of Reformed theology during the formative Göttingen years was not, in other words, an entirely *ad fontes* event.

To approach the subject, this chapter explores §1 of Barth's Göttingen lectures on prolegomena to dogmatics, vis-à-vis his definition of dogmatics as a science and the object of dogmatics. In this early section of the lectures readers find Barth's first serious historical and dogmatic efforts conjoined. He offered a description and assessment of Reformed orthodox theology on the definition of dogmatics and then related this discussion to Schleiermacher and other modern definitions. While he was critical of the tradition on the one hand, in fact attempting to connect the early Protestant scholastics to later Schleiermacherian developments, on the other hand he sought to use the tradition positively for his own theological formulations. The sources and themes found in this text are of abiding relevance to historical theologians and Barth scholars alike. Critical issues to be explored include the accuracy of Barth's historical narrative, the issue of dependence on nineteenth-century historiography, and an assessment of his positive appropriation of the sources.

The *Göttingen Dogmatics*: the general structure and prolegomena

The Göttingen lecture cycle or *Urdogmatik* (original dogmatics), as it has been called, is a monument to historical theology applied to constructive dogmatics. During the summer semester of 1924, Barth began a series of lectures in systematic theology, forced by the predominantly Lutheran faculty to construe his instruction along Reformed doctrinal lines.[10] As the Honorary Professor for Reformed Theology (*Honorarprofessor für reformierte Theologie*) Barth hesitantly agreed to the course title 'Instruction in the Christian Religion', with its

---

9. For a summary and critique of the historiography of Protestant orthodoxy, see R. A. Muller, *After Calvin: Studies in the Development of a Theological Tradition* (Oxford: Oxford University Press, 2003); C. R. Trueman and R. S. Clark (eds.), *Protestant Scholasticism: Essays in Reassessment* (Carlisle: Paternoster, 1999).

10. *GD*. For the complete series available only in German, see K. Barth, *Unterricht in der christlichen Religion*, 3 vols., ed. Hinrich Stoevesandt (Zurich: Theologischer Verlag, 1985, 1990, 2003). On the conflict, see K. Barth and E. Thurneysen, *Karl Barth – Eduard Thurneysen Briefwechsel*, vol. 2: *1921–1930* (Zurich: Theologischer Verlag Zurich, 1974), p. 221; ET, *Revolutionary Theology in the Making: Barth–Thurneysen Correspondence, 1914–1925*, trans. J. D. Smart (London: Epworth, 1964), p. 166.

obvious allusion to John Calvin's classic text.[11] At that point in his career he
was eager to press on with the task of dogmatics in order to meet the growing
expectations of naysayers and curious parties that the 'Barth-movement'
move beyond polemics and announce to the world 'the B and C that come
after A'.[12] In Barth's own thinking there were many questions as to the form
and content this remedial alphabet should take. At that point in the 1920s the
former pastor from Safenwil and newly minted professor had not yet become
'the colossus of European Protestant thinkers', as he has been called, and he
had yet to prove himself a serious systematician.[13] In many ways he was still
in the process of emerging from nineteenth-century liberalism, casting about
for direction and help to construct his own positive theology. The question
he faced with regard to the 1920s lectures was how to teach a specifically
Reformed dogmatics? Where should one start, with what sources and from what
authority?[14]

Given the nature of the academic theology on which Barth had cut his
teeth (Kant, Schleiermacher, Herrmann, Harnack etc.), the question of how
to begin a systematic theology that prioritized the Word of God (as a revelation outside human possibilities) was a serious one. It was in this way that the
sourcebooks of Reformed theology edited by nineteenth-century historiographers Heinrich Heppe, Alexander Schweizer and others became significant
for Barth.[15] With the help of these collections he found himself in a haven of
the theology of the Reformed church and received the necessary aid he
desired in building a basic theological system. So fundamental were these
texts, especially Heppe's compendium or reader's digest version of Reformed
theology, that Barth's Göttingen lectures have been described as something
akin to a medieval *Sentences* commentary, that is, a close reading of a textbook
of theology offered to students along with commentary, explanation and

---

11. See E. Busch, *Karl Barth: His Life from Letters and Autobiographical Texts*, trans. J.
    Bowden (Philadelphia: Fortress, 1976), pp. 155ff.; see also Barth and Thurneysen,
    Revolutionary Theology, pp. 163, 166–167, 181–182.

12. Barth and Thurneysen, *Revolutionary Theology*, p. 167.

13. J. Webster, *Barth* (London: Continuum, 2000), p. 113.

14. See the autobiographical account in K. Barth, 'Foreword', in H. Heppe, *Reformed
    Dogmatics: Set out and Illustrated from the Sources*, trans. G. T. Thomson, ed. E. Bizer
    (London: George Allen & Unwin, 1950), p. v.

15. H. Heppe, *Die Dogmatik der evangelisch-reformierten Kirche* (Elberfeld: Friedrichs, 1861);
    Alexander Schweizer, *Die Glaubenslehre der evangelisch-reformierten Kirche dargestellt und
    aus den Quellen belegt*, 2 vols. (Zurich, 1844–7).

counterpoint. In this case, Barth substituted Heppe's *Reformed Dogmatics* for Peter Lombard's *Sentences*, thus allowing for significant historical–theological interaction and dialogue with Protestant orthodoxy.[16] Anticipating our conclusion, the importance of the nineteenth century can already be seen here; Barth's recovery of Reformed theology in Göttingen was synonymous with his discovery of Heppe and a coterie of nineteenth-century historiographers of the tradition.[17] The point may be a subtle one, but is nonetheless important. As the rest of this chapter will bear out, the encounter with nineteenth-century *reconstructions* of Protestant orthodoxy led to a number of historiographical inaccuracies and errors, none the least of which was a revival of the faulty but widespread 'Calvin versus the Calvinists' thesis.[18] This was even the case with Barth's reliance on the conservative, Dutch, neo-Calvinist, Herman Bavinck, as will be seen in §1. Before proceeding to the Prolegomena however, a general account of the overall structure of the dogmatics is in order.

The entire lecture cycle comprised eight parts: four parts of prolegomena and four parts of the system, treating respectively the doctrines of God,

---

16. B. L. McCormack, 'A Scholastic of a Higher Order: The Development of Karl Barth's Theology, 1921–31' (PhD diss., Princeton Theological Seminary, 1989), pp. 558–677.

17. See the Lutheran sourcebook compiled by H. Schmid, *Die Dogmatik der evangelisch-lutherischen Kirche dargestellt und aus den Quellen belegt*, 7th ed. (Gütersloh: Bertelsmann, 1893); ET, *The Doctrinal Theology of the Evangelical Lutheran Church, Verified from the Original Sources*, 2nd ed. (Philadelphia: Lutheran Publication Society, 1889). Upon his arrival in Göttingen in 1921, Barth purchased E. F. K. Müller's compilation of Reformed Confessions and familiarized himself with historical treatments by Heppe, Schweizer, Gottlob Schrenk, Herman Bavinck, and August Tholuck among others.

18. See C. R. Trueman, 'Calvin and Calvinism', in D. K. McKim (ed.), *The Cambridge Companion to John Calvin* (Cambridge: Cambridge University Press, 2004), pp. 225–244; R. A. Muller, *The Unaccommodated Calvin: Studies in the Foundation of a Theological Tradition* (Oxford: Oxford University Press, 2000), pp. 3–17; Muller, *After Calvin*, pp. 3–21; W. J. van Asselt and E. Dekker (eds.), *Reformation and Scholasticism: An Ecumenical Enterprise* (Grand Rapids: Baker Academic, 2001), pp. 14–21. Critical issues for the historiography of Protestant orthodoxy include the definitions of the terms 'scholastic' and 'orthodox', the relationship of orthodoxy to the Reformation, the question of philosophy, rationalism and theological method, the problem of central dogma interpretations of theological development, anachronistic readings of the tradition and more (see Muller, *After Calvin*, p. 71).

humanity, reconciliation and redemption.[19] Contrary to Colin Gunton's claim that Barth was never a systematic theologian in the scholastic sense, it is more appropriate to think that he learned the dogmatic trade from nineteenth-century historical theologians.[20] As part of his education from scholasticism, Barth acquired a taste for treating dogmatics as an orderly and scholarly enterprise. John Webster argues that during Barth's early development he profoundly internalized 'the thought structure of classical dogmatics'.[21]

The preliminary lectures moved to 'achieve a basic understanding of the theme, the necessity and the course of such reXection'.[22] They were especially intended to 'deal with the determination of the object, the conception, and the methods' of theology, with the grand theme of 'The Word of God' taking precedence throughout.[23] Worried about the Scylla of liberalism on the one hand and the Charybdis of classical Protestantism on the other, Barth announced that his 'guiding principle' would be 'not to attempt too much and not to accomplish too little, so as not to fall into any speculative or barbarically orthodox hole'.[24] It was important to begin with prolegomena and remain there for some time, in Barth's view, because the demise of pre-critical theology required it. The reasoning was that the more modern theologians

> lost sight of their theme and became unsure of their cause, [thus] beginning the tragic retreat which in the theology of Schleiermacher ended with total capitulation, there flourished introductions, prolegomena, debates about scripture, inspiration, revelation, miracles, religion, and reason . . . [25]

He further lamented 'the fact that an introduction to dogmatics is generally regarded as necessary, at times in the form of a so-called philosophy of religion, is a symptom that we do not live in a classical age of theology'.[26]

---

19. Busch, *Karl Barth*, pp. 153ff.; D. Migliore, 'Karl Barth's First Lectures in Dogmatics: Instruction in the Christian Religion', in *GD*, p. xliii.
20. C. Gunton, 'Karl Barth's Doctrine of Election as Part of His Doctrine of God', *JTS* 25 (1974), p. 389.
21. *Barth*, p. 6.
22. *GD*, p. 3.
23. Barth and Thurneysen, *Revolutionary Theology*, pp. 167–168.
24. Ibid., p. 167.
25. *GD*, p. 19.
26. Ibid., p. 18.

A science needs prolegomena when it is no longer sure of its presuppositions, when it has to reach agreement on them, when it has to work at showing with what right and with what means it can do what it wants to do, when it does not any longer, or, more hopefully put, when it does not yet understand the self-evident things with which any science commences.[27]

Although Barth himself may have been confident of the self-evident presuppositions needed to begin, the movement of the introduction revealed his keen awareness that theologians young and old should 'take only the smallest steps' in terrain that is 'difficult both in general and in detail'.[28] In accordance with Barth's small steps, this study will examine only a brief section of the Introduction.

Dogmatics as the science of the Word of God

Nineteenth-century dogmatics: finding common ground

The discussion of dogmatics as the science of the Word of God in section two of §1 introduced a litany of standard nineteenth-century definitions of theology. Barth began by calling attention to the similarity of his thesis, that dogmatics is 'scientific reflection on the Word of God', with representative positions of modern dogmaticians.[29] The point of contact, he suggested, lay in the shared conception of dogmatics as *science*, or *scientific* reflection (*wissenschaftliche Besinnung*), as employed by diverse thinkers from Schleiermacher to Alexander Schweizer, Richard Rothe, Richard Lipsius, Friedrich Nitzsch, Julius Kaftan, Wilhelm Herrmann, Hans Hinrich Wendt, and Ernst Troeltsch.[30] It soon became clear, however, that this apparent agreement caused Barth some discomfort, and so he moved to find a more precise formula and qualify the terms in view.

Before the modern era, the question of whether theology should be considered a science was engaged thoroughly by the medievals, typically by

---

27. Ibid. The validity of this statement could be questioned. One limitation of Heppe's summary was that it minimized extant prolegomena and gave readers the impression that the locus was virtually non-existent in the pre-critical era.
28. Ibid., p. 7.
29. Ibid.
30. Ibid., pp. 7–8.

recourse to classical, Aristotelian categories.[31] But in the sixteenth and seventeenth centuries the entire discussion was retooled by the Protestant scholastics to reflect both the teaching of the past and also the advances and new insights of the Reformation (e.g. *sola scriptura* [Scripture alone]).[32] Later, with the rise of Enlightenment thought and modern science, however, from the eighteenth century onward, the notion of theology as science developed new connotations and faced many objections from theologians, philosophers and scientists alike. In many ways, the issue emerged as one of the more significant problems for modern dogmaticians to tackle in relation to modern metaphysics, epistemology and Enlightenment philosophies of science.[33] Barth similarly identified this topic as one of the presuppositions of dogmatics that

---

31. Richard Muller notes that the medieval scholastics such as Alexander of Hales and Thomas Aquinas took up the five Aristotelian categories of knowing – 'understanding or intelligence (*intelligentia*), knowledge or science (*scientia*), wisdom or discernment (*sapientia*), prudence or discretion (*prudentia*), and art or technique (*ars*)' – in order to work out a careful position on the nature of the theological discipline and the quality of its knowledge; see R. A. Muller, *Post-Reformation Reformed Dogmatics: The Rise and Development of Reformed Orthodoxy, ca. 1520 to ca. 1725* (Grand Rapids: Baker Academic, 2003), vol. 1, p. 326. Most importantly, they asked whether theology was a kind of 'metaphysics'/'physics' (*scientia*) or 'ethics' (*prudentia*) (p. 325).

32. In reply to a series of prolegomenal questions (What is the object of theology? In what way can God be said to be the object? What is the genus of theological knowledge: scientific, ethical, wisdom etc.? Is theology theoretical or practical? In what sense is theology a science?), the Protestant scholastics, in conversation with Scotist critiques of *scientia* and Franciscan emphases on the practical rather than theoretical nature of theology, reworked the basic Thomist understanding of dogmatics as science. In particular, the orthodox were slow to 'equate theology precisely with any human discipline', taking any equation to be purely analogical (Muller, *Post-Reformation Reformed Dogmatic*, vol. 1, p. 338). Therefore, a range of positions was prevalent in the tradition, alternating between theology as a kind of science (see Lambert Daneau, Lucas Trelcatius [the younger], William Perkins, John Stoughton and Antonius Walaeus) and theology as wisdom (see Franciscus Junius, Johannes Scharpius, Johann Heinrich Alsted, Amandus Polanus and Francis Turretin). From his presentation, Barth seems not to have been aware of the nuances of these discussions.

33. See J. Kaftan, *Zur Dogmatik: Seiben Abhandlungen aus der 'Zeitschrift für Theologie und Kirche'* (Tübingen: J. C. B. Mohr [Paul Siebeck], 1904).

was problematic in his day and, as a consequence, had to be relearned to some extent. His discussion made rather curious uses of medieval and post-Reformation developments and constituted the first substantial historical–theological interaction in the Göttingen lectures.

Barth's insistence that 'Dogmatics is not fiction . . . It is science' struck a common chord with Hans Wendt's indication that 'science' is a discipline that applies methods in order to establish the 'objective truth of knowledge'.[34] Adding to this, Barth wanted to equate the descriptors 'scientific' and 'objective', 'objectivity being the closest possible adjustment of knowledge to the distinctiveness of its object'.[35] On this view, a science that presses after objectivity certifies its own authenticity and criterion of truth by its connection and close relation to the object under consideration. The object itself then guarantees the truth of the science, provided that, in the case of theology, the object be understood as having given of itself for reflection. Barth explained:

> The most fitting means to establish objective truth, the most certain way to achieve coherence in knowledge, the freest critical norm, and the most logical grounding of all knowledge will in every field of science be the truth itself, which we do not have to produce but which is given to us.[36]

Despite modern confusion surrounding the terms 'scientific' and 'objective', Barth wanted to uphold the definition of dogmatics as science. Although he could have stimulated his thinking and refined his definition with help from the scholastics, he made no reference or appeal at this point to the numerous and lengthy Reformed orthodox discussions of the topic available in primary sources. Thus far, only nineteenth-century interlocutors were in view. Moving under his own power, then, Barth pressed the point of the *self*-revealed nature or sheer givenness of the object of theology as a protective hedge against crasser notions of God as an object of science, able to be humanly controlled or manipulated as on a microscope slide or in a Petri dish. For Barth, the objective character of revealed truth did not 'preclude its scientific character' but 'included it'.[37] Given these provisos, Barth accepted the proximity and even agreement of his definition with the variety of modern ones.

---

34. *GD*, p. 8.
35. Ibid.
36. Ibid.
37. Ibid.

Modern anthropocentric dogmatics: Barth's dissent

Agreement with the modern tradition was exhausted in due course, however, and so, quickly enough, Barth began to catalogue his disagreement with the nineteenth-century definitions in view. The real point of contention concerned the *object* of theological science. His dissent was governed by the fact that he took over for constructive use what he called 'an older dogmatic tradition' with its honoured object of dogmatics being the Word of God.[38] The entire discussion represented the first in the Göttingen lectures of Barth's significant interaction with post-Reformation Reformed and Lutheran sources, a fact that has too often been overlooked in secondary literature. Even while borrowing from the Reformed orthodox tradition, however, the problems he identified in the modern views he also blamed on post-Reformation predecessors.

Turning first to the complaint levelled against the modern definitions, Barth rejected their various objects of theology as anthropocentric and insufficient to meet the requirements of a fully Christian doctrine of revelation, that is, a doctrine of revelation that depended solely upon the fact of its divine givenness. Instead of identifying revelation or God's Word as the object of theology, Barth complained that 'all those other definitions speak more or less expressly of faith, religion, or the religious-consciousness, sometimes with an explicit limitation to present-day faith'.[39] These were not legitimate objects for theology, in his view, because they ignored the supremacy of God in theology, the implications of the Godness of God for churchly reflection, and the fundamental importance of the Word of God for dogmatic efforts. The anthropocentric objects represented the tragic inversion of the subject–object relationship in theology and allowed humanity the pride of place in the articulation of the Christian faith. By reference to the 'present-day' orientation of theology to the religious consciousness (which amounted to establishing 'man' and his piety as the object of theological reflection), Barth intended his listeners to draw connections to Friedrich Schleiermacher, the great Father of modern neo-Protestantism.[40] Before offering his corrective to these modern definitions, by way of the 'older tradition', he next offered an explanatory genealogy of the subjective, anthropocentric and Schleiermacherian trajectory.

---

38. Ibid.
39. Ibid., p. 9.
40. See Friedrich Schleiermacher, *The Christian Faith*, trans. and ed. H. R. Mackintosh and J. S. Stewart, ET of the 2nd German ed. (Edinburgh: T. & T. Clark, 1968), §§6, 19, 29.

A genealogy of modern problems

Identifying lines of continuity

Barth proposed a genealogical thesis that drew a line of anthropocentric continuity back from Schleiermacher, through pietism, to the post-Reformation Reformed and Lutheran scholastics. The problematic definitions of nineteenth-century *Vermittlungstheologie* (mediation theology) were the result, in his view, of seeds sown in the earlier orthodox period and did 'not date only from Schleiermacher'.[41] In making this claim, Barth was very careful to exonerate the Reformation proper from charges of anthropocentrism. He contended, in other words, that the definitions which displaced God and turned instead to the human subject (or 'religion' in general) to find the object for dogmatic reflection relied on a tradition that went 'back by way of pietism to Protestant orthodoxy. *Not to Zwingli and Calvin*, one must say, in spite of the bad impression that might be made by a first glimpse of titles like *Commentary on True and False Religion* or *Institutes of the Christian Religion*.'[42]

Because of the recurrence of the 'Calvin versus the Calvinist' debate about the development of the Reformed tradition, it is crucial to point out that Barth protected the magisterial Reformers but blamed Protestant orthodoxy for the woes that befell the nineteenth century, for the blind alleys and even what he called the 'gigantic swindle' of Schleiermacher's theology.[43] This kind of discontinuity thesis, which in contemporary scholarship has been thoroughly rebutted, posited a tradition of later 'Calvinists' who allegedly overturned and betrayed Calvin's theology. In this vein, Barth vindicated Zwingli and Calvin, commenting that 'we have only to read the first pages' of their books 'to be convinced that we do *not* have here a theology of religious consciousness'.[44] The only way in which 'human awareness of God' could be the 'object of theology' for the Reformers was, on Barth's reading of Calvin, 'only insofar as insight into our poverty, nakedness, and ruin through the fall compel us to ask after God'.[45] Calvin, therefore, was assuredly *not* the progenitor of the Schleiermacherian tradition on this score. In keeping with the Calvin versus the Calvinists routine, however, Barth then insisted that Reformed orthodoxy broke from Calvin and laid the groundwork for, of all things, neo-Protestant

---

41. *GD*, p. 9.
42. Ibid. (italics mine).
43. Barth and Thurneysen, *Revolutionary Theology*, pp. 167–168.
44. *GD*, p. 9 (italics mine).
45. Ibid.

liberalism. The likelihood of this claim and its origins requires consideration in due course.

Turning from the general historical thesis to the details, Barth found developments in English Calvinism and later Lutheran scholasticism to be the source of modern ills. He pointed up the English theologian William Ames (1575–1633, a theologian of what is known as the Early orthodox era) and the tradition of Reformed covenant theology following the Dutch theologian Johannes Cocceius (1603–69, High orthodox era), along with the Lutheran theologian Abraham Calov (1612–86, High orthodox era), as responsible for the developments that eventuated in the centring of theological reflection on humanity.[46] Barth explained in a pivotal paragraph:

> It seems to be in English Presbyterianism that we are to seek the source of that tradition. In Franeker at the beginning of the 17th century it found a champion in the Englishman Amesius, the teacher of Cocceius. For him, living to God through Christ, religion, and the cultus were the themes of theology. The Lutheran Abraham Calovius took the same line in Wittenberg in the second half of the century, finding the object of dogmatics in those who are being brought to salvation.[47]

The stumbling block for Barth involved the traditions' use of human piety, religion and the church as primary 'objects' for theology, in that this bore more than a passing similarity with Schleiermacher's approach. Then closing the interpretative gap between Schleiermacher and this ignoble line of post-Reformation thinkers, Barth concluded the genealogy:

> Schleiermacher's Copernican revolution, which the formulas that I have quoted reflect, was the culmination of an older development rather than the initiation of a new one. He gave classical and even canonical form to a view which from those beginnings had come to increasingly more forceful expression throughout the 18th century, the view that theology in general and dogmatics in particular is the science of religion, the science of statements of pious experience such as is found in the Christian church . . .[48]

---

46. Chronologies of the post-Reformation eras (Early, High and Late) and biographical sketches of orthodox theologians can be found in Muller, *After Calvin*, pp. 4–7; R. D. Preus, *The Theology of Post-Reformation Lutheranism*, vol. 1: *A Study of Theological Prolegomena* (St. Louis: Concordia, 1970), pp. 44–66.

47. *GD*, p. 9.

48. Ibid.

Having thereby asserted both a *discontinuity* thesis concerning the Reformation and Protestant orthodoxy and an anthropocentric *continuity* claim linking Protestant orthodoxy to neo-Protestant liberalism, Barth turned without further ado to his own theological correction and counterpoint. Before following to the constructive discussion, however, a number of issues require attention and testing, including (1) the question of the historical connection between Reformed orthodoxy, pietism and Schleiermacher, (2) the implied central dogma thesis at work in Barth's claims, (3) the criticism of the Lutheran Abraham Calovius, and especially (4) the censure of William Ames and, by implication, Johannes Cocceius. In each case, we shall see the marked influence of nineteenth-century historiographers. Throughout, the persistence of Calvin versus the Calvinists arguments requires brief critique, especially given the fact that Barth mediated a form of this argument to subsequent generations.[49]

Nineteenth-century source dependence
The relationship of Reformed orthodoxy to pietism and Schleiermacher
The first aspect of Barth's discussion to consider briefly is the question of the relationship of Schleiermacher to pietism and pietism to Protestant orthodoxy. While few would doubt that Schleiermacher was an heir to the Moravian pietist tradition in many respects (Barth's colleague Emil Brunner certainly thought so), the problem of the exact origin of pietism has remained a contentious issue, one thoroughly debated throughout the nineteenth century and not likely to be settled here.[50] Suffice it to say, it should not be taken for granted

---

49. R. T. Kendall, e.g., similarly argued that English Calvinism from William Perkins to the Westminster Assembly represented a departure from the theology of Calvin. Allegedly taking its cue from Theodore Beza, Calvinism is supposed to have turned introspectively towards the human subject, thereby producing an insufficient doctrine of faith and assurance and the doctrine of limited atonement; see R. T. Kendall, 'The Nature of Saving Faith from William Perkins (d. 1602) to the Westminster Assembly (1643–9)' (DPhil diss., University of Oxford, 1976), published as *Calvin and English Calvinism to 1649* (Carlisle: Paternoster, 1997). For a helpful critique of Kendall, see P. Helm, *Calvin and the Calvinists* (Edinburgh: Banner of Truth Trust, 1982); Muller, *After Calvin*, pp. 63–80, 81–102.

50. See M. Redeker, *Schleiermacher: Life and Thought*, trans. J. Wallhausser (Philadelphia: Fortress, 1973), pp. 6–24. One view is that pietism was a reactionary movement within the orthodox tradition. A more plausible theory is that pietism's origins are

that pietism emerged out of Protestant orthodoxy, except perhaps as a polemical reaction to the confessional character of the tradition. If anything, pietism is best understood as the product of the simultaneous demise of orthodoxy and rise of philosophical rationalism in the late eighteenth century.[51] In this way, it is possible to direct suspicions away from origins in orthodoxy and instead relate pietism closely with the anti-creedal, anti-catholic impulse of the Radical Reformation, which also tended towards a hybrid of rationalism and mysticism.

The implied central dogma interpretation

In the mid-nineteenth century Alexander Schweizer (1808–88) offered a way of connecting Protestant orthodoxy to the theology of Schleiermacher. Schweizer espoused a 'central dogma' interpretation of doctrinal history, a view arguing that Reformed theology possessed in the doctrine of predestination an inner principle, logic, or central dogma according to which it organically developed in history. On this view, Schleiermacher's doctrine of *Abhängigkeitsgefühl* (feeling of absolute dependence) was in fact the fruition and goal of the earlier tradition's doctrine of predestination.[52] The progress of orthodoxy through a pietist phase to Schleiermacher was, then, the perfectly natural outworking of Reformed theology's own specific nature.

The fact that several of the orthodox sources quoted by Barth in §1 came from Schweizer's *Lehrbuch* (textbook) is evidence enough that Barth was aware of the historiographer's work.[53] As such, Schweizer was crucial to Barth's

---

Footnote 50 (*continued*)

traceable in part to medieval mysticism, Socinianism and the Radical Reformation (see A. Ritschl, *Geschichte des Pietismus*, 3 vols. (Berlin: de Gruyter, 1966). Emil Brunner's interpretation of Schleiermacher was published the same year as Barth's lectures on prolegomena. He described Schleiermacher as a sub-Christian, mystical philosopher, descended from both pietism and medieval mysticism; see E. Brunner, *Mystik und das Wort: Der Gegensatz zwischen moderner Religionsauffassung und christlichem Glauben dargestellt an der Theologie Schleiermachers* (Tübingen: J. C. B. Mohr [Paul Siebeck], 1924.

51. See B. Hägglund, *History of Theology*, trans. G. J. Lund, 3rd ed. (St. Louis: Concordia, 1968), pp. 325ff.; Muller, *Post-Reformation Reformed Dogmatics*, vol. 1, pp. 81ff.

52. See A. Schweizer, *Die Protestantischen Zentraldogmen in ihrer Entwicklung innerhalb der reformierten Kirche*, 2 vols. (Zurich: Orell, Füssli, 1854–6).

53. *GD*, p. 10. Schweizer was among sources Barth read (Barth to Thurneysen, 20 April 1924, in K. Barth and E. Thurneysen, *Karl Barth – Eduard Thurneysen*

KARL BARTH AS HISTORICAL THEOLOGIAN

lecture preparation and it is likely that his genealogical ideas influenced Barth's understanding of the tradition to some extent. Even though in some places Barth proved wary of his claims, Schweizer was nonetheless an integral source for the *Göttingen Dogmatics* and contributed to the idea that Schleiermacher descended organically from Reformed orthodoxy.[54]

The criticism of Abraham Calovius

In relation to the anti-Calov sentiment expressed in the genealogy, the nineteenth-century pietist theologian August Tholuck (1799–1877) also informed Barth to some extent. Historian Robert Preus has singled out Tholuck as one of the 'highly censorious' nineteenth-century theologians who evidenced serious dislike for the orthodox Lutheran theologian Abraham Calov.[55] According to Preus, Tholuck appreciated the earlier Lutheran scholastic Johann Gerhard, but unfairly 'despised Calov', preferring the 'spirit in Wittenberg in the first half of the 17th century' and then deploring 'the spirit during the second half'.[56] More to the point, in his *Geschichte des Rationalismus* Tholuck described his view that 'orthodoxy was the cause of the Enlightenment and of rationalism'.[57] This view proved influential on Barth, who depended on Tholuck's arguments and even cited this particular text later in the lectures.[58] Further establishing Barth's awareness, Eberhard Busch notes that there were numerous references to Tholuck in the first edition of *Der Römerbrief* and that Barth had read his biography in 1919 as he was developing

_____

  Briefwechsel, vol. 2: *1921–1930*. Zurich: Theologischer Verlag, 1974), p. 243; Barth and
  Thurneysen, *Revolutionary Theology*, p. 176; note, the ET mistakenly dates the letter 20
  March).

54. See also B. L. McCormack, 'The Sum of the Gospel: The Doctrine of Election in the
  Theologies of Alexander Schweizer and Karl Barth', in D. Willis and M. Welker (eds.),
  Toward the Future of Reformed Theology (Grand Rapids: Eerdmans, 1999), pp. 470–493.

55. *Theology*, p. 19, citing A. Tholuck, *Der Geist der Lutherischen Theologen Wittenbergs im
  Verlaufe des 17. Jahrhunderts* (Hamburg: F. & A. Parther, 1852); *Geschichte des
  Rationalismus*, vol. 1: *Geschichte des Pietismus und des ersten Studiums der Aufklärung*
  (Berlin: Wiegandt & Grieben, 1865).

56. Ibid.

57. Ibid. Against Tholuck's theory, see M. I. Klauber, *Between Reformed Scholasticism and
  Pan-Protestantism: Jean-Alphonse Turretin (1671–1737) and Enlightened Orthodoxy at the
  Academy of Geneva* (Toronto: Susquehanna University Press, 1994).

58. Barth cited Tholuck in §22 (Barth, *Unterricht in der christlichen Religion*, vol. 2,
  p. 356).

his critique of pietism.[59] Unfortunately, there is not the space here to treat Tholuck's views on the history of Protestantism and the Enlightenment; his claims, as well as other nineteenth-century theses on the origins of rationalism, have been handled sufficiently by other scholars.[60]

Despite all these connections, however, Schweizer and Tholuck were not the pivotal sources for Barth's charge against Calov and prejudice against later Lutheranism. A thorough analysis of the rest of Barth's prolegomena reveals that the most immediate source for Barth's comments throughout was Herman Bavinck (1854–1921). In fact, the late nineteenth-century Dutch theologian was the primary historiographer heavily consulted throughout §1.[61]

Bavinck's narrative and Johannes Cocceius

Turning our attention to Barth's use of Bavinck, we see that although Barth interacted with Luther, Zwingli, Calvin and the nineteenth-century dogmaticians from primary source texts, he lifted the Ames quotation and Calov reference directly from Herman Bavinck's *Gereformeerde Dogmatiek*, thus suggesting that he borrowed the historical-genealogical thesis from Bavinck as well.[62] It is important to introduce Bavinck's interpretation of the Reformed tradition in this regard in order to identify points of continuity and discontinuity with Barth's thesis. An examination of Bavinck's text suggests that Barth grasped something of the general, historical description, but also missed important details that led him to exaggerate and radicalize Bavinck's analysis on two counts.

Bavinck's interpretation in *Reformed Dogmatics* rehearsed a number of medieval views on the object of theology as part of the introduction to prolegomena, beginning with Augustine and Lombard and moving to the

---

59. *Karl Barth and the Pietists: The Young Karl Barth's Critique of Pietism and Its Response,* trans. D. W. Bloesch (Downers Grove: IVP, 2004), p. 36. Barth also penned a chapter on Tholuck's revivalist theology in *Protestant Theology in the Nineteenth Century*, pp. 494–504.

60. See Preus, *Theology,* vols. 1, 2.

61. A biographical sketch can be found in H. Bavinck, *In the Beginning: Foundations of Creation Theology,* trans. J. Vriend, ed. J. Bolt (Grand Rapids: Baker Books, 1999), pp. 9–20.

62. Barth cited Bavinck throughout this section. See H. Bavinck, *Gereformeerde Dogmatiek,* 4 vols., 2nd ed. (Kampen: J. H. Bas, 1911); ET, *Reformed Dogmatics,* vol. 1: *Prolegomena,* trans. J. Vriend, ed. J. Bolt (Grand Rapids: Baker Academic, 2003). Unless otherwise noted the ET will be quoted.

'improved' positions of Alexander of Hales, Bonaventure and Hugh of St Victor. Their definitions of theology were variously related to God, Christ and his church, or more generally to the work of salvation.[63] But Bavinck also cited Abraham Calov as a Lutheran representative opposed to the notion that God could be the object of theology, because the limitations of human existence in this life on earth proved too great a barrier to the knowledge of God.[64] As

---

63. *Reformed Dogmatics*, vol. 1, p. 34. Bavinck did not present a sophisticated summary of medieval discussions or their importance for Reformation and post-Reformation theology. For instance, he only hinted at the difference between a more inclusive Thomist definition of the object of theology (namely, a definition that included God and created things) and the narrower and soteriologically oriented definition of Hugh of St Victor (cf. Muller, *Post-Reformation Reformed Dogmatics*, vol. 1, p. 312). Furthermore, he ignored developments by the Augustinian theologians Gregory of Rimini and Giles of Rome in their consideration of God in an absolute sense as he is known in himself and God in a restricted sense as he reveals himself to be the saviour (ibid.). These discussions became the basis for Lutheran and Reformed developments of the object of theology as God 'for us' (*erga nos*) rather than God 'in himself' (*in se*). Very few Reformation insights – such as the distinction between the hidden and revealed God, the theology of the cross, and the *duplex cognitio Dei* (twofold knowledge of God) – and even fewer Reformed orthodox additions were incorporated into Bavinck's summary.

64. *Reformed Dogmatics*, vol. 1, pp. 34–35. Barth seems to have missed Bavinck's citations of the English Puritan John Owen and Johannes Cocceius among others for supporting the view that God is the object of theology 'primarily' and creatures only 'secondarily', 'according to the respect in which they are related to God as to their source and end' (Bavinck, *Reformed Dogmatics*, vol. 1, p. 34). Nevertheless, Bavinck did fail to describe the essential continuity of Calov's ideas with the rest of Lutheran and Reformed orthodoxy. E.g. Bavinck reported Calov's argument that 'theology on earth' strives after the knowledge of God but that what it attains is 'very different from theology in heaven' (pp. 34–35). This thinking was crucial to Calov's position on the object and kind of knowledge available in theology. At the root of his discussion was the distinction between God's knowledge of himself (*theologia archetypa*) and God's knowledge revealed to man (*theologia ectypa*). This ectypal theology was then subdivided into four further kinds: (1) the theology of pilgrims here on earth who are not yet glorified (*theologia viatorum*), (2) the theology of the saints in heaven (*theologia beatorum*), (3) the theology of angels (*theologia angelorum*), and (4) the theology of Christ or the unique

a result of this conclusion, Bavinck summarized Calov's determination that the 'real object of theology is man "insofar as he is to be brought to salvation", or the religion prescribed by God in his Word'.[65] Turning next to Reformed developments, Bavinck continued, 'Similarly, some Reformed theologians described "living for God through Christ, religion, the worship of God", as the content of dogmatics.'[66] While this quotation came from William Ames's *The Marrow of Theology*, Bavinck also cited Peter van Mastricht (1630–1706), Johannes Marckius (1656–1713), Bernhard de Moor (1710 to ca. 1765) and Franz Burmann (1632–79).[67] Having finished with his historical overview, Bavinck concluded with a note that doubtlessly informed Barth's genealogy:

Foonote 64 (*continued*)

> knowledge of Christ that he possesses as the God-man (*theologia Christi* or *theologia unionis*). The motivation for Calov's statements, then, was the realization that theological knowledge is possible only because of revelation and the fact that God chooses to reveal himself to man primarily in the context of human salvation. The limitations on human knowledge (because of the Creator–creature distinction and the doctrine of sin) provided restrictions for the discussion of the object of theology. Therefore, Calov's gravitation towards humanity in the context of soteriology reflected not a growing anthropocentrism, but basic theological-epistemological insights in continuity with much of the rest of Lutheran and Reformed scholasticism (see a Reformed example in J. Wollebius, 'Compendium Theologiae Christianae', in J. W. Beardslee III [ed.], *Reformed Dogmatics* [Grand Rapids: Baker, 1965], 1.1). The only essential difference between the Lutherans and the Reformed was the *theologia Christi* (see Muller, *Post-Reformation Reformed Dogmatics*, vol. 1, pp. 248–255; Preus, *Theology*, pp. 112–114, 167–173). In conclusion, Bavinck provided insufficient information for the kind of theological judgments drawn. In the first place, it simply is not possible to break Calov (or Ames) off from the rest of the tradition. Secondly, the Ames and Calov definitions can be explained easily so that they relate to Luther's and Calvin's basic views and even, perhaps ironically, to what Barth and Bavinck themselves wanted to say constructively about the object of theology.

65. *Reformed Dogmatics*, vol. 1, p. 35, citing A. Calovius, *Isagoge ad theologian* (1662), pp. 283 ff., 291 ff.

66. Ibid. Ames's definition of theology associated him with earlier tendencies to describe theology as an essentially practical discipline, even as 'art' (see Muller, *Post-Reformation Reformed Dogmatics*, vol. 1, pp. 323, 340 ff.).

67. Biographical sketches can be found in Muller, *Post-Reformation Reformed Dogmatics*, vol. 1, pp. 40–52.

Thus, step by step, the subjective practical notion of theology began to find acceptance. This tendency was strongly promoted by the philosophy of Immanuel Kant . . . On the basis of other considerations, Schleiermacher arrived at a similar conclusion.[68]

With this much of Bavinck's presentation in view, Barth does seem to have represented the general sense of the historical excursus. One further point of continuity should be mentioned.

One of the more striking aspects of Barth's genealogy was the effort that he made to point out various negative connections to Johannes Cocceius and, by association, to problematic modern views.[69] First, at the outset Barth linked Cocceius to William Ames and what he deemed to be an improper object for theology.[70] Later, then, when Barth constructively borrowed from the tradition, he somewhat randomly mentioned, as if to garner support, that the theologian he was positively appropriating was a 'contentious opponent of Cocceius'.[71] The question remains, did Barth absorb this anti-Cocceian sentiment from Bavinck?

At first glance, the section in Bavinck from which Barth gathered his Ames–Calov material makes no mention of Cocceius. However, in the first several chapters of introduction, Bavinck did connect these figures to Cocceius and the modern tradition after him. It is clear that Bavinck possessed a determined anti-Cocceian bias, as seen in his view that Cocceian federal theology was 'problematic' because its 'theological starting point is not God but

---

68. *Reformed Dogmatics*, vol. 1, p. 35.

69. *GD*, p. 9. Barth also dealt with Cocceius in a short historical excursus in §24 ('God and Man in Covenant'), *Unterricht in der christlichen Religion*, vol. 2, pp. 382–385. The treatment there was almost entirely dependent upon Gottlob Schrenk's *Gottesreich und Bund im älteren Protestantismus vornehmlich bei Johannes Coccejus: Zugleich ein Beitrag zur Geschichte des Pietismus und der heilsgeschichtlichen Theologie* (Darmstadt: Wissenschaftliche Buchgesellschaft, 1923, repr. 1967). Barth read Schrenk's book upon its publication in 1923 and adopted its interpretation of Cocceius (see Barth and Thurneysen, *Briefwechsel*, vol. 2, pp. 129–130). Shrenk was a forerunner to J. W. Baker's thesis that Heinrich Bullinger invented covenant theology apart from Calvin. This thesis has been criticized by C. P. Venema, *Heinrich Bullinger and the Doctrine of Predestination: Author of 'the Other Reformed Tradition'?* (Grand Rapids: Baker Academic, 2002).

70. *GD*, p. 10.

71. Ibid.

humanity's need for covenantal fellowship, for salvation'.[72] Bavinck pressed the issue and in the very next sentence related Cocceius to Kant and 'modern philosophy', where 'morality and religious feeling became the starting point and subject matter of theology'.[73] It would seem, then, for Bavinck that Cocceius was responsible in part for the anthropocentric turn of modern theology.

In the scholarship on Reformed orthodoxy, Cocceius has been a much-maligned figure. Readers of the *Church Dogmatics* will surely recognize many of the oft-repeated nineteenth-century grievances, especially the charge in Barth's history of covenant theology that Cocceius was in some sense responsible for theology's capitulation to modern philosophy and historicism.[74] Fortunately, recent work has carefully corrected these misconceptions and explicated Cocceius' theology from primary sources.[75] It can only be asserted here that Bavinck, and Barth with him, misunderstood Cocceius' role in the development of Protestant theological history.

In relation to Cocceius and the Calvin-versus-the-Calvinists thesis, Bavinck summarized Reformed dogmatic history as the gradual departure of seventeenth-century 'Reformed theologians such as Junius, Zanchius and Polanus' away from 'Calvin's "biblical theology" to a more scholastic one paralleling the development of the Middle Ages'.[76] This era, Bavinck argued, responded to

---

72. *Reformed Dogmatics*, vol. 1, p. 61. Bavinck's anti-Cocceian attitude probably arose from his own supralapsarian tendencies, which led him to align with representatives of this position (Franciscus Gomarus and Gisbertus Voetius) *pace* the infralapsarian Cocceius. Bavinck also criticized the exegetical arguments of several Reformed orthodox theologians, including Cocceius, for the doctrine of the *pactum salutis* (council of peace or covenant of redemption) and the historicizing of 'that which is eternal' (ibid., p. 185).

73. Ibid., p. 61.

74. *CD* IV/1, pp. 54ff.

75. See W. J. van Asselt, *The Federal Theology of Johannes Cocceius (1603–1669)*, trans. R. A Blacketer (Leiden: E. J. Brill, 2001), p. 228.

76. *Reformed Dogmatics*, vol. 1, p. 61. Bavinck did not acknowledge that scholasticism was merely a method appropriate to the schools, one that continued to handle piety and biblical studies but formulated the material in a different setting and for changing academic and polemical purposes. Bavinck's caricature contended that scholasticism 'surfaced in Reformed theology toward the end of the sixteenth century' because 'people lost interest in the simple treatment of dogma as we find it in Calvin' (ibid., p. 180). Scholasticism was elsewhere described as 'philosophical

the challenges of Rationalism, mysticism, Anabaptism, Socinianism, Arminianism and Cartesianism, but not without capitulation, especially, in his view, when it came to the champion of covenant or federal theology. Bavinck took it that 'the federalist theology of Johannes Cocceius' became an ally of Cartesian philosophy and led, lamentably, to the eclipse of the Precisionist theology of Giserbertus Voetius.[77]

From these statements it is evident that Barth followed Bavinck's historical survey very closely indeed. Barth took away from his reading the notion that Ames, Cocceius and Calov taught that dogmatics was the accumulation of statements about the Christian's pious, salvific experience of God, thus making humanity the object of theology.[78] To break off the analysis here, however, would be to ignore the points of discontinuity in Barth's interpretation from Bavinck's, to skip over Barth's exaggeration of the Schleiermacher-continuity argument. It would also be to ignore the way in which Barth misread Bavinck and missed important qualifications in the course of the historical discussion.

The exaggerated reading of Bavinck

We have seen thus far that Barth relied on Bavinck's historical analysis in order to join supposed subjectivist strands of English Calvinism and Cocceian theology with modernity, all the while bracketing off the Reformation from what he perceived to be Enlightenment ailments. In keeping with what would

---

terminology' and a set of 'futile academic questions' that ignored the presentation of 'truth in a simpler form' (ibid., p. 181). Throughout, Bavinck played on a false antithesis between a 'simple', 'thoroughly biblical and practical' Calvin and a pedantic, philosophical, Protestant scholasticism (ibid., p. 175). A thorough critique of this view is available in D. C. Steinmetz, 'The Scholastic Calvin', in Trueman and Clark, *Protestant Scholasticism*, pp. 16–30; Muller, *After Calvin*, pp. 25–46.

77. *Reformed Dogmatics*, vol. 1, p. 175. Bavinck exaggerated Cocceius' use of philosophy and Descartes; see Van Asselt, *Johannes Cocceius*, pp. 72–105.

78. It is important to critique Bavinck's summary on at least two counts. First, Bavinck presented few doctrinal positions actually held by the scholastics relative to prolegomena. Second, he inadequately described the development and codification of Reformed scholasticism out of the Reformation proper into the era of confessionalism and orthodoxy. This mistreatment negatively impacted Barth's understanding of the tradition such that he could only reproduce in his own lectures several inaccurate, nineteenth-century glosses on Protestant theological history.

become a general pattern for Barth's use of the tradition, he radicalized his reading, in this case hyper-extending the possible line of development to neo-Protestantism. Barth had it that the 'tragic retreat' begun by Reformed orthodoxy ended in 'the theology of Schleiermacher' as the 'total capitulation' of Protestantism to anthropocentric interests.[79] But in exaggerating this claim, Barth had not quite informed his lectures with a nuanced reading of Bavinck. For instance, Barth supplemented his reading by making the very existence of the *locus* of prolegomena the result of anthropocentric concerns. In other words, he argued that while Zwingli and Calvin had not devoted 'more than a few pages to the concept and method of their science', the orthodox gradually 'lost sight of their theme' until they began to elaborate the prolegomenal *locus*.[80] Thus, he explained, 'there flourished introductions' and prolegomena became a cottage-industry, 'an enterprise', for Barth, that necessarily arose out of the inescapable situation theology inhabited, 'especially Protestant theology', in the post-critical era.[81]

In addition to accentuating the culmination thesis, Barth also revised the historical narrative in a way that failed to recognize the significance Bavinck had attributed to Immanuel Kant. Bavinck's text actually indicated that a substantive shift had occurred in Kant and the new intellectual climate of the Enlightenment. In Bavinck's view, any suggestion that a trajectory had been set in motion by Ames or other Protestant scholastics had to be tempered by the admission that the study of man and creation as objects of theology was not wrong per se, and certainly had not been articulated by the orthodox in the same way as by Schleiermacher.[82] Acquitting the post-Reformation of gross anthropocentrism, Bavinck explained that '*after Kant* and Schleiermacher this definition acquired *another meaning*'.[83] In other words, throughout Bavinck's text, when the origins of the peculiarly 'modern' approach to subjectivity in theology were discussed, it was relative to Kant, Hegel and the philosophical revolutions of the Enlightenment. Despite possible forerunners in Ames, Cocceius or Calov, Bavinck's presen-

---

79. *GD*, p. 19.

80. Ibid., pp. 9, 19.

81. Ibid., p. 19.

82. *Reformed Dogmatics*, vol. 1, p. 36. On the existence of early Reformed prolegomena and its continuity with the Reformation, see W. J. van Asselt, 'The Fundamental Meaning of Theology: Archetypal and Ectypal Theology in Seventeenth-Century Reformed Thought', *WTJ* 64 (2002), pp. 319–336.

83. *Reformed Dogmatics*, vol. 1, p. 36 (italics mine).

tation repeatedly emphasized the significant change that occurred with the inauguration of modern critical epistemology, even calling it a 'great reversal' that had only recently shifted the foundation of theology exclusively to the 'religious subject'.[84] Barth's claim, then, that 'Schleiermacher's Copernican revolution . . . was the culmination of an older development rather than the initiation of a new one' was not entirely the spirit one imbibes from Bavinck.[85]

Barth's own valuation and acceptance of Kant was evident in section two of §1, where he acknowledged that his own view of dogmatics was not exactly the same as a definition of theology 'as a science of God'.[86] The reason for nuance involved the peculiar acceptance of Kantian boundaries for religious thought. Barth admitted, 'In my view the modern objections to this latter definition are right, namely, that it confuses dogmatics with a metaphysics that has become impossible since Kant, and that it does not give faith its proper place in fixing the object.'[87] Herein, then, is one example of a possible inconsistency in Barth's understanding of Kant's significance. On the one hand, he wanted to recognize Kant as a watershed in his critique of metaphysics, offering still-valid epistemological strictures for contemporary theology. On the other hand, however, he did not allow that the Copernican revolution in philosophy had thereby disrupted any meaningful thread of continuity that might have existed from Ames to Schleiermacher.

Constructive use of the Reformed tradition

Turning finally to Barth's positive use of the Reformed tradition, we find that the nineteenth-century mediators continued to play an important role even beyond historical analysis. Bavinck in particular, but also Schweizer, did not

----

84. Ibid., pp. 32, 66. Bavinck reminded readers that the 'philosophical reversal in philosophy, represented by Kant, Schleiermacher, and Hegel' entailed the production of 'yet another theological method – the subjective' in such a way that 'experience replaced knowledge as the foundation of theology' (ibid., p. 59). Elsewhere, Bavinck spoke of the 'major difference' between classical Protestant theology and everything 'since Schleiermacher', meaning the decisive turn 'from the object to the subject' (ibid., p. 88).
85. *GD*, p. 9.
86. Ibid., p. 10.
87. Ibid.

recede from view, although Barth did not always cite them explicitly.[88] Of utmost importance to Barth in this section was the articulation of a governing condition for the doctrine of revelation, one that quickly became an enduring Barthian adage: only God can make God known in theology. This truth, he insisted from the outset, needed to be established in the prolegomena, naming the appropriate object for dogmatic reflection as a 'first word'. In order to accomplish this, and following his earlier intention, he took over 'an older dogmatic tradition' and announced that dogmatics is 'reflection on *the Word of God*' and not on faith, human piety or any other triviality'.[89] Far from adopting Schleiermacher's position, Barth forwarded a dictum from Martin Luther that he lifted from Bavinck without citation. He explained, 'I oppose to it [namely, the modern Schleiermacherian definition] the view that I find expressed in Luther's saying that God's Word – and no one else, not even an angel – must establish articles of faith; and if not an angel, then certainly not I, a man with my pious experience.'[90] And then, lest students gain the impression that he had disavowed the entire Protestant orthodox tradition because of harmful trajectories set in motion by their object of theology, Barth affirmed the definition

---

88. §1 amounted to a commentary on the following passage in Bavinck: 'God cannot be known by us apart from revelation received in faith. Dogmatics seeks nothing other than to be true to the faith-knowledge given in this revelation. Dogmatics is thus not the science of faith or of religion but the science about God. The task of the dogmatician is to think God's thoughts after him and to trace their unity. This is a task that must be done in the confidence that God has spoken, in humble submission to the church's teaching tradition, and for communicating the gospel's message to the world' (Bavinck, *Reformed Dogmatics*, vol. 1, p. 25).

89. *GD*, pp. 8–9 (italics mine).

90. Ibid., p. 10, citing the Schmalkaldic Articles, 2.2. Barth quoted this Luther reference from Bavinck, where he also found the Ursinus saying. A comparison of Bavinck's text with Barth's is telling. Bavinck wrote, 'But the Reformation recognizes no truth other than that which is given on the authority of God in holy Scripture. "The Word of God grounds the articles of faith and beyond that no one, not even an angel" [cf. Schmalkaldic Articles, 2.2.]. Dogmas, articles of faith, are only those truths "which are properly set forth in Scripture as things to be believed" [cf. Andreas Hyperius]. It is only those "propositions [*sententiae*] which must be believed on account of a mandate from God" [cf. Ursinus]. Among Reformed theologians, therefore, the following proposition returns again and again: "the principle into which all theological dogmas are distilled is: God has said it"' (*Reformed Dogmatics*, vol. 1, p. 30).

given by Zacharias Ursinus (1534–83, Early orthodox era) and Bavinck. He continued, 'I find it also expressed in the statement of Ursinus that dogmas are things we must believe or obey because God commands them, so that the principle behind every theological dogma is *Deus dixit* [God has spoken].'[91]

Still refusing to rest content with these two authorities in view (Luther's dictum and Ursinus' definition), Barth borrowed two additional Reformed definitions of theology from Samuel Maresius (1599–1673, High orthodox era) and Campegius Vitringa (1695–1722, Late orthodox era), both taken from Alexander Schweizer's *Glaubenslehre* (dogmatics):

> I also find it expressed in the saying of M. Maresius, the contentious opponent of Cocceius, to the effect that the doctrine of true religion is disclosed to us by God to his own glory and our salvation. God is the author, the final end is his glory, and the secondary end is our salvation.[92]

Here we see that the emphasis on the *givenness* of revelation was reasserted. With the God-reveals-God principle at work, Barth could then make some allowance for the inclusion of faith in the definition of dogmatics, provided it was carefully qualified. To make this point, Vitringa was cited from Schweizer:

> Campegius Vitringa (d. 1722) has left a fine definition of a theologian as one who speaks the truth about God to the glory of God. I can adopt this so long as we understand by 'truth' the Word that God himself and God alone has spoken, so that the correlation of God and faith is not destroyed or restricted by the interposition of a truth that we humans have rationally or irrationally established, but is secured by an intervening *Deus dixit*.[93]

The appropriation of Maresius and Vitringa centred on the typically 'Calvinist' emphasis on the glory of God both in God's prerogative in the disclosure of

---

91. *GD*, p. 10. Barth found both the Luther and Ursinus quotations in Bavinck. The reference to believing things because God commands them (in Bavinck: 'a mandate from God') was a quotation from Ursinus (see above note), but the *Deus dixit* statement in Bavinck was meant to be a summary of Reformed orthodox teaching and did not specifically cite Ursinus (*Reformed Dogmatics*, vol. 1, p. 30). Incidentally, Bavinck attributes a nearly identical 'mandate from God' phrase to Amandus Polanus a few pages later (ibid., p. 33).

92. *GD*, p. 10.

93. Ibid.

revelation and in the human task of theological reflection. Pertaining to the object of theology, there could be no doubt that on Barth's borrowed view dogmatics 'must find its first, primary, and principle theme in this generative basis, in this confidential turning and address of God, without which faith is nonsense'.[94] Moving then to the relationship between theology and revelation, he joined the *Deus dixit* concept of Ursinus and Bavinck with the definition of Vitringa. Barth instructed students that revelation is what secures the 'correlation of God and faith', which is the only basis upon which a dogmatician may even dare to speak of God.[95] The fact that the God who reveals himself is also a God who creates faith is the hinge upon which the possibility of dogmatics turns.[96] Because God does these things, because he is the revealing subject of revelation, Barth insisted, the idea of God as the 'object of scholarly metaphysics' was prohibited and the Feuerbachian notion of 'viewing God as the product of faith instead of vice versa' could be excluded.[97]

The remarkable thing about the passages quoted above is that one of the pre-eminent themes of Barth's theology, the *Deus dixit*, made its very first appearance in the prolegomena here, as the result of Barth's reading of Bavinck and consideration of the older tradition. And as he strove to clarify the meaning of his lecture to this point, to put things 'differently and more materially', he continued to rely on the broader Reformation and post-Reformation traditions, not to mention Bavinck. He explained to students, 'Let us accept provisionally, if not without reservation, the common Protestant definition of faith as trust.'[98] Taken in a legal sense and related to the biblical motif of 'promise', as the Reformers were wont to do, Barth resolutely maintained that trust should be connected to a 'given word' that is 'its basis and origin'.[99]

Conclusion: Barth and the Reformed tradition

In a concluding comment at the end of a rather lengthy introductory section, Barth made one final veiled reference to Bavinck by noting Julius Kaftan's

---

94. Ibid., p. 12.
95. Ibid., pp. 10, 12.
96. See Bavinck, *Reformed Dogmatics*, vol. 1, p. 40.
97. *GD*, pp. 11, 12.
98. Ibid.
99. Ibid., citing Bavinck, *Reformed Dogmatics*, vol. 1, p. 44.

request that dogmaticians 'relearn how to speak in an absolute tone'.[100] For Barth, the process of re-education thus far consisted of accumulating older Reformed teachings from collections by Tholuck, Schweizer and Bavinck. But as we have seen, the gathering of sources also included a collection of nine-teenth-century misreadings of the tradition. As such, a summary of Barth's relationship to classical Reformed theology in §1 of the *Göttingen Dogmatics* amounts to an account of his interaction with these post-critical conveyers of the tradition. Although Bavinck all but disappeared from the source list after §1, Heppe, Schweizer and the rest grew in importance.

The lessons to take away from this careful reading of Barth's historical and systematic theology can be summarized as follows.

1. In terms of Barth's supposed 'recovery' of a Reformed identity, it bears repeating that his understanding of the Protestant orthodox tradition at this point was entirely dependent on later historiography and was therefore not particularly deep or sophisticated. Although he did ask the first traditional questions of classical Protestant prolegomena (Is theology a science? What is its object?), and the names of Protestant orthodox theologians appeared, very few details of Reformed scholastic teaching came into view.

2. Unfortunately, Protestant doctrinal history fared little better. The narra-tive Barth inherited also lacked nuance and the exaggerated reading of Bavinck only served to blur the picture further. Perhaps it is surprising for evangelicals today, but it would seem that Herman Bavinck, a Reformed thinker typically known for his congeniality towards confessional orthodoxy, played a significant role in pointing Barth towards the genealogical thesis of subjectiv-ity. Taking his cue from Bavinck, Barth reiterated a faulty historiographical bias against Johannes Cocceius, William Ames and English Puritanism, a bias that appeared in much of his later work and was passed down to numerous Barthian interpreters of Reformed theology. Although it can be tedious work, Barth interpreters can no longer shy away from the mass of post-Reformation secondary literature (including the critique of the 'Calvin versus the Calvinists' argument and the body of scholarship on Cocceian federal theology); for, no real understanding of Barth's interpretation of Reformed theology can be had until the historiographical difficulties are untangled. Exposition of Barth and historiographical correction must go hand in hand.

3. And finally, Barth's constructive appropriation of the tradition in §1 can best be described as somewhat idiosyncratic and ahistorical. Although nearly all of his efforts in section two were put towards overcoming Schleiermacher

---

100. *GD*, p. 14.

and Feuerbach, one irony is that the two definitions Barth borrowed from Reformed orthodoxy he lifted directly from Alexander Schweizer, Schleiermacher's best-known epigone. In many ways, then, Barth attempted to harvest pre-critical sources for post-critical problems. And so, in Barth's break from neo-Protestantism, Kant continued to dictate the terms of the theological discussion. Nevertheless, even with the stylized version of the tradition available to him in Schweizer, Barth did use orthodox sources for his own formulation of the object of theology and discussion of the question of dogmatics as science, confirming his thesis that God is the subject of revelation, and God's Word the object of theological science.

4. KARL BARTH AND COVENANT THEOLOGY

A. T. B. McGowan

Introduction

The purpose of this chapter is to state and assess Barth's use of the covenant concept in his theology. It is, of course, not possible in one chapter to cover all that Barth wrote on the subject of covenant, so closely is the theme interwoven into every aspect of his thinking. That being the case, we shall concentrate on the section in the *Church Dogmatics* where Barth expounds his understanding of the covenant concept in theology.[1] After providing an overview of that section we shall then focus more specifically on his analysis and critique of covenant theology.[2] Next, we shall examine how two of his successors took up this critique and developed it. Finally, we shall conclude with some assessment of the strengths and weaknesses of Barth's argument.

Reformed theology prior to Barth

All Christian theologians must find a place for 'covenant' in their systems, since

---

1. *CD* IV/1, pp. 3–78.
2. I use 'covenant theology' and 'federal theology' as interchangeable terms.

it is such a recurring, even dominant, concept in the Scriptures. It was, however, in the Calvinist strand of Reformation theology that the concept came to be the central means of expressing the relationship between God and humanity. Calvin himself used the term as an overarching concept, focusing on the covenant of grace,[3] but, by the end of the seventeenth century, a detailed and somewhat complex theology had been worked out, with a covenant of works, a covenant of redemption and a covenant of grace.[4] There has been a long dispute as to whether Calvin himself would have approved of this development of his thought,[5] but recently a compelling case has been made for the argument that the seeds of the later development (particularly the idea of a covenant of works) are already there in Calvin.[6] From Calvin, this 'covenant theology' was developed further by the Heidelberg theologians Caspar Olevianus (1536–87) and Zacharias Ursinus (1534–83), was popularized by William Perkins (1558–1602) and was significantly advanced by the

3. See J. Calvin, *Institutes of the Christian Religion*, ed. F. L. Battles (Philadelphia: Westminster, 1977), 2.10 and 2.11.

4. For an analysis of this development, see *inter alia* D. A. Weir, *The Origins of the Federal Theology in Sixteenth-Century Reformation Thought* (Oxford: Clarendon, 1990); C. S. McCoy and J. W. Baker, *Fountainhead of Federalism: Heinrich Bullinger and the Covenantal Tradition* (Louisville: Westminster John Knox, 1991); D. N. J. Poole, *Stages of Religious Faith in the Classical Reformation Tradition: The Covenant Approach to the* Ordo Salutis (Lampeter: Edwin Mellen, 1995).

5. Samples of that literature include B. Hall, 'Calvin against the Calvinists', in G. E. Duffield (ed.), *John Calvin* (Grand Rapids: Eerdmans, 1966), pp. 12–37; H. Rolston III, 'Responsible Man in Reformed Theology: Calvin versus the Westminster Confession', *SJT* 23 (1970), pp. 129–156; *John Calvin versus the Westminster Confession* (Richmond, Va.: John Knox, 1972); R. T. Kendall, *Calvin and English Calvinism to 1649* (Oxford: Oxford University Press, 1979); M. C. Bell, 'Calvin and the Extent of the Atonement', *EQ* 55 (1983), pp. 115–123; P. Helm, Calvin and the Calvinists (Edinburgh: Banner of Truth, 1982); 'Calvin and the Covenant: Unity and Discontinuity', *EQ* 55 (1983), pp. 65–81; R. A. Muller, *Christ and the Decree* (Durham, N. C.: Labyrinth, 1986); 'Calvin and the "Calvinists": Assessing Continuities and Discontinuities between the Reformation and Orthodoxy', *CTJ* 30 (1995), pp. 345–375; *CTJ* 31 (1996), pp. 125–160; also a number of the essays in C. R. Trueman and R. S. Clark (eds.), *Protestant Scholasticism: Essays in Reassessment* (Carlisle: Paternoster, 1999).

6. P. A. Lillback, *The Binding of God: Calvin's Role in the Development of Covenant Theology* (Grand Rapids: Baker, 2001).

later German theologian Johannes Cocceius (1603–69). By the end of the seventeenth century, not least due to the Westminster Confession of Faith and its
Congregationalist and Baptist variants, covenant theology had become the
dominant theological position within Reformed theology. In the course of this
development, however, covenant theology was expressed in different ways,
such that there is no one definitive covenant theology, although most of the
key elements are agreed.

Covenant theology has been subjected to criticism from a range of perspectives through the centuries but the critique of Barth and his successors is
undoubtedly the most sustained and the most trenchant. This is because, as we
shall see, they view covenant theology as a dangerous innovation that undermines and ultimately destroys a theology of grace. In particular, they argue that
covenant theology removes Christ from his central place in God's reconciliation and leads to a skewed understanding of various doctrines, especially the
doctrines of predestination, atonement and assurance.

Barth's use of the covenant concept

Although Barth does not build his theology on the foundation of a three-
covenant system as developed by earlier Reformed theologians, it should not
be imagined that thereby he neglects the theme. Quite the reverse is the case.
Indeed, he probably speaks more about covenant than any other recent theologian, apart from those in the school of covenant theology. Barth builds the
idea of covenant into the central themes of his dogmatic theology. Not only
does he relate covenant to the doctrine of election, although in a somewhat
different way than others in the Reformed tradition; he also relates it carefully
to every aspect of God's gracious action in Christ. Everything is drawn
together such that God's grace is the basis for the covenant, election is the outworking of the covenant, creation prepares the ground for the covenant and
reconciliation (especially atonement) is the fulfilment of the covenant. As John
Webster says, for Barth, 'Creation, covenant and Trinity are indissolubly united
in the church's confession.'[7]

In order to understand Barth's use of the covenant concept, we turn now
to his extended exposition of the subject in §57 of his *Church Dogmatics*, entitled 'The Work of God the Reconciler'. It is here, in his exposition of the doctrine of reconciliation, that Barth begins to open up in detail both his general

---

7. *Barth* (London: Continuum, 2000) p. 98.

understanding of the theme of covenant and his critique of the older covenant theology. True to the overall direction of his work, Barth makes it clear that we cannot begin a treatment of reconciliation by speaking about covenant; rather, we must begin by speaking about God. Only when we have described God's free act of reconciliation in Christ can we turn to consider the covenantal relationship God has set in place as part of the outworking of his sovereign and gracious electing action. For that reason, he begins this section with an exposition of the theme 'God with us'.[8] His intention is to demonstrate that 'the covenant fulfilled in the atonement' is the heart and centre of the church's dogmatics.[9] It is difficult to find a better summary of Barth's exposition of this theme 'God with us' than has been provided by Geoffrey Bromiley:

> What does 'God with us' mean? Barth lists seven successive implications which provide critical clues to the understanding of reconciliation. (1) It means God's being in his act on which our being reposes (6f.). (2) It means God's act aimed at a specific and central goal (7f.). (3) It means an act dealing with man's salvation (8f.). (4) It means an act grounded in God's eternal purpose and taking precedence even to the work of creation (9f.). (5) It means an act on behalf of those who have forfeited their creaturely existence and have no claim to salvation, that is, of undeserving sinners (10–12). (6) It means God's personal identification with us and therefore not just a restoration but rather the very coming of salvation (12–14). (7) It means our being with God ('we with God') as we are lifted up, given a place, awakened to our true being, and made free for God in virtue of his being with us (14–16). Nor is all this a mere idea. It is a history that finds fulfilment in the name of Jesus Christ, not as a sign or symbol, but as an authentic reality.[10]

With that background, Barth turns to the theme of covenant. He begins by saying very clearly that 'reconciliation is the fulfilment of the covenant between God and man'.[11] It is not a coincidence that Barth has no volume devoted to the human condition, the fall and sin. Rather, he sets all of these in the context of reconciliation. For him, the covenant between God and humanity is an eternal, gracious, unilateral covenant that has always promised redemption and reconciliation to all who are in Christ. He defines it in this way: 'The fellowship which originally existed between God and man, which was

---

8. *CD* IV/1, pp. 3–21.

9. Ibid., p. 3.

10. *Introduction to the Theology of Karl Barth* (Edinburgh: T. & T. Clark, 1979), p. 176.

11. *CD* IV/1, p. 22.

then disturbed and jeopardised, the purpose of which is now fulfilled in Jesus Christ and in the work of reconciliation, we describe as the covenant.'[12]

Barth then provides a long exegetical study, examining the use of the word 'covenant' in the Scriptures.[13] Despite the fact that there is some uncertainty as to the proper etymology and interpretation of both the Hebrew *běrît* and the Greek *diathēkē*, Barth is able to draw certain conclusions from the biblical evidence. His primary conclusion is that the covenant with Israel is established by God himself and is therefore a sovereign, gracious covenant. It is also supremely personal, involving the actions of God and of Israel. Recognizing that there are many covenants in the Old Testament (with Noah, Abraham, Moses, David etc.) he rejects the notion that these are all expressions of one underlying or more fundamental covenant. He writes:

> The autonomy and importance which the Old Testament literature gives to each of these many events, quite irrespective of their mutual relationship, seems to make it impossible to try to find some pragmatic, historical connexion.[14]

Nevertheless, there is a unity among them in that they are all expressions of the gracious action of a sovereign, electing God. Barth is also at pains to point out that nothing in our understanding of covenant must lead us to the conclusion that somehow God is under obligation because of the covenant, or is restricted in his action. The eternal freedom of the sovereign God is a fundamental thesis that must not be lost in expounding his relationship with his creatures. In other words, the covenant is unilateral in its essence, although bilateral in its outworking. In this context he even quotes Jacques Ellul to the effect that the covenant is 'a contract in which one of the parties makes the arrangements and the other simply agrees'.[15] In using this terminology, Barth specifically rejects the notion of a 'mutually binding contract'. But even the use of this language of 'contract' was later rejected by scholars in the Barthian tradition, who preferred to accuse the covenant theologians of thinking contractually and thus failing to see that the covenant was primarily gracious, based on love and not law.[16]

---

12. Ibid.
13. Ibid., pp. 22–24.
14. Ibid., p. 24.
15. Ibid, p. 25.
16. J. B. Torrance, 'The Covenant Concept in Scottish Theology and Politics and its Legacy', *SJT* 34 (1981), pp. 225–243.

Barth then goes on to make three important points in relation to his under-standing of covenant. The first is that the covenant is with the whole human race. This stands in marked difference to the covenant theology that sees the covenant as made with elect individuals, albeit with a more general reference in respect of the historical nation of Israel. Barth argues for his wider inter-pretation by beginning with the first covenant mentioned in Scripture, the covenant made with Noah, in which the whole human race is included.[17] He recognizes that the covenant made with Abraham and his descendents in Genesis 12 is restricted to the nation of Israel and thus two covenants are established in 'concentric circles', the outer one being with Noah and the inner one with Abraham. He does not accept, however, that the covenant with Noah is purely to do with the preservation of the race, whereas the covenant with Abraham has to do with grace and salvation. He points out that the Abrahamic covenant had elements of the preservation of Israel in it but, more significantly, he wants to argue that the covenant with Noah was essentially gracious since it involved God's unconditional promise to be faithful to the human race and to refrain from destroying them, despite their sin and dis-obedience. Hence he can write:

> Therefore the Noachic covenant – in a way which remarkably is much more
> perceptible than in the case of the covenant or covenants with Israel – is already a
> covenant of grace in the twofold sense of the concept grace: the free and utterly
> unmerited self-obligation of God to the human race which had completely fallen
> away from Him, but which as such is still pledged to Him . . . and as the sign of the
> longsuffering of God obviously also the promise of the future divine coming which
> will far transcend the mere preserving of the race.[18]

Barth believes that because this covenant is not an aspect of God's general rev-elation but represents a specific decision and action of God in relation to fallen humanity, then even although it is not part of the 'inner circle' of redemptive covenantal agreement, nevertheless it is 'an activity on the basis of which the nations preserved by God cannot be excluded from his redemptive work. In this sense the race, as a whole, is in covenant.'[19]

The second point Barth makes is that the covenant must be understood in terms of the mission of Israel. The intention here is to demonstrate that the

---

17. *CD* IV/1, pp. 26–27.

18. Ibid., p. 27.

19. Ibid.

covenant is not to be understood as a private arrangement between God and one historical nation. Israel's mission was to be a 'light to the nations' and a 'light to the Gentiles' and so God's redemptive purpose, although initially communicated to and in some senses vested in Israel, was intended for all the nations. Barth exegetes the passages in Isaiah and elsewhere where these and similar expressions occur and also widens the discussion to consider the eschatological significance of the fulfilment of Israel's mission in the coming of the Messiah, the declaration of the gospel to the Gentiles and the climax of all of this in the day of Yahweh. That last day, the day of the 'conclusion of the covenant' must not be seen simply as a time of judgment. Rather:

> The last time, the day of Yahweh, will indeed be the day of final judgement – the prophets of a false confidence must make no mistake about that. But as such it will also be the day of Israel's redemption – the day when the covenant which Yahweh has made with it finds its positive fulfilment.[20]

The third point Barth makes is that the covenant made with Israel transposes into the new covenant in Jesus Christ and can be understood fully only in that context. This new covenant was already anticipated in the prophecy of Jeremiah (chs. 31–32). In order to stress the unity and continuity of the covenants, Barth points out that almost precisely the same formula is found in Jeremiah as is found in the establishment of the covenants with Abraham, Moses and Joshua, namely, 'I will be your God and you will be my people.' This new, eternal covenant would not replace these older covenants but would rather bring them to fulfilment and completion. What then happens to the covenant with Israel? Barth writes:

> What happens to this covenant with the conclusion of a new and eternal covenant is rather . . . that it is upheld, that is, lifted up to its true level, that it is given its proper form, and that far from being destroyed it is maintained and confirmed. There is no question of a dissolution but rather of a revelation of the real purpose and nature of that first covenant.[21]

For Barth, the 'most remarkable thing of all' about this new covenant is that it will become a 'perfect covenant' because sin and God's opposition to it will finally be a thing of the past:

---

20. Ibid., p. 31.
21. Ibid., p. 33.

> This ending and new beginning will be posited in the fact that God not only exercises patience as in the Noachic covenant, but that He remits guilt, that He does not remember sin, and that in this way and on this basis He not only allows an unmerited continuation of life, again as in the Noachic covenant, but reduces to order, and in a sense compulsorily places in the freedom of obedience which we owe Him as His covenant partners.[22]

By moving from the covenant with Noah, to the prophecy of Jeremiah 31, and then on to the new covenant in Christ, Barth's whole intention is to demonstrate that the covenant is universal in its design, scope and implications. Thus, he can conclude, 'In the light of this passage in Jeremiah 31 we are indeed enabled and summoned to give to the concept of the covenant the universal meaning which it acquired in the form which it manifestly assumed in Jesus Christ.'[23]

Barth is never satisfied with his exposition of a doctrine unless it can be demonstrated to have a Christological focus, so, having completed the extended exegetical analysis of the notion of covenant, especially in the Old Testament, he now turns to speak of Christ. Christ is the one who brings the covenant to its place of fulfilment and completion, especially in his atonement. Indeed, Jesus Christ is 'the eschatological realisation of the will of God for Israel and therefore the whole race. And as such He is also the revelation of this divine will and therefore of the covenant.'[24] Again, Barth stresses that this covenant, now brought to fruition in Christ, is for the whole race. God's covenantal purposes for humankind that, from the beginning, have had as their intention the salvation of humanity, are now revealed in Christ. Being both God and man, he is able to reconcile humanity by his atonement. This helps us to understand, says Barth, that 'God does not at first occupy a position of neutrality in relation to man.'[25] Rather, God from all eternity has willed the salvation of humanity and in every situation has 'pledged himself' to humanity. The words 'I will be your God and you shall be my people' are not simply a historical statement made on several occasions but rather a revelation of God's eternal purpose in relation to his creatures. This binding and pledging of himself to humanity is the covenant and is the 'presupposition of the atonement' itself.[26]

In calling this covenant the 'covenant of grace', Barth argues that three

---

22. Ibid.
23. Ibid., p. 34.
24. Ibid., pp. 34–35.
25. Ibid., p. 37.
26. Ibid., p. 38.

things are being affirmed. First, it affirms the freedom of God in establishing and maintaining the covenant. Because of sin, humanity is unable to find reconciliation with God and so it must be provided from outside, from God himself. By our sin we have alienated ourselves from God and caused a breach in the fellowship with God. We have no rights in the situation and can make no demands: we are utterly at his mercy. Only God can act to deal with this situation and there are no factors operating upon him that can force him to take such action. He is entirely free in his self-determination to be our God and in his invitation for us to become his people.

The second implication of speaking about a covenant of grace conditions the first point, but only slightly. Indeed, no external factors limit the sovereign freedom of God to act graciously towards the human race he has created, but his own nature compels him. In other words, when we speak about a covenant of grace, we are actually making an affirmation about the nature of God himself. God does not simply pass on favours or benefits he might equally well have chosen to deny. Rather, the covenant of grace God makes with all humanity is an expression of his inner nature and true identity. It is himself he gives to humanity and not simply benefits. That is why the fullest explanation of the atonement is that it is the coming of God himself who acts out on this earth the salvation that springs from his essential being. Being and act can never be separated.

The third implication of speaking about the covenant as a covenant of grace is that the obligation on the part of humanity is simply one of gratitude. As we saw earlier, the covenant is unilateral: it represents the free and gracious action of a sovereign God whose heart of love reaches out to the human race he has created. It is not a covenant to which we as human beings contribute anything. All that is required of us is gratitude.[27] In one of those marvellous passages where Barth the preacher seems to take over, he explains that one of the implications of this is that we must not think of ourselves differently than God has come to think of us in Christ. Barth writes:

> By deciding for us God has decided concerning us. We are therefore prevented from thinking otherwise about ourselves, from seeing or understanding or explaining man any other way, than as the being engaged and covenanted to God, and therefore simply but strictly engaged and covenanted to thanks. Just as there is no God but the God of the covenant, there is no man but the man of the covenant: the man who as such is destined and called to give thanks.[28]

---

27. Ibid., p. 41.
28. Ibid., p. 43.

For many people who find themselves struggling to believe that they have truly been found by God in Christ, this is a marvellous pastoral application of the meaning of the covenant of grace.

At this point Barth adds a word of caution and warning. Nothing he has said about the covenant of grace can be discovered by natural theology. Only in Christ can we find the revelation of God's saving action. Indeed, 'Apart from and without Jesus Christ we can say nothing at all about God and man and their relationship one with another.'[29] At one level Barth is saying that revelation is vital for us to have any knowledge or understanding of what God has done for us in Christ, but at a deeper level he is arguing that the covenant of grace is grounded in the being of God and in his eternal decision to become a man for us. This has huge implications, not least that 'Ontologically, therefore, the covenant of grace is already included and grounded in Jesus Christ, in the human form and human contact which God willed to give His Word from all eternity.'[30] The covenant of grace is revealed only in Christ and especially in his atonement, the culmination of the covenant.

Barth on covenant theology

After this exposition of his general understanding of the theme of covenant, Barth turns more directly to a historical analysis and critique of the older covenant theology, which he calls 'federal theology'.[31] He does not attempt to trace the historical development of federal theology, although he does note some of the key figures in its earliest development and he does recognize that it was the 'ruling orthodoxy' of the Reformed churches in the second half of the seventeenth century.

Barth regards the federal theology as representing a significant improvement on what had gone before, both in medieval Catholicism and in the early Protestant scholastic tradition. In particular, he likes the way in which the federal theologians did not see the doctrines of the Christian faith as a series of propositional statements to be connected logically and theologically but rather viewed the message of Scripture more dynamically, viewing their task as the presentation and analysis of the history of God's relationship to humanity. In this sense they were following Calvin himself who also understood the-

29. Ibid., p. 45.
30. Ibid.
31. Ibid., pp. 54–66.

ology in this dynamic manner.[32] Unfortunately, from Barth's perspective there was a fatal flaw in this approach: the federal theologians viewed the atonement as one event in a series of events, rather than as 'the event' that gives meaning to everything else. As Barth says:

> They overlooked the fact that in all the forms of its attestation this single and complete event is a special event which has to be understood in a special way. Because of the difference of the attestation it cannot be broken up into a series of different covenant acts, or acts of redemption, which follow one another step by step, and then reassembled into a single whole. The Federal theologians did not notice that for all the exclusiveness with which they read the Scriptures, in this analysis and synthesis of the occurrence between God and man they were going beyond Scripture and missing its real content.[33]

Barth goes on to speak of some of the earliest occurrences of the covenant theology, in Zwingli and in Bullinger, who were using the structure of covenant to undergird their theology of infant baptism. Barth is not convinced that they were successful in this but he does identify in their expression of the covenant a universal significance of which he heartily approves. He goes on to demonstrate that in the more developed forms of federal theology this universalism was lost. In this later federal theology, the covenant of grace applies only to the elect. Instead of seeing a universal atonement as the climax of the covenant, the atonement becomes the means by which God secures the salvation of those elect individuals with whom (and only with whom) he was in covenant. Barth regards this as a 'blind alley' that departed from the earlier 'very remarkable form' of federal theology.[34] As Barth later said, this means that the covenant of grace thus becomes at best 'a secondary and subsequent divine arrangement' rather than 'the beginning of all the ways of God'.[35]

What led to this blind alley? Barth believes that the problems arose principally through the introduction of a two-covenant system, a covenant of *works* and a covenant of *grace*, for which he blames Ursinus, although there is increasing evidence to suggest that the idea predates Ursinus.[36] He notes that this gradually became the normative position within Reformed theology, receiving

---

32. Ibid., p. 55.
33. Ibid., p. 56.
34. Ibid., p. 58.
35. Ibid., p. 66.
36. See Weir's historical analysis, *Origins of Federal Theology*.

covenantal status in the Westminster Confession of Faith. Barth spells out the developed covenant theology in its two-covenant form, using the writings of Cocceius as his core text. Indeed, he says that Cocceius 'represents the Federal theology in a form which is not only the most perfect, but also the ripest and strongest and most impressive'.[37] Despite this, however, Barth regards him as having made fundamental theological mistakes, especially in his regarding the covenant of grace only in negative terms as an abrogation of the covenant of works.

Barth's most serious criticism of Cocceius, however, is that his understanding of the covenant of grace led to the necessity for an inter-trinitarian covenant, which, in later covenant theology, would be called the covenant of redemption. This inter-trinitarian covenant was held to be the basis for the covenant of grace. The Father and the Son covenant together to the effect that if the Son will agree to become incarnate and receive from the Father the punishment for sin on behalf of the elect, then the Father will forgive the sins of the elect and impute to them the righteousness of Christ. Barth's trinitarian theology will not allow him even to contemplate such a notion. He is quite dismissive of such a theology:

> This is mythology, for which there is no place in a right understanding of the doctrine of the Trinity as the doctrine of the three modes of being of the one God, which is how it was understood and presented in Reformed orthodoxy itself.[38]

Having presented his critique of the older federal theology, Barth then completes the picture by speaking of reconciliation as the fulfilment of the covenant.[39]

In order for us to see the full extent of Barth's critique of covenant theology, however, it is necessary for us to move beyond the *Church Dogmatics* itself and to consider an earlier work by Barth. In *The Theology of the Reformed Confessions*,[40] we see a criticism that has only tangentially appeared so far, namely that covenant theology has an anthropological basis rather than a theological basis.

Barth articulated his opposition to the anthropological approach of

---

37. *CD* IV/1, p. 60.

38. Ibid., p. 65.

39. Ibid., pp. 67–78.

40. Columbia Series in Reformed Theology, trans. D. L. Guder and J. J. Guder (Louisville: Westminster John Knox, 2002 [1923]).

covenant theology in the early stages of his theological development, when he gave a series of lectures on the theology of the Reformed confessions. This book, only recently available in English for the first time, contains a series of lectures Barth gave in Göttingen in 1923 (he had taken up his appointment as Professor there in 1921). In these lectures we catch a glimpse of the early Barth as he goes back behind the liberal theology in which he was schooled but has now abandoned, in order to explore his own Reformed tradition. It is interesting to see in these lectures Barth's strong affirmation of the need for confessional orthodoxy and his critique of liberal theology for having abandoned this. The relevance of the book for our present purposes, however, is that already at this early period we find Barth spelling out his main problem with covenant theology, namely its emphasis on anthropology. For Barth, it is vital to emphasize the priority of theology over anthropology, a theme that will remain central in his later, more mature thought.

We see the first clear exposition of this problem when he deals with the Westminster Confession of Faith (hereafter WCF). He sets the scene by arguing that the significance of a Reformed confession lies not in itself but rather in that which is beyond itself, that to which it points, namely to the Word of God. Having established that principle, he is critical of confessions that fail in this regard. It is in this context that he expresses his high regard for the Scots Confession of 1560 and also his astonishment that we Scots would exchange it for the WCF![41] Why did he prefer the Scots Confession? Simply, because he believed that the WCF, with its emphasis on the application of redemption and the quest for assurance, places the focus too much on anthropology instead of theology.[42]

Barth makes the same criticism of the Canons of Dort, although not without first praising Dort for its core instincts. He writes, 'There is no way to deny that what is expressed in the canons of Dort is the authentic concern of the Reformation. Their case against the Remonstrants is entirely justified and consistent from the perspective of Luther and Calvin.'[43] It was absolutely necessary to emphasize the freedom of God in his sovereign election. Unfortunately, from Barth's perspective, this fundamentally correct instinct was damaged by their concern with the question as to whether or not particular individuals were elect. He says, 'There is no doubting that they respond with the *Reformation* answer to this question. But in my view, the actual interest in

---

41. Ibid., pp. 134–136.
42. Ibid., pp. 150–151.
43. Ibid., p. 215.

this *question* was the first crack in the wall of the church itself.'[44] Barth goes on to explain what he means:

> They were thinking anthropologically rather than theologically when they made the 'absolute decree' [*decretum absolutum*], which is a profound statement about God, into a doctrine not just about humanity but about this or that person – even if they did so with logical consistency. The doctrine of a 'limited number' [*numerus clausus*] of the elect is, in particular, not good doctrine; it ties God down to particular people when the meaning of the entire doctrine is precisely the freedom of God.[45]

Barth goes so far as to call the decisions of the Synod of Dort 'the *mausoleum* of the early Reformed movement'.[46] Despite this, he has grave misgivings about the WCF, which he compares unfavourably with the Canons of Dort. For he writes:

> But I would like to add that the canons of Dort are much superior to the Westminster Confession. Especially the dangerous doctrine of the assurance of election is presented here in a balanced way and does not emerge as the central point and crown of the entire thing, as is the case in the intolerable approach of the English.[47]

To complete Barth's critique of covenant theology, I make one final point, drawn from his study *Christ and Adam: Man and Humanity in Romans 5*.[48] In this little book Barth deals with the parallel between Christ and Adam in Romans 5, a key text in covenant theology. The point to be noted is that Barth will not allow Adam to have the priority. In most expressions of covenant theology, Adam is dealt with first as the federal head of the race and then later Christ is presented as the federal head of the elect, whom God by this means rescues from eternal punishment. Thus, Christ is the second (or last) Adam. Barth writes:

> The relationship between Adam and us reveals not the primary but only the secondary anthropological truth and ordering principle. The primary anthropological truth and ordering principle, which only mirrors itself in that relationship, is made

---

44. Ibid., p. 216.
45. Ibid.,
46. Ibid., p. 212.
47. Ibid., p. 216.
48. Trans. T. A. Smail (New York: Collier, 1962).

clear only through the relationship between Christ and us. Adam is, as is said in v.14, *typos tou mellontos*, the type of Him who was to come. Man's essential and original nature is to be found, therefore, not in Adam but in Christ. In Adam we can only find it prefigured. Adam can therefore be interpreted only in the light of Christ, and not the other way round.[49]

In summary, then, Barth's critique of covenant theology consists of seven main points. (1) Covenant theology divides the single unique 'event' of Christ into a series of covenantal arrangements, thus denying the fundamental significance of 'the event'. (2) In its later forms, covenant theology denies the universality of the covenant of grace and becomes particularized in a set of elect individuals. (3) Rather than understanding the covenant of grace as the outworking of God's electing purpose for all humanity, covenant theology understands the covenant of grace as a secondary arrangement necessary only because of the failure of the original covenant of works. (4) Covenant theology views the atonement not as the climax of the universal implications of the covenant but as a means of effecting the salvation of the elect. (5) Covenant theology requires an inter-trinitarian covenant that undermines the doctrine of the Trinity. (6) Covenant theology has an anthropological rather than a theological approach to salvation. (7) In covenant theology Adam is given priority over Christ.

The Torrance brothers on covenant theology

Many scholars have taken up the various themes in Barth's theology, but few scholars in the Barthian tradition of theology have done more to advance Barth's critique of covenant theology than J. B. Torrance and his brother T. F. Torrance. Indeed, it might fairly be said that James Torrance in particular had a single-minded passion for this subject and devoted most of his academic career to an assault on the covenant theology.[50] He did this not for any abstract

---

49. Ibid., pp. 39–40.
50. For a selection of his writings on this subject, see J. B. Torrance, 'The Contribution of McLeod Campbell to Scottish Theology', *SJT* 26 (1973), pp. 295–311; 'Covenant Concept in Scottish Theology'; 'Strengths and Weaknesses of the Westminster Theology', in A. I. Heron (ed.), *The Westminster Confession in the Church Today* (Edinburgh: St Andrew, 1982), pp. 40–53; 'The Incarnation and Limited Atonement', *EQ* 55 (1983), pp. 83–94.

academic or intellectual reasons but out of a deep personal conviction that the gospel itself was fundamentally damaged by covenant theology and that we must reject this theology if we are truly to proclaim Christ.

In the writings of J. B. Torrance are several recurring themes, some of which are found in Barth but that Torrance spelled out in more detail. First, he argued that by placing the doctrine of election at the beginning of the theological *corpus* and by defining it as God's choice of certain individuals and the rejection of certain other individuals, election becomes the controlling dogma and everything else is worked out from that starting point. Secondly, he argued that by defining election as referring to individuals rather than to Christ, the result is limited atonement and a denial of the universal scope of Christ's atoning death. Thirdly, he argued that the doctrine of assurance is fatally damaged by this view of election because the question becomes 'How do I know that I am elect?' This results in people looking inward to themselves for 'signs of election', instead of looking outward to Christ. Torrance had a deep appreciation for John McLeod Campbell, who rejected the doctrines of election and limited atonement as defined by traditional covenant theology precisely because he discerned a lack of assurance among the members of his congregation and traced this back to these central federal doctrines. Fourthly, covenant theology puts nature before grace, and justice before love, thus inverting the biblical order. Fifthly, covenant theology makes the mistake of confusing covenant and contract, leading to a bilateral covenant whereby grace is obtained when certain conditions have been met, most notably repentance.

T. F. Torrance shared his brother's critique of covenant theology and elements of that shared critique can be seen at various points in his writing. It was, however, in one of his last publications that it comes most fully to the surface. Having been asked to contribute to a history of New College, Edinburgh, he ended up writing a book on the history of Scottish theology![51] The book consists of a long spelling out of a core thesis, namely that the gracious and biblical theology of John Calvin, John Knox and the early Reformers was fundamentally damaged by the development of covenant theology, which is not a legitimate development from that early Reformed theology but is, in fact, a serious aberration.

This 'older Scottish tradition', as represented for example by the Scots Confession of 1560, was incarnational and inclusivist, like the theology of Athanasius, and held to a universal atonement, like Calvin. Unfortunately,

---

51. *Scottish Theology: From John Knox to John McLeod Campbell* (Edinburgh: T. & T. Clark, 1996).

there was a return to a scholastic theological model through the creation of federal theology by High Calvinists such as Perkins, Rutherford, Dickson and Durham, a conditionalist, legalistic and contractual theology that emphasized limited atonement and led to every conceivable problem, particularly the lack of assurance among Christians. John McLeod Campbell, recognizing this error, restored the 'older Scottish tradition' and suffered the consequences.

Response to Barth on covenant theology

Having presented at some length Barth's understanding of how the concept of covenant ought to function in a Reformed dogmatics and having observed both his own critique of covenant theology and that of the Torrance brothers, it is necessary now to move towards some assessment of these views. I do so from the perspective of one who affirms the core teaching of covenant theology, although I have sought to offer modifications to the system, not least that I prefer to call it 'headship theology', for reasons spelled out elsewhere.[52] In offering this assessment I want to begin by commending four aspects of Barth's exposition of the covenant concept, including aspects of his critique of covenant theology that are well founded and ought to provide a necessary corrective to some forms of that theological system.

Points of agreement

First, as we noted at the beginning, Barth does not use the covenant concept as a mere subsection within his general understanding of salvation, but rather he integrates the theme theologically into every area of his dogmatics. This is a huge undertaking and emphasizes the seriousness with which he takes the fact that, according to the Scriptures, God's dealings with humanity must be conceived of in covenantal terms. This also means that his view of covenant is internally self-consistent, even if it may be criticized from other theological perspectives. The architectonic structure of his dogmatics is truly impressive and one has to agree that some of his critics lack the deep theological rigour involved in this integrative work, opting instead for a somewhat shallow theological method that does not deeply imbed the covenant concept into the core theological structure of their dogmatics.

---

52. A. T. B. McGowan, 'In Defence of "Headship Theology"', in J. A. Grant and A. I. Wilson (eds.), *The God of Covenant: Biblical, Theological and Contemporary Perspectives* (Leicester: Apollos, 2005), pp. 178–199.

Secondly, Barth is right to affirm that the covenant is unilateral in nature, established by God with a sovereign freedom. The covenant is not a bilateral, conditional covenant. In this context, he is also right to affirm the unity of the covenants. There is a unity in the covenantal dealing of God with humanity that must not be undermined by unnecessarily polarizing covenants of works and grace.[53]

Thirdly, Barth is right to insist upon the priority of grace over law. This is one point, however, where Barth and J. B. Torrance would have benefited from recognizing the various strands within covenant theology. The difference between these strands on issues of law and grace are quite significant. For example, Torrance says that covenant theology involved giving priority to law over grace and that it is based 'on contract law rather than on the grace and love of God',[54] but this is not generally true. Some covenant theologians have indeed suggested that law has priority over grace, arguing that grace is entirely a response to the fall. Some of them have insisted that we must not speak about grace until the proto-gospel of Genesis 3:15. This was a matter of serious dispute between two recent Reformed theologians, John Murray and Meredith G. Kline. Like Barth and Torrance, although for different reasons, Murray insisted on the priority of grace over law, as the famous covenant theologian Thomas Boston had done before him.[55] He was right to do so and so we reject the conclusions of one writer, who compared Murray and Kline and argued that Kline's position was to be preferred.[56] Perhaps the principal lesson to be learned here is that if covenant theologians do make the mistake of arguing that law precedes grace, then they are opening the door for a most destructive (perhaps even fatal) analysis of their position.

---

53. See my chapter 'The Unity of the Covenant', in J. A. Pipa and C. N. Willborn (eds.), *The Covenant: God's Voluntary Condescension* (Taylors, S. C.: Presbyterian, 2005), pp. 1–13.

54. See the pamphlet by Torrance, *A Critique of Federal Theology in the Light of the Gospel: Was John Calvin a "Federal" Theologian?* (Victoria: Burning Bush Society of Victoria, 1997).

55. See A. T. B. McGowan, 'Scottish Covenant Theology', in idem, *Covenant: God's Voluntary Condescension*, pp. 61–72, in which I advocate Murray's understanding of covenant theology; and also McGowan, 'Headship Theology', pp. 178–199, where I compare and assess Murray and Kline.

56. Jeong Koo Jeon, *Covenant Theology: John Murray's and Meredith Kline's Response to the Historical Development of Federal Theology in Reformed Thought* (Lanham, Md.: University Press of America, 1999).

Fourthly, Barth was right to insist that there is no inter-trinitarian covenant. This is a weakness in covenant theology that demonstrates a failure to integrate properly its understanding of covenant with its doctrine of the Trinity. Interestingly, Thomas Boston also rejected the notion of an inter-trinitarian covenant. In taking this position, we are not thereby accepting the Barthian view of atonement, which sees the reconciliation between God and humanity taking place ontologically in the person of Christ with the emphasis on the incarnation, rather than forensically through penal substitutionary atonement, where the emphasis is placed on the cross. I do believe that there is an encounter between the Father and the Son on the cross, whereby the Son is punished by the Father in our place. I do not believe, however, that this necessitates an inter-trinitarian covenant.

Points of disagreement

Having noted these points of agreement, we must now turn to six points of disagreement.

First, I must take issue with Barth's argument that the federal theologians were wrong to structure the 'event' of redemption as a series of events (or covenants). As we saw, Barth believed that the one 'event' of Christ cannot be divided and there can be no revelation of God except through this 'event'. This betrays Barth's unwillingness, observable throughout his writings, to speak of revelation other than in and through Christ. This is an understandable concern and I share Barth's rejection of natural theology in all its forms. But, as the writer to the Hebrews says, this God did speak through prophets and apostles before the final speaking in Jesus Christ (Heb. 1:1–2). In my view, the federal theologians were simply taking seriously the redemptive history God reveals to us in the Scriptures and that Barth, not the covenant theologians, is the one who has missed 'the real content'[57] of Scripture.

Secondly, Barth's critique of covenant theology is too tightly focused on one individual (Cocceius), representing one tradition within covenant theology. Covenant theology is not a monolithic structure agreed in all its elements by all its adherents. One of the problems with both Barth and the Torrances is that *some* of their criticisms are legitimate in respect of *some* expressions of covenant theology but are definitely *not* legitimate in respect of every strand of covenant theology. There are many covenant theologians who do not hold in its entirety to the position espoused by Cocceius, Barth's primary source for an understanding of covenant theology. There were (and

---

57. *CD* IV/1, p. 56.

are) various strands of covenant theology, but Barth does not distinguish these various strands. For example, some covenant theologians believed that the Mosaic covenant was a republication of the covenant of works, but John Murray did not, for good reasons.

Thirdly, I must disagree with Barth's understanding of Christ the Mediator. Barth argues that even if there had been no fall, Christ would still have come as Mediator. This implies that there is some ontological breach or gulf that has to be bridged between God and humanity, rather than the moral breach of the fall. Even some of those such as J. L. Scott, who are generally sympathetic to Barth's overall critique of covenant theology find it difficult to accept his argument at this point because it seems to fly in the face of the teaching of Scripture.[58] For example, Scott asks:

> [I]s it not going too far to use the word Mediator of the relationship of Christ to unfallen man? Is there any reference in Scripture which clearly and unambiguously states that the 'eternal purpose' of God for an unfallen world would have been that the Word should become flesh?[59]

After suggesting some passages of Scripture that seem to suggest otherwise, Scott concludes, 'Can we then say with dogmatic assurance that without human sin there would have been no cross, but there would certainly have been Jesus Christ the God-man?'[60] It is my view that without the fall, human beings do not require a Mediator.

Fourthly, I must disagree with Barth's attempt to make the covenant with Noah the primary expression of God's relationship with humanity. In order to widen the covenant beyond simply the scope of Israel and to argue that God's covenant with humanity is a universal covenant, Barth takes the covenant with Noah to be the primary covenant and works out most of his subsequent argument from that basis. In the biblical witness, however, it is the Abrahamic covenant that is quoted again and again through the subsequent generations and that seems to form the basis for a true understanding of the nature of God's dealings with humanity. Barth, however, takes a different approach. As we saw, when he is expounding his understanding of the new covenant, he sets it in the context of the covenant with Noah and not the covenant with Abraham. This flies in the face of the New Testament

---

58. 'The Covenant in the Theology of Karl Barth', *SJT* 17.2 (1964), pp. 182–198.

59. Ibid., p. 196.

60. Ibid., pp. 196–197.

teaching about the new covenant, which both Paul and the writer to the Hebrews set firmly in the context of the covenants with Abraham and Moses. In other words, Barth's argument that the covenant (and therefore the atonement) is universal, based on an exegesis of the covenant with Noah, is not persuasive. It asks the 'outer circle' (as he calls it) of God's covenantal dealings to do theological work for which it was not intended. Far more persuasive is John Murray's analysis of the relationship between the various biblical covenants.[61]

Fifthly, I disagree with Barth's development of a Christological view of predestination. Once again, Barth's intention is to maintain a universal focus for the reconciliation that takes place in Christ. If predestination has to do only with some individuals and not with every human being, then the outworking of God's electing grace will naturally take the form it does in covenant theology and will result in limited atonement. As most covenant theologians have argued, Christ died only for the elect, since otherwise there would be a double payment for sin by those who go to hell. To avoid this conclusion, Barth must argue that Christ is the one who is predestined and that he is both the electing God and the elect man. I am not suggesting that this is the reason why Barth arrived at his Christological understanding of predestination. I accept that he reached his position out of deep-seated convictions about the nature of God and his grace. It is, however, a crucial element in his opposition to covenant theology and I believe that in this matter he has departed from the teaching of Scripture as well as from Calvin and the Reformed tradition.

Sixthly, I would argue that Barth has failed to provide a satisfying account of the relationship between Christ and Adam. This is undoubtedly the most significant of my criticisms because it takes us to the very nub of the conflict between Barth and covenant theology. Covenant theologians argue that the relationship between Adam and Christ, as spelled out by Paul in Romans 5:12–21 and 1 Corinthians 15:12–34 (esp. vv. 21–22), requires us to structure our theology in a particular way. These passages tell us that through the actions of the one man Adam we all became sinners and through the actions of the one man Christ we become righteous. How are we to explain this connection? It is very difficult to read those passages in Paul without concluding that God entered into a relationship with humanity in Adam, such that Adam's disobedience brought judgment not only upon himself but upon all those he represented as he stood before God in Genesis 2 (namely, all humanity yet unborn).

61. *The Covenant of Grace* (London: Tyndale, 1954).

Similarly, it seems clear that God has entered into a new relationship with humanity in Christ such that what was done by Adam was reversed by Christ. Given the weaknesses of an Augustinian account of the transmission of sin, how are we to make sense of the imputation of Adam's sin and the imputation of Christ's righteousness if we do not accept some form of covenant theology? The recapitulation theory of Irenaeus is helpful in some limited ways but it does not properly handle imputation. I am not denying that there are some difficulties in the way these matters have sometimes been handled in covenant theology, but my view is that most of these difficulties are removed by talking about headship theology, where the focus is firmly on two men, Adam and Christ, rather than on two covenants. We must also take care to emphasize the importance of union with Christ and not see this as an alternative account to that of headship and imputation.

Barth's natural instinct to give priority to Christ over Adam is understandable. Adam was a 'type' of the one who was to come and therefore in some fundamental sense we must view Adam in the light of Christ. Nevertheless, Christ is also the second (or last) Adam. In his desire to be Christocentric, Barth has failed to take the biblical account of history seriously. Indeed, it can perhaps be argued that one of the overall weaknesses of Barth's theology is a lack of proper 'grounding' in the redemptive-historical context set out for us in Scripture. We also understand Barth's anxiety about the primacy of grace. As we noted earlier, the traditional account of the relationship between Adam and Christ in covenant theology has sometimes been guilty of giving the priority to law over grace and has sometimes spoken unwisely about 'merit'. I would argue, however, that these are problems that can be (and in the cases of some covenant theologians have been) sorted. These concerns certainly do not justify abandoning any concept of headship theology. In any case, as I have argued, the alternative proposals are deeply unsatisfying.

Conclusions

In the light of my analysis of Barth's exposition of the covenant concept and my assessment of his critique of covenant theology I must now draw some conclusions. There are perhaps three things to be said. (1) Barth's theology remains the most serious challenge to the tradition of covenant theology, not least because it seeks to integrate the doctrine of God with the exposition of reconciliation in Christ that covenant theologians have often failed to do. (2) While there are clearly aspects of Barth's thinking on covenant that I believe to be mistaken, nevertheless there are lessons to be learned from Barth and those in his tradition, lessons that act as a useful corrective to some expressions of traditional covenant theology. (3) I remain convinced that it is possible to develop a covenant theology that is both biblically grounded and theologically sophisticated, and nothing in the criticisms levelled by Barth and the Torrances has damaged this fundamental conviction.

5. THE DAY OF GOD'S MERCY: ROMANS 9 – 11 IN BARTH'S DOCTRINE OF ELECTION

David Gibson

Introduction

In the *Göttingen Dogmatics*, Karl Barth comments on his 'one incisive deviation' from the Reformed doctrine of predestination:

> And I for my part am fully aware that it is no secondary matter if I deviate here but that it will have the most far-reaching consequences. This is the rent in the cloak of my orthodoxy, for which undoubtedly I would at least have been beaten with rods in old-time Geneva.[1]

If Barth felt like this about his doctrine of election as it stood in 1924–5, then the personal reflection on his mature exposition of election in *Church Dogmatics* II/2 (1942) is not surprising: 'To think of the contents of this volume gives me much pleasure, but even greater anxiety.'[2] However much Barth may have felt he was departing from the Reformed tradition in the *Göttingen Dogmatics*, it was nothing compared to the colossal shift that appears in II/2 of the *Church Dogmatics*. His treatment of election in Göttingen contains notable similarities

---

1. *GD*, p. 453.
2. *CD* II/2, p. x.

to this tradition (Rom. 9 'teaches eternal, unconditional, twofold predestin-ation'[3]), with the stated deviation being the account of temporality. Here Barth rejects a concept of election as a decree occurring in a pre-temporal past to save a 'fixed number'. He prefers instead an actualistic understanding of election whereby God is involved in a continual interaction with individuals in the present as part of the divine decision of electing and rejecting.[4] But by 1942 everything is different. In *CD* II/2 Barth explicitly rejects not just his earlier moment-by-moment actualism in offering a more complex account of eternity and time, but also the classical landscape of eternal, individual, double predes-tination. While wishing to stand in the Reformed tradition and adopt many of its foundational premises, Barth now offers a radical reorientation of the doc-trine to a Christological centre that issues in a completely new understanding of both election and double predestination. 'It is arguably the classic instance in the *Church Dogmatics* of Barth working out his conviction that the church's talk of Jesus Christ is to furnish the ground and content of all theological doc-trine.'[5]

There are many reasons for this development in Barth's thought.[6] One simple and often overlooked reason that Barth himself gives is exegesis. The publication of *CD* II/2 gave Barth 'much pleasure, but even greater anxiety', for, as he comments in the preface:

> I would have preferred to follow Calvin's doctrine of predestination much more closely instead of departing from it so radically . . . But I could not and cannot do so. As I let the Bible itself speak to me on these matters, as I meditated upon what I seemed to hear, I was driven irresistibly to reconstruction.[7]

---

3. *GD*, p. 453.

4. S. McDonald argues that this doctrine of election remains influential for Barth in the volumes of *Church Dogmatics* prior to II/2; see her 'Barth's "Other" Doctrine of Election in the *Church Dogmatics*', *IJST* 9.2 (2007), pp. 134–147.

5. J. Webster, *Barth* (London: Continuum, 2000), p. 88.

6. Cf. B. L. McCormack, *Karl Barth's Critically Realistic Dialectical Theology: Its Genesis and Development 1909–1936* (Oxford: Clarendon, 1995), pp. 453–463. Note McCormack's recent modification to this developmental paradigm in 'Seek God where he May Be Found: A Response to Edwin Chr. van Driel', *SJT* 60.1 (2007), pp. 62–79; cf. also M. Gockel, *Barth and Schleiermacher on the Doctrine of Election: A Systematic-Theological Comparison* (Oxford: Oxford University Press, 2006), pp. 158–197.

7. *CD* II/2, p. x.

The claim to have been driven by attending to Scripture is vindicated by the sheer length and detail of the biblical exegesis that occupies Barth in II/2. These small-print sections raise many important questions, not least among them: how cogent is Barth's exegetical reconstruction?

In this chapter I shall examine one strand from *CD* II/2: the election of the community in Romans 9 – 11. Arguably, the main aim of this exegesis is to overcome the (alleged) focus on the individual in the classic Reformed doctrine of election. By placing Christology and humanity in proper relation to each other, Barth's doctrine of election begins with Jesus Christ as both the electing God and the elected man; then moves to see the one community of God (Israel and the church) as a witness to the election of Christ; and only then comes to treat the election of the individual. I shall suggest that, in his effort to correct the Reformed tradition, Barth reads Romans 9 – 11 in concert with a Christologically redefined concept of double predestination in such a way that in key places the text begins to warp under the Christological weight it is made to bear. The result is an exegetical treatment that is by turns brilliant and complex, but also ultimately unsuccessful.

I shall proceed in four stages. First, I shall outline Barth's hermeneutical framework for this exegesis, both in its immediate and broader contexts. This treatment will necessarily be very compressed but aims to allow Barth's exegesis its own explanatory power. Second, as the heart of the chapter, I shall consider a range of exegetical issues from two portions of Romans 9. Third, I shall respond to one way in which his exegesis might plausibly be defended. Finally, I shall offer some concluding thoughts about the implications of this example of Barth's exegesis, both for the church's use of Scripture and for wider discussions about Barth on election. Throughout, my critique aims to be more Pauline (1 Tim. 5:1) than old-time Genevan.

The hermeneutical framework

Barth's exegesis of Romans 9 – 11 can be understood only in the light of many features of its context; I shall outline two of the most important. The first is Barth's doctrine of Scripture. The second is Barth's opening moves in the doctrine of election in II/2, §§32–33, prior to his discussion of the election of the community in §34.[8]

---

8. It is doubtful whether Barth would have cared much for talk of his hermeneutical 'framework'. I do not suggest that Barth merely imposes a set of a prioris on to his

The doctrine of Scripture

In establishing his central thesis that 'God's eternal will is the election of Jesus Christ',[9] Barth pauses to make some epistemological observations about the basis for his radically Christocentric doctrine of election. He suggests that the fundamental difference between his doctrine and that of the 'older theologians' is based on the fact that the latter carried out their exegesis 'in line with a highly questionable general hermeneutical principle which we ourselves cannot follow'.[10] These theologians rightly 'taught us that in the word which calls and justifies and sanctifies us, the word which forms the content of the biblical witness, we must recognise in all seriousness the Word of God', and also that 'we must seek and will assuredly find (the in every respect) perfect and unsurpassable Word of God in the name and person of Jesus Christ'.[11] However, in the matter of predestination, these interpreters ignored their own best insights: 'in some inexplicable way there suddenly seemed to open up before them the vista of heights and depths beyond and behind the Word which calls and justifies and sanctifies us, the Word which they could never extol enough as the source of all our knowledge of God and man'.[12] Their questionable hermeneutical principle was thus the implicit conviction that in fact there can be a knowledge of the predestinating God which is not identical to the knowledge of Jesus Christ. In opposition to this hermeneutic, Barth sets up his own:

---

exegetical endeavours. 'So listen to my last piece of advice: exegesis, exegesis and yet more exegesis! Keep to the Word, to the Scripture that has been given us' – this was Barth's parting exhortation to his Bonn students in 1935 (E. Busch, *Karl Barth: His Life from Letters and Autobiographical Texts*, trans. John Bowden [Grand Rapids: Eerdmans, 1994], p. 259). Barth would have argued that any hermeneutical approach he adopted was itself exegetically derived, and note the suggestion that there is no place for a 'conceptually formulated principle of theology' in *CD* (H. Kirschstein, *Der Souveräne Gott und die Heilige Schrift: Einführung in die Biblische Hermeneutic Karl Barths* [Aachen: Shaker, 1998], p. 23, quoting P. Lange). Instead of a concept, Barth has a Name. Nevertheless, there is a complex interaction of doctrinal concerns and exegetical moves in his reading of Rom. 9 – 11, and, given the way the exegesis is presented as part of an argument that contains his explicit description of a hermeneutical principle or decision (*Entscheidung*), to speak of Barth's framework is not misleading.

9. *CD* II/2, p. 146.

10. Ibid., p. 150.

11. Ibid.

12. Ibid., p. 151.

> Like all other passages, [the scriptural passages on predestination] must be read in the
> context of the whole Bible, *and that means with an understanding that the Word of God is the*
> *content of the Bible.* The exegesis of these passages depends on whether or not we have
> determined that our exposition should be true to the context in which they stand and are
> intended to be read . . . [I]n the exegesis of the biblical passages which treat directly of
> election we have to look in the same direction as we must always look in biblical exegesis.
> We must hold by the fact that the Word which calls us, the Word which forms the content
> of Scripture, is itself and as such the (in every respect) perfect and unsurpassable Word
> of God, the Word which exhausts and reveals our whole knowledge of God.[13]

Jesus Christ is the content of the biblical witness, such that exegesis for Barth
is only rightly practised when it derives from and results in the knowledge of
Jesus Christ. In this light, there can be no exegesis of election that is 'divorced
from the name and person to which the whole content of the Bible relates as
to the exhaustive self-revelation of God'.[14]

These observations – the developments of the intervening years notwithstanding – are in harmony with Barth's substantive reflections on Scripture.
Earlier in the *Church Dogmatics* Barth had developed a bibliology well known
for its 'indirect identity' thesis: Scripture is a witness to revelation but is not in
and of itself revelation. Barth both distinguishes the biblical text from revelation, and yet also identifies the text with it on the basis of the fact that revelation is always an event, an act of the free and gracious God.[15] In that event,
'the biblical word becomes God's Word'.[16] Barth's theology of Scripture is an
extended reflection on this relation between the human words and the divine
Word, and for our purposes some comments from the end of his treatment in
CD I/2 ('Freedom Under the Word') are especially pertinent.

In a rich discussion of the processes of scriptural interpretation, Barth asks
why it is that we must subordinate ourselves to the scriptural witness. The
answer is theological: we are sinners, utterly dependent on God's grace to us,
and only the content of the Bible explains this particular relation between man
and God. This is the theological principle of hermeneutics.

> But it is certain that biblical hermeneutics must be controlled by this special
> fundamental principle because the content of the Bible imperatively requires it. The

---

13. Ibid., p. 152 (emphasis added).
14. Ibid., p. 153.
15. *CD* I/2, p. 463.
16. *CD* I/1, p. 113.

content of the Bible, and the object of its witness, is Jesus Christ as the name of the God who deals graciously with man the sinner . . . The Bible says all sorts of things, certainly; but in all this multiplicity and variety, it says in truth only one thing – just this: the name of Jesus Christ, concealed under the name Israel in the Old Testament and revealed under his own name in the New Testament . . . The Bible becomes clear when it is clear that it says this one thing: that it proclaims the name Jesus Christ and therefore proclaims God in his richness and mercy, and man in his need and helplessness . . . [W]e can properly interpret the Bible only when we perceive and show that what it says is said from the point of view of the concealed and revealed name of Jesus Christ.[17]

Barth goes on to discuss the individual phases of scriptural interpretation and presses home the above point even further. The object of the biblical text is 'mirrored in the prophetic-apostolic word' so that the aim of exegesis is 'to form a picture of what has taken place on the spot to which the words of the author refer'.[18] Barth is clear that this object is singular: 'The object of the biblical texts is quite simply the name Jesus Christ, and these texts can be understood only when understood as determined by this object.'[19] So at the very least in Barth's exegesis of Romans 9 – 11 we should expect to find the text itself witnessing to the name of Jesus Christ, with Barth aiming to expound carefully how the particular words of this particular text teach us that name. By the time we arrive at Romans 9 – 11 in *CD* II/2, the Jesus Christ this text witnesses to has already taken centre-stage in Barth's doctrine of election.

The doctrine of election

If the Reformed tradition spoke of Christ and the decree, for Barth Christ *is* the decree: 'God's eternal will is the election of Jesus Christ'. The heart of this argument is that Jesus Christ is the electing God and the elected man. This makes Jesus both the subject of election (the one doing the choosing) and the object of election (the one chosen). In a brilliant treatment of the infralapsarian–supralapsarian debate, Barth argues for his own version of supralapsarianism; other positions go astray by not recognizing that objects of election such as the community and the individual exist subordinately to the election of Christ himself.[20] The implications of this 'purified' supralapsarianism for

---

17. *CD* I/2, p. 720.
18. Ibid., p. 724.
19. Ibid., p. 727.
20. *CD* II/2, pp. 127–145.

Barth cannot be underestimated. The self-determination that takes place within the divine being to make Christ the elect man is the determination from which the entire covenant of grace flows, so that creation itself is predicated on the divine decision to be God for us in this particular way: humanity comes to exist because Christ is already the electing God and the elected man.[21] So Barth's supralapsarianism is expressed when he argues that God 'elects the people of Israel *for the purpose* of assuming its flesh and blood' and that 'the election of Israel occurred *for the sake* of the Son of God and Man'.[22] This immanent Christological ground for election provides a theological and onto-logical basis for two hermeneutical moves in Barth's exegesis of Romans 9 – 11.

First, Barth states, 'Now just as the electing God is one and elected man is one, i.e., Jesus, so also the community as the primary object of the one elec-tion which has taken place and takes place in Jesus Christ is one.'[23] By being the elected *man* as well as the electing God, the object of Christ's election must necessarily be one. That is to say, Christ cannot elect 'two humanities' but only one, and therefore, despite variations in form or appearance, the election of humanity cannot be other than the election of one united community. So Barth has done away with the possibility that there could be any portion of humanity in Israel or the church – or even (as becomes clear later) outside either group – that is not elect.

The second hermeneutical move in Barth's argument is an extension of the first: the 'twofold determination' of Jesus Christ is applied to the one com-munity of God. Barth has already argued that the elect man Jesus was predes-tined to suffer and to die. On this basis, God's electing will must be twofold, 'containing within itself both a Yes and a No'.[24] This twofold determination means that God says 'Yes' to humanity and 'No' to himself: 'in the election of Jesus Christ, which is the eternal will of God, God has ascribed to man . . . election, salvation and life; and to himself he has ascribed . . . reprobation, perdition and death'.[25] Thus, for Barth *the election of the community of God is the*

---

21. Webster argues that precisely because the *Church Dogmatics* is an exposition of the statement 'God is', it is also all along the line an anthropology, given the way Barth understands how God is; cf. Barth's *Ethics of Reconciliation* (Cambridge: Cambridge University Press, 1995), pp. 2–5, 47–51.

22. *CD* II/2, pp. 207, 296 (emphases added).

23. Ibid., p. 197.

24. Ibid., p. 161.

25. Ibid., p. 163.

witness of history to the election of Jesus Christ. What God chooses for himself in Christ – rejection and judgment – he determines for one form of the community (Israel); what God determines for humankind in Christ – fellowship and mercy – he determines for another form of the community (the church). Israel in its historical existence must bear witness to what God has determined for himself in Christ (judgment); the church in its historical existence must bear witness to what God has determined for humanity in Christ (mercy).[26] 'And it is in the twofold determination of Christ himself that this difference has its basis.'[27] Through the lens of this radical redefinition of the Reformed view of double predestination – the double determination of Christ becomes the double determination of the community – Barth's exegesis of Romans 9 – 11 describes the one elect community, Israel and the church, irreversibly joined on the basis of their double witness to the election of Jesus Christ.

When these two hermeneutical moves in the doctrine of election are read in conjunction with the thesis of indirect identity between the biblical words and revelation, a further significant point emerges. This is well stated by Douglas Sharp:

> [Barth's] exegesis [of Rom. 9 – 11] presupposes the identity of revelation/incarnation and election, and can be seen to consist in the interpretation of an objective reality (Israel and the Church) which he finds imaged in the text. The truly significant element of the exegesis is the fact that it is not so much the interpretation of biblical revelation as it is an interpretation of a medium which is itself an interpretation of revelation. This is to say that the exegesis of Romans 9–11 is an interpretation of an interpretation. Jesus Christ is *the* revelation, and Barth views the existence of the community as an interpretation of that revelation. Thus Barth interprets the community in its two forms in terms of the primary reality of Jesus Christ's election.[28]

In this way Barth's doctrine of Scripture and his doctrine of election undergird his distinctive approach to Romans 9 – 11. Barth operates with clear convictions both about what Scripture actually is as divine address and what it does: by describing the election of Israel and the church, the text images and thereby witnesses to the election of Jesus Christ. Although a full evaluation of

---

26. Ibid., p. 198.
27. Ibid., p. 199.
28. *The Hermeneutics of Election: The Significance of the Doctrine in Barth's Church Dogmatics* (Lanham, Md.: University Press of America, 1990), p. 140.

this hermeneutical framework is beyond our scope, one way to probe its via-bility is by examining its effects when brought into relation with Barth's exe-gesis of the biblical text. John Webster suggests that Barth's 'interpretation of Scripture is certainly not without question, especially when he allowed it to be commandeered by doctrinal interests'.[29] I shall now try to show that Barth's exegesis of Romans 9 – 11 is one such case where this complex interaction of doctrinal concerns raises serious questions.

Two examples

Salvation or vocation? Romans 9:1–9

From the outset, one major implication of Barth's approach to Romans 9 – 11 is that these chapters are read through an explicitly vocational rather than a soteriological lens. The issue for Barth is not whether Israel, or individuals from Israel, will be saved; the matter at hand is the divine calling given to Israel to be the form of the community that resists its election and so testifies to God's judgment. Jesus (as crucified Messiah of Israel) is 'the authentic witness of the judgment that God takes upon himself by choosing fellowship with man', and therefore Israel is called to 'exhibit', to 'attest', to 'reflect', to 'witness' to God's judgment on man. Jesus (as risen Lord of the church) is 'the authentic witness of the mercy in which God in choosing man for fellowship with himself turns towards him his own glory', and in this way the church is called to witness to God's mercy.[30] Israel and the church are elect for specific forms of service. For Barth this means that the election of Israel is never in doubt and it is impossi-ble for the salvific election of any Jew to be undone. This is ultimately because of the election of Jesus Christ. 'Behind and above the human obduracy char-acteristic of the Israelite form of the community there stands indeed the divine rejection, but there stands also God's election in which he has determined himself to take upon himself the rejection.'[31] This argument for two forms of the community reflecting the twofold determination of Jesus Christ obscures

---

29. 'Barth, Karl', in K. Vanhoozer (ed.), *Dictionary of Theological Interpretation of the Bible* (Grand Rapids: Baker, 2005), p. 84.

30. *CD* II/2, p. 198.

31. Ibid., p. 200. There is, of course, no strict dichotomy between vocational and soteriological concerns here. But, because the soteriological question is ultimately dealt with in the election of Jesus Christ, then for Barth, Paul's concern regarding Israel has to be almost exclusively in the realm of what Israel is called to witness to;

the explicitly soteriological focus of these chapters. I shall outline three key factors from the opening verses.

First, Barth does not engage sufficiently with the *anathema* clause in 9:3 and what it contributes to the logic of Paul's argument. At the start of chapter 9, something causes Paul to have 'great sorrow and unceasing anguish in my heart' (v. 2). Then in verse 3 he states, 'For I could wish that I myself were accursed and cut off from Christ (*anathema . . . apo tou Christou*) for the sake of my brothers (*hyper tōn adelphōn mou*), my kinsmen according to the flesh (*tōn syngenōn mou kata sarka*)', ESV. Barth's understanding of these verses is that Paul's suffering is caused by the unbelief of his kinsfolk. But rather than seeing a division here between Paul and his people, Barth is keen to stress their unity:

> The unbelief of his 'kinsmen' (v. 3) seeks to separate him from them. But this cannot succeed. Even in their unbelief they are and remain his 'brethren'. His faith, the church's faith in Jesus Christ, unites him with them.[32]

For Barth, Israel's unbelief is a 'dreadful denial' of its unalterable election and Paul is willing to be *anathema* to bring about an end to Israel's persistent rejection of the Messiah.

However, as numerous commentators note, Paul's wish to be accursed and cut off from Christ for the sake of his people only really makes sense if this is the position in which his people now stand.[33] Paul appears to believe that his people 'are in a plight as serious as the one he is willing to enter for their sake'.[34]

---

cf. ibid., p. 205, where Christ is 'the living head' of all unbelieving and 'dead' Israel. Or again, 'But [the Jews] cannot again reverse what for the sake of man and therefore for their sakes God has put right in this Jesus Christ . . . By their resistance to their election they cannot create any fact that finally turns the scale against their own election, separating them from the love of God in Jesus Christ, cancelling the eternal decree of God' (ibid., p. 209).

32. Ibid., p. 202.

33. D. Moo, *Romans*, NICNT (Grand Rapids: Eerdmans, 1996), pp. 557–558; J. Piper, *The Justification of God*, 2nd ed. (Grand Rapids: Baker, 1993), p. 45; J. Munck, *Christ and Israel* (Philadelphia: Fortress, 1967), pp. 27–28; T. Schreiner, *Romans*, BECNT (Grand Rapids: Baker, 1998), p. 481; P. Stuhlmacher, *Paul's Letter to the Romans*, trans. S. Hafemann (Louisville: Westminster John Knox, 1994), p. 145.

34. Piper, *Justification*, p. 45. J. D. G. Dunn comments, 'Whether Paul intended his readers to understand that Israel was *anathema* . . . is more than open to question', but he offers no convincing objection (*Romans 9–16*, WBC [Waco: Word, 1988], pp. 524–525).

Whether we understand *hyper* in representative or substitutionary terms, Paul's desire (if such were possible) is to be *anathema* on their behalf. Nowhere in the passage does Paul explicitly spell out the cause of his intense grief; however, on the basis of the *gar* (for) in verse 3 it again seems most likely that what has caused the pain is the *anathema* Paul sees Israel now standing under. This gains even more plausibility in the light of the meaning of *anathema*. In the LXX *anathema* translates *ḥērem*, which conveys the sense of 'something devoted to God' either positively as an offering, or negatively as set aside for destruction.[35] Paul uses the term in three other places (1 Cor. 12:3; 16:22; Gal. 1:8–9) and each time it is used negatively, as it clearly is here. C. E. B. Cranfield says that for Paul 'to be *anathema . . .* is to be delivered over to the divine wrath, accursed. Here in Romans 9:3 *anathema einai* clearly means "to forfeit final salvation."'[36] The implicit contention and the cause of Paul's grief is that this is what Israel has forfeited. Numerous other details in the argument of Romans 9 – 11 suggest that the question of salvation for Israel remains the crucial issue: the use of *tekna tou theou* (children of God) and *tekna tēs epangelias* (children of promise) in 9:7–9, terms that elsewhere in Paul refer to those who are saved (Rom. 8:16, 21; Gal. 4:28; Phil. 2:15); in 9:11–12, the standard soteriological terms of *erga* (works) and *kalein* (to call); *apōleia* (destruction) and *doxa* (glory) in 9:22–23, both used elsewhere by Paul to describe ultimate eschatological ends (Phil. 1:28; 2 Thess. 2:3; Rom. 8:18; 1 Thess. 2:12);[37] and the repeated explicit references to Israel and salvation (Rom. 9:27; 10:1, 13; 11:14, 26). These considerations point clearly to a salvific focus on Israel as opposed to a vocational one, which is at odds with Barth's reading.

The second factor to consider here is the immense theological weight Barth accords to *hoitines eisin Israēlitai* (they are Israelites) in verse 4. Arguing that even in their unbelief Israelites remain Paul's brethren, Barth states that

> this brotherhood and solidarity has (vv. 4–5) its objective basis in the fact that these 'kinsmen according to the flesh' have not ceased to be Israelites and therefore bearers of the name given to Jacob ('wrestler with God'), and real wrestlers with God according to the meaning of this name, any more than Paul himself has with his faith.[38]

---

35. BDAG, p. 63.

36. *Romans*, vol. 2, ICC (Edinburgh: T. & T. Clark, 1979), p. 457. On the significance of being *anathema . . . apo tou Christou*, Cranfield says, 'Nothing less than the eschatological sentence of exclusion from Christ's presence (cf. Mt 7:23; 25:42) is involved' (p. 458).

37. Schreiner, *Romans*, pp. 481–482.

38. *CD* II/2, p. 203.

For Barth the significant point here is that the name 'Israelites' unites Israel both to Paul and into an ongoing relationship with God. But does this not move too quickly over the preceding descriptions Paul has given of his relation to these Israelites in verse 3? There Paul describes them as 'my brothers, my kinsmen according to the flesh (*tōn adelphōn mou tōn syngenōn mou kata sarka*)', ESV. Cranfield argues that because in Paul *adelphoi* refers almost invariably to those who belong to the family of God, then the application here to unbelieving Jews means that Paul 'recognizes them still, in spite of their unbelief, as fellow-members of the people of God . . . Unbelieving Israel is within the elect community, not outside of it.' Cranfield further comments that the addition of *tōn syngenōn mou kata sarka* cannot mean that the 'bond of Jewish nationality is *merely* a fleshly matter: in view of vv. 4–5 it is clear that Paul cannot have intended any disparagement of the Jews by it'.[39] This position is precisely the same as Barth's. However, the question to put to this reading is this: if the positive reading of *kata sarka* in verse 3 is based on what follows it in verses 4–5, then must we not also consider what follows this in verses 6–9, where 'Israel' is further qualified with a term drawn from verse 3? In verse 7, referring to Israel, Paul clearly states that it is not *ta tekna tēs sarkos* (the children of the flesh) who are the children of God but *ta tekna tēs epangelias* (the children of the promise), and in this light it is very likely that in verse 3 Paul is giving an initial hint that he is capable of thinking about Israel in terms that involve a clear salvific distinction.[40] Given the content of verses 6–9, it is hard to see support for Barth's assertion that the Israel according to the flesh is as much 'a real wrestler with God' according to its name as Paul is as a believer in Christ. Here the lines of distinction are blurred for Barth but Paul draws them more sharply.[41]

This leads directly to the third point. That there is a distinction within Israel is something all interpreters admit, including Barth. But how should this distinction be understood? Barth takes it to be fundamentally a distinction between Israel and the church. Not all of those who bear the name Israel were also appointed to become members of the church.

---

39. *Romans*, vol. 2, pp. 458–459.
40. Cf. C. K. Barrett, *A Commentary on The Epistle to the Romans* (London: Harper & Row, 1957), p. 176.
41. Cf. C. A. Evans, 'Paul and the Prophets: Prophetic Criticism in the Epistle to the Romans (with special reference to Romans 9 – 11)', in S. K. Soderlund and N. T. Wright (eds.), *Romans and the People of God* (Grand Rapids: Eerdmans, 1999), pp. 123–124.

They were certainly appointed members of the elected community of God. This is
something that none of this race can be deprived of; this is something that not one of
this race can decline, not even if his name is Caiaphas or indeed Judas Iscariot; this is
what Jews, one and all, are by birth. But they were not all appointed members of the
church hidden in Israel and revealed in Jesus Christ . . . That is, they are not the true
Israel, i.e., the Israel which recognises Israel's true determination by accepting its proper
place in the church, which realises the mercy of God by joining in the church's praise.[42]

Barth is explicit that by 'church' he means 'the true spiritual Israel'.[43] But we
note again that the distinction between natural Israel and spiritual Israel (the
church) is not a soteriological distinction but a vocational one. The spiritual
Israel are those who perform the church's calling of proclaiming God's mercy
instead of the fleshly Israel's calling (proclaiming God's judgment). This
means that in his treatment of rejection Barth is always operating with 'a very
carefully circumscribed exclusion'.[44] In the treatment of Jacob and Esau that
follows, Barth will go on to argue that 'Even [Israel's] rejected members are
not forsaken, but after, as before, share in the special care and guidance of the
electing God.'[45] By operating with a concept of a single elect community on
the basis of Jesus Christ's election, Barth's constant refrain is that Israel, in displaying 'the sheer, stark judgment of God' nevertheless is incapable of doing
anything that separates her 'from the love of God in Jesus Christ, cancelling
the eternal decree of God'.[46]

We have to ask how convincing this is as a reading of Paul's dividing line. If
we are right about the import of the *anathema* clause, the general soteriological
terminology and in particular the soteric distinction between *tekna tēs sarkos* and
tekna tou theou / tēs epangelias, it is much more likely that the division Paul is outlining here is one which explains how there can be a saved Israel and an unsaved

42. *CD* II/2, p. 214.

43. Ibid. Barth comments here that, strictly speaking, only Jesus is the true Israel and
    that it is only in him that all others are elected. S. Grindheim criticizes a similar
    position held by N. T. Wright, that in this way the people of God narrows down to
    one person: 'This is eisegesis. Paul's argument drives towards the saved remnant,
    not the saving remnant'; see *The Crux of Election: Paul's Critique of the Jewish Confidence
    in the Election of Israel* (Tübingen: Mohr Siebeck, 2005), p. 144, n. 27.

44. A. Paddison, 'Karl Barth's Theological Exegesis of Romans 9–11 in the Light of
    Jewish–Christian Understanding', *JSNT* 28.4 (2006), p. 474.

45. *CD* II/2, p. 217.

46. Ibid., pp. 208–209.

Israel. Although I do not have the space for a detailed presentation, I suggest
the shape of Paul's argument runs something like this: The natural response to
the great saving promises of Romans 8:28–39 is to ask how dependable they
are given that the saving promises to Israel do not appear to have been
fulfilled.[47] Paul is in agony because by rejecting their Messiah his people are
thereby excluded from salvation. But how can this be reconciled with the fact
that Israel possesses all the privileges of eschatological salvation (9:4–5)? Does
this mean that the word of God (understood as the sum total of the privileges
in 9:4–5) has failed?[48] In 9:6 Paul begins to explain precisely why the word of
God has not failed, and at the heart of his unfolding answer is the presupposition that 'salvation was never promised to every ethnic Israelite'.[49] This is evidenced in the winnowing process Paul elaborates in 9:6–13, best understood as
a distinction between an ethnic Israel and an elect Israel (or between an ethnically elect Israel and an ethnically *and* salvifically elect Israel).[50]

Mercy and hardening: Romans 9:14–23

In his treatment of these verses the Christological bent of Barth's exegesis
comes to the fore explicitly. I shall focus particularly on verses 14–18 while
drawing attention to similar issues in verses 19–23.

After the rhetorical question in verse 14 that asks if God's discriminating
purposes mean that he is unrighteous, Barth naturally takes verse 15 to be
Paul's offer of proof that God is in fact righteous to act in this way. The quotation of Exodus 33:19 ('I will have mercy on whom I will have mercy, and I
will have compassion on whom I will have compassion') Barth understands to
be a paraphrase of the divine name given in Exodus 3:14. Due to this convergence of Exodus 3:14 and 33:19, Barth then offers a striking interpretation of
the quotation:

---

47. On this link between Rom. 1 – 8 and 9 – 11, cf. L. Goppelt, *Christologie und Ethik*
    (Gottingen: Vandenhoeck & Ruprecht, 1968), pp. 180–182.
48. For this understanding of the privileges and *ho logos tou theou* (the word of God),
    see Piper, *Justification*, pp. 21–44, 49.
49. Schreiner, *Romans*, p. 472. Cf. S. Hafemann, 'The Salvation of Israel in Romans
    11:25–32: A Response to Krister Stendahl', *ExAud* 4 (1988), pp. 38–58: 'Since God
    never promised to save all ethnic Israelites, the rejection of Jesus by the majority in
    Paul's day caused no problem for the integrity of God's word' (p. 44).
50. Cf. esp. M. Cranford, 'Election and Ethnicity: Paul's View of Israel in Romans
    9:1–13', *JSNT* 50 (1993), pp. 27–41. His criticisms of Cranfield's view of the
    distinction within Israel (pp. 36–37) apply equally to Barth.

According to this revealed name of his, God's nature consists in the fact that he renews, establishes and glorifies himself by his own future; or materially, that he renews, establishes and glorifies his being by his future being, or even more materially, his mercy by his future mercy, his compassion by his future compassion.[51]

This interpretation emphasizes the future tenses:

But what Ex. 33:19 says here has a still richer content. God's nature consists in the fact that as he freely shows mercy, so he will again show mercy. His righteousness indeed consists in the fact that he not only is but always becomes again the merciful One, that he does not cease to show mercy, but by what he will do in his mercy establishes the truth of what he does and already has done in his mercy.[52]

God's future mercy establishes the present and past showing of mercy: this is how God's nature is indexed and it is the vindication of his righteousness. It is not hard to see where Barth is going with this reading. The temporal sequence of God showing mercy to Abraham, then Isaac, then Jacob, then Moses, provides examples of God's repeated commitment to follow mercy with mercy, but these point merely in one direction:

All renewal, establishment and glorification of his present (his mercy already shown) by his own future (his mercy yet to be shown), and therefore the life corresponding to his nature in the realm of his creation and in covenant with man, are finally effective and visible in their perfect and at the same time original form, and the day of his future dawns, in the fact that he has mercy on the man Jesus and in him on all men by becoming man himself, by taking up and taking away man's burden in order to clothe man with his own glory. In view of the day of this one man in whom God will renew, establish and glorify his righteousness (the righteousness of his mercy) by suffering himself the judgment which overtakes man, the Israel from which this One will be taken is subject to the order: 'I will be he that I am', and the Church is continually separated within Israel. Is there any appropriate standpoint from which we can legitimately complain of this order and accuse it as unrighteous?[53]

So Barth understands verse 15 to offer a Christological answer to the ques-

---

51. *CD* II/2, p. 218.
52. Ibid., p. 219.
53. Ibid.

tion of verse 14. God is not unjust because the day of his mercy has dawned in Jesus Christ.

This interpretation of verse 15 now occupies a determining role in Barth's exegesis of the following verses. He argues that the righteousness of the divine mercy in verses 15–16 is what Paul now seeks to apply to those who are rejected: Ishmael, Esau and Pharaoh. Barth is not merely claiming that God's showing mercy to some and not others means that God is nevertheless still righteous. Rather verse 15 means that the rejected are also the recipients of God's mercy, albeit in a different way than was the case with Isaac, Jacob and Moses. The first part of Barth's case here is to note that where we might have expected a *de* (but) at the start of verse 17 to show that Pharaoh is contrasted with Moses, we instead have a *gar* (for) to show that the word of God to Pharaoh is actually set alongside that given to Moses.[54] But, given that Barth also understands Pharaoh here to be functioning as an example of the rebellious Israel of Paul's day, how is this related to God's mercy? Barth explains:

> Not every act of God's mercy is necessarily followed by a further one – for in that case how would it be mercy, how would it be the mercy of God? That one act of mercy should follow another is a matter for the free decision of him who is merciful, which might equally well cause a failure in this sequence. This is the negative side of the truth of v. 15. And it is on its negative side that it affects Ishmael, Esau and Pharaoh. But in the first place this has the following positive significance. In the relation of his history to that of Israel, there is an original act of God's mercy towards Pharaoh also.[55]

That God is merciful towards Pharaoh too is what Barth understands the context of Exodus 9:16 (quoted in Rom. 9:17) to teach. The point, then, is that although God refuses to renew this original act of mercy to Pharaoh by the event of a further one, nevertheless, the following applies:

> Even while he is refused what is given to Moses, because both acts occur in the same freedom, Pharaoh is still in the same sphere as Moses. The original mercy of God is not turned in vain even towards him, but with a very definite and positive purpose. He, too, has a function in the service of the God who bears this name.[56]

---

54. Ibid., p. 220.

55. Ibid.

56. Ibid.

What Barth is doing here is providing a typological explanation of how Israel can still be elect while determined by God to serve a negative purpose, that of witnessing to God's judgment. Just as Pharaoh received mercy from God but not its renewal, so Israel received original electing mercy but, in being refused its renewal, suffers not soteriological loss but a shift (albeit negative) in vocational purpose. This exegesis has a decisive impact on Barth's interpretation of verse 18:

> Before expounding [v. 18] in the sense of the classical doctrine of predestination attention should have been paid to the fact that here the twofold *thelei* [he wills] cannot possibly be regarded neutrally, i.e., as an indeterminately free willing which now takes the one direction and now the other. To be sure, this willing of God is free. But it is not for that reason indeterminate. It is determined in the sense given by God's name (v. 15). And it is determined in the sense that it has this twofold direction. On both sides, although in different forms, God wills one and the same thing. The contradiction of *eleei* [he has mercy] and *sklērynei* [he hardens] is bracketed by this *thelei* [he wills], the one purpose of God in the election of his community. As will be stated in Rom. 11:32 with complete unambiguity, this purpose is the purpose of his mercy. It is just this which, according to vv. 15–17, both Moses and Pharaoh must carry out. They do so in different ways and to this extent the single will of God has a differentiated form.[57]

By way of response to this exegesis I shall make four points.

Christology
Kevin Vanhoozer has recently suggested:

> Barth's decision to read all of Scripture as a unified witness to God's Word and his concomitant tendency to read the Bible as a literary whole leads him to focus on large canonical patterns and to make typological connections in a way that makes evangelical exegetes trained to read in a grammatical-historical fashion uneasy.[58]

It may be queried whether the dichotomized terms of contrast here are really apposite (in either direction), but as a first movement in our evaluation some

---

57. Ibid., p. 221.
58. 'A Person of the Book? Barth on Biblical Authority and Interpretation', in Sung Wook Chung (ed.), *Karl Barth and Evangelical Theology* (Carlisle: Paternoster, 2006), p. 47.

unease with Barth's canonical-Christological understanding of verse 15 is surely warranted.

It is clear that Barth understands the Exodus quotation in verse 15 to be fundamentally a declaration about the nature and freedom of God. But the primary point of both Exodus 33:19 and Paul's use of it is precisely to *stress* this divine freedom, rather than to point forward to a particular example of mercy and compassion with the kind of specificity Barth suggests. The issue turns partly on the force of the verbs *ḥānan* (be gracious) and *rāḥam* (be merciful), where the emphasis of the future tense (vav consecutive and imperfect) does not fall primarily on the time. It also turns on the relation of this clause in Exodus 33:19 to that which immediately precedes it: 'I will proclaim my name, the LORD, in your presence'. One of the most detailed studies of these verses in their Old Testament context is provided by John Piper. He follows Childs, Hyatt and Driver to argue that 'I will have mercy on whom I will have mercy, and I will have compassion on whom I will have compassion' is an example of the Hebrew *idem per idem* (the same by the same) formula:

> By leaving the action unspecified the force of this idiom is to preserve the freedom of the subject to perform the action in whatever way he pleases. By simply repeating the action without adding any stipulations the *idem per idem* formula makes clear that the way the action is executed is determined by the will of the subject . . .[God] is stressing that there are no stipulations outside his own council or will which determine the disposal of his mercy and grace.[59]

Further, following Childs, Piper contends that this formula, coming as it does directly after 'I will proclaim my name, the LORD, in your presence', functions to interpret the essence of the divine name.[60] If this is granted, we may say that the verbs in Exodus 33:19 are therefore principial of the divine being, rather than temporally specific about the divine action.

Of course, the novelty in Barth's account is not merely that he wants to specify a future act of mercy, but that he specifies the day of God's future as the mercy shown to all humankind in Jesus. Here we see Barth's fundamental hermeneutical *Entscheidung* (decision): 'we can properly interpret the Bible only when we perceive and show that what it says is said from the point of view of the concealed and revealed name of Jesus Christ'.[61] But even if we were to

---

59. *Justification*, p. 82; cf. pp. 75–90.
60. Ibid., p. 84.
61. *CD* I/2, p. 720.

grant that, ultimately, the divine name does find its canonical fulfilment in the revelation of Jesus Christ, how convincing is it to accept that this is actually Paul's point here? In particular, how likely is it that Paul is putting forward Jesus as the answer to the question of verse 14?

We may observe two similar Christological claims. In verse 19 Paul envisages an interlocutor asking why God still finds fault with humanity even though he is the one who freely hardens. Barth holds that the question is both pointless and irrelevant, not because God possesses supreme or 'indeterminate' power, but because his power is wholly determined by the 'purpose on which God has decided with respect to man in Jesus'.[62] Therefore he understands Paul to respond in verse 20 like this:

> The tenor of the answer hidden in the counter-question of v. 20 is: 'In any case whether you are a friend of God like Moses, or an enemy of God like Pharaoh, whether your name is Isaac or Ishmael, Jacob or Esau, you are the man on account of whose sin and for whose sin Jesus Christ has died on the cross for the justification of God, and for whose justification he has been raised from the dead' (Rom. 4:25). This man – the man who is concerned in this twofold justification achieved in Jesus Christ, who is confronted with this twofold justification – cannot possibly make the challenge of v. 19.[63]

Instead of verse 20 being a sharp reminder of human ignorance and mortality, Barth says it is a response to the man who is unaware that he is justified in Jesus Christ.

Barth turns next to the analogy of the potter and the ultimate ends of the 'vessels of mercy' (*skeuē eleous*) and 'vessels of wrath' (*skeuē orgēs*) in Romans 9:20–23. Barth explains that the reason the *skeuē orgēs* exist is so that, leading up to the day of Jesus Christ, the history of Israel can function as 'an increasingly close succession of intimations of this judgment'.[64] On the basis of *ēnenken* ([God] bore) as the principal verb in verse 22, Barth understands the main point of the verse to be God's patience, his long-suffering towards the objects of wrath on the way to the day of Jesus Christ:

> Because he bore in his own Son the rejection which falls on mankind, the fact of Ishmael's rejection, of Esau's, of Pharaoh's, of all Israel's also, is in the end

---

62. *CD* II/2, p. 223.
63. Ibid.
64. Ibid., p. 226.

superseded and limited; it is characterised as a rejection borne by God. 'To bear' in this context means more accurately to bear forward, to bear to an expected end. It is for the sake of him who is to come, for the sake of the Lamb of God who will bear away the sin of the world (Jn. 1:29), that the sustaining long-suffering of God (cf. Rom. 3:25f.) which befalls the 'vessels of wrath' is possible and necessary.[65]

So Barth's Christology is tightly woven into the fabric of his exegetical decisions, with the result that not just whole verses (as in vv. 15 and 19) but also specific words (as above) derive their meaning from a pool of Christological conceptualities. But unless one is operating with Barth's commitment to the election of Jesus Christ having a twofold determination of judgment and mercy which are both imaged in two forms of the one community, it is extremely hard to understand how a reader would ever unearth either the Christological tenor 'hidden in the counter-question of v. 20', or the reference to the death of Jesus in the *ēnenken* of verse 22. However we wish to construe the relationship between Barth's actual exegesis and his doctrinal presuppositions, at this point the latter are dominating the former. Paddison argues that because of Barth's conviction that all of Scripture speaks of Christ from beginning to end, then 'criticizing Barth by focusing on the relative absence of Christ in Romans 9 – 11 will represent nothing more than talking past him, rather than talking *with* him'.[66] But more than an assertion of method is required to substantiate individual exegetical decisions. The question that must be asked of any hermeneutical framework is whether there are details in the parts that might alter or readjust the conception of the whole. It will not suffice simply to start with a conception of the whole and then show how this is present in the parts. If all of Scripture speaks of Christ from beginning to end, but Romans 9 – 11 says relatively little about Christ, then the question is not how do we therefore find Christ *in* the passage, but rather, how does the affirmation of the Christological focus of Scripture need to be qualified so as to *allow* a passage like Romans 9 – 11 to say relatively little about Christ? Romans 9 – 11 is an exposition of the causes and results, present and future, of belief and unbelief in Israel's Messiah. It speaks of Christ by drawing out the implications of his gospel for Jew and Gentile, but this does not necessitate making details of the text refer to Christ himself when Paul more obviously intends them to refer to other realities.

This problem is underscored when we observe that the mere presence of

---

65. Ibid.
66. 'Theological Exegesis', p. 483.

Christology in these verses is not all that Barth claims. In his treatment of verse
15, we note the clear universality in the day of God's mercy. God

> has mercy on the man Jesus *and in him on all men* by becoming man himself . . . God is
> righteous in the fact that when he shows mercy to Israel – *for the sake of all men and all
> Israel as well* – he is concerned with his future act of mercy.[67]

In Barth's treatment of verses 19–20 likewise, the death and resurrection of
Jesus apply equally to both the elected and the rejected *in a way that actually justifies them all*. But even if we were to grant that in these verses Paul is indeed
pointing to Jesus Christ, then given the context of a discriminating purpose
that exists in God's free willing (9:6–13), the relative pronouns of 9:15 (*hon an*,
'on whom') which might suggest the application of this discriminating
purpose to some and not others, and the flow of the argument that separates
not just Moses from Pharaoh but also vessels of honour (prepared for glory)
from vessels of dishonour (fitted for destruction), the universal note in these
parts of the text is surely discordant. It is not just that Christology fits uneasily
here; the one Barth finds is even less likely. Clearly, Barth is operating with the
conception of Christology and election he developed earlier in his argument,
but it is fair to say that this view of God's mercy in Christ as universally actual
is assumed without exegetical argument.[68]

Mercy
Returning to verses 14–18, we may consider a second point. It is important for
Barth's argument to see Pharaoh as explicitly a recipient of God's mercy,
despite the ensuing negative purpose he serves. Although it is grammatically
possible that the *gar* in verse 17 refers back to verses 15–16 (so that Pharaoh is
alongside Moses rather than contrasted to him), the inference that Paul draws
from the quotation of Exodus 9:16 in verse 17 is clearly not another example
of mercy but this time one of hardening, as verse 18 makes clear. In verse 18
Paul draws a conclusion from verse 17 that is not explicit in verse 17 itself (God
hardens whom he wills), and this shows that he is working with a very strong
sense of the context of Exodus 9:16, where hardening is prominent (cf. Exod.
4:21; 7:3, 22; 8:15; 9:12, 35; 10:1, 20, 27; 11:10; 13:15; 14:4, 8, 17).[69] This understanding of the context is much more to the fore than the aspect Barth empha-

---

67. *CD* II/2, p. 219 (emphasis added).
68. Cf. *CD* II/2, pp. 161–175.
69. Dunn, *Romans 9–16*, p. 554.

sizes. The aim of verse 17 therefore goes in a different direction from the issue of mercy, and in this light the *gar* likely refers back primarily to verse 14: 'The "for" introducing verse 17 may, then, function as does its counterpart in verse 15 and indicate that verses 17–18 contain a second reason to reject the accusation that God is unjust.'[70] This also best explains why verse 19 follows verse 18. The rhetorical question about why God still finds fault is much more comprehensible following a statement about Pharaoh as an example of God's free hardening than as a further example of God's free mercy.

Another part of Barth's strategy is to see in the context of Exodus 9:16 God's mercy to Pharaoh: 'For by now I could have put out my hand and struck you [Exod. 9:15] . . . But for this purpose [Exod. 9:16] . . .', ESV. This patience is God's 'original' act of mercy towards Pharaoh. But there are some problems with Barth's construal of both the Hebrew and Paul's use of the LXX. While he is correct that Paul's rendering of Exodus 9:16 in Romans 9:17 ('that I might show my power in you', ESV) corresponds more to the LXX than the MT, it is not the case that Paul derived *exēgeira se* (I have raised you up) from the LXX, as Barth appears to suggest. Instead of *exēgeira* the LXX has *dietērēthēs* (you were preserved), with Paul's translation arguably more closely reflecting the perfect hiphil *he'ĕmadtîkā*. In the absence of a detailed discussion of these issues,[71] suffice it to say that a strong case can be made that the sense of the hiphil of *'āmad* leans much more towards Pharaoh being 'raised up' or 'appointed' than it does being 'preserved'. Paul's intention, then, is to emphasize *God's* initiative in the story of Pharaoh's hard-heartedness so as to prepare directly for the conclusion of verse 18.[72] In his interpretation of verse 17 Barth is of course beginning to point forward to 9:22, to God's bearing in patience with the objects of wrath, and this kind of observation is not without merit. But Paul's point in these verses is that in God's patience wholly *different* objects serve the *same* end (God's glory), and this is why God bears with the vessels of wrath. Indeed, Paul argues that this is why God raised up and hardened Pharaoh. There is no indication at all that in this bearing with the objects of wrath they are therefore also 'in the same sphere' as the recipients of mercy. Robert Jewett argues that Paul employs the hardening of Pharaoh, widely accepted throughout the biblical literature,

> to make the much more controversial case that God's mercy is sovereign. Paul was convinced that the refusal of this sovereign grace revealed in the gospel placed his

---

70. Moo, *Romans*, p. 594; cf. Piper, *Justification*, pp. 158–159.

71. For this, cf. esp. Cranfield, *Romans*, vol. 2, pp. 485–487; Piper, *Justification*, 159–175.

72. R. Jewett, *Romans: A Commentary* (Minneapolis: Fortress, 2007), p. 584.

Jewish compatriots in 'the position of Pharaoh,' incredibly reversing their status before God.[73]

Hardening

That we should understand the difference between mercy and hardening in such absolute terms is confirmed, thirdly, by the precise meaning of the 'harden' (*sklērynō*) terminology. Barth takes 'hardening' to be 'the isolation of the original and the withholding of the special new act of mercy'.[74] But note how on this definition hardening is still explained as something that happens ultimately within the sphere of electing mercy. Any definition of 'harden' as the strong soteriological opposite to 'mercy' is excluded; Barth's definition is a theological gloss when there are further exegetical matters to consider. In brief, these include the connection between 'mercy'/'hardening' in verse 18 and the unfolding argument about honourable/dishonourable vessels leading to some being prepared for mercy and glory, and others for wrath and destruction (so that here 'hardening' is clearly something that results in destruction); the use of the cognate *sklērotēs* in Romans 2:5 to describe a state that leads to ultimate condemnation; the use of synonymous terms for 'harden' in Romans 11:7 (*pōroō*) and 11:25 (*pōrōsis*), to indicate a condition that excludes from salvation.[75] Alongside this note the specifically soteriological import of mercy (*eleos*): Romans 11:30–32; 15:9; Ephesians 2:4; 1 Timothy 1:13, 16.[76]

Clarity

The three issues raised above combine to suggest one more. Despite the detail of Barth's treatment of Romans 9:14–23, it is hard to avoid the impression that it remains vague on crucial issues. As well as his handling of the tradition,[77] and

---

73. Ibid., p. 586.

74. *CD* II/2, p. 221.

75. Cf. Moo, *Romans*, pp. 596–598; Piper, *Justification*, pp. 175–178. For a detailed treatment of Rom. 9:17 in its OT context, see G. K. Beale, 'An Exegetical and Theological Consideration of the Hardening of Pharaoh's Heart in Exodus 4–14 and Romans 9', *TrinJ* 5.2 (1984), pp. 129–154 (see esp. pp. 152–154).

76. Schreiner, *Romans*, p. 511.

77. Barth refers to 'the classical doctrine of predestination' four times in *CD* II/2, pp. 221–223, but on each occasion offers no examples in the tradition of the point he is arguing against. The result is a vague characterization that invariably misleads. Taking Calvin as an example, I observe two points. First, the charge of seeing the

the language of the renewal or non-renewal of mercy, consider the very strong meanings Barth attaches to the hardening terminology, which he nevertheless wishes to bracket within God's mercy. He relates *sklērynein* to 'the prefiguration of judgment' and 'the curse and punishment of God', but always as determined for those who are first of all mercifully elect.[78] Here Barth comments, 'If it is self-evident that for [Moses and Pharaoh] it means personally something very different to be dealt with and used by God in these different ways, there is no mention of that here.'[79] He then criticizes the classical doctrine of

scope of Rom. 9:18 'in the personal situation and destiny of Moses and Pharaoh' is inaccurate as a description of Calvin's treatment. He does view Pharaoh as an example of divine reprobation, but does not view Moses as an example of divine election. Rather, for Calvin the important issue is not Moses himself but the words said to Moses that are principial of God's nature (*Calvin's New Testament Commentaries*, ed. D. W. Torrance and T. F. Torrance, 12 vols. [Grand Rapids: Eerdmans, 1959–72], vol. 8, pp. 202–206). Calvin certainly sees double predestination of individuals in Rom. 9 – 11. This, however, is Paul's illustration of principle within the main argument, which Calvin takes to be God's faithfulness to his covenant with Israel (ibid., pp. 190–261; cf. 'Theme of the Epistle', pp. 9–10). Secondly, Barth attributes to the classical doctrine of predestination 'an absolute power of disposal belonging to God' (*CD* II/2, p. 222). The *decretum absolutum* (absolute decree) is 'an indeterminate power of God' and, over against such a God, who deals with his people 'according to the caprices of his omnipotence', Barth posits instead a God who acts in accordance with the divine name revealed in Rom. 9:15 (ibid., p. 221; cf. p. 223). This discussion is the exegetical rationale for Barth's earlier rejection of a general doctrine of God that views him as 'omnipotent Will . . . irresistibly efficacious power *in abstracto* [in the abstract], naked freedom and sovereignty' (ibid., p. 44). But the concept of 'absolute might' is explicitly rejected by Calvin in his doctrine of election. He refers to it as a 'fiction' (*Institutes of the Christian Religion*, ed. J. T. McNeill, trans. F. L. Battles [Philadelphia: Westminster, 1960], 3.23.2). In his exegesis of Rom. 9:21, Calvin says, 'The word right does not mean that the maker has power or strength to do what he pleases, but that this power to act rightly belongs to him. Paul does not want to claim for God an inordinate power, but the power which he should rightly be given' (*Romans*, p. 210). God is not 'self-determined' for Calvin in the way that he is for Barth, but Calvin never separates God's will from God's character. Cf. P. Helm, *John Calvin's Ideas* (Oxford: Oxford University Press, 2004), pp. 312–346.

78. *CD* II/2, pp. 221–222.

79. Ibid., p. 221.

predestination for being worried about such matters. Over against this view he asserts:

> But the point at issue here is precisely how the diversity of the personal situation and destiny of Israelite man, which, conditioned by the divine predetermination, is so characteristic of the history and life of the chosen people Israel, does not contradict but corresponds to the election of Israel and the righteousness and mercy of its God.[80]

It is not clear what this means in real terms. It is one thing to comment that the issue of Moses' or Pharaoh's personal destinies are not the main point in view; it is another altogether to suggest that what it actually means for God to use them in different ways does not have an important bearing on vital matters in the doctrine of election. If the personal situation and destiny of individuals is characteristic of the whole, and these characteristics include judgment and curse and punishment, what meaning do these terms carry if they do not really signify ultimate loss? Likewise, on the vessels of wrath 'fitted for destruction' (*katērtismena eis apōleian*, v. 22), one way of countering a traditional exegesis at this point is to suggest that in the light of God's patience with the vessels of wrath they will eventually come to repentance and so be saved.[81] But Barth does not argue this. As he sees it, these vessels stand typologically in Paul's argument both for Israel itself in its service of prefiguring God's judgment, and Israel as reduced to One in delivering up its Messiah to death.[82] The vessels of wrath really do experience destruction, with Israel's experience of judgment throughout its history being 'in the end superseded and limited' in the judgment borne by Christ.[83] But what does it actually mean to be destroyed only vocationally? Paul always uses *apōleia* to refer to final condemnation (Phil. 1:28; 3:19; 2 Thess. 2:3; 1 Tim 6:9),[84] and the objects of this *apōleia* in Romans

---

80. Ibid.
81. Cranfield, *Romans*, vol. 2, p. 497: 'it is God's purpose that the *skeuē orgēs* [vessels of wrath] should become *skeuē eleous* [vessels of mercy]'; cf. also Jewett, *Romans*, pp. 595–596.
82. *CD* II/2, p. 226; cf. also p. 228, where correspondingly 'The vessel of mercy . . . is primarily the Lord Jesus Christ risen from the dead.'
83. Ibid.
84. Cf. Moo, who also points to the cognate verb *apollymi* (to perish) and its use in Rom. 2:12, 1 Cor. 1:18, 2 Cor. 2:15, 4:3 with the same eschatological and soteriological connotations (*Romans*, p. 607).

9:22 are plural. There is no hint at all here that Paul is thinking of Jesus as bearing it in a way that somehow limits its force or effect on those who prefigure it.

At this point Barth's overall thesis – that the election of Jesus is imaged in the election of the community with the attendant result that none in the community can be separated from the love of God in Christ – exerts such a pressure that the details of the text have distorted under its weight. Rhetorically powerful and compelling in its intensity, Barth's argument is not the direction in which Romans 9 points.

The argument of Romans 9 – 11

So far my discussion of Barth's exegesis has focused on his treatment of key details in Romans 9. I have suggested that Barth does not succeed in supporting his doctrine of election from this passage. At this point, however, it could be argued that the tenor of Romans 9 – 11 as a whole is actually in Barth's favour. This is one way in which Barth's exegesis might be defended, perhaps as follows: even if some of Barth's Christological exegesis in Romans 9 is problematic, to be wrong on some of the particulars does not necessitate being wrong overall. Specifically, Romans 9 – 11 needs to be interpreted from the vantage point of the end of Paul's argument in chapter 11. There we discover that a number of details in chapter 9 receive crucial further elaboration. Hardening, for example, is temporary (11:25); by being hardened Israel serves the purpose of bringing in the Gentiles so that Barth's main lens of a vocation for Israel seems to be endorsed (11:11–12); and God's ultimate purpose is now clearly revealed to be the display of his mercy (11:32).

We have seen that Barth does aim to read Romans 9 in the light of Romans 11: 'As will be stated in Rom. 11:32 with complete unambiguity, this purpose [in the election of the community] is the purpose of his mercy.'[85] So it could be argued that Barth's exegesis grasps the whole in a way in which more traditional interpretations do not. Variations on this holistic approach to Romans 9 – 11 are commonplace. For Dunn, 'the talk of Pharaoh's hardening evidently prepares for the later talk of Israel's hardening (pōroō/pōrōsis – 11:7, 25), which Paul sees as a partial and temporary phase of God's purpose'.[86] Francis Watson says that 'The texts marshalled in Romans 9 give a provisional, penultimate

---

85. *CD* II/2, p. 221; cf. also p. 15.

86. *Romans 9–16*, p. 555.

account of the divine electing purpose. They are not the last word.'[87] Cranfield goes further:

> We shall misunderstand these chapters if we fail to recognise that their key-word is 'mercy'. Paul is here concerned . . . to show that Israel's disobedience, together with the divine judgment which it merits and procures, is surrounded on all sides by the divine mercy.[88]

Arguments like these suggest that Barth could be wrong in some details but remain basically right overall. Although a complete response would require a detailed study of Romans 9 – 11 in its entirety, I shall register here a few cautionary remarks against this conclusion.

First, mercy does not function in Romans 9 – 11 in the hermeneutically absolute way Barth claims it does – and it is Barth himself who shows us this. His exegesis of 11:32 does not prove what he needs it to prove, namely that ultimately none stand outside the sphere of God's electing mercy. The reason for this shortcoming is that his exegesis of 11:32 is actually quite conventional. Barth holds (perhaps surprisingly) that the *pas Israēl* of 11:26 'does not mean the totality of all Jewish individuals' but rather is 'the community of those elected by God in and with Jesus Christ both from Jews and also from Gentiles, the whole church'.[89] This is important for his interpretation of 11:32. Here Barth says:

> Again, there is no question of an unqualified totality but of the *pas Israēl* of v. 26 . . . The Gentiles had been shut up in the natural disobedience in which God had

---

87. *Paul, Judaism and the Gentiles: Beyond the New Perspective* (Grand Rapids: Eerdmans, forthcoming).

88. *Romans*, vol. 2, p. 448.

89. *CD* II/2, p. 300. Although Barth does not think that the *pas Israēl* who will be saved refers to the totality of all Jewish individuals, this does not mean that he now agrees with my argument that Paul teaches it was never God's intention to save every single ethnic Israelite. A few lines later Barth says that *pas Israēl* includes 'the elect from Israel (in the narrower sense of the word)' who obtain a share in the divine deliverance, 'thus attesting and establishing the genuineness of the election of the people of Israel as such by the restoration of the natural order' (ibid.; emphasis added). The role of *pas Israēl* in the argument is to establish that Israel as a whole is never outside the sphere of God's mercy.

previously left them. And the Jews are shut up in the unnatural disobedience into which God has now plunged them by hardening their hearts. Both are shut up by God in the same prison. But the prison opens and again they are all together.[90]

This reading of 11:32 is once again surprisingly traditional. In the recognition that *tous pantas* (all) in verse 32 has a specific focus in context on Jew and Gentile (rather than a universal application), and even then does not entail application to every single Jew or Gentile, Barth's view is the same as Calvin's.[91] But if we accept that the mercy being shown to all does not mean that mercy is thereby necessarily shown to every single individual within the Jew–Gentile groupings, then the significance of 11:32 for the argument of 9:18 is seriously altered. For on this interpretation of 11:32 there is no contradiction at all between God's having mercy on some and hardening some in a strictly antithetical way (9:18), and his showing mercy to all. If Barth's interpretation of 11:26, 32 is a measure of his attempt to wrestle honestly with the meaning of each text as he finds it, then it is also a sign that his reading of chapter 9, even in the light of chapter 11, still does not have the force he requires.[92] At the same time, following Barth in his understanding of 11:32 means that we may actually safeguard his insight that Romans 9 – 11 does progress towards a conclusion that sees God's mercy as the climax of the argument. Barth is surely right in one of his fundamental convictions: throughout Romans 9 – 11 election and rejection, mercy and hardening, do not operate in the divine will in a strictly symmetrical way. God's hardening of some and the display of his wrath serve the ultimate end of a display of his glory on the vessels of mercy. This much emerges in Romans 9:22–23, and here an aspect of the conclusion of Romans 11 is already anticipated.[93] But the important point to retain in this

---

90. Ibid., p. 305.

91. Calvin, *Romans*, p. 258.

92. Barth is explicit that here God's mercy is directed to the community. Interestingly, Cranfield, who is indebted to Barth throughout his treatment of Rom. 9 – 11, goes much further in outlining a possible universal sense to *tous pantas* in 11:32 (*Romans*, vol. 2, p. 588). Certainly, something like the meaning he suggests for 11:32 is required for a Barthian conception of Rom. 9 – 11 to succeed, but Cranfield's exegesis is unwarranted. Cf. I. H. Marshall, 'The New Testament Does *Not* Teach Universal Salvation', in R. A. Parry and C. H. Partridge (eds.), *Universal Salvation? The Current Debate* (Carlisle: Paternoster, 2003), pp. 55–76.

93. Cranfield, *Romans*, vol. 2, pp. 496–497, shows convincingly why the grammar of Rom. 9:22–23 suggests this; cf. also Piper, *Justification*, pp. 188–189, 214–216.

presentation is that the display of God's glory in mercy entails the existence of objects of hardening and vessels of wrath that remain outside the sphere of electing mercy.

The fact that mercy is not hermeneutically absolute in chapter 11 (in the sense required by Barth) ensures that a second point follows: the temporary nature of hardening hinted at throughout 11:11–24, and made explicit in 11:25–26, should not be understood as absolute either. The fact that the time of hardening comes to an end and 'all Israel will be saved (*pas Israēl sōthēsetai*)', ESV, in 11:26 does not mean that the argument of Romans 9 (God hardens some as vessels of wrath prepared for destruction) refers only to a temporary hardening. As we have seen, this is Dunn's view: because of 11:26–32, Pharaoh's hardening must be temporary. This imports the climax of Paul's argument back into its earlier stages. But as Grindheim observes, 'At this juncture [in Rom. 9] Israel is compared to Pharaoh, whose hardening was not temporary.'[94] The issue here turns on grasping the distinction between what Paul sees as happening to individuals within Israel throughout its history, and what he sees as happening to Israel as a corporate entity at a future point in time. Throughout Israel's history, Paul sees a winnowing process, with some in Israel hardened and being Israel in a way that shows they are not Israel (9:6); with regard to Israel's future he envisages a day when the hardened 'part' will give way to the saved 'all'. But the point is that this is in the future. It is a conviction that the hardening of Israel will not last forever, not an assertion that the hardening of all Israelites throughout history was only temporary.

Connected to this is the issue of what Paul means by *pas Israēl* in 11:26. Unless the *pas* here refers necessarily to every single Israelite, there is nothing in 11:25–26 which requires that we understand the future lifting of hardening 'for the part of Israel' (*apo merous tō Israēl*) as meaning that the hardening of every single Israelite is temporary. But most recent commentators are agreed here that *pas Israēl* does not mean every single Israelite.[95] The use of the phrase in the LXX would seem to suggest this (Josh. 7:25; 1 Sam. 7:5; 25:1; 2 Sam. 16:22; 1 Kgs 12:1; 2 Chr. 12:1; Dan. 9:11). This means that we may say with Moo:

> In contrast to [11:]7b–10, Paul is in verses 11–32 clearly thinking about Israel from a corporate perspective: The hardening of Israel as a national group, Paul argues,

---

94. *Crux*, p. 147, n. 41. He offers sound advice against reading too much of ch. 11 into the argument of ch. 9; cf. p. 147, n. 42; p. 148, n. 47.

95. Cf. Cranfield, *Romans*, vol. 2, p. 577; Dunn, *Romans 9–16*, p. 681; Moo, *Romans*, p. 722, n. 55.

is temporary; but this says nothing about the permanence of his hardening of individuals within Israel.[96]

This argument is of course dependent on other exegetical decisions within chapter 11 that may be contested, but my point here is that a fully coherent reading of Romans 9 – 11 as a whole is possible which does not demand that we see all hardening as temporary. Barth likewise holds that in 11:26 *pas Israēl* does not refer to every single Israelite,[97] and on the terms of this argument there is no support for a reading back of the lifting of hardening in chapter 11 into the hardening of chapter 9.

Conclusion

There are other striking examples of Barth's Christological exegesis of Romans 9 – 11 that I have been unable to consider.[98] However, I have sketched the hermeneutical framework for Barth's exegesis and found that he approaches the text with the conviction that its content must be the name of Jesus Christ. Further, Jesus Christ must be described according to the double-determination of his election. Barth articulates his thesis by claiming that the text of Romans 9 – 11 refers us to the day of God's mercy to all humankind which has now dawned in Jesus Christ.

Although I have questioned the adequacy of Barth's Christological reading, this should not be taken to mean that there is nothing to be gained from careful attention to his approach. Barth's exegesis appears as part of an attempt to do something eminently worthwhile: providing a close reading of the biblical materials in an explicitly dogmatic context. If there are problems along the way in Barth's account, this is not because of what he attempted to do but rather because of the particular way in which he did it. His efforts here are a monument to refusing to treat the text in narrowly historicist or even biblicist terms, but rather as a unified testimony to Jesus Christ. Such an approach has benefits beyond the purpose originally envisaged by Barth for his exegesis. Paddison

---

96. *Romans*, p. 681; cf. Schreiner, *Romans*, pp. 511–512, 621–622.

97. *CD* II/2, pp. 299–300.

98. E.g. he argues that the 'holy root' (*rhiza hagia*) of Israel in 11:16 is Jesus, the last and as such first member of Israel, 'the man beloved of God, in whom his love to every man was decreed from all eternity and became an event in time' (*CD* II/2, p. 285).

argues that Barth's treatment of Romans 9 – 11 gives an explicitly Christological foundation to all Jewish–Christian dialogue and that Barth, though often derided for making negative comments about the status of the Jewish religion, can make a good claim to be simply engaging the contours of Paul's argument.[99] Nevertheless, we have also seen that in a range of exegetical decisions concerning Romans 9 it is extremely hard to avoid the impression that the dogmatic context commandeers the exegesis. Paul's agony at his fellow Jews being 'accursed and cut off from Christ (*anathema apo tou Christou*)', ESV, is relativized to being an agony at the form of service they are performing but that is nevertheless incapable of affecting eternal destiny. Hardening is relativized to taking place always within the sphere of ultimate mercy. If the exegesis of chapter 9 does not support these interpretations, then neither do they gain validity from Romans 9 – 11 as a whole.

In this light, two final comments. Brevard S. Childs, after suggesting that Barth offers the most ambitious attempt in the twentieth century to construct church dogmatics on the foundation of biblical exegesis, states:

> Yet for various reasons Barth's exegesis, for all its brilliant insights and massive stimulus, remained a 'virtuoso performance' . . . which could not be duplicated and which left little lasting impact either on the biblical academy or on the church. Here the contrast with the enduring biblical contribution of the Reformers is painfully evident.[100]

More than a little danger lurks in such generalities and certainly Barth would have given short shrift to attempts merely to duplicate his exegesis. But as applied to Barth's exegesis of Romans 9 – 11, the point made by Childs is a properly ecclesial one. Could a reader not possessing Barth's individual brilliance or a commitment to his wholly unique doctrine of election ever find the text to say what Barth claims it says? On the answer to this question hangs the utility of Barth's exegesis for a range of church practices, not least preaching. Francis Watson has observed that 'Underlying the myriad individual, more or less *ad hoc* questions evoked by a systematic theology, there is a single question of principle: how far does this theology help us to read the bible?'[101] In many instances, what Barth

---

99. 'Theological Exegesis', pp. 482–486.

100. 'Toward Recovering Theological Exegesis', *ProEccl* 6 (1997), p. 19; cited in R. E. Burnett, *Karl Barth's Theological Exegesis: The Hermeneutical Principles of the Römerbrief Period* (Grand Rapids: Eerdmans, 2004), p. 9.

101. '"America's Theologian": an Appreciation of Robert Jenson's Systematic Theology', *SJT* 55.2 (2002), pp. 201–223 (p. 215).

posits as a Christological reference in the text, I suggest is rather a Christological inference from his system. Where the text is Christologically totalized, the result is a Christology in danger of not being textually governed. This opens Barth's exegesis to the charge of operating under what (in a different context) D. A. Carson has suggested is 'the tyranny of the dominant':[102] the Christological motif is employed in such a way that it drowns out complementary but distinct aspects of the biblical witness. In this way, and at this point in his project, Barth's theology does not help us to hear the clear teaching of Scripture.

Second, regardless of whether or not my critique has convinced the reader of the problems in Barth's account, I hope that it will draw attention to the vital significance of Barth's exegetical efforts in his reconstruction of the doctrine of election. What Barth actually means at critical points in his doctrine of election is contested. The deep structures of his thought are hotly debated by Barth scholars, mainly in ontological or metaphysical categories. The danger here is that the discussion ignores the exegetical contours of his argument. But Barth was explicit about the significance of his exegesis: 'I have grounds for thinking that to some my meaning will be clearer in these passages than in the main body of the text.'[103] It is likely that where Barth's doctrine of election is debated without attention to his practice as an exegete, and specifically to the very question that mattered most to him – 'Does it stand in Scripture?'[104] – then a debate occurs within parameters that Barth himself would not have recognized.[105]

© David Gibson, 2008

---

102. *The Gospel According to John* (Leicester: IVP, 1991), p. 439.
103. *CD* II/2, p. x.
104. Cf. Burnett, *Theological Exegesis*, p. 10, where Burnett also relays the anecdote from one of Barth's seminars in the 1950s, when Barth interrupted some of his students engaged in a protracted debate about his method: 'If I understand what I am trying to do in the *Church Dogmatics*, it is to listen to what Scripture is saying and to tell you what I hear.'
105. I am grateful to my *Doktorvater*, Prof. Francis Watson, and to Prof. John Webster and Jonathan Gibson for their comments on an earlier draft of this chapter. Dr Rob Price provided invaluable help in a number of areas. I am also grateful to Dr Simon Gathercole for his comments and for helpful discussions about many issues in Rom. 9 – 11.

6. WITNESS TO THE WORD: ON BARTH'S DOCTRINE OF SCRIPTURE

Mark D. Thompson

Searching for the real Karl Barth

Karl Barth once complained that he existed in far too many minds as a cartoon summary, 'hastily dashed off by some person at some time, and for the sake of convenience, just as hastily accepted, and then copied endlessly'.[1] Undoubtedly, he had a point when he made that remark more than fifty years ago. Yet even a cursory glance at the plethora of books and articles on his theology published since suggests his complaint could just as easily be repeated today and perhaps with even more validity. On the one hand, there are those who continue to portray him as the arch-enemy of evangelical theology, someone whose ideas are to be avoided at all costs. His theology is heady stuff, alluring but most definitely dangerous. For such people engagement with Barth's theological concerns is highly suspect. 'Barthianism' must be recognized as one of the great heresies of the twentieth century and when Barth is mentioned, little positive can be said beyond the usual introductory pleasantries. On the other hand, some still present him as the greatest evangelical

---

1. 'Foreword to the English Edition', in O. Weber, *Karl Barth's Church Dogmatics: An Introductory Report on Volumes I:1 to III:4*, trans. A. C. Cochrane (London: Lutterworth, 1953), p. 7.

theologian of the twentieth century, whose challenge to classic evangelical theology is very largely the product of small and defensive minds. 'In him a church father has walked amongst us' is one extravagant assessment.[2] For such people, engagement with Barth very often takes the form of wholehearted embrace followed by the development of his ideas in new directions. Furthermore, it is suggested that a reappropriation of Barth's theology promises to be the most effective way of breathing new life into what has become a tired and marginalized academic discipline.

Nothing is to be gained by pretending Barth is someone he is not or that his work represents something it does not. In the first instance, Barth, like all of us, was a child of his time. His theological work regularly intersected with the wider context of his world, a world convulsed by extraordinary events and engaged in a frantic search for sounder intellectual and social moorings. It should never be forgotten that his famous 'change of mind' took place in the midst of the Great War, almost within earshot of the battlefields that soaked up the blood of a generation. Similarly, the opening volume of his most lasting achievement, the great *Church Dogmatics*, first appeared in bookshops just as Germany headed almost inexorably into the darkness of Nazism. Barth's monumental courage in both of those contexts, challenging the proud German theological tradition in the wake of its unrestrained capitulation to the Kaiser's militarism and resisting the Führer's attempts to harness the German churches for his own sinister purposes, arises out of and in turn feeds into his theological endeavours. His is a robust, almost aggressive theology, unwilling to cower before the demands of the world or the theological consensus of his teachers and peers. It is not in the slightest defensive. The principal drafter of the Barmen Declaration, the author of a little theological piece simply titled *Nein!* (*No!*) knew how and when to hold his ground. And in his studies in dogmatics he unfolded the why.

Barth was also a child of nineteenth-century theology as well as being one of its most trenchant critics. He once described himself as having absorbed the theology of one of his teachers, Wilhelm Herrmann, 'through all my pores'.[3] Careful examination of Herrmann's theology reveals an astonishing

---

2. J. Godsey, 'Introduction', in K. Barth, *How I Changed My Mind* (Richmond, Va.: John Knox, 1966), p. 9.

3. E. Busch, *Karl Barth: His Life from Letters and Autobiographical Texts* (London: SCM, 1976), p. 45. In 1925 Barth delivered a lecture in which he explained, 'I cannot deny that through the years I have become a somewhat surprising disciple of Herrmann. "Much is altered here, the dishes differ and the wine is changed." But I could never

number of resonances with the later work of his most famous pupil. Herrmann's protest that Christian faith must be freed from all worldly justifications, his insistence on the self-authentication of the central religious experience, and his determination to maintain a focus on the person of Jesus Christ, all find an echo in Barth's own theology. Of course, each of these was developed in new ways and freshly anchored in more fundamental convictions about the sovereign freedom of God and his trinitarian being. There really was a revolution. But while Barth challenged so much that Herrmann held dear, he did not do away with everything. Some of the assumptions of nineteenth-century historical and theological criticism survived unscathed.

It is also of particular importance that Barth's new directions were set in the midst of a sustained engagement with the text of the Bible.[4] Entering into this 'strange new world' provided him with both the reason and the resources to mount a substantial and fundamental challenge to the prevailing theological consensus.[5] His friend Eduard Thurneysen later wrote of their common journey in the second decade of the twentieth century:

> We read the Bible in a new way. We read it more respectfully, more as an eternal Word addressed to us and to our time. We criticised it less. We read it with the eyes of shipwrecked people, whose all had gone overboard. The Bible appeared in a new

---

Footnote 3 (*continued*)

    inwardly agree that I had really turned away from my teacher. Nor can I so agree today' ('The Principles of Dogmatics according to Wilhelm Herrmann', in idem, *Theology and Church*, trans. L. P. Smith [New York: Harper & Row, 1962], pp. 238–239).

4. His contemporaries were left in no doubt that his theology, while undoubtedly affected by his context, was nonetheless 'not to be explained in terms of the collapse of the war but in terms of a new reading of Scripture' (D. Bonhoeffer, 'The History of Systematic Theology in the Twentieth Century' [Bonn, 1931/1932], repr. in *Dietrich Bonhoeffer Werke*, 16 vols. [Munich: C. Kaiser, 1986–98], vol. 11, pp. 194–195; cited in A. Pangritz, *Karl Barth in the Theology of Dietrich Bonhoeffer*, trans. B. Rumscheidt and M. Rumscheidt [Grand Rapids: Eerdmans, 2000], p. 36).

5. It should be said that such a challenge on the basis of the same resource, the Bible, had been mounted repeatedly from outside the European theological context. However, both the scale of Barth's assault and the fact that it was mounted by one trained and endorsed within that context (and who wrote in German!) gave Barth's criticisms a hearing others never received.

light. Beyond all interpretations, its genuine word began to speak again: the word of forgiveness, the Gospel of the coming Kingdom.[6]

Barth himself explained the impact of this fresh engagement with the Bible:

> By 1916 a number of us of the younger generation had hesitantly set out to introduce a theology better than that of the nineteenth century and of the turn of the century – better in the sense that in it God, in his unique position over against man, and especially religious man, might clearly be given that honour we believed we found him to have in the Bible.[7]

This concern to reform both the content and the method of mainstream theology in line with the teaching of Scripture is present throughout Barth's writing. It explains the extent of exegetical comment in the *Church Dogmatics*. Very few systematic theologians have devoted as much space in their theological work to extended interactions with the biblical text. The same concern finds expression in the famous opening of the Barmen Declaration, with its insistence that 'Jesus Christ, *as he is testified to us in the Holy Scripture*, is the one Word of God, whom we are to hear, whom we are to trust and obey in life and in death.'[8] All the various appropriations of Jesus Christ are to be tested by the witness of the Bible. A little less well known is his parting advice to the Bible study he ran at the University of Bonn upon being forced by the German authorities to leave: '[E]xegesis, exegesis, exegesis! Keep to the Word, to the scripture that has been given us.'[9] Barth certainly would not have endorsed any suggestion that such a preoccupation with the teaching of Scripture was a declension from vital, living Christianity. In his own words, 'strangely enough Christianity has always been and only been a living religion when it is not ashamed to be actually and seriously a book religion'.[10] In public and in private

6. Cited in J. McConnachie, *The Barthian Theology and the Man of Today* (London: Hodder & Stoughton, 1933), p. 94.

7. 'A Thank-You and a Bow – Kierkegaard's Reveille: Speech on Being Awarded the Sonning Prize (1963)', in M. Rumscheidt (ed.), *Fragments Grave and Gray*, trans. E. Mosbacher (London: Collins, 1971), p. 97.

8. Art. 1, extracted in K. Scholder, *The Churches and the Third Reich*, vol. 2 (London: SCM, 1988), pp. 148–149 (emphasis mine).

9. Busch, *Karl Barth*, p. 259.

10. *CD* I/2, p. 495.

he insisted that Holy Scripture 'is normative for me'.[11] He called on others to follow his own practice and warned 'do not stop testing and correcting your insights by holy scripture'.[12]

In this connection it is significant that Barth lectured so often and so extensively on the biblical text. His exegetical work was not limited to excurses within his *Church Dogmatics*. True, not much of this has yet been published let alone translated for the English-speaking world. However, one recent study of Barth's use of the Bible has brought the extent of this work to light.[13] While Professor of Reformed Theology at the University of Göttingen (1921–5), Barth offered fifteen lecture courses, of which seven were exegetical. At Münster where he was, most interestingly, Professor of Dogmatics and New Testament Exegesis (1925–30), Barth lectured on the Gospel of John and Philippians, Colossians and James. At the University of Bonn he lectured on Colossians and 1 Peter. To this we could add his regular preaching in churches and in the prison at Basel. In practice and throughout his remarkable teaching career, Barth remained deeply attentive to the words of Scripture.

These preliminary observations, these significant 'background conditions', provide an important context for responsible engagement with Barth's doctrine of Scripture. Indeed, acknowledgment of such a context is perhaps the first step in letting Barth be himself, free from either adulation or suspicion, both of which have too often marred discussions of his theology in general and his doctrine of Scripture in particular. He must be allowed to define himself, to set the limits of his own theological associations. Barth's conscious separation from theological liberalism is well known. He could speak of 'the wolves of the eighteenth and nineteenth century'.[14] Yet he just as vehemently refused even to engage American evangelicals such as Gordon H. Clark, Fred H. Klooster and Cornelius Van Til, since they only wanted 'to confirm the judgement they have already passed on me'.[15] He later lamented the fact that

11. E.g. Barth to Prof. Hiderobu Kuwada of Tokyo, 22 Jan. 1963, in *Karl Barth Letters 1961–1968*, trans. G. W. Bromiley (Grand Rapids: Eerdmans, 1981), p. 89.

12. Barth to H. Israelsen of Copenhagen, 12 July 1963, in *Letters*, p. 108.

13. I am grateful for the work of John Webster, which is reflected in this paragraph: J. Webster, 'Reading the Bible: The Example of Barth and Bonhoeffer', in idem, *Word and Church: Essays in Church Dogmatics* (Edinburgh: T. & T. Clark, 2001), p. 89.

14. *CD* I/2, p. 525.

15. Barth to Dr Geoffrey W. Bromiley of Pasadena, 1 June 1961, in *Letters*, pp. 7–8. Barth had in mind the assessment made of him (and Brunner) by Van Til fifteen

books like J. A. T. Robinson's *Honest to God!* forced him to make common cause with 'some finally very distasteful fundamentalists'.[16] Respect for Barth must start here with the lines he himself drew between his own theological position and that of others.

A second critical step is an appreciation of Barth's theological concerns. As well as protesting that some had precipitately made up their minds about him, often on the basis of very little firsthand engagement with his work, he lamented the fact they did not 'focus on the reason for my statements'.[17] Barth's conviction that Christian theology is both unified and coherent, with a singular focus on the person of Jesus Christ, often meant that prior theological commitments played a vital role in the shaping of individual doctrines. More often than not he had a well-thought-through reason for expressing a particular insight in this way and not another. That reason may not be unassailable, but it will most certainly be carefully considered. So much so, that one recent and brilliant study of his thought suggests, 'we really first understand Barth's work only when we do not merely understand this work but what it is that motivates it'.[18]

In the quest to let Barth be Barth, a third critical step is to gain a familiarity with his method of argument. It has sometimes been likened to the style of one of his beloved Mozart concertos, teasing out a theme and then returning to it from a range of different angles. For those schooled in the linear method of argument with its determined movement from premise to conclusion, Barth's style is strange and off-putting.[19] He is 'constantly circling around his subject, in order to follow it in the dynamics which inheres in it'.[20] As another leading account puts it, 'the force of the "argument" gradually accumulates,

---

years earlier as 'the new foe' (C. Van Til, *The New Modernism: An Appraisal of the Theology of Barth and Brunner* [Philadelphia: Presbyterian & Reformed, 1946], p. 378). This criticism by Van Til, which at points flies so directly in the face of the evidence as to be absurd, was based almost entirely on Barth's abortive *Christliche Dogmatik im Entwurf* (Munich: C. Kaiser, 1927).

16. Barth to Prof. Friedrich Wilhelm Kantzenbach of Neuendettelsau, 4 April 1964, in *Letters*, p. 156.

17. Barth to Bromiley, 1 June 1961, in *Letters*, p. 7.

18. E. Busch, *The Great Passion: An Introduction to Karl Barth's Theology*, trans. G. W. Bromiley, ed. D. L. Guder and J. J. Guder (Grand Rapids: Eerdmans, 2004), p. 40.

19. This initial sense of alienation is compounded by Barth's fondness for dialectical explanation and paradox.

20. Busch, *Passion*, p. 39.

swelling towards a conclusion rather than reaching it by taking measured steps'.[21] This method of accumulation takes time and is at least part of the explanation for the extraordinary prolixity of the *Church Dogmatics* in particular. It is easy to get lost in the mass of verbiage.[22] However, as Eberhard Busch has once again shown, there is 'an inner sequence' and 'a characteristic rhythm' to Barth's work.[23] Equally important and perhaps contrary to what many expect or even demand of him, Barth explicitly refused to see himself as providing the final word on any subject:

> [I]n dogmatics strictly speaking there are no comprehensive views, no final
> conclusions and results. There is only the investigation and teaching which take place
> in the act of dogmatic work and which, strictly speaking, must continually begin again
> at the beginning in every point.[24]

The necessity of this lengthy introduction to an examination of Barth's doctrine of Scripture arises from the simple fact that, given the monumental extent of his theological output, many in the English-speaking world have gained access to Barth's theology either through the work of his admiring students or else through the trenchant criticism of his opponents. In such circumstances a measure of distortion is almost inevitable.[25] Indeed, when it comes to Barth's doctrine of Scripture, one recent study argued that many of the problems classic evangelicalism has had with his account arise from 'theological misinterpretation of his multi-leveled dynamism regarding "the Word of God"', stemming not least from misrepresentations of his work by those most enthusiastic about it.[26] There are sometimes difficulties with the conduits

---

21. J. Webster, *Karl Barth* (London: Continuum, 2000), p. 50.

22. Hans Frei insisted that this feature of Barth's work is not merely accidental. His task of reconstructing the theological task involved the reinstatement of a theological language that necessitated expansive, even leisurely, employment; see H. Frei, *Types of Christian Theology* (New Haven: Yale University Press, 1992), pp. 152–153. See also Webster, *Karl Barth*, p. 50.

23. *Passion*, p. 41.

24. *CD* I/2, p. 868.

25. Note e.g. George Hunsinger's analysis of various 'readings' of Barth by Balthasar, T. F. Torrance, Berkouwer, Jenson and Hartwell: Hunsinger, *How to Read Karl Barth: The Shape of His Theology* (New York: Oxford University Press, 1991), pp. 3–23.

26. J. D. Morrison, 'Barth, Barthians and Evangelicals: Reassessing the Question of the Relation of Holy Scripture and the Word of God', *TrinJ* NS 25 (2004), pp. 187–213.

of Barth's thought into the world of Anglophone theology. For this reason, a determined effort must be made to engage directly with Barth across the massive range of his contribution – what some have called 'a canonical reading' – in order to ensure that it is indeed *his* doctrine of Scripture to which we are responding. Barth himself seemed to think this was reasonable:

> I do not expect anyone to agree with me – still less that he say nice things about me. But since it now happens that there are those who have so much to say about me, without presumption I might expect that they had first informed themselves about me and therefore had read me, and moreover, had read me calmly and in some measure completely.[27]

Barth's leading concerns

It has been suggested that 'properly speaking . . . Barth does not have a doctrine of scripture, but more a "scripture principle"'.[28] That observation, on the face of it, would seem somewhat difficult to sustain. Besides the almost three hundred pages in the second part-volume of the *Church Dogmatics* entitled 'Holy Scripture', Barth wrote repeatedly about the nature of Scripture and its relation to the Word as the self-revelation of the triune God.[29] Furthermore,

---

Note also the somewhat less than convincing (and, one might say, somewhat predictable) conclusion of Kevin Vanhoozer: 'The differences between Barth and evangelicals on the matter of the Bible being the Word of God stem from mutual misunderstandings that can be accounted for in terms of speech-act theory' (K. J. Vanhoozer, 'A Person of the Book? Barth on Biblical Authority and Interpretation', in Sung Wook Chung [ed.], *Karl Barth and Evangelical Theology* [Carlisle: Paternoster, 2006], p. 57).

27. 'Foreword', in Weber, *Barth's Church Dogmatics*, p. 8.

28. J. Webster, 'Karl Barth', in J. P. Greenman and T. Larson (eds.), *Reading Romans through the Centuries: From the Early Church to Karl Barth* (Grand Rapids: Brazos, 2005), p. 206.

29. Among the most significant expositions of his doctrine of the Word of God (in chronological order) are 'The Strange New World within the Bible' (1916), in *The Word of God and the Word of Man*, trans. D. Horton (Gloucester, Mass.: Peter Smith, 1956), pp. 28–50; *Christliche Dogmatik im Entwurf*, ed. G. Sauter (Zurich: Theologischer Verlag, 1982 [1927]), pp. 33–69, 435–530; *GD*, pp. 45–68, 201–249; *CD* I/1 (1932), pp. 47–292; 'Revelation' (1934), in *God in Action: Theological Addresses*,

aware that his teaching on this subject was a source for concern on the part of some, he sought to clarify what he was saying in successive accounts of the doctrine. He spoke of 'the old uneasiness smouldering in the conservative camp . . . concerning what I have supposedly been heard to say about the authority of the Bible and the relationship of *Geschichte* [the interpretation of *Historie*] and *Historie* [that which is reported as fact]'.[30] However, it is true that 'what Barth has to say about the nature of scripture is a function of other, more primary, dogmatic convictions'.[31] The reasons for many of his statements on the nature of Scripture can be traced to the particular account of God and his self-revelation that provide their most important context. Following Barth's own lead, then, it is important that we trace these reasons, these theological concerns, and the impact they have on his account of the Christian doctrine of Scripture.

The lordship of God

The pre-eminent concern of Barth in all his writing from around 1914 onwards was the sovereign freedom of God. He insisted that in all his acts, the triune God remains the Lord. He cannot be circumscribed, he cannot be comprehensively analysed and he certainly cannot be 'mastered'. This critical category of lordship is inextricable from any Christian talk about God, whether the topic of interest is God in relation to creation, reconciliation or redemption. God is always and irrefutably the Lord. Barth considered this perspective to be vital when we come to consider divine revelation: 'God reveals Himself as the Lord . . . Revelation is the revelation of lordship and therewith it is the revelation of God.'[32]

There is some variety in the way in which Barth would describe what he

---

Footnote 29 (*continued*)

trans. E. G. Homrighausen and K. J. Ernst (Edinburgh: T. & T. Clark, 1937), pp. 3–19; *CD* I/2 (1938), pp. 457–740; 'The Authority and Significance of the Bible: Twelve Theses' (1947), in *God Here and Now*, trans. P. M. van Buren (London: Routledge, 1964), pp. 55–74; 'The Christian Understanding of Revelation' (1948), in *Against the Stream: Shorter Post-War Writings 1946–52*, trans. S. Godman, ed. R. G. Smith (London: SCM, 1954), pp. 203–240; *CD* IV/3 (1959), pp. 38–165; *Evangelical Theology: An Introduction*, trans. G. Foley (Edinburgh: T. & T. Clark, 1963), pp. 15–36.

30. *Evangelical Theology*, p. xi.

31. Webster, 'Karl Barth', p. 206.

32. *CD* I/1, p. 306.

meant by lordship. For instance, in the preface to the second edition of his Romans commentary, from 1921, he quoted Kierkegaard's 'infinite qualitative distinction' between time and eternity. This he saw as having both a negative and positive significance: "'God is in heaven and thou art on earth." The relation between such a God and such a man, and the relation between such a man and such a God, is for me the theme of the Bible . . .'[33] This fundamental reality demands a particular stance on the part of the Christian and especially the theologian. In the lectures on dogmatics delivered in Göttingen just three years later, Barth spoke of how, in order to be real, 'our certainty about God must always lie in God's hands'.[34] Later, in the *Church Dogmatics*, he could explore the idea of the hiddenness and mystery of revelation as a way of conveying the same idea:

> for the point of God's speech is not to occasion specific thoughts or a specific attitude but through the clarity which God gives us, and which induces both these in us, to bind us to Himself. This happens, however, as we are constantly set before our limit, i.e., before His mystery.[35]

However, two particular ways of speaking about God's lordship and its implications for revelation and for the doctrine of Scripture recur throughout Barth's theological work. The first of these is his insistence that God remains *subject* in the act of revelation. The revelation of God is not an object that can be grasped by human ingenuity, probed and prodded in order to come to a better or more precise knowledge of its nature and its use. It is not a human phenomenon or something towards which we might address ourselves. Barth is quite emphatic: 'Revelation means the knowledge of God through God and from God.'[36] Revelation always travels in this direction. It is always *Deus dixit* (God has spoken). '*God* is the subject even when we hear his Word in the witness of the prophets and apostles.'[37] The word of God cannot be separated from the God who speaks it and indeed from the act or event of his speaking. Here Barth is quite clearly and explicitly countering the theological tradition in which he was trained. To suggest that revelation arises

---

33. *The Epistle to the Romans*, trans. E. C. Hoskyns (London: Oxford University Press, 1968), p. 10.

34. *GD*, p. 67.

35. *CD* I/1, p. 175; cf. p. 321.

36. *GD*, p. 61.

37. Ibid., p. 62.

out of human feeling or experience ('whatever finds me'[38]) 'makes God an object *without* God'.[39] But, as he said in an early address on the Bible, it tells us

> not how we should talk with God but what he says to us; not how we find the way to him, but how he has sought and found the way to us; not the right relation in which we must place ourselves to him, but the covenant he has made with all who are Abraham's spiritual children and which he has sealed once and for all in Jesus Christ.[40]

Basic to Barth's understanding of divine lordship is an appreciation of God's *absolute freedom*: 'Godhead in the Bible means freedom, ontic and noetic autonomy . . . It is thus, as One who is free, as the only One who is free, that God has lordship in the Bible.'[41] God is free from constraint of any kind and he will not be controlled by his creatures. It is this language of freedom that becomes the primary vehicle for much of Barth's argument when it comes to God's lordship in revelation and especially with regard to Scripture. Any genuine knowledge of God is founded on 'the free decision of the eternal and unchangeable God', his prior decision to *be known*.[42] But God is also free to decide when and where he is known. 'Revelation is simply the freedom of God's grace.'[43] So when it comes to Scripture, while we are right to say that we are bound to these texts and can expect to hear God's word only here, God always remains free with regard to them.

> The Bible is God's Word to the extent that God causes it to be His Word, to the extent that He speaks through it . . . we cannot abstract from the free action of God in and by which He causes it to be true to us and for us here and now that the biblical word of man is His own Word.[44]

---

38. S. T. Coleridge, *Confessions of an Inquiring Spirit* (New York: Chelsea House, 1983 [1840]), p. 42; cf. F. D. E. Schleiermacher, *The Christian Faith*, 2nd ed., trans. D. M. Baillie, H. R. Mackintosh et al. (Edinburgh: T. & T. Clark, 1999 [1831]), p. 51.
39. *GD*, p. 61 (emphasis original).
40. 'Strange New World', p. 43.
41. *CD* I/1, p. 307.
42. 'Revelation', p. 11.
43. *CD* I/1, p. 117.
44. Ibid., pp. 109, 110.

Viewed from another angle, this is what constitutes 'the inaccessible mystery of the free grace in which the Spirit of God is present and active before and above and in the Bible'.[45]

This is in large measure why Barth is so careful to distinguish his own position from those who appeal to the text of Scripture as the word of God without any reference to the sovereignly free decision of God that it should be so. To speak like this is to risk treating God as object rather than subject and to suggest that we might have some kind of autonomous purchase on God himself and hence truth about him. This is the unfortunate development Barth claimed took place in connection with the doctrine of biblical inspiration during the post-Reformation period:

> This new understanding of biblical inspiration meant simply that the statement that the Bible is the Word of God was now transformed . . . from a statement about the free grace of God into a statement about the nature of the Bible as exposed to human inquiry brought under human control. The Bible as the Word of God surreptitiously became a part of natural knowledge of God, i.e., of that knowledge of God which man can have without the free grace of God, by his own power, and with direct insight and assurance.[46]

Barth's reading of the post-Reformation orthodox may well have been proven tendentious and unhelpfully influenced by the work of Heinrich Heppe.[47] He may also have imported a notion of lordship as absolute freedom that has been determined apart from and prior to God's own expression of his freedom in creation, covenant, incarnation and the commissioning of Scripture.[48] At points Barth appears to risk an overemphasis on the *will* of God as the focal

---

45. *CD* I/2, p. 504.

46. *CD* I/2, pp. 522–523.

47. R. A. Muller, *Post-Reformation Reformed Dogmatics: The Rise and Development of Reformed Orthodoxy, ca. 1520 to ca. 1725*, vol. 2: *Holy Scripture, the Cognitive Foundation of Theology*, 2nd ed. (Grand Rapids: Baker, 2003), esp. pp. 67, 155, 184–185. The reference to Heppe follows Barth's acknowledged debt to H. Heppe, *Reformed Dogmatics, Set out and Illustrated from the Sources*, rev. and ed. E. Bizer (London: George Allen & Unwin, 1950 [1861]).

48. N. Wolterstorff, *Divine Discourse: Philosophical Reflections on the Claim that God Speaks* (Cambridge: Cambridge University Press, 1995), p. 75. Is Barth's formulation perhaps an unfortunate development of Kierkegaard's infinite qualitative distinction?

point of his transcendent lordship. However, his concern that God's lordship not be compromised by a doctrine of Scripture that ascribes to this text the inherent quality of perfection and even divinity, failing to insist that the authority and dignity of Scripture is inextricably tied to the authority and dignity of God, is a concern that ought to be addressed. I do not engage with this text purely for its own sake. And yet, God's sovereign freedom is not to be pitted against his faithfulness. God cannot lie (Titus 1:2) and has bound himself to human beings by the blood of the new covenant (Mark 14:24; Heb. 10:29). 'If we are faithless, he remains faithful – for he *cannot* deny himself' (2 Tim. 2:13; my emphasis[49]). There is a divine necessity arising from his character and borne by his promise. While Barth would no doubt agree that God must himself determine the nature of his own lordship,[50] he does not appear to consider that God might bind himself to the word he speaks and that he commissions the prophets and apostles to write. Barth is certainly right to say the Bible 'directs us to God'. His next sentence is more difficult to sustain in the light of how God has in fact dealt with us: 'But God can and will direct us only to himself.'[51]

The centrality of Christ

The radically Christological concentration of Barth's entire theological enterprise is well known:

> [W]ithin theological thinking generally unconditional priority must be given to thinking which is attentive to the existence of the living person of Jesus Christ (just because it is this existence), so that *per definitionem* [by definition] christological thinking forms the unconditional basis for all other theological thinking . . . The obligation to give to christological thinking this unconditional precedence, this function of a basis in the strict sense, seems to me to be imposed quite simply by the character of the living person Jesus Christ as the almighty Mediator whom it must follow.[52]

For Barth, the focus of attention must always be Christ himself, not a Christological principle. All theology must look to the one indicated by John the Baptist's 'prodigious index finger', recalling the copy of Grünewald's

---

49. All Scripture quotations in this chapter are from the ESV.
50. *CD* IV/1, p. 186.
51. *GD*, p. 58.
52. *CD* IV/3, p. 175.

'Crucifixion' that watched over Barth each day as he laboured over the *Church Dogmatics*.[53] As early as 1920 he insisted, 'it is this hand which is in evidence in the Bible'.[54]

Perhaps no other statement of Barth more powerfully captures his concern to point all theology in this direction than the words quoted earlier, the famous opening of the Barmen Declaration, which he drafted in 1934: 'Jesus Christ, as He is attested to us in Holy Scripture, is the one Word of God, whom we have to hear and whom we have to obey in life and in death.'[55] Over and against all other purported words of God, and especially any appeal to creaturely realities as indicating or mediating the person and purposes of God, Christians insist upon the person of Jesus Christ. Precisely because in the man Jesus Christ we are in fact dealing with God himself and no mere creaturely mediation of him, Jesus must remain the focus of our attention. Fourteen years later, when the political threat that provoked this declaration had been removed, Barth would still argue that 'when it refers to God's revelation as the Word of God, Christianity means Jesus Christ'.[56]

For Barth, this is a critical perspective from which to appreciate what Scripture in fact is and what it is not. With the Reformers he insisted that the singularity of the Bible 'consists in and is established by the fact that it is the book of Christ'.[57] Indeed, he went further in emphasizing that 'the witness of Holy Scripture to itself consists simply in the fact that it is witness to Jesus Christ'.[58] To contemplate the nature of Scripture apart from this key element of witness beyond itself and in a specific direction actually does violence to

---

53. *CD* I/1, p. 112; Busch, *Karl Barth*, p. 116.

54. 'Biblical Questions, Insights, and Vistas' (1920), in *Word of God*, p. 65.

55. See above n. 8.

56. 'Christian Understanding', p. 214. 'No human word, even if it is spoken with God's commission and in God's service, can as such speak in this way or say or accomplish these things. God's direct presence is needed for this. God Himself must come and speak' (*CD* IV/3, p. 98).

57. *CD* I/1, p. 109. Luther and Calvin may both have said much more than this about the singularity of the Bible, but certainly never less. E.g. M. Luther, 'A Brief Instruction on what to Look for and Expect in the Gospels' (1522), in *Luther's Works*, ed. J. Pelikan and H. T. Lehmann, 55 vols. (St. Louis: Concordia; Philadelphia: Fortress, 1955–86), vol. 35, p. 122; J. Calvin, *Institutes of the Christian Religion*, trans. F. L. Battles, ed. J. T. McNeill, 2 vols. (Philadelphia: Westminster, 1960 [1559]), 1.1–9, pp. 35–96.

58. *CD* I/2, 485.

the text that finds its truth, power and validity precisely in this witness.[59] Did not Jesus himself say that the Scriptures 'bear witness about *me*' (John 5:39–40; my emphasis) and commission his apostles as '*my* witnesses' (Acts 1:8; my emphasis)?

There is, of course, clear biblical warrant for speaking about Jesus as the Word of God (John 1:1–18; 1 John 1:1–4). However, following Luther's lead, Barth spoke of the threefold form of the Word of God: 'one Word only in this threefold form . . . one and the same whether we understand it as revelation, Bible, or proclamation. There is no distinction of *degree* or *value* between the three forms.'[60] Nevertheless, both Barth and Luther saw a difference of *kind* between Jesus as the Word of God on the one hand and both Scripture and Christian preaching as the Word of God on the other. Luther insisted that only one form of the Word of God is in substance God.[61] Barth agreed. Precisely because Jesus is God with us (*Immanuel*) we may speak of him as the Word of God or revelation without any reservation or qualification. 'Revelation in fact does not differ from the person of Jesus Christ nor from the reconciliation accomplished in Him. To say revelation is to say "The Word became flesh".'[62] Barth, however, critically misunderstood Luther at this point and went much further.[63] He insisted that whereas Jesus Christ as this revela-

---

59. 'Authority', p. 58.

60. *CD* I/1, p. 120 (emphasis mine). Luther's use of the 'threefold' description of the Word of God, which differs at a number of important points from that of Barth, is found in his comments on Ps. 45:1 in the 'Dictata super Psalterium' (1513–15), in Pelikan and Lehmann, *Luther's Works*, vol. 10, p. 220; cf. M. D. Thompson, *A Sure Ground on Which to Stand: The Relation of Authority and Interpretative Method in Luther's Approach to Scripture* (Carlisle: Paternoster, 2004), pp. 70–73.

61. *Substantialiter Deus*. Luther, 'Tabletalk #5177' (1540), in Pelikan and Lehmann, *Luther's Works*, vol. 54, p. 395. This is quite clearly also what Luther had in mind when he wrote, 'God and the Scripture of God are two things, no less than the Creator and the creature of God are two things', a sentence that has been abused in much subsequent discussion of Luther's view of Scripture. Luther, 'On the Bondage of the Will', in Pelikan and Lehmann, *Luther's Works*, vol. 33, p. 25. See Thompson, *Sure Ground*, pp. 68–90, 105–106.

62. *CD* I/1, p. 119.

63. Barth's misappropriation of Luther is most clear in his citation of a fragment of a sentence from one of Luther's postils, misreading the referent of the pronoun, and building upon this a discussion of how Scripture 'only holds, encloses, limits and surrounds' God's Word (see *CD* I/2, p. 492); cf. Thompson, *Sure Ground*, pp. 88–90.

tion is God's Word originally and directly, 'the Bible and Church proclamation are derivatively and indirectly'.

> The underlying and basic third form of the Word of God, which we have tried to pin down in the concept of revelation, is what has forced us constantly to keep this proviso in mind in our analysis of the concepts of proclamation and Scripture. Underlying the Word of God not as proclamation and Scripture alone but as God's revelation in proclamation and Scripture, we must understand it in its identity with God Himself. God's revelation is Jesus Christ, the Son of God.[64]

One of the notorious difficulties in coming to grips with Barth's treatment of the Word of God is holding together his statements about the unity of the three forms of the Word of God with this obvious distinction he makes between the Word as the self-revelation of God in Jesus Christ (its third form 'or materially we should rather say its first form'[65]) and the other two forms, namely Scripture and Christian preaching. The one is a witness to nothing other than itself. Revelation is not something predicated of it but simply another way of designating it.[66] In contrast, the other two are first and foremost witnesses to revelation rather than revelation itself. 'The Bible is God's Word as it bears witness to revelation, and proclamation is God's Word as it really promises revelation.'[67] And yet Barth can also say just ten pages later that 'to the extent that the Bible really attests revelation it is no less the Word of God than revelation itself'.[68] Barth himself understood the tension between these statements. However, he did not consider that this tension was one of his making and drew attention in this context to the doctrine of the triunity of God, with its basic determinations and mutual relationships, the same 'decisive difficulty' and also the same 'decisive clarity'.[69] This, then, is precisely what

---

64. *CD* I/1, p. 137.
65. Ibid., p. 120.
66. Ibid., p. 118.
67. Ibid., p. 111.
68. Ibid., p. 121. A page earlier (p. 120) he had insisted, 'there is no distinction of degree or value between the three forms'.
69. Ibid., p. 121; cf. 'If revelation is to be taken seriously as God's presence, if there is to be a valid belief in revelation, then in no sense can Christ and the Spirit be subordinate hypostases. In the predicate and object of the concept of revelation we must again have, and to no less a degree, the subject itself. Revelation and revealing must be equal to the revealer' (*CD* I/1, p. 353).

one should expect if the Word of God is in fact the self-revelation of the personal, triune God. The very shape of revelation is determined by the one who is revealed, the triune God himself. At Göttingen Barth had even spoken of one *Word* but three *addresses*, with unmistakable allusion to the trinitarian formula.[70] Yet, as is the case with the persons of the Trinity, confusion is as problematic as separation. To fail to distinguish between the forms of the one Word of God, no less between revelation and the Bible than between the Bible and church proclamation, would be to dishonour the unique sense in which Christ is the Word of God.

In slightly different words, this is Barth's famous – and to many problematic – distinction between a direct relation of Jesus Christ and revelation on one hand, but only an indirect relation between revelation and the Bible on the other. At one point Barth even insists that we 'do the Bible poor and unwelcome honour if we equate it directly with this other, with revelation itself'.[71] He is at pains to make clear that this does not prevent revelation and the Bible from becoming one 'in the event of God's Word'.[72] However, at the same time he repeatedly argues that the Bible must be distinguished from revelation: 'A real witness is not identical with that to which it witnesses, but it sets it before us.'[73] Perhaps it is significant that from Barth's point of view, what is being held together is a limitation and a positive element, 'a distinctiveness from revelation, in so far as it is only a human word about it, and its unity with it, in so far as revelation is the basis, object and content of this word'.[74] Barth is not attempting to hold together 'indirect relation' and 'direct relation', but rather 'indirect relation' and 'unity with'. In his view, to claim a direct relation would be to risk divinizing the text. 'Again it is quite impossible that there should be a direct identity between the human word of Scripture and the Word of God, and therefore between the creaturely reality in itself and as such the reality of God the Creator.'[75] Here would be bibliolatry indeed. So while other factors are undoubtedly at work at this point, it is chiefly Barth's desire to preserve the singular honour due to Jesus Christ, which causes him to qualify his talk about the Bible as the Word of God: 'the Bible is not the Word of God on

---

70. *GD*, p. 14.
71. *CD* I/1, p. 112.
72. Ibid., p. 113.
73. *CD* I/2, p. 463.
74. Ibid.
75. Ibid., p. 499.

earth in the same way as Jesus Christ, very God and very man, is that Word in heaven'.[76]

Barth's Christological concentration is one of the immensely attractive features of his theology. It resonates both with classic evangelical theology's strong emphasis on the centrality of Jesus and the biblical identification of him as the one in whom we have 'every spiritual blessing in the heavenly places' (Eph. 1:3). A doctrine of Scripture that leaves Jesus at its periphery could hardly lay claim to being genuinely evangelical.[77] Just as sub-evangelical is a practice of biblical interpretation and exposition that terminates on the text itself: at best simply assuming the next step; at worst neglecting it altogether. However, was Barth really Christological enough?[78] Can his approach really account for Jesus' own stance towards the Scriptures of his day and the commissioned witness of his apostles? As we have already noted, Jesus did indeed call on the Pharisees to recognize that the Old Testament Scripture testified to him (John 5:39–40), yet he could also speak of the words recorded by Moses as, without qualification, the word of God which was set aside by their appeal to tradition (Matt. 15:1–9). How should we understand Jesus' own appeal to the words of Deuteronomy in his encounter with the satan in the wilderness? The way these texts are used by Jesus suggests they are more than simply a testimony to Jesus or a prophetic indication of how he would behave when faced with temptation (Matt. 4:1–11). They are in fact the word from God that settles the issue at hand. Similarly, while Jesus certainly calls on his apostles to be 'my witnesses' (Acts 1:8), this involves not only speaking of him but 'teaching them to observe all that I have commanded you' (Matt. 28:20).[79] The apostle Paul, commissioned by the risen Christ, could rejoice in how his preaching was received for what it in fact is, the word of God and not simply as the word of men testifying to the word of God (1 Thess. 2:13). In contrast, Barth appears to overplay the

---

76. Ibid., p. 513.

77. F. Watson, 'An Evangelical Response', in P. Helm and C. R. Trueman (eds.), *The Trustworthiness of God: Perspectives on the Nature of Scripture* (Grand Rapids: Eerdmans; Leicester: Apollos, 2002), p. 288.

78. See M. D. Thompson, *A Clear and Present Word: The Clarity of Scripture* (Leicester: Apollos, 2006), pp. 76, 82–87.

79. We cannot pursue here the important truth that there are commands even in the NT. Not everything is in the indicative mood, a fact sometimes lost in Barth's own exegesis and in that of those who follow him. It is not necessarily a denial of grace to call for radical obedience.

distinction between *Deus dixit* and *Paulus dixit*, notwithstanding his insistence that they 'become one and the same thing in the event of the Word of God'.[80] At issue here is, in the final analysis, the nature and result of biblical inspiration.

The personal and dynamic character of divine revelation (and inspiration)

For Barth, God's self-expression in his Word is, by definition, irradicably personal. God intends to make *himself* known to men and women – not just truth about him but *himself*. This in turn means that revelation must be understood in active and dynamic terms, as an event or encounter and not simply as a deposit of information:

> Only within this I–Thou relation, in which one speaks and another is spoken to, in which there is communication and reception, only in full *action* is revelation revelation. When we do not think of revelation as such, that is, one person speaking and another spoken to, God revealing himself to us and we to whom he reveals himself; when revelation is seen from the standpoint of the non-involved spectator, then it amounts to nonrevelation.[81]

This is, of course, a corollary of the insight that God always remain *subject* rather than mere object when it comes to revelation: 'He is the subject who acts in His revelation. This act of revelation is a token of His being and the expression of His nature.'[82] If revelation could be rightly conceived as a concrete deposit of truth or information about God that by its very existence in the creaturely world no longer remains solely at the disposal of God, but instead is open to examination and testing by human methods and criteria, then God's lordship would be open to challenge at precisely this point. Rebellious men and women might claim to have 'mastered' God's word. They might even attempt to dethrone God by construing the deposit as the self-interested expression of a particular human religious experience rather than as the word of God. Even more seriously, God would be directing us to something other than himself.

However, Barth insists that God's word is not a thing that can be observed

---

80. *CD* I/1, p. 113; cf. *GD*, pp. 56–57, where Barth seems to assume that an equation of *Deus dixit* and *Paulus dixit* necessarily involves the notion of God's dictation of the words and stylistic features with a parallel being drawn to the Delphic oracles.
81. Ibid., p. 58 (emphasis original).
82. Barth, 'Christian Understanding', p. 209.

and described from a position of human neutrality. In the first place, God's word of address to human beings confronts us and unmasks such supposed neutrality as pretence or self-delusion. 'Neutrality towards the Word of God is impossible; we cannot say Yes and No at the same time . . . it is impossible to adopt the attitude of a mere onlooker towards it.'[83] Secondly, and for Barth perhaps more importantly, the personal address of particular human beings by the word of God cannot be contained by attempts at distillation or systematization in propositional form, even when this is attempted by those seeking to honour God by taking his word seriously. God's word is God's act. Speaking his word is something that God does. In this sense it is an event rather than an object. 'What God speaks is never known or true anywhere in abstraction from God Himself.'[84]

A number of significant features of Barth's doctrine of Scripture are tied to this basic conviction that divine revelation is personal and dynamic. First of all, this insistence on the word of God as an event – the speech of God as the act of God – draws attention to the power of the word of God to shape all reality:

> The distinction between word and act is that mere word is the mere self-expression of a person, while act is the resultant active alteration in the world around. Mere word is passive, act is an active participation in history. But this kind of distinction does not apply to the Word of God. As mere Word it is act. As mere Word it is the divine person, the person of the Lord of history, whose self-expression is as such an alteration, and indeed an absolute alteration of the world, whose *passio* [suffering] in history is as such *actio* [act].[85]

Barth is surely right to point to the creative fiat of God, the redemptive call of God, the life-generating promise of forgiveness, the word that calls Lazarus from the grave and banishes demons from the life of a man. Long before speech-act philosophy was proposed as the panacea for all our theological ills, the Bible itself insisted that God's word changes things. It accomplishes God's purpose (Isa. 55:10–11), calls forth and nourishes faith (Rom. 10:17), it sustains the life of the universe (Heb. 1:3). As Paul advised Timothy, the sacred writings 'are able to make you wise for salvation through faith in Christ Jesus' (2 Tim. 3:15). Any account of the word of God that suggests it needs to be

---

83. Ibid., p. 215.
84. *CD* I/1, p. 137.
85. Ibid., p. 144.

supplemented in order to be effective is deeply problematic.[86] God's word may certainly be despised and rejected. A negative response is possible.[87] Yet the absurdity and perversity of such a stance before the word of the living God who created and sustains their own lives underscores the culpability of those who adopt it. With Peter we must recognize it is possible to twist Scripture to one's 'own destruction' (2 Pet. 3:16). The word of God always accomplishes its purpose and sometimes that purpose is judgment (Isa. 6:9–10; Mark 4:11–12).

Secondly, given that Barth identifies revelation as the event of God's word addressing actual men and women throughout human history, it is not surprising that his doctrine of Scripture must embrace both inspiration and illumination and hold them in the closest possible relation. God's active lordship in revelation does not cease with the Spirit's production of the biblical text. By the same Spirit he enables its reception as well. God sovereignly decides in these human words to address a particular man or woman (and, through proclamation, the church made up of such men and women) at a particular time and in a particular place. As he argued at Göttingen:

> We have thus to see how provisional and relative is the separation between the Spirit in scripture and the Spirit in us, between the outer and the inner aspects, the then and now, the there and here. Once we isolate either aspect, we pervert things . . . In relation to the Holy Spirit, then, we have to say that we must view inspiration as a single, timeless – or rather, contemporary – act of God (its communication, too, is really an act) in *both* the biblical authors *and* ourselves . . . We are not to distinguish between the light the Bible sheds and the eye that perceives this light.[88]

On this issue too Barth considers that a misstep was taken in the century after the Reformation. Under the guise of a heightened supernaturalism, Reformed and Lutheran theologians of that period fixed inspiration to the biblical text alone and separated the living witness of the Spirit in Scripture from the internal testimony of the Holy Spirit.[89] The act or event of *inspiration* was transformed into a general, uniform and permanent attribute of the biblical text: *inspiredness.* Claiming too much for the Bible and distinguishing too sharply

---

86. 'The Word of God does not need to be supplemented by an act. The Word is itself the act of God' (*CD* I/1, p. 143).
87. 'Christian Understanding', p. 216.
88. *GD*, pp. 224, 225; cf. *CD* I/1, p. 149.
89. *CD* I/2, p. 523.

between the moment of its production and every moment since would later prove to be counter-productive, resulting in 'the catastrophic crash of orthodoxy in the eighteenth century'.[90] Once again there is a certain degree of caricature here – to distinguish is not always to separate and it is in fact difficult to identify a theologian in the Reformed tradition who located the Spirit's involvement with the biblical text solely at the point of its inscripturation.[91] Barth himself has been accused (quite reasonably in my view) of having collapsed the Spirit's illumination into the concept of revelation.[92] Furthermore, we might ask whether he has given sufficient weight to the simple exegetical fact that the only biblical use of *theopneustos* [God-breathed = inspired by God] is attached to *pasa graphē* [all Scripture]; that is, this particular activity of God focuses on the biblical *text* rather than the biblical *authors* or Bible *readers*. Does he move too quickly from 2 Timothy 3 to 2 Peter 1? Is he entirely right to use 1 Corinthians 2 and 2 Corinthians 3 as interpretative keys to the more explicit statements about Scripture in 2 Timothy 3 and 2 Peter 1? However, despite these questions it is worth applauding the fact that Barth's protest has been instrumental in ensuring that a new and proper emphasis has been placed on God's presence in and with his word: the Bible, unlike any other piece of literature, is always read in the presence of its author. An influential contemporary account puts it this way: 'To read [holy Scripture] is to be caught up by the truth-bestowing Spirit of God.'[93]

A third feature is the way Barth's account raises questions about the nature of Scripture *in itself* (if indeed it is appropriate to speak in this way), prior to a

---

90. *CD* I/1, p. 124.

91. R. A. Muller's work *Post-Reformation Reformed Dogmatics* constitutes an important corrective here.

92. One thinks at once of statements such as 'this self-disclosure in its totality [creation of the witness and bearing witness to its truth to men] is *theopneustia*, the inspiration of the word of the prophets and apostles' (*CD* I/2, p. 516). See the critique of R. Nicole, 'The Neo-orthodox Reduction', in G. Lewis and B. Demarest (eds.), *Challenges to Inerrancy: A Theological Response* (Chicago: Moody, 1984), p. 132; P. Helm, *Divine Revelation* (London: Marshall, Morgan & Scott, 1982), p. 42; Wolterstorff, *Divine Discourse*, pp. 72–73; T. Ward, *Word and Supplement: Speech Acts, Biblical Texts, and the Sufficiency of Scripture* (Oxford: Oxford University Press, 2002), p. 120. See also the questions raised by T. F. Torrance's development of Barth's ideas in Thompson, *Clear and Present*, p. 74, n. 78.

93. J. Webster, *Holy Scripture: A Dogmatic Sketch* (Cambridge: Cambridge University Press, 2003), p. 95.

Christian reading of it or the Spirit's work in bringing its witness to the human heart. Barth strongly denied that Scripture is the word of God because we believe it to be so. It is not constituted as such by our faith.[94] Rather, the Bible becomes God's word because of God's sovereign decision that it be so.

> The *Deus dixit* is true . . . where it *is* true, i.e., where and when God, in speaking once and for all, wills according to His eternal counsel that it be true, where and when God by His activating, ratifying and fulfilling of the word of the Bible and preaching lets it become true.[95]

In speaking about the Bible as an effective witness to revelation, Barth cited the case of the Pool of Bethesda, which became a means of healing only when it was disturbed by the angel (John 5:1–9).[96] And yet Barth could insist in the Göttingen lectures that the unavoidable insight remains 'that the Bible cannot come to be God's Word if it is not this already'.[97] How are we to reconcile these perspectives? Does the 'event of revelation' transform the human words of the biblical text into something they otherwise are not, does it actualize what they already are, or is there perhaps a more fundamental problem with applying the being and becoming ontology to the Bible?[98] At this point, though, it

---

94. 'It does not become God's Word because we accord it faith but in the fact that it becomes revelation to us' (*CD* I/1, p. 110); 'the inspiration of the Bible cannot be reduced to our faith in it, even though we understand this faith as the gift and work of God in us . . . certainly it is not our faith which makes the Bible the Word of God' (*CD* I/2, p. 534).

95. *CD* I/1, p. 120.

96. Ibid., p. 111.

97. *GD*, p. 219.

98. The attractive suggestion of Bruce McCormack, that the issue is largely resolved by realizing that for Barth all being is becoming, even if not everything becomes what it is in the same way, is somewhat less than convincing in the light of Barth's explicit statements. Furthermore, application of this ontological formula raises very significant questions. It may indeed be right to say that Barth's use of this language was motivated by a concern to preserve the reality of the incarnation of the eternal Son and address how divine immutability can be maintained in the face of this ostensive 'change in God'. However, the differences between the person of Christ and the text of Scripture are more extensive than simply the way each becomes what they are (hypostatic union in one case and divine inspiration in the other). Luther was right: only one form of the word is in fact God, and this is

is important to realize that Barth considered a personal and dynamic account of the word of God to be something that distinguished him from the 'fundamentalists'. In a colloquium in 1955 he was asked precisely this: 'What differentiates your understanding of the Word of God from that of a fundamentalist?' He replied, 'For me the Word of God is a *happening*, not a thing. Therefore the Bible must *become* the Word of God, and it does this through the work of the Spirit.'[99]

The genuine humanity of the biblical text

Barth was clearly sensitive to any suggestion that the evangelical doctrine of Scripture might be construed as docetic – paying lip service to the humanity of the biblical texts while at the same time undermining this by a one-sided concentration on their origin in God and hence their 'divine character'. On the one hand, he considered such accounts to be ultimately incoherent: 'one would have to make a *sacrificum intellectus* [sacrifice of the intellect] in order to say: the Bible, as it stands, is revelation: it is therefore in reality not a human document at all but a divine document'.[100] On the other, they represent a failure to take the Bible seriously on its own terms, as it is presented to us. In such accounts the miracle of the Bible is transformed from God's gracious determination to use words such as these in making himself known to us – words written by men with all that this means – into the production of a perfect text that directly and unproblematically addresses us as the word of God. By now it ought to come as no surprise that Barth attributes this transformation of the Protestant 'Scripture Principle' to the theologians of the seventeenth and early eighteenth centuries and the doctrine of verbal inspiration:

---

surely highly significant in any discussion of Scripture's ontology. McCormack's own account seems to accept some of the historical and theological caricature we have seen in Barth, e.g. the suggestion that if inspiration were tied to a fixed state of affairs this would amount to something being true of the Bible apart from God. Once more we are brought back to the relation of inspiration and illumination and the issue of the Spirit's ongoing involvement with this unique text. See B. L. McCormack, 'The Being of Holy Scripture Is in Becoming: Karl Barth in Conversation with American Evangelical Criticism', in V. Bacote, L. C. Miguélez and D. L. Okholm (eds.), *Evangelicals and Scripture: Tradition, Authority and Hermeneutics* (Downers Grove: IVP, 2004), pp. 55–75.

99. J. D. Godsey (ed.), *Karl Barth's Table Talk* (Edinburgh: Oliver & Boyd, 1963), p. 26.
100. 'Christian Understanding', pp. 222–223.

> Later Protestant orthodoxy did incalculable damage with its doctrine of inspiration in
> which it did not accept the paradox that in scripture God's Word is given to us in the
> concealment of true and authentic human words, when it removed the salutary
> barrier between scripture and revelation, when it adopted pagan ideas and made the
> authors of the Bible into amanuenses, pens, or flutes of the Holy Spirit, and thus
> found in the Bible an open and directly given revelation, as though this were not a
> contradiction in terms . . . To deny the hiddenness of revelation even in scripture is
> to deny revelation itself, and with it the Word of God.[101]

Once again Barth's account of seventeenth-century Reformed and
Lutheran theology is difficult to sustain in the light of more thorough
research into the period.[102] Was there really a widespread denial that the
words of Scripture are 'true and authentic human words'? Furthermore, to
the extent that he is attempting to echo Luther's famous talk of God's hiddenness 'under the form of the contrary', his account is open to significant
challenge.[103] Nevertheless, it should be freely acknowledged that throughout the entire history of Christian theology, no less in the evangelical tradition than in others, incautious language has been employed under
headings such as 'the perfections of Scripture' and even 'the divinity of
Scripture'. As Barth recognized, the great Fathers of the early church (e.g.
Irenaeus, Gregory and Augustine) are not free from blame in this regard.[104]
It has always proven possible to present the humanity of the text – its
human authorship, human language and the reflection of a range of human
literary conventions, alongside the simple reality of its historical and cultural location – as merely incidental. Barth's protest needs to be heard at
this point.

In contrast, Barth himself insisted that by God's gracious act, a miracle
occurs: entirely human words that share the fragility and even 'the distorted
nature' of their environment become the word of God. Their 'secularity'
cannot and should not be avoided. In these very words as they are, God
addresses the church and the world. 'If God did not speak to us in secular

---

101. *GD*, pp. 58–59. Note Barth's explicit debt to the conclusions of Heinrich Heppe,
      Alexander Schweizer, Heinrich Schmid and C. E. Luthardt for his portrayal of
      Protestant orthodoxy in the footnotes to the published English edition of these
      lectures.
102. Muller, *Post-Reformation Reformed Dogmatics*, esp. pp. 239–242, 245–248.
103. Thompson, *Sure Ground*, pp. 206–207.
104. *CD* I/2, pp. 517–519.

form, He would not speak to us at all.'[105] The analogy between the humanity of Christ and the humanity of the Scriptures is critical as far as Barth is concerned. Just as the Son was incarnate in human flesh as it actually exists in the world this side of the fall — with all its weakness and indeed mortality — so God's Word exists in the world in the form of broken and in one sense inappropriate human words. Barth was prepared to say:

> Its form is not a suitable but an unsuitable medium for God's self-presentation. It does not correspond to the matter but contradicts it. It does not unveil but veils it . . . The form of God's Word, then, is in fact the form of the cosmos which stands in contradiction to God.[106]

Humanity, genuine humanity as it is under the conditions of our world, is not in a pristine condition and so to take seriously the humanity of the biblical text means to accept that God has chosen to use this text warts and all. This is the miracle of *theopneustia* as Barth sees it: a conditioned and limited word, which must remain as such because it is a genuinely human word, becomes by God's grace a real and effective witness to Christ.

A determination to take the humanity of Scripture seriously, combined with his conviction that this must be our humanity and not some ideal version of it, led Barth to reject any suggestion of biblical infallibility or inerrancy while at the same time strongly maintaining the authority of Scripture over church and reason. Barth wrote of 'the vulnerability of the Bible', acknowledging without embarrassment that 'its capacity for error also extends to its religious or theological content'.[107] Generations of evangelical theologians have reacted in horror, but, given Barth's own assumptions about the humanity of the text and its capacity to convey God's word only by the miracle of God's revelatory act, it should come as no surprise. For him, this is something we cannot possibly deny 'if we are not to take away this humanity, if we are not to be guilty of Docetism'.[108] At one point, it is true, Barth qualified this 'capacity for error' with 'within certain limits and therefore relatively'; however, he did not explain what these limits are other than the gracious decision of God. Furthermore, within two pages he was able to write, '*At every point* it is the vulnerable word of man.'[109]

---

105. *CD* I/1, p. 168.
106. Ibid., p. 166.
107. *CD* I/2, p. 509.
108. Ibid., p. 510.
109. Ibid., pp. 510, 512 (emphasis mine).

Care is needed in engaging Barth on this issue. It is important to emphasize again that these observations did not, for him, lead to a dismissal of biblical *authority*, either in principle or in practice.[110] He refused to identify actual errors in the Bible. Obsession with the question from either direction could itself be an act of rebellion:

> If God was not ashamed of the fallibility of all the human words of the Bible, of their historical and scientific inaccuracies, their theological contradictions, the uncertainty of their tradition, and, above all, their Judaism, but adopted and made use of these expressions in all their fallibility, we do not need to be ashamed when He wills to renew it to us in all its fallibility as witness, and it is mere self-will and disobedience to try to find some infallible elements in the Bible.[111]

What is more, his own extended meditations on the authority of Holy Scripture over the church and over human reason follow immediately in the *Church Dogmatics* his comments on the humanity of the biblical text and his reconfiguration of the doctrine of inspiration. He resolutely insists that all our thought and talk of God must be shaped by the teaching of Scripture. While God is not bound to the Bible, we most certainly are.[112]

Nevertheless, Barth's account of the humanity of Scripture is problematic at a number of levels. First of all, his claim that human words are 'an unsuitable medium for God's self-presentation' must be challenged on the basis of God's choice to use words in order to make himself known. The blessing and command in the Garden, the call of Abraham, Moses, Samuel and the others, the words spoken on Mount Sinai and the voice from heaven heard when Jesus was baptized and again at his transfiguration – all these suggest God makes human words suitable for this purpose by his very use of them. Certainly the human words are not themselves God. They are always part of our creaturely reality. However, God is the first and last speaker of human words according to the biblical account and it is God himself who initiates the transition from the spoken to the written form of those words (Exod. 24:12; 31:18). A theological account of human language as a gift of God and of human beings as

---

110. Geoffrey Bromiley has suggested that Barth saw it as 'a crippling mistake to suspend authority on the human ability to establish inerrancy' (G. W. Bromiley, 'The Authority of Scripture in Karl Barth', in D. A. Carson and J. D. Woodbridge [eds.], *Hermeneutics, Authority and Canon* [Grand Rapids: Zondervan, 1986], p. 293).
111. *CD* I/2, p. 531. Note when this originally appeared in German: 1938!
112. 'We are tied to these texts' (ibid., p. 492).

the created speech-partners of God, neither of which realities are eliminated by the fall or even by the complications following the incident at Babel, raises serious questions about Barth's claim.[113]

Secondly, Barth moves too quickly from genuine humanity existing under the conditions of the fall to the necessity of error and contradiction. The capacity for error does not always lead to actual error even in our everyday dealings with each other. Even with our limited perspectives and sinful dispositions we are able to speak the truth from time to time. Furthermore, the real humanity of the incarnate Son did most certainly involve tiredness, hunger and mortality but it did not prevent him always doing that which pleased his Father (John 8:29) and always speaking 'the truth that I heard from God' (John 8:40). Given an understanding of the Spirit's work that superintends the production of the text without bypassing the human author's personality, mind or will, and given that truth can be expressed perspectivally – that is, we do not need to know everything or to speak from a position of absolute objectivity or neutrality in order to speak truly – what exactly would be docetic about an infallible text should we be given one?

Thirdly, it is not at all clear why the miracle of God using fallible and indeed faulty human words as his own word is preferable to the miracle of the Spirit so superintending the entire process of a human writer's development, experience and literary expression that he or she freely writes the words that God intended. We need not suggest that everything the prophets or apostles said in their lives was the authoritative word of God. We can acknowledge their fallibility and sinfulness as men. We can take very seriously their historical and cultural location. It is the text of Scripture that is *theopneustos*, the product of that work of the Spirit who moved these men without turning them into mere amanuenses. Barth's uncritical acceptance of the nineteenth-century caricature of verbal inspiration as mechanical dictation and his insistence that if the prophets and apostles are not fallible 'even when they speak and write of God's revelation' then 'it is not a miracle that they speak the Word of God'[114] are both extraordinarily reductionist. His suggestion that an affirmation of biblical infallibility involves resisting the sovereignty of grace is very difficult to take seriously.[115]

---

113. For an outline of such an account in response to contemporary apophatic approaches to the knowledge of God, see M. D. Thompson, *Too Big for Words? The Transcendent God and Finite Human Language* (London: Latimer Trust, 2006).

114. *CD* I/2, p. 529.

115. Ibid.

Finally, Barth gives no account of Scripture's own testimony concerning its truthfulness and reliability. Here again the stance of Jesus Christ towards the Old Testament is critical. His appeal to the text of the Old Testament as the reliable expression of God's character and God's purposes can be traced throughout the Gospels. The temptation narratives (Matt. 4:1–11), the stance he takes before the prophecy of Isaiah in the synagogue in Nazareth (Luke 4:16–21), his appeal to Old Testament prophecy, which *must* be fulfilled (Luke 22:37; 24:44; John 15:25) and his debate with the Pharisees about precise expressions within the Old Testament text (Matt. 22:32, 43–45; John 10:34–35) – all of this is hard to reconcile with a view of the humanity of the Old Testament authors as something that must be miraculously overcome and of their words as fallible, fragile and fallen but nevertheless graciously used by God in his encounter with men and women through the ages. And yet this is not to say that Jesus neglected or denied the human authorship of these texts (e.g. Matt. 8:4; 15:7; 24:15; Mark 7:10; 12:35–37; John 12:39–41). He evidently believed both their truthfulness and their humanity to be necessary and significant.

Learning from Barth without morphing into him

Karl Barth strongly disapproved of the equivocation of so many of his critics, the 'yes . . . but' that characterized so many treatments of his theology (and still does). 'If we are to face each other squarely', he explained to one no doubt polite questioner, 'you must not meet me with such a "Yes, but –"; you must answer with a complete and unequivocal No!'[116] The problem with this require-ment is that when it comes to the doctrine of Scripture, Barth has so many good things to say. His concerns are reasonable, even when we disagree with the way he explains them or with what he sees as threatening them. The lord-ship of God, the centrality of Christ, the personal and dynamic character of God's revelation and the genuine humanity of the Scriptures – all of these are emphases evangelical theologians have themselves endorsed repeatedly. In addition, his practical commitment to the authority of Scripture, demonstrated by page after page of exegesis in the *Church Dogmatics* (admittedly at some points rather idiosyncratic and unconvincing) and by his serious advice to those students he left behind in Bonn in 1935, reminds us that the person with whom we are engaging is not an enemy but a fellow disciple of Jesus Christ.

---

116. *God in Action*, p. 121.

However, at each point there are difficulties with Barth's account. It would seem that elements of the historical and theological criticism of nineteenth-century liberalism have survived his revolution. His commitment to God's absolute and unconditional freedom and his embrace of a particular way of understanding being and becoming fit awkwardly with the biblical presentation of God as one who freely binds himself to his promise and of God's Word as an inspired text that cannot be broken (John 10:35). His emphasis on the person of Jesus Christ takes insufficient account of Jesus' own stance towards the Old Testament. His unfolding of the implications of Scripture's genuine humanity assumes the necessity of error and the basic unsuitability of human language as a vehicle of divine revelation. His use of certain historical sources, most notably the post-Reformation theologians but also Luther and others, is at points highly tendentious. Most important of all, in the final analysis his account of the doctrine of Scripture fails to do justice to Scripture's self-attestation.

Karl Barth should be read and read extensively on revelation and the Christian doctrine of Scripture. There is much to learn and appreciate in what he has to say. We need not feel compelled to hunt out every error in order to dismiss him nor that we must defend him from every criticism. Certainly, we do not need to replicate his theology or to transpose it into the idiom of the early twenty-first century. Barth's ministry to classic evangelical theology is, I suggest, of an entirely different order. Through honest and careful attentiveness to Barth's proposals and the concerns that shape them, we can be stimulated – perhaps even provoked – to present a more robust evangelical doctrine of Scripture that does not leave the gates open to the barbarians and addresses his other concerns, while at the same time stating clearly that the Bible we have in our hands is without qualification the word of the living God that is utterly reliable and true and normative for all our talk about God. We can and must give Barth his unequivocal 'No!' at important points. Nevertheless, we can still thank God for the way this servant sought to honour his Lord and live under the authority of his Word.

7. A PRIVATE LOVE? KARL BARTH AND THE TRIUNE GOD

Michael J. Ovey

> The doctrine of the Trinity is what basically distinguishes the Christian doctrine of God as Christian, and therefore what already distinguishes the Christian concept of revelation as Christian, in contrast to all other possible doctrines of God or concepts of revelation.
>
> (Karl Barth, *Church Dogmatics*)

> [A] system which is at once compelling and alienating . . .
>
> (Rowan Williams, 'Barth on the Triune God')

Introduction

'[F]ascinated exasperation':[1] Rowan Williams's reaction reflects the enigmatic quality of Karl Barth's theology. Thus, for evangelicals Barth is both the trenchant critic of liberal Protestantism in his Romans Commentary, yet also one who arguably retained too much, even too uncritically, of liberal Protestantism's critical scholarship on the Bible. This enigmatic quality persists

---

1. R. Williams, 'Barth on the Triune God', in S. W. Sykes (ed.), *Karl Barth: Studies of his Theological Method* (Oxford: Clarendon, 1979), p. 192.

in Barth's trinitarian theology. R. Olson writes of a renaissance of trinitarian theology under Barth's influence, as against a nineteenth-century liberal Protestant attitude that '[f]or all practical purposes . . . had become unitarian by the turn of the century'.[2] Yet notoriously, J. Moltmann thinks Barth's approach a triumph for Sabellian modalism, notwithstanding Barth's repudiation of 'modalism',[3] something colourably close to unitarian positions; nor is Moltmann alone.[4]

The question of how far Barth is from such positions informs much of what follows, and this chapter advances three positions related to this issue. First, Barth defines modalism more narrowly than patristic theologians did. Secondly, Barth's distinctive language that the Persons are repetitions, drawn from Anselm's *Letter on the Incarnation of the Word*, is misconceived and rests on a misconception of Anselm's argument. Thirdly, the language of reflexiveness in intra-trinitarian relations, connected with the idea of the Persons as repetitions, is not what the New Testament accounts seem to reveal.

Karl Barth's place in revitalized trinitarian theology

First, though, it is necessary to explain Olson's contention that Barth is central in a renaissance, at least in academic theology, of trinitarian thinking. The ordering of some classic theologies in the Western tradition postponed

---

2. 'The Triumphs and Tragedies of Twentieth Century Christian Theology', *Christian Scholar's Review* 29.4 (2000), p. 665.

3. *The Trinity and the Kingdom of God: The Doctrine of God*, trans. M. Kohl (London: SCM, 1981), p. 139. For Barth's repudiation, see e.g. *CD* I/1, p. 470.

4. See also W. Pannenberg, *Systematic Theology*, vol. 1, trans. G. W. Bromiley (Edinburgh: T. & T. Clark; Grand Rapids: Eerdmans, 1991), pp. 282, 295; C. M. LaCugna, *God for Us: The Trinity and Christian Life* (New York: HarperCollins, 2004), p. 252. More mutedly, C. Gunton sees similar problems; see his 'The Triune God and the Freedom of the Creature', in S. W. Sykes (ed.), *Karl Barth: Centenary Essays* (Cambridge: Cambridge University Press, 1989), pp. 46–68. Others disagree; e.g. G. W. Bromiley, *Introduction to the Theology of Karl Barth* (Edinburgh: T. & T. Clark, 1979), p. 16; A. J. Torrance, 'The Trinity', in J. Webster (ed.), *The Cambridge Companion to Karl Barth* (Cambridge: Cambridge University Press, 2000), pp. 72–91; G. Hunsinger, '*Mysterium Trinitatis*: Karl Barth's Conception of Eternity', in idem, *Disruptive Grace: Studies in the Theology of Karl Barth* (Grand Rapids: Eerdmans, 2000), p. 191, n. 7.

detailed consideration of the Trinity.[5] This could imply that trinitarian theology is an addendum to the doctrine of God proper,[6] an attitude one can see
unfolding and developing in Schleiermacher's theology, where God as Trinity
seems an appendix, and culminating in the position of Ritschl and Harnack,
which readily suggests that trinitarian theology is essentially speculative, conducted under the influence of Hellenistic metaphysics.[7] As such, Nicene trinitarian theology may not be authentically Christian. Necessarily, this would
suggest that Christian orthodoxy is wider than the *anathemata* (the accursed
things) of Nicaea 325 contemplate.

Barth's challenge to this post-Ritschlian trajectory is commendable. He insists
that the doctrine of the Trinity is no mere addition, but distinguishes the
Christian God.[8] Barth pursues this thought, arguing that the doctrine of the
Trinity stands 'at the head of all dogmatics',[9] for it is from knowing the one who
reveals that we know that the Scripture he gives us is holy.[10] This significantly
nuances traditional Protestant orderings of systematic theology, which not
infrequently began with questions of Scripture as essential prolegomena. Barth
argues that the doctrine of the Trinity belongs precisely in prolegomena, because
it is foundational, a presupposition for any subsequent dogmatic discussion.[11]

This perspective is significant for two further reasons: first, if Barth follows
his own programme, then errors or obscurities in his own trinitarian theology,
designed to stand at the head of his dogmatics, may have far-reaching implications.[12] Secondly, this perspective affects how we encounter non-trinitarian
but allegedly monotheistic faiths: such faiths, Barth implies, do not deal with

---

5. Such criticism classically cites Aquinas' *Summa theologiae* (see also *Summa contra
    gentiles*), but similar points can be made of J. Calvin, *Institutes of the Christian Religion*;
    F. Turretin, *Institutes of Elenctic Theology*; and B. Pictet, *Christian Theology*. Naturally,
    none of these would have accepted that trinitarian dogma was a 'mere' addendum.
6. See R. Letham, *The Holy Trinity* (Philipsburg: Presbyterian & Reformed, 2004), pp.
    271–272.
7. Olson's useful summary, 'Triumphs and Tragedies', p. 665.
8. *CD* I/1, p. 301.
9. Ibid., p. 300.
10. Ibid.
11. It is 'the presupposition of the basic principles that must be set forth in dogmatics
    proper' (*GD*, p. 96).
12. D. W. Jowers notes that if Barth holds heretical views on the Trinity, this would
    'discredit' the whole *Church Dogmatics*; see 'The Reproach of Modalism: A
    Difficulty for Karl Barth's Doctrine of the Trinity', *SJT* 56.2 (2003), p. 231.

God as he really is. Barth's position entails political and social consequences as Christians deal with Muslims and Jews today.

Some relevant characteristics of Karl Barth's theology

Of course, Barth's trinitarian theology does not occur in a vacuum. G. Hunsinger rightly points out the difficulty of finding a single overarching theme in Barth, but helpfully draws attention to the way some major motifs constantly recur in Barth's project.[13] Three motifs are of particular interest here:[14] personalism, antipathy to natural theology and divine freedom.

To begin with personalism, Barth makes much play of 'I–Thou' relations, a network of ideas especially associated with M. Buber.[15] However, Barth has not surreptitiously allowed autonomous human reflection a governing position here.[16] I–Thou relations between God and human beings are definitely Christianized. Hunsinger comments, 'We are made capable in Jesus Christ of what for us (as mere creatures and especially as sinners) would otherwise be impossible, an I–Thou relationship (or pattern of relationships) in the eternal life of the triune God.'[17]

God makes himself so present that humans 'can say Thou to Him and pray to Him'.[18] God addresses us in Jesus, but the mode of address is personalist. For God 'speaks as an I and addresses by a Thou'.[19] This aspect of personal relationship is fundamental for Barth. Humans were created for this: as humans, our 'creaturely being is a being in encounter – between I and thou'.[20] Further, this manner of being comprises our resemblance to the being of our Creator.[21]

---

13. Hunsinger's motifs are actualism, particularism, objectivism, personalism, realism and rationalism; see his *How to Read Karl Barth: The Shape of His Theology* (New York: Oxford University Press, 1991), pp. 3–4.
14. This departs from Hunsinger's classification.
15. In particular, in *I and Thou*, trans. R. G. Smith (Edinburgh: T. & T. Clark, 1958).
16. Hunsinger indicates that Barth was more open to scrutinizing non-Christian thought than some think, discerning and testing it (*How to Read*, pp. 63 ff.).
17. Ibid., p. 42.
18. *CD* I/1, p. 316.
19. Ibid., p. 307.
20. *CD* III/2, p. 203. *CD* III/2 features extensive discussion of I–Thou relations.
21. Ibid., p. 203: 'and in this humanity [of existing as I–Thou beings] it is a likeness of the being of its Creator'.

One way in which Barth has reconfigured Buber's original conception is through the central idea of God as I addressing us in Christ as Thou's. However, we must turn now to other ways in which Barth nuances his personalist account.

Barth's well-known antipathy to natural theology appears in his trinitarian theology too. He closes the traditional door to naturalist speculation in trinitarian theology in his discussion of traces of the Trinity in nature.[22] He comments that while a 'trinitarian' (i.e. threefold) structure can be seen in natural phenomena, this is not necessarily revelation of the Trinity. He writes, 'That there are *vestigia trinitatis* [traces of the Trinity] is undeniable of course; the only question is, of which Trinity?'[23] His point is that we would have to apply some a priori judgment to state that, say, a shamrock illustrated the Trinity.[24] Instead, we must rely on how the Trinity actually has been revealed, that is, in Jesus Christ.

This feature, though, underlines something special about the I–Thou relation between the triune God and a human being. In I–Thou relations between ourselves there is, among other things, mutual self-disclosure.[25] Certainly, our I–Thou encounters with God feature self-disclosure: we must listen to his revelation of himself. Yet an asymmetry arises because God is not dependent on our self-disclosure of ourselves. Barth is aware of discontinuity between these two types of I–Thou relations, noting the importance of divine freedom in explaining it.[26]

Finally, there is the divine freedom. God is never an It to us. This goes further than merely asserting that God is a Thou, to be treated as essentially personal. Instead, as well as never merely being an object for our scrutiny and investigation, God reveals himself as Lord and, as such, free. Barth writes, 'It is thus, as one who is free, as the only one who is free, that God has lordship in the Bible.'[27]

Naturally, these three motifs interrelate. Yet, in a sense, the last, the divine

---

22. *CD* I/1, pp. 334ff.

23. Ibid., p. 343.

24. See A. J. Torrance on the self-ratifying nature of finding God elsewhere than through his revelation ('Trinity', p. 75).

25. In *CD* III/2, pp. 250ff., Barth movingly discusses three qualities in 'being in encounter': (1) one 'looks the other in the eye' (pp. 250ff.); (2) 'mutual speech and hearing' (pp. 252ff.); (3) 'mutual assistance in the act of being' (pp. 260ff.). Mutual self-disclosure belongs in the second category.

26. *CD* III/2, p. 220.

27. *CD* I/1, p. 307

freedom is decisively influential. For I–Thou relationships that feature God as Lord are personal, yet radically different from I–Thou relationships between humans, because we are simply not 'Lord' to each other. Similarly, the impossibility of natural theology and the necessity for this I–Thou relation to be asymmetrically structured around revelation from one party arises from God being the free Lord.

Karl Barth's trinitarian theology outlined

We turn now to some distinctive features of Barth's presentation of trinitarian theology, although for reasons that appear later we must exercise caution not to assume that Barth always held the same position, nor that his positions were completely coherent.

Revelation as the root of the Trinity

For Barth the Trinity is revelation, not speculation.[28] He characteristically states, 'The basis or root of the doctrine of the Trinity, if it has one and is thus legitimate dogma – and it does have one and is thus legitimate dogma – lies in revelation.'[29]

This does not mean merely that the Trinity is a revealed truth. That would be uncontroversial with the theologians whose failure to present the Trinity as prolegomenal he criticizes. Instead, he contends that revelation itself is trinitarian in structure:

> God's word is God Himself in His revelation. For God reveals Himself as the Lord
> and according to Scripture this signifies for the concept of revelation that God
> Himself in unimpaired unity yet also in unimpaired distinction is Revealer, Revelation
> and Revealedness.[30]

This key statement outlines some important elements.

First, the statement 'God's Word is God Himself' suggests that God and his Word are in some way identical. Later statements confirm this. Thus:

---

28. Cf. *GD*, p. 102: 'In sum, I would say that the issue in the doctrine of the Trinity is revelation.' Both *CD* I/1 and *GD* emphasize that the Trinity unfolds the maxim *Deus dixit* (God has spoken).

29. *CD* I/1, p. 311.

30. Ibid., p. 295.

> If we really want to understand revelation in terms of its subject, i.e., God, then the
> first [thing] we have to realize is that this subject, God the Revealer, is identical with
> His act in revelation and also identical with its effect.[31]

One would expect something along these lines given the Nicene concept of
homoousios, which entails that the attributes of nature of the three Persons are
identical.[32] Nevertheless, Barth's willingness to use these terms prepares us for
another marked terminology, that of the Second and Third Persons as 'repetitions' of the First.

Secondly, the phrase 'God's Word is God *Himself*' (emphasis added) suggests Barth may think in terms of a single subject. Some commentators do so construe Barth. Williams writes:

> [I]n I/1, Barth proposed that the event of revelation, although in a sense pluriform, is
> most simply and basically the utterance of a subject (the Father) about himself: in Christ,
> this utterance is projected outwards to men as a true predication about the Father.[33]

Letham also comments, 'Barth's stress is on the oneness of God. It is
"himself" he reveals.'[34] We shall return to this question of what Letham terms
'unipersonality'.[35]

Thirdly, the structure of revealer, revelation and revealedness is clearly tripartite, yet perhaps distinctively 'linear'.[36] For the movement appears to be as follows:

Father ——▶ Son ——▶ Spirit

For revealedness apparently arises immediately out of revelation. Admittedly,

---

31. Ibid., p. 296.
32. For Barth's difficulties with 'Person', see below.
33. 'Barth on the Triune God', p. 180.
34. *Holy Trinity*, p. 274. Cf. J. Thurmer, 'The Analogy of the Trinity', *SJT* 34.6 (1981),
    p. 513, and Pannenberg, *Systematic Theology*, vol. 1, pp. 282, 294, who relate this
    revelation schema to Augustine's psychological analogy of the Trinity. So too
    C. Mostert, 'Barth and Pannenberg on Method, Revelation and Trinity', in
    G. Thompson and C. Mostert (eds.), *Karl Barth: A Future for Postmodern Theology?*
    (Hindmarsh, Australia: Australian Theological Forum, 2000), p. 92.
35. *Holy Trinity*, pp. 275, 278.
36. Williams, 'Barth on the Triune God', p. 180.

'revealedness' seems obscure, but is best taken as the effect or application of revelation.[37] If application of revelation is apt, then seeing a direct logical dependence of revealedness on revelation seems justifiable, and Williams's term 'linear' is felicitous.[38]

Lastly, this seminal statement is not simply in terms of the threefold structure of revelation but also deals with the content of that revelation, that God is Lord.

The importance of trinitarian theology

I have already touched on Barth's contention that the doctrine of the Trinity stands 'at the head of all dogmatics'.[39] Given that revelation functions as the root of the doctrine of the Trinity, it is now clearer why Barth insists on this – any dogmatic discussion, if it is not to be human speculation, must be related to revelation, and revelation is now seen to be trinitarianly structured. This inverts the 'Ritschlian trajectory', which readily saw trinitarian doctrine as alien and Hellenizing. Such views naturally made it possible to conduct Christian theology without substantial reference to the Trinity. By relating the Trinity so strongly to revelation, Barth effectively reverses this so that Christian theology can be conducted only with reference to the Trinity.

Trinity as God is Lord

Barth relates revelation to God's lordship. This unfolds in several ways, lordship relating to content, mode and result.

Thus, most obviously, lordship is the *content* of revelation. Barth writes, 'We may sum all this up in the statement that God reveals Himself as the Lord.'[40] He uses the scriptural and creedal ascription to Jesus of the lordship term *Kyrios* to develop this.[41] He argues the term indicates deity: '*Kyrios* means God – there can be no real doubt about that.'[42]

---

37. See *CD* I/1, pp. 296, 298.
38. Space precludes discussion of the merits of a 'linear' Trinity with respect to the Spirit. But this way of putting things has resonances with Athanasius' *Letters to Serapion*, which draw parallels between the Father–Son relationship and the Son–Spirit relationship. In this way the relation of Son and Spirit is strongly to the fore, appropriately enough given the upper-room discourse in John's Gospel.
39. *CD* I/1, p. 300.
40. Ibid., p. 306.
41. Ibid., p. 400. Barth used the theme of Jesus as *Kyrios* similarly in *GD*, pp. 110ff.
42. *GD*, p. 110.

However, lordship is also the *mode* of revelation.[43] Revelation is a lordly act, a way of acting towards us. Thus, Barth can say, 'In the event which God describes as revelation God deals with man as the Lord . . .'[44] This lordship is hierarchical: 'We are speaking of lordship when one person brings himself to the awareness of another, an I to a Thou, as the bearer of power, when a superior will makes its power known.'[45]

However, lordship in revelation deals also with *result*. Revelation establishes an I–Thou relation, but one, understandably enough, where one I is Lord: 'To acquire a Lord is to acquire what man does in God when he receives His revelation . . .'[46] This suggests that unless one acquires God as Lord, one has not received his revelation.

This stress on lordship raises disquiet for some. Williams comments, 'power, lordship, the master–slave relationship, all play an uncomfortably large part in Barth's system'.[47] Yet Barth's concern for God is noteworthy. Lordship for him carries an important corollary: 'Lordship means freedom.'[48] Thus, revelation, because it has these lordship characteristics, does not result in God becoming an It, an object to dominate and control.

Barth might therefore reply to such criticisms that, far from undermining relationship,[49] he upholds the only relationship humans may properly have with God and that properly maintains the distinction between creature and Creator.[50] Moreover, Barth's clear relating of lordship to divine freedom poses the question whether human repudiation of divine lordship is not related to human objections to divine freedom.

---

43. Cf. *CD* I/1, p. 314: 'God reveals Himself as the Lord; in this statement we have summed up our understanding of the form and the content of the biblical revelation.'

44. Ibid., p. 384.

45. Ibid.

46. Ibid., p. 306.

47. 'Barth on the Triune God', pp. 189–190.

48. *CD* I/1, p. 306.

49. Williams speaks of the lack of 'adult relationship' with God ('Barth on the Triune God', p. 192).

50. Barth insists the covenant relationship of creation is unalterable: 'Sin is not creative. It cannot replace the creature of God by a different reality. It cannot, therefore, annul the covenant' (*CD* II/2, p. 206).

The Holy Spirit

Barth's account of the Holy Spirit is closely tied to revelation and lordship. Revelation becomes manifest to us through the Spirit,[51] but this is not a revelation with independent, different, content.[52] Since the Spirit is genuinely Lord, the revelation he makes manifest does not become ours to master.[53] Rather, Barth argues, 'By the doctrine of the deity and autonomy of the Spirit's divine mode of being man is, as it were, challenged in his own house.'[54]

Barth adds prophetically that the difficulties here are not simply intellectual, but include our wish for this not to be true.[55] Barth's account also has several other noteworthy features.

He argues that the Spirit proceeds from Father and Son, upholding the *filioque* clause of the Western version of the Niceno-Constantinopolitan Creed.[56] Both positive and negative reasons are at work. To support the *filioque*, Barth uses criteria of revelation, that the revealed economy of salvation is indicative of divine relations. Thus:

> But we have constantly followed the rule, which we regard as basic, that statements about the divine modes of being antecedent in themselves cannot be different in content from those that are made about their reality in revelation.[57]

The obvious references here would include John 15:26, where the Spirit's sending is associated with Jesus.

Further, Eastern denials of the *filioque* represent for Barth a speculative method:

> For us the Eastern rejection of the *Filioque* is already suspect from the formal standpoint because it is patently a speculation which interprets individual verses of the Bible in isolation, because it bears no relation to the reality of God in revelation and faith.[58]

---

51. *CD* I/1, p. 449.
52. Ibid., pp. 452–453.
53. Ibid., p. 468.
54. Ibid.
55. Ibid.
56. Ibid., p. 477. Cf. 'He is the eternal Spirit of the Father and the Son' (*GD*, p. 87).
57. *CD* I/1, p. 479.
58. Ibid., p. 480.

This objection is very grave for Barth, because speculative methods on such a subject approach denying divine lordship and freedom in revelation.

However, this quotation also hints at the role of the Spirit more generally. Barth argues in favour of the *filioque* that it 'expresses recognition of the communion between the Father and the Son'.[59] This takes us to another important feature.

Following strongly, perhaps even developing, Augustinian lines of thought, Barth envisages the Spirit as the bond or communion between Father and Son. Thus, in *Church Dogmatics*, he starts to explore the proposition 'We believe in the Holy Ghost, the Lord' from the Niceno-Constantinopolitan Creed:

> This togetherness or communion of the Father and the Son is the Holy Spirit. The specific element in the divine mode of being of the Holy Spirit thus consists, paradoxically enough, in the fact that He is the common factor in the mode of being of God the Father and that of God the Son. He is what is common to them, not in so far as they are the one God, but in so far as they are the Father and the Son.[60]

He then explains

> He [the Spirit] is the *vinculum pacis* [bond of peace] (Eph. 4:3). The *amor* [love], the *caritas* [affection], the mutual *donum* [gift], between the Father and the Son, as it has often been put in the train of Augustine. He is thus the love in which God (loves Himself, i.e., loves Himself as the Father and as the Son and) as the Father loves the Son and as the Son loves the Father.[61]

Yet this Augustinian strand receives a particular nuance from the conception that the Spirit is 'neutral'. *Pneuma* is, after all, a neuter noun. He is definitely divine, for he is 'Lord', but:

> He is it all in a neutral way, neutral in the sense of distinct, i.e., distinct from the Father and the Son whose modes of being are reciprocal, but neuter also in the sense of being related, i.e., related to the Father and the Son, whose reciprocity is not a being against, but a being to and from one another.[62]

---

59. Ibid.
60. Ibid., p. 469.
61. Ibid., p. 470.
62. Ibid., p. 469.

Space precludes investigation of serious questions which this view generates, in particular whether this depersonalizes the Spirit, since the larger question of modalism in Barth, which is addressed below, is in some ways a prior question.[63]

Allegiance to Nicene orthodoxy

Barth's expositions of trinitarian doctrine in both the *Göttingen Dogmatics* and the *Church Dogmatics* follow the Niceno-Constantinopolitan Creed, thereby treating it as highly significant.[64] This is reinforced by his defence in both works of *homoousios*,[65] and although he departs in the *Church Dogmatics* from the Nicene terminology of 'person' in favour of 'mode of being',[66] this is to preserve the patristic concept originally expressed by the term.[67]

These considerations suggest that Barth envisaged his trinitarian theology as essentially consistent with patristic Nicene theology and steered a route between the traditional patristic dangers of subordinationism and Sabellianism.[68] He analyses these ancient heresies afresh, seeing both as eliminating authentic I–Thou relations between us and God, in favour of a relationship in which God has been objectified as less than Lord.[69]

God as unipersonal

We now approach the vexed question of unipersonality. Barth clearly envisages God as in some sense personal:

> For it follows from the Trinitarian understanding of the God revealed in Scripture that this one God is to be understood not just as impersonal lordship, i.e., as power, but as the Lord, not just as absolute Spirit but as person, i.e., as I existing in and for

---

63. Other obvious questions are whether the *vinculum amoris* (bond of love) view undermines the *filioque* position and the doctrine of the Spirit as *homoousios* with the other Persons.

64. Note his comment that the second article of the Niceno-Constantinopolitan Creed is 'the most important record of the Church dogma of the deity of Christ' (*CD* I/1, p. 423).

65. E.g. *CD* I/1, p. 439; *GD*, p. 122.

66. *CD* I/1, p. 355.

67. He thinks the term 'person' has changed its meaning: *CD* I/1, p. 357; cf. Barth, *Dogmatics in Outline*, trans. G. T. Thomson (London: SCM, 1949), pp. 42–43.

68. *CD* I/1, pp. 381–382.

69. Ibid.

itself with its own thought and will. This is how He meets us in His revelation. This is how He is thrice God as Father, Son and Spirit.[70]

This 'I-ness' in God is, of course, logically necessary if he is to have I–Thou relations with human beings. Predictably, Barth's concern is again the divine freedom and lordship – by asserting that God is personal we avoid God becoming an It.[71]

However, the question is whether the triune God is one I or three. In the *Göttingen Dogmatics* Barth had written:

> Three subjects of revelation then? Yes indeed, one cannot avoid working out and establishing this thought . . . three subjects of revelation, three persons, *prosopa*, or *hypostases* of the one divine substance, *ousia*, or *essentia*.[72]

However, the *Church Dogmatics* strikes a different note on the idea of God's personhood: 'But in it we are not speaking of three divine I's, but thrice of the one divine I.' He then construes *homoousios* in the Niceno-Constantinopolitan Creed: 'It forces us really to understand the "persons" as modes of being, i.e. not as two subjects but as twice the same subject (in indissoluble twofoldness of course, as may be inferred from the context of the creed) . . .'[73]

Potentially, this raises an issue not merely of development, but of inconsistency.[74] While there are continuities (Barth repudiates modalism in both works),[75] by the time Barth reaches the *homoousios* discussion in the *Church Dogmatics* he is unhappy to use simple plurals about the subject of divine action, but insists it is the same subject, ultimately thrice. This contrasts sharply with the *Göttingen Dogmatics*, which uses just such plurals of the subject of divine action.[76]

Which position represents Barth's 'doctrine of the Trinity'? The *Church Dogmatics* is best taken as the settled position. Not only was this written after the *Göttingen Dogmatics*,[77] but the position of the *Church Dogmatics* occurs in

---

70. Ibid., pp. 358–359.
71. Ibid., p. 351.
72. *GD*, p. 100.
73. *CD* I/1, p. 439.
74. Letham hints at this (*Holy Trinity*, p. 275).
75. *GD*, p. 101; *CD* I/1, p. 382.
76. It is unclear whether Barth recognized a shift had occurred.
77. *GD* is based on lectures from 1924 to 1925; *CD* from 1932 onwards.

other later work. Thus, Barth says in *Dogmatics in Outline*:

> But when we speak to-day of person, involuntarily and almost irresistibly the idea
> arises of something rather like the way in which we men are persons. And actually
> this idea is as ill-suited as possible to describe what God the Father, the Son and the
> Holy Spirit is. Calvin once mockingly suggested that we should not imagine the triune
> God as all the artists have depicted Him, three manikins or *marmousets*. That is not the
> Trinity. But when the Christian Church speaks of the triune God, it means that God
> is not just in one way, but that He is the Father and the Son and the Holy Spirit.
> Three times the One and the Same, threefold, but above all triune, He, the Father,
> the Son and the Holy Spirit, in Himself and in the highest and in His revelation.[78]

This statement is striking: '*He* [emphasis added] is the Father and the Son
and the Holy Spirit'.[79] This readily points to a single subject and prompts four
observations.

First, because there is only a single subject, Barth speaks about this single
divine subject's triune life as reflexive. For example, Barth writes of the trinitarian processions, 'He brings forth Himself and in two distinctive ways He is
brought forth by Himself. He possesses Himself as Father, i.e., as pure Giver,
as Son, i.e., Receiver and Giver, and as Spirit, i.e., as pure Receiver.'[80] For Barth,
as one Person begets or breathes another, God is bringing forth himself. Intra-
trinitarian relations have, it seems, become reflexive: God deals with himself.[81]

However, secondly, this singleness of subject does not exclude plurality
altogether, because Barth speaks insistently of three different 'modes of
being'. The following passage displays both the single subject idea and the
plurality of modes of being:

> In all three modes of being God is the one God both in Himself and in relation to
> the world and man. But this one God is God three times in different ways, so
> different that it is only in this threefold difference that He is God, so different that this
> difference, this being in these three modes of being, is absolutely essential to Him, so
> different, then, that this difference is irremovable.[82]

---

78. *Dogmatics in Outline*, pp. 42–43.

79. Ibid., p. 43.

80. *CD* I/1, p. 364.

81. Cf. *CD* III/2, p. 218: 'He posits Himself, is posited by Himself, and conforms
    Himself in both respects, as His own origin and His own goal.'

82. *CD* I/1, p. 360.

Thirdly, this single subject, reflexive approach permits Barth to reverse the normal order of the Athanasian Creed. That creed speaks in these terms: 'The Father is God, the Son is God . . .', so that the Person is grammatical subject and 'God' is the predicate. Barth reverses this, to make 'God' the subject and the Person the predicate.[83] Thus:

> The One God, God in the highest, the Only God, is the Father. In pronouncing this word, in saying Father along with the first article of the Confession, we are straightway bound to look ahead to the second, He is the Son, and to the third, He is the Holy Spirit.[84]

Fourthly, this single-subject approach is closely associated with understanding the trinitarian Persons as repetitions: 'The name of Father, Son and Spirit means that God is the one God in threefold repetition . . . He is the one God in each repetition.'[85] Barth takes this language of repetition from Anselm's letter *On the Incarnation of the Word* 15.[86]

Barth feels uncomfortable with the traditional trinitarian terminology of 'Person', because he thinks this term has now greatly changed its meaning. He writes:

> What is called 'personality' in the conceptual vocabulary of the 19th century is distinguished from the patristic and mediaeval *persona* by the addition of the attribute of self-consciousness. This really complicates the whole issue.[87]

Hence Barth argues that Nicene discussions of three 'Persons' are not assert-

---

83. Anselm anticipated Barth here (*Letter on the Incarnation of the Word* 2), worth noting because Barth heavily uses another set of terminology from the same letter: see below.

84. *Dogmatics in Outline*, p. 42. Cf. the statement in *CD* I/1, p. 477: '[F]or God himself is the Father, the Son, and the Spirit'.

85. *CD* I/1, p. 350.

86. Ibid. A. J. Torrance rightly notes the stress on repetition, but the description of this as a metaphor perhaps understates Barth's use of repetition ideas ('Trinity', pp. 80–81). B. L. McCormack likewise articulates Barth's Trinity as 'an eternal repetition of himself in eternity'; see 'Grace and Being: The Role of God's Gracious Election in Karl Barth's Theological Ontology', in J. Webster (ed.), *Cambridge Companion to Karl Barth*, p. 103.

87. *CD* I/1, p. 357; cf. Barth, *Dogmatics in Outline*, pp. 42–43.

ing 'there are three personalities in God'.[88] Given this shift in meaning, Barth prefers 'mode of being' as expressing what 'Person' once did.[89]

Thus, while the three modes of being are genuine, irremovable differentiations in God, they do not amount to three different subjects or self-consciousnesses. We should not prematurely assume that 'subject' and 'self-consciousness' are synonyms.

Evaluation

Summary

All this reveals a trinitarian theology that by the *Göttingen Dogmatics* featured revelation as a key concept in deriving and understanding the Trinity. This is maintained and developed in the *Church Dogmatics* and later, but on the basis of one divine subject who exists in threefold repetition rather than as three divine subjects. This mature theology can be described as 'Augustinian' in at least four respects. Barth holds to the *filioque*, to the Spirit as the *vinculum amoris*, to unity of operation,[90] and to the terminological misgivings Augustine voices over 'Person'.[91] Letham observes that by the *Church Dogmatics* Barth's fear was tritheism,[92] which produces a strong emphasis on God's unity, something with strong Augustinian overtones.

However, the simple label 'Augustinian' is inadequate. Most obviously, Augustine finally retained the term 'Person', whereas Barth substitutes for it 'mode of being', something readily associated with the Cappadocians' terminology of *tropos hyparcheos*. Barth's trinitarian thought could be described as having some Augustinian characteristics, but a Cappadocian terminological twist.

Positives

Barth's stress on revelation is in many respects most welcome. His emphasis helps rescue trinitarian thinking from being an essentially speculative or alien import, and reasserts it as authentically Christian. Rather, his emphasis on the

---

88. *CD* I/1, p. 351. He thinks three 'personalities' would be tritheism.
89. Ibid., p. 355.
90. Inseparable operation is, of course, found in the Cappadocians, e.g. Gregory of Nyssa, *Letter to Ablabius*. Augustine, however, makes great use of it.
91. See e.g. Augustine, *The Trinity* 7.10, 11.
92. *Holy Trinity*, p. 275.

revelation of the Trinity challenges those who deny or marginalize trinitarian thinking whether their theology is not essentially speculative.

Likewise, Barth structures his discussion around the Niceno-Constantinopolitan Creed and thus constantly interacts with it. The arguments of the *Göttingen Dogmatics* and *Church Dogmatics* I/1 could therefore partly be seen as prolonged, if sometimes controversial, interaction with the creed. There is a seriousness to Barth's engagement with, and no wish to depart lightly from, that tradition.

Barth not merely asserts the importance of trinitarian thought in *Church Dogmatics* I/1, but deploys it in his account of divine–human relations. Those relations are cast in I–Thou terms,[93] and the divine 'I' in those relations is established on the basis of a trinitarian scheme of the threefold divine 'I' in his lordship. The Trinity, then, is basic to human existence in family, society, polity, church and so forth, for we are established as 'beings in encounter',[94] beings who engage in I–Thou relations. Much trinitarian thought has since made similar connections, including such fierce critics of Barth as J. Moltmann.[95]

Barth emphasizes that what the Persons are, as Father, Son and Spirit, they are antecedently to revelation.[96] This means that the immanent Trinity cannot for Barth be subsumed into the economic Trinity. This preservation of an immanent Trinity matters for two reasons related to divine freedom. First, it means that God, even though revealed, is not mastered to become

93. See notably *CD* III/2.

94. Ibid., p. 203.

95. Admittedly, not necessarily for Barth's reasons.

96. Of the Father, see *CD* I/1, pp. 384, 391–392; of the Son, see *CD* I/1, pp. 399, 416; of the Spirit, see *CD* I/1, pp. 448, 466.

97. E.g. *CD* I/1, p. 324; cf. P. D. Molnar, *Divine Freedom and the Doctrine of the Immanent Trinity in Dialogue with Karl Barth and Contemporary Theology* (London: T. & T. Clark, 2000), p. ix. B. L. McCormack has recently proposed that Barth should really have been committed to the view that election (God towards us) grounds the trinitarian processions (cf. 'Grace and Being', p. 103). Molnar's *Divine Freedom* is in part an answer to this thinking. K. Hector pursued McCormack's argument with modifications in 'God's Triunity and Self-Determination: A Conversation with Karl Barth, Bruce McCormack and Paul Molnar', *IJST* 7.3 (2005), pp. 246–261. P. D. Molnar has replied in 'The Trinity, Election, and God's Ontological Freedom: A Response to Kevin W. Hector', *IJST* 8.3 (2006), pp. 294–306. At least three different questions are at issue here: (1) did Barth actually think election grounded the trinitarian processions? (2) should Barth have been logically committed to thinking

an It or tool by being revealed.[97] Secondly, this tends to prevent the Creator–creature relation becoming necessary for God.[98]

Another important positive consequence stems from the Persons being who they are antecedently. It precludes views that see the trinitarian relations as contingent, so that the trinitarian identities are identities the Persons enter, but are not necessary or essential to them. That would anyway fit poorly with Barth's account of a single subject, but, worse, would tend to subvert revelation. For one is left asking what lies behind the contingent identities – that hinterland is not revealed. In particular, his approach rules out accounts proposing the Trinity is somehow established by historical events.[99]

Negative questions

Concept or content of revelation?

Barth famously remarked, 'We arrive at the doctrine of the Trinity by no other way than that of an analysis of the concept of revelation.'[100] But this term 'concept' provokes precisely the question whether Barth's revelation basis is really an analysis of a concept rather than of content, that is, of the revelation that actually occurred.[101]

The prime question here concerns the identity of the revealer. Williams wrote that for Barth 'the event of revelation . . . is most simply and basically the utterance of a subject (the Father) about himself'.[102] This might suggest that the Father is the revealer. In fact, Barth's position seems more nuanced. Answering the ques-

---

election grounded the trinitarian processions given what he thinks elsewhere? (3) what are the ramifications of grounding the trinitarian processions in election? Space precludes discussion of the Molnar–McCormack debate, although C. Kaiser, 'The Ontological Trinity in the Context of Historical Religions', *SJT* 29.4 (1976), pp. 301–310, very usefully discusses the independence of the *opera ad intra* (generation, procession) from the *opera ad extra* (creation, revelation) in Athanasius' thinking (pp. 305–306). This bears on the third of these questions.

98. See e.g. *CD* I/1, pp. 420–421, on the way the antecedence of the Son prevents this.

99. The obvious candidate is Moltmann, *Trinity and Kingdom of God*; but see also LaCugna, *God for Us*.

100. *CD* I/1, p. 312.

101. Williams is alive to the distinction, though rightly noting that Barth would not have felt he was dealing only with the concept ('Barth on the Triune God', p. 152).

102. Ibid., p. 180.

tion 'Who is the revealer?', a more prominent formula would run along lines that God reveals himself as Lord in revealing himself as Father and as Son and as Spirit.[103] It is striking that revelation here is reflexive: God reveals himself,[104] although the proposal that God is a single subject ultimately requires this.

Yet the New Testament seems to return a slightly different answer to the question 'Who is the revealer?' For at different points Father, Son and Spirit all appear as revealers. Thus, Jesus identifies his Father as revealer in Matthew 11:25 and also in John 5:37 and 8:18.[105] Equally, though, Jesus appears as revealer. Jesus' extended prayer in John 17 underlines his role as revealer, for he states he has revealed the Father's name (vv. 6 and 26).[106] Likewise, the Spirit appears as revealer, both as the one who inspires the Scriptures,[107] but also as one who illuminates and applies the truth about Jesus.[108] It is not clear, though, why this is not simply an action as a revealer, rather than, as in Barth's schema, being designated as revealedness.

Does it matter that Barth glosses the answer to 'Who is the revealer?' in reflexive terms rather than retaining the individuated, particular answers in terms of the Persons as revealers? Has he lost anything? After all, revelation as an external act of the Trinity may well be covered by the maxim that external works of the Trinity are undivided.[109] Moreover, there is a reflexive element in the Son's revelation in John's Gospel: the Son reveals himself as Son (see e.g. John 5:17ff.).

---

103. See *CD* I/1, p. 295 ('God reveals himself as the Lord'); paralleled at pp. 306, 320 ('He reveals Himself as the Son'); p. 324 ('God reveals Himself as the Father'); p. 448 ('The one God reveals Himself according to Scripture as the Redeemer [the Spirit]'); p. 381 ('But it is God who reveals Himself equally as the Father in His self-veiling and holiness, as the Son in His self-unveiling and mercy, and as the Spirit in His self-impartation and love').

104. Cf. Letham, who has a similar reflexive formulation (*Holy Trinity*, p. 274).

105. The Father provides 'testimony', part of John's revelation vocabulary. Note also Jesus' response to Peter's confession as a revelation by the Father (Matt. 16:17), while at the transfiguration Jesus is designated as Son by the voice from heaven (Matt. 17:5).

106. Note also John 1:18, he 'who is in the bosom of the Father' (NKJV) reveals, and the Johannine theme that Jesus speaks what the Father gives him to say; cf. Jesus as revealer in Matt. 11:27.

107. E.g. Mark 12:36; 1 Pet. 1:11.

108. E.g. 1 Cor. 12:1–3.

109. Found in both Greek and Latin theologians, but emphatically with Augustine.

KARL BARTH AND THE TRIUNE GOD

Several observations should be made in response to the contention that Barth has lost nothing by his reflexive formula. First, the great advocate of inseparable operation, Augustine, is nuanced in his statements. He roots inseparable operation in the inseparable relations of the Persons, stating 'just as Father and Son and Holy Spirit are inseparable, so do they work inseparably'.[110] However, Augustine is also concerned to assert distinction. Thus, he stresses it was the Son, not the others, who was incarnate; the Spirit, not the others, who descended at Pentecost and so forth. This too is rooted in the eternal relations, for the relations are relations with distinctions between the Persons.[111] Augustine's full-orbed account thus speaks of operations that are, in particular cases, distinctively of one Person, but 'not without' the other Persons.[112] It is not enough, then, to appeal to inseparable operation to defend Barth here: one must also ask whether the personal distinctions have been maintained.

Secondly, while the Son may reveal himself as Son, one must remember that 'Son' is a relational term: Jesus reveals himself as someone's son. His self-revelation as Son is not merely reflexive, then, but also of another, as the Jews see in John 5:18.

Thirdly, the New Testament data suggest the Persons reveal each other. Each is the content of revelation.[113] The obvious point is that glossing the revelation of a son by his father as essentially a self-revelation means that the revelation was not by one of another. It is not what it seems to be. We shall return to this point when considering modalism below. Yet it needs to be noted that at points exactly the plurality of subjects and the non-reflexive nature of revelation by the Persons is vital. Thus, in John 8:12–21 Jesus develops the theme of testimony, a central Johannine category of revelation. He is charged in 8:13 with testifying 'about himself' (*peri seautou*). Jesus answers that, though he testifies about himself, his testimony is true (v. 14) and refers (v. 17) to the well-known law that requires corroboration by two or more witnesses.[114] He argues that he bears witness and his Father also bears witness, which satisfies the corroboration requirement. A. Köstenberger comments that 'Jesus states plainly

---

110. *Trinity* 1.7.

111. Ibid.

112. See e.g. Sermon 52 for development of this terminology.

113. The Spirit also is the content of revelation: the Son reveals the Spirit as he introduces him as another paraclete (John 14:16) and explains something of the Spirit's own revelatory role in John 14 – 16.

114. See Num. 35:30; Deut. 17:6; 19:15.

that he and his Father are the two witnesses that attest to his truthfulness.'[115]

There is a difficulty here. If one glosses revelation as self-revelation by one single subject, then it is very hard to see how there is not ultimately just one revealer and, in Johannine terms (since 'witness' is a revelation category for John),[116] just one witness. If there is ultimately only one witness/revealer, then the corroboration requirement is not met, and Jesus' implied command to accept him falls to the ground, for his testimony is invalid. Similarly, in John 5:31 Jesus notes that if he simply bore witness 'to himself' (*peri emautou*), his testimony would not be true. From verse 32 he develops the testimony that others bear, including (v. 37) that of his Father. Again mere self-testimony would eradicate the force of Jesus' point.

Thus, a suspicion arises that Barth's formula obscures the particulars of the interrelations of the Persons, and this affects the content of revelation. The details of the New Testament take us to revelation that is reciprocal (one Person of another), rather than reflexive (a single subject of himself). Nor does Barth's one subject, reflexive formula sit easily with Jesus' own discussion of the revelation he brings.

The Lord who loves in freedom?

Barth emphasizes that revelation must be related to the lordship of God,[117] which involves his free action.[118] The revealed lordship is not loveless but involves an imparting and giving of love.[119] However, this is a self-giving freedom: 'He remains free in His working, in giving Himself.'[120]

However, this prompts reflections similar to those arising concerning revelation. First, this free giving is again phrased reflexively, a giving of himself. The question is whether this involves a loss of trinitarian specificity, for climactic passages of divine giving are phrased as the Father giving the Son. The obvious example is John 3:16. The risk is that with the loss of specificity something about the Father's love in particular is not so much denied as obscured. Our adoptive heavenly Father displays love of this quality, that he does for us what he does not ask Abraham, the earthly father, to do: give his own Son to death.

---

115. *John* (Grand Rapids: Baker Academic, 2004), p. 256; cf. R. E. Brown, *The Gospel according to John*, vol. 1 (London: Geoffrey Chapman, 1971), p. 341.

116. This is used for convenience to refer to the author of the Fourth Gospel.

117. *CD* I/1, p. 306.

118. Ibid.

119. Ibid., p. 381.

120. Ibid., p. 371.

Secondly, the giving of the Son is indeed a free giving, for God wills this. Barth rightly stresses that God's love *towards us* has this essentially gracious, willed quality. Yet the obvious question here is whether the love *between the Persons* is similarly free. The difficulty here is that love between Father and Son seems so fundamental to their relationship in the New Testament.[121] Moreover Athanasius articulated the Nicene position that the relation between Father and Son was not constituted by will,[122] and this Athanasian approach seems to preclude the idea that the Father–Son relation features a giving of love to each other in freedom. Yet, if revelation is of the Lord who loves in freedom and only that, then obviously one asks how we know that God's intra-trinitarian love is not an essentially contingent love in freedom. Barth's references to the Persons as being what they are antecedently do not sit easily with a contingent trinity, yet it is not easy to see how this coheres with his own accounts of the content of revelation.

Thirdly, we must ask whether summarizing the content of revelation as lordship is not too restrictive. John's Gospel again is instructive. John 20:31 sets out the Gospel's purpose as leading to belief that Jesus is the Christ, the Son of God.[123] This certainly includes lordship, as Barth rightly indicates, but by this stage of the Gospel the designation of Sonship has come to define Jesus in relation to his Father, in terms, that is, of intra-trinitarian relationships. In John, Jesus is revealed not merely in his relation to us, as life-giver and future judge (John 5:21–22) but also in his relation to the Father. Clearly, the first category, what God is to us, is vital, as Barth rightly stresses, but the second matters too. In fact, it forms the basis of the Son's relation to us: for the Son who gives life and is to be our judge is this by the gift of the Father and in the Father's love (John 5:20). The Son's identity to us as Lord rests on the intra-trinitarian relations, which are rightly seen as love, but dubiously as love given in freedom.

In fact, Barth's own case seems to require revelation of something more

---

121. Thus, Jesus in John 5:19ff. develops his relationship with the Father in terms emphasizing the Father's love to him, which issues in the entrusting of life-giving and judgment.

122. Athanasius, *Orations against the Arians* 3.60–65. Arians attempted to impose the dilemma that the Son was Son either by the Father's will (and so not truly God), or by necessity imposed on the Father (which was absurd). Athanasius refused the dilemma, stating the Son was Son, neither by will, nor by constraint, but by nature (*kata physin*) (62–67).

123. An alternative translation might run, 'that the Christ, the Son of God, is Jesus'.

than lordship. Lordship readily tends to define God in relation to us. Barth writes, for instance, 'To be Lord means being what God is in His revelation to man.'[124] This obviously risks rooting who God is eternally in what he is in relation to us, which in turn creates pressures to see humanity and creation as necessary for God to be what he is. An unpleasant dilemma lurks here: either to admit God depends on creation to be what he is, lord;[125] or to deny that lordship reveals anything eternal about God. The first alternative violates one of Barth's prime values, God's sovereign freedom from creation. The second alternative subverts revelation as telling us anything essential about God.

Unipersonality and reflexive love

Love of self, not love of other
The issue of reflexivity is raised both by revelation and God's lordship as giving in freedom: for Barth, God reveals himself and gives himself. It is no surprise to find that this reflexivity extends to God's intra-trinitarian love. This too becomes reflexive. Barth writes, 'He [the Spirit] is thus the love in which God (loves Himself, i.e., loves Himself as the Father and as the Son and) as the Father loves the Son and as the Son loves the Father.'[126] This reflects both the idea of the Spirit as the *vinculum amoris* but also that he is the communion in a reflexive, self-love. This is clearly a coherent, indeed inevitable, position to take once one postulates a single divine subject.

Modalist?
The obvious question is whether this is modalist.[127] The *Church Dogmatics*

---

124. *CD* I/1, p. 306. Note here the Molnar–McCormack debate referred to in n. 97 above.
125. This is not unknown: Origen followed something like this line; see *First Principles* 1.2.9.
126. *CD* I/1, p. 470.
127. Jowers lists four grounds on which Barth is charged with modalism: (1) giving ontological priority to unity; (2) a Hegelian Idealist modalism; (3) advocacy of the doctrine of appropriations; (4) the terminological shift from Person to mode of being ('Reproach of Modalism', pp. 241–246). It is unfortunate that the question of the single subject and reflexivity is not dealt with. See also A. J. Torrance, where the full weight of criticism on modalist grounds is not developed at any length in terms of a single subject in reflexive relationship ('Trinity', pp. 81–83). Hunsinger

clearly repudiates modalism,[128] and for some the charge is preposterous. Thus, Hunsinger writes, 'In any case, modalism can be charged against Barth only out of ignorance, incompetence or (willful) misunderstanding.'[129]

However some definitional precision is required before Hunsinger's trenchant dismissal can be shared. Barth objects to modalism because it destroys or relativizes revelation,[130] and references to what constitutes modalism must be seen in this light. For example, 'If we are dealing with His revelation, we are dealing with God Himself and not, as modalists in all ages have thought, with an entity distinct from Him.'[131]

This other entity, distinct from what is given in revelation, is a fourth,[132] and Barth repudiates the idea of a fourth entity: 'The position is not that we have to seek the true God beyond these three moments in a higher being in which He is not Father, Son and Spirit.'[133]

However, real difficulties lurk here. Is Barth's definition of modalism self-evident?[134] Patristic definitions of types of modalism (Sabellianism, Noetianism etc.) are not so restrictive. Such definitions envisage modalism or monarchianism arising when the Father and Son are treated as the same. Augustine delineates Noetians thus: 'Noetians are named from one Noetus who used to say that Christ himself (*eumdem ipsum*) was Father and Holy Spirit.'[135]

---

    likewise suggests objections arise from (1) the terminological shift and (2) the connection of God's free subjectivity with the divine *ousia* (*'Mysterium'*, p. 191, n. 7).

128. E.g. *CD* I/1, pp. 311, 382, 396; *GD*, p. 101. Jowers documents the force of Barth's repudiation ('Reproach of Modalism', pp. 237–240).

129. *'Mysterium'*, p. 191, n. 7.

130. *CD* I/1, p. 382; *GD*, p. 101.

131. *CD* I/1, p. 311.

132. Cf. *CD* I/1 and the reference to modalism as involving a 'neutral, undifferentiated fourth' (p. 396). See Jowers: 'Barth claims modalists posit a quaternity instead of a trinity' ('Reproach of Modalism', p. 239); and A. J. Torrance who also, following E. Jüngel, sees modalism as involving a hidden fourth ('Trinity', pp. 81–82). Hunsinger has a different turn of phrase (cf. *'Mysterium'*, p. 191, n. 7), which is discussed below.

133. *CD* I/1, p. 382.

134. Jowers approaches this question when he writes that Barth opposes 'at least what he conceives of as modalism' ('Reproach of Modalism', p. 238). But this does not ask the question whether Barth's definition matches those of others.

135. *Heresies* 36. Cf. also *Tractates on the Gospel of John* 70.2 (on John 14:7–10), and *Against Maximinus the Arian* 1.13.

Nor is Augustine unrepresentative here, for Hippolytus earlier described Noetian belief likewise as identifying Father and Son.[136] Tertullian similarly insists that the Father is not identical with the Son, as monarchians suggest.[137] The issue is not a hidden fourth, but rather the blurring of distinctions between Father, Son and Spirit.[138]

Does this matter? After all, while the Fathers may not define modalism as involving a hidden fourth, Barth does not simply assert that the Father is 'the same' as the Son: he envisages some difference. However, the question is whether the kind of difference Barth asserts between Father and Son would satisfy patristic opponents of modalism.[139]

Of Barth's defenders on this topic, Hunsinger seems aware that modalism is not necessarily defined as postulating a fourth entity,[140] for he writes, 'Modalism . . . means that the trinitarian *hypostases* are merely manifestations of God in history, but not essential distinctions within the eternal Godhead itself.'[141]

The key term here is 'essential distinctions'. It must be admitted that the adjective 'essential' is scarcely ideal in this context. If Hunsinger means literally 'pertaining to the essence', then he has obliterated the difference between modalism and Nicene orthodoxy. For Nicene orthodoxy says there are no distinctions of *essence*: denial of such distinctions of 'essence' is precisely what the Nicene *homoousios* defends, since *ousia* is in Latin terms 'substance' or 'essence'.

Presumably, Hunsinger did not mean to conflate Nicene theology with modalism, and the obvious alternative construal is that 'essential' here is not employed in its technical trinitarian sense, but simply being used loosely, to mean something like 'very important'. This, though, leaves unclear whether

---

136. *Against Noetus*, e.g. 1.2; 2.3; 2.7

137. *Against Praxeas* 10.

138. As J. N. D. Kelly notes; see *Early Christian Doctrines* (London: A. & C. Black, 1977), p. 115. G. L. Prestige notes the way Origen sees Sabellianism as teaching there is a single Person; see *God in Patristic Thought* (London: SPCK, 1959).

139. Thus, Sabellius recognized difference between the operations in the economy; see Kelly, *Early Christian Doctrines*, p. 122. The point was they were not differences that respected the Persons.

140. Although, one must recall that Barth is right that a fourth entity can constitute modalism.

141. '*Mysterium*', p. 191, n. 7. He does not appear to notice that his definition differs from Barth's.

Barth's conceptions of 'very important distinctions' match the conceptions of Hippolytus, Tertullian and others on what are the 'very important distinctions'. The underlying issue is whether asserting 'very important distinctions', but denying those distinctions actually constitute plural subjects, would satisfy patristic critics of modalism in its monarchian forms.[142]

Misgiving here centres on Barth's reflexive language. Barth writes of the divine generation: 'He brings forth Himself and in two distinctive ways He is brought forth by Himself.'[143] Yet Tertullian appears to think that just such reflexive language about generation is modalist:

> He himself, say they [the monarchians], made himself (*se . . . sibi fecit*) his own Son. Nay but father makes son, and son makes father, and those who become what they are by relationship with another cannot by any means so become by relationship with themselves (*semetipsis sibi*), as that a father should make himself his own son (*pater se sibi filium faciat*) or a son cause himself to be his own father.[144]

Tertullian argues this kind of modalism, constituted by a unipersonal God acting on himself in different ways, is obnoxious because, among other things, it destroys revelation. This appears vividly in Tertullian's account of prayers by the Son on earth to the Father:

> The Son makes request from earth, the Father makes a promise from heaven. Why do you make both Father and Son a liar? If it is the case that either the Father was speaking to the Son from heaven, while being himself the Son upon earth, or that the Son was praying to the Father while being himself the Father in heaven, how is it that the Son should also, by making request of the Father, make request of himself (*a semetipso*) . . .?[145]

Tertullian adds that a god who really turns out to be one under these circumstances is a *deum versipellem* (chameleon or skin-changing).[146] For the prayers apparently comprise, using Barth's terms, an I–Thou relationship, but, on

---

142. Hunsinger sees the accusation of modalism as relying in part on a link between divine subjectivity and *ousia* ('*Mysterium*', p. 191, n. 7). This does not adequately present the problem that revolves around the issue of a single subjectivity.

143. *CD* I/1, p. 364.

144. *Against Praxeas* 10.

145. Ibid. 23.

146. Ibid.

monarchian assumptions, this is not true because there is really only one 'I'. Barth too has just one divine 'I'.

It is difficult at this point to see how Barth could have accepted the exegesis of John 10:30 ('I and the Father are one') that is offered by Tertullian and Hippolytus.[147] They both reject the monarchian modalist idea that this verse can be rendered 'I and the Father are one person', pointing to the use of the plural *esmen* (we are) rather than the singular *eimi* (I am) and the neuter *hen* (one thing) rather than the masculine *heis* (one person). These grammatical points are well made and modern commentators raise similar considerations.[148] Yet if Father and Son are modes of existence of one divine subject, then Tertullian's question seems natural: why did John in 10:30 not write *heis* rather than *hen*? For to speak of the 'subject', whether human or divine, seems to demand a masculine or feminine rather than neuter form. Certainly, God in 'I–Thou' relation to us would not be adequately conveyed by a neuter form.

For Tertullian, Hippolytus and other opponents of modalistic monarchianism, then, modalism in a vicious sense arose when the three Persons given in revelation were reduced to one, so that generation was reflexive, and prayers were reflexive.[149] It was not just if there was a hidden fourth.

One might respond that Barth retains room for an 'I–Thou' relationship in the prayers of the incarnation, but the 'I' of Jesus is a human 'I' only. This, though, will scarcely do, for the 'I' that speaks in the Gospels (and in John in particular) is addressed by others as God and in particular as Lord (Thomas' confession: John 20:28). The 'I' of Jesus consistently portrays itself as the divine Son (see e.g. John 5:17ff.). To reduce this 'I' to being purely human both does violence to what the economy reveals, and also, as the Nicenes charged against the Arians, involves blasphemy, since divine honours are both paid to what is on this hypothesis the purely creaturely 'I' of Jesus by Thomas and also expected by Jesus himself (John 5:23).

Another response runs that Barth is not alone, but merely teasing out a

---

147. Ibid. 22; Hippolytus, *Against Noetus* 7.1; Augustine, *Tractate* 48.9–10. John 10:30 was a lynchpin in modalist argument, judging by *Against Praxeas* and *Against Noetus*.

148. E.g. Köstenberger, *John*, p. 312, n. 72; D. A. Carson, *The Gospel According to John* (Leicester: IVP, 1991), p. 394; Brown, *Gospel according to John*, p. 403.

149. Hence Hunsinger does not grasp precisely the force of the criticism of Barth. He sees the accusation of modalism as relying in part on a link between divine subjectivity and *ousia* ('*Mysterium*', p. 191, n. 7). For Tertullian, Hippolytus and others the problem revolves rather around the issue of a single subjectivity. Apart from anything else, *ousia* had not then acquired its later technical significance.

legitimate strand in Christian orthodoxy, by working with Anselm's idea of a 'repetition of eternity in eternity', the grandiloquent phrase Barth culls from Anselm's *Letter on the Incarnation of the Word*. This takes us to the adequacy of Barth's emphatic 'repetition' language.

We must begin by noting that Anselm, when commenting on the Father and Son as different Persons, repudiates reflexive language: 'For a father is always the father of some-one, and a son the son of some-one, nor is a father ever the father of his very self (*semetipsius*), or a son the son of his very self (*semetipsius*).'[150]

Furthermore, Anselm's phrase *repetatur aeternitas in aeternitate* (repeat eternity in eternity),[151] rendered by Barth *repetitio aeternitatis in aeternitate* (a repetition of eternity in eternity),[152] bears closer investigation. While arguing that the Trinity is not 'a plurality of individuals',[153] Barth applies this language of repetition to the *Persons*: 'The name of Father, Son and Spirit means that God is the one God in threefold repetition . . . He is the one God in each repetition.'[154]

Yet Anselm's original use occurs in discussing not the *Persons*, but the unity of the divine *nature*. *Incarnation* 15 begins by talking about the 'highest nature' (*summa natura*). From there Anselm talks of God as 'pure eternity' (*simplex aeternitas*), in contrast to there being 'several eternities' (*aeternitates . . . plures*). He then argues there is but one eternity, not several. He reasons that several eternities would be either within or outside each other. He first eliminates the possibility of several eternities outside each other, and then proceeds to the other alternative, eternity 'in' (as in 'within') eternity. The phrase *repetatur aeternitas in aeternitate* occurs at this point in the following sentence: 'And if one asserts that there are several eternities within one another, such a one ought to know that there is only one and the same eternity, however many times eternity may be replicated upon itself.'[155] The phrase Barth uses actually occurs, then, in a concession where Anselm argues that even if eternity is repeated 'in' (as in 'within') eternity, this is still only one eternity. Notwithstanding any repetition, there is, in fact, one and the same eternity. Anselm's reason is that a 'nature' (*natura*)

---

150. *Incarnation* 3.

151. Ibid. 15.

152. *CD* I/1, p. 350.

153. Ibid.

154. Ibid. Jowers cites the passage but does not dwell on the implications of taking the Persons as repetitions of one subject ('Reproach of Modalism', p. 234).

155. 'Si vero in se invicem plures esse dicuntur, sciendum est quia quotienscumque repetatur aeternitas in aeternitate, non est nisi una et eadem aeternitas.'

replicated upon itself is in a higher unity than one that admits plurality of itself. From here Anselm then discusses one omnipotence.

This brief account prompts four reflections. First, Barth has taken Anselm's argument about the unity of the divine nature and transferred it to the Persons. Anselm is not discussing the relations of the Persons. Nor is it attractive to envisage Anselm as using terms loosely here: his defence of the incarnation depends on employing 'nature' and 'person' in technical and mutually exclusive senses.[156]

Secondly, if one follows through Barth's correlation of *aeternitas* with Person, then Anselm would be arguing for only one Person, for he is certainly arguing for only one eternity. However, this would be fatal for Anselm's overall argument. For the *Incarnation* is responding to Roscelin's discussion that the Father is incarnate with the Son. Anselm resists this on the basis that there is one nature but several Persons in God, and the incarnation involves one of those Persons, not all, and not the nature, assuming a further nature.[157] His rebuttal of Roscelin depends on plurality of Persons, not unity of Persons. Barth's construction of Anselm opens the door to Roscelin in exactly the way that Anselm wished to close.

Thirdly, by adopting Anselm's reference to the repetition of eternity in/within eternity, and applying it to the Persons,[158] Barth seems to be committing himself to a trajectory that would ultimately eliminate plurality of persons. Barth's argument, on any view, requires some plurality of Persons. But Anselm's 'repetition of eternity' argument is not meant to establish a plurality, but to deny it: even if one were to have a replication of eternities, ultimately there is only one ('there is only one and the same eternity' [*non est nisi una et eadem aeternitas*]). It is, of course, precisely such rendering of the Persons as 'one and the same' that the Fathers from Tertullian to Augustine see as modalist.

Fourthly, as a related point, Barth also seems to be committing himself to a trajectory that would ultimately eliminate personal distinction.[159] To begin with, 'repetition' is not a happy term, since the Nicene idea of personal distinctions does not permit us to say that the Son is a repetition of the Father, and nothing more. Repetition by itself obliterates distinction both as between

---

156. The distinction between person and nature is in view at the start of *Incarnation* 16.
157. See e.g. ibid. 11.
158. *CD* I/1, p. 350: 'The so-called "persons" are a *repetitio aeternitatis in aeternitate . . .*'
159. Jowers understandably dismisses the idea that Barth was a 'conscious modalist' ('Reproach of Modalism', p. 240). That, though, is not quite the issue.

Father and Son, but also as between Son and Spirit. Nicene tradition does not see the Spirit as another Son, nor the spiration of the Spirit as merely another begetting.

In any case, strictly, if we were to substitute 'Father' for 'eternity' in the phrase *repetatur aeternitas in aeternitate*, then we would quite plausibly be committed to saying, 'The Father is repeated in the Father,' and there would thus be two Fathers. This is not Nicene orthodoxy, nor would Barth wish to say this, but it is not clear how this can be avoided once the language of eternity repeating within eternity is applied to the Persons. Even if it were phrased differently, as in 'God is repeated,' again one would have to ask how this repetition manifests the Personal distinctions in which the Father is not the Son and so on. For Anselm is clear that there is only one eternity (*simplex aeternitas*), in contrast to several.

It is tempting to respond that Barth is not open to this criticism, since he does, after all, use the term *tropos hyparcheos* as an alternative to Person. This alternative term has a Cappadocian pedigree, and the Cappadocians are sometimes thought of as irreproachable upholders of personal distinction. However, this response is not convincing. As a term *tropos hyparcheos* tells us only about a mode of being: it is not self-interpreting so as to say what the mode of being in question actually is. Sabellius could say that, in a sense, he subscribed to modes of being.

The question therefore arises whether Barth and the Cappadocians invest *tropos hyparcheos* with the same meaning. For the Cappadocians, such terms are used in contexts where they are stressing what is individuated in the Persons, not what they are in common.[160] Barth, though, as we have seen, has invested *tropos hyparcheos* with the sense of 'repetition' based on a text of Anselm that is discussing *natura*. The one nature is precisely what the Persons have in common, not what they are in their distinction. Moreover, Gregory of Nyssa at least makes use, at least to some extent, of the analogy of three men to the three Persons when discussing personal distinction, something suspiciously close to what Barth emphatically rejects.[161]

One must conclude that Barth's repetition language, founded in Anselm's *Incarnation* 15, is not enough to safeguard the Personal distinctions, but rather undercuts distinction.

The area where this reflexive trinitarian conception, with its modalist tendency, causes most concern is the intra-trinitarian love. Jesus in John 5:19ff.

---

160. Note here Gregory of Nyssa, *Letter to Ablabius*.

161. E.g. *Dogmatics in Outline*, pp. 42–43.

discusses his relationship with his Father, and in verse 20 tells us that the Father loves the Son. One immediately feels the force of objections such as Tertullian's to a modalist reading of the verse that would gloss it as 'God loves himself' or 'The Father loves himself as the Son.' Revelation in the economy would have ceased to take place and a division is created between God in the economy (other-personed love by one subject of another) and God immanently (reflexive love by one subject of himself).

Simply in terms of what constitutes love, reflexive self-love seems very different from other-personed love. Richard of St Victor articulated this:

> For nothing is better than charity; nothing is more perfect than charity. However, no one is properly said to have charity on the basis of his own private love of himself. And so it is necessary for love to be directed toward another for it to be charity. Therefore, where a plurality of persons is lacking, charity cannot exist.[162]

Yet Jesus goes on to develop how his Father loves him in John 5:21–29 and his description seems very far from a reflexive 'private love' of self. For he does this by reference to what the Father gives him, gifts that revolve around the themes of life and judgment.[163] Thus, the Father has given judgment to the Son (vv. 22 and 27) and has also granted life-in-himself to the Son (v. 26), on which basis it is unsurprising that Jesus can give life to others (v. 21; cf. 6:57). Since the quality of life-in-himself is the very kind of life the Father has, it is right to see this gift of life to the Son in verse 26 as a giving outside space and time.[164] Giving, then, is a feature of the Father's relationship towards the Son both in the economy of creation and redemption and also in eternity. Gift is in general a natural enough association for love: one gives to those one loves.

However, it seems odd to characterize gift as a reflexive action. Not only does the text of John 5 speak, at least on the surface, of two subjects, one, the

---

162. *Trinity* 3.2.

163. Appropriately, since the issue in ch. 5 is a healing on the Sabbath and life and judgment are the prerogative powers of God, which are properly exercised on the Sabbath.

164. D. A. Carson writes, 'The impartation of life-in-himself to the Son must be an act belonging to eternity, of a piece with the Father/Son relationship, which is itself of a piece with the relationship between the Word and God' (*Gospel according to John*, p. 256).

Father as giver, the other, the Son as recipient, but the ideas of generosity seem to require two subjects.

Moreover, to reduce this to self-love and self-giving significantly alters the way the Father specifically is characterized. R. A. Culpepper rightly argues that John does not give a list of divine attributes, but establishes divine character through narration.[165] The Father's narrated actions therefore help establish his character. Yet by construing the actions of the Father as reflexive rather than other-person centred, Barth subtly alters the Father's character. It is perfectly true that Barth tells us of a self-giving God, in the sense of giving to us, but it is very difficult to see how his unipersonal structure permits space for the Father specifically to be eternally generous and giving to another, his Son.

Moreover, Jesus elsewhere understands the Father's love for him in ways that seem to presuppose two subjects, not one subject acting reflexively in two modes of being. Thus, in John 10:17 Jesus describes the Father's love as evoked by Jesus' self-sacrificial giving of his life. As Augustine noted, Jesus' passion is something he, not the other Persons, endures, although not without them.[166] Jesus' self-sacrifice is also something he endures in obedience to the Father's will. At this point, the Father's love in John 10:17 looks like the responsive love of one subject towards another for an action that that other subject undergoes.

Further, Jesus' 'High Priestly' prayer of John 17 is not only in prayer form, which as Tertullian notes, seems to demand two subjects, but also asks that the world may know that the Father loves believers even as he loves the Son. (*ēgapēsas autous kathōs eme ēgapēsas*). Jesus clearly envisages a comparison of the Father's love for believers and his love for the Son. Yet his love for believers is manifestly in I–Thou terms, which seems to require two subjects. If there is to be a comparison, then the obvious reading of Jesus' understanding of the Father's love for him is that it is a love of one subject for another, not a reflexive love.

This must be put in the broader context of our own adoptive sonship. Our sonship clearly involves two subjects. In what sense is the Second Person truly a son, if he and his Father are not two subjects? It is not enough to reply that there is a relation of generation or origin, for the data of revelation is more specific: Scripture uses – repeatedly – a specific relation of generation, sonship. One is naturally driven to ask, if divine sonship is so different from all our other experiences of sonship, what exactly is conveyed to us by the use of this term?

---

165. *The Gospel and Letters of John* (Nashville: Abingdon, 1998), p. 88.
166. *Trinity* 1.7.

Conclusion

Barth's contribution to trinitarian theology is mixed. Positively – and all this must be highly valued – he has reasserted Christian monotheism by making the doctrine of the Trinity foundational, as well as fruitfully insisting that this doctrine must be related to God's lordship and freedom, that it forms the basis for our own relations with God and that it must be based on what actually was revealed.

Yet this contribution is undermined in Barth's later work because of his commitment to the notion of a single divine subject, such that the Persons, or modes of being, are repetitions. The idea of repetitions has its ostensible source in Anselm's *Letter on the Incarnation* but represents a reading of Anselm that wrenches Anselm's argument from its original context to fatal effect, applying to the Persons what Anselm discussed in relation to nature. This commitment means God's intra-trinitarian life is reflexive, rather than being reciprocal and mutual as between three correlative subjects. Such reflexive ideas seem to fall within patristic notions of modalism, while Barth's repudiation of modalism rests on a definition that is differently drawn from the patristic sources, with no real discussion of this difference.

This concept of reflexive repetition subverts Barth's commitment to the content of revelation, for, as Tertullian had noted, the revelation in the economy of the incarnation takes us apparently to three divine subjects. Barth's commitment to I–Thou relations is likewise undermined, for, given a single divine subject, it is difficult to see how God can eternally be a Being-in-encounter. At best, this seems only something that he can become, a potential that is realized only with the creation of other 'Thou's' to whom he can be an 'I'. This in turn tends to undermine the commitment to God's being in freedom, for he seems to need creatures in order to be a fully realized Being-in-encounter. Finally, the great casualty is the divine love, and most specifically the revelation of the Father. His love and generosity are rewritten from the revelation of an I–Thou relation to his Son to become a 'private love of himself'.

Jowers rightly foresaw that trinitarian shortcomings could have wide ramifications for Barth's structure.[167] This is so. Three areas may be mentioned here. First, Christology: given Barth's commitment to a single divine subject, a pressing question becomes, 'Who is the Jesus who speaks to people and speaks to his Father?' For if there is one divine subject and one divine self-

---

167. 'Reproach of Modalism', p. 231.

consciousness, what is the self-consciousness in Jesus? Is it human or divine, and are there one or two self-consciousnesses? Secondly, there is the question of Barth's doctrine of election. If Jesus is both the subject of election and its object,[168] and if this depends on Barth's idea of a single subject acting reflexively,[169] and if this understanding is modalist within patristic definitions, as I have shown, then one must ask whether Barth's doctrine of election is not likewise modalist. Thirdly, there are pastoral consequences to be considered, for, as Barth would remind us, theology is a task for the church. Barth's eternal intra-trinitarian love of God is different from the love found in the economy and arguably far less satisfactorily grounds it. Most significant of all, the eternal character of a Christian's adoptive Father has subtly changed: instead of an eternal love of I and Thou, it has become reflexive, a 'private love of himself'.

---

168. See e. g. McCormack 'Grace and Being', pp. 93–94.
169. Ibid., p. 104, citing *CD* IV/1, p. 65.

8. KARL BARTH AND THE DOCTRINE OF THE ATONEMENT

Garry J. Williams

Introduction

This exploration of Karl Barth's understanding of the death of the Lord Jesus Christ will cover some of the wider aspects of *Versöhnung* as 'reconciliation' before moving to consider the way in which he understands the cross as 'atonement'.[1] In particular, given the historic Reformed emphasis on penal substitutionary atonement, attention will focus on Barth's account of Christ's death as penal satisfaction to God. These issues will be considered within the wider context of Barth's understanding of the doctrine of God and his perfections, the election of Jesus Christ, and the covenant of grace. When this

---

1. There are debates surrounding the twofold translation of the term *Versöhnung*, but it is valid to distinguish, as G. W. Bromiley does, between the wider and narrower sense, especially when the context indicates the scope of the intended reference. Bromiley explains his procedure in *CD* IV/1, p. vii. For an objection to Bromiley's approach, see A. B. Come, *An Introduction to Barth's* Dogmatics *for Preachers* (London: SCM, 1963), pp. 200–201. It is hard not to suspect that Come's argument is as much motivated by his evident allergy to what he terms *de haut en bas*, the 'fundamentalist theory of atonement as penal satisfaction' (p. 201), as it is by linguistic considerations.

contextual explanation of Barth's understanding of the atonement is complete, I shall outline a Reformed response to it.

Exposition

Barth as a Reformed theologian

The basis for identifying Barth as in some sense a Reformed theologian can be seen plainly in his biography. It also emerges in the substance of his doctrine of reconciliation, both in his view of the place of the Bible in dogmatics and in the way he criticizes other theological traditions. Barth believes in a form of the principle of *sola Scriptura* (Scripture alone), albeit redefined to accord with his own understanding of the nature of the Bible. He makes this point forcefully in his treatment of election, where in his own mind he departs most markedly from the Reformed tradition. In this context he speaks of 'the basic rule of all Church dogmatics':

> No single item of Christian doctrine is legitimately grounded, or rightly developed or expounded, unless it can of itself be understood and explained as a part of the responsibility laid upon the hearing and teaching Church towards the self-revelation of God attested in Holy Scripture.[2]

Accordingly, Barth follows the Reformers in rejecting Roman Catholicism. His particular concern with Roman Catholic theology is the manner in which it seeks to give control of divine grace to the human creature by dividing it into different types. Thus, he resists distinctions drawn between internal and external grace, between *gratia operans* (operating grace) and *gratia cooperans* (cooperating grace).[3] These, he believes, serve to give control of the external means of grace to creatures. Instead, Barth insists on a single, sovereignly effective grace, and asks, 'Is grace as such ever *sufficiens* [sufficient] without being *efficax* [efficient]? Is it ever effective objectively without being effective subjectively?'[4]

A similar desire to vindicate grace motivates Barth's negative reaction to Arminianism and Lutheranism. Both alike, he argues, exalt man over God by teaching that divine election is based on foreknown faith (*praevisa fides*). A keynote of Barth's theology in its opposition to Arminianism is his emphasis

---

2. *CD* II/2, p. 35. See also p. 148.
3. *CD* IV/1, p. 85.
4. Ibid., p. 86.

on the freedom of God, who is who he is 'not as limited and conditioned by our freedom, but in the exalted freedom of his grace'.[5]

Coupled with his emphasis on divine revelation through the Bible is Barth's famous hostility to natural theology, particularly in the form in which it was found in nineteenth-century liberalism. Barth is here still very much the author of *Die Römerbrief.* He emphasizes that we must not collapse the distance between man and God by viewing Jesus Christ as 'the highest evolutionary continuation' of the 'reality of the world and man'.[6] Such a deduction would invert the proper relationship between Jesus Christ and His creation: 'He does not derive from it: it derives from Him.'[7]

We also find in Barth a riposte to the existentialist theology of his own day. He speaks at the outset of *Church Dogmatics* IV/1 of his 'intensive, although for the most part quiet, debate with Rudolf Bultmann'.[8] Here his concern is above all with the collapse of Christology into anthropology.

Barth thus located himself within the Reformed tradition in his positive emphasis on the Bible, and in his criticism of other theological positions. This location is significant for the exposition and criticism that follows, since it suggests that when we bring to him questions generated from within historic Reformed theology, we are not doing something alien to his own intentions. Barth believed that the Reformed tradition asked the right questions and had the right fundamental theological instincts, but he judged that its own interests could be better served if significant parts of its doctrine, most notably the doctrine of election, were reconstructed. If therefore we press him with challenges from within the Reformed tradition, we are testing him by a standard he himself favoured. For this reason, the ensuing exposition lays out some of the significant aspects in Barth's doctrine when viewed from a classical Reformed perspective.

The centrality of Jesus Christ as reconciliation

Barth maintains that the doctrine of reconciliation is 'the heart of the message received by and laid upon the Christian community and therefore . . . the heart of the Church's dogmatics'. The theology of the Christian church has as its circumference the doctrines of creation and the last things, 'but the covenant fulfilled in the atonement is its centre'.[9] If reconciliation is misunderstood,

---

5. Ibid., p. 39.
6. Ibid., p. 49.
7. Ibid., p. 50.
8. Ibid., p. ix.
9. Ibid., p. 3.

then the consequences are far-reaching: 'To fail here is to fail everywhere.'[10]

Barth emphasizes that Jesus Christ is the centre of reconciliation because it is Jesus Christ who *is* reconciliation. Jesus Christ, he asserts, is 'God in the work of reconciliation'.[11] The very nature of the covenant is in Christ: 'Ontologically, therefore, the covenant of grace is already included and grounded in Jesus Christ, in the human form and human content which God willed to give His Word from all eternity.'[12] So too the atonement: 'Jesus Christ is the actuality of the atonement.'[13] For Barth it is not any formal principle that is the heart of the Christian faith, but Jesus Christ himself: 'the Christian message (in all its content) means Jesus Christ'.[14] Hence, while he endorses Luther's doctrine of justification, he does so with this reservation: 'Only Jesus Christ Himself can be the principle of the doctrine of reconciliation, not justification or any other of the true but secondary forms of His grace.'[15] We do well to remember that the sometimes labyrinthine argument of *Church Dogmatics* IV is at root governed by what John Webster describes as this 'single, and relatively simple, conviction: that Jesus Christ is the summation of God's ways with the world and the world's dealings with God'.[16]

When Barth asserts that Jesus Christ is *Versöhnung* and covenant, he does not mean that the eternal Son of God *as* God is the one in or by whom these realities are found. Rather, he means they are found in Jesus Christ, very God and very man. He emphatically denies we should seek the eternal ground of reconciliation in the Son of God prior to his incarnation, the *Logos asarkos*:

> What is the point of a regress to Him as the supposed basis of the being and knowledge of all things? In any case, how can we make such a regress? The second 'person' of the Godhead in Himself and as such is not God the Reconciler.[17]

---

10. Ibid., p. ix.

11. Ibid., p. 22.

12. Ibid., p. 45; cf. p. 54.

13. Ibid., p. 136.

14. Ibid., p. 20.

15. Ibid., p. 145; cf. also *CD* IV/3.1, p. 173, for Barth's negative comment on G. C. Berkouwer's emphasis on the principle of grace in *The Triumph of Grace in the Theology of Karl Barth* (Grand Rapids: Eerdmans, 1956): 'We are concerned with the living person of Jesus Christ. Strictly, it is not grace, but He Himself as its Bearer, Bringer and Revealer, who is the Victory.'

16. *Barth* (London: Continuum, 2000), p. 137.

17. *CD* IV/1, p. 52.

Barth's great fear here is idolatry: 'Under the title of a *logos asarkos* we pay homage to a *Deus absconditus* [hidden God] and therefore to some image of God which we have made for ourselves.'[18] His concern for the centrality of the incarnate Christ is illustrated by his rejection of the Reformed doctrine of the covenant of redemption between the Father and the Son. Barth thinks that this doctrine entails speaking directly of the *Logos asarkos*, whereas the decree of election should be identified with the incarnate Christ:

> In the divine act of predestination there pre-exists the Jesus Christ who as the Son of the eternal Father and the child of the Virgin Mary will become and be the Mediator of the covenant between God and man, the One who accomplishes the act of atonement.[19]

Similarly, Christ is the eternal covenant: 'He who in Scripture is attested to be very God and very man is also the eternal *testamentum* [testament], the eternal *sponsio* [surety], the eternal *pactum* [covenant], between God and man.'[20] In this deeply significant alteration to the Reformed conception of the divine decree, Barth argues that the incarnate Jesus Christ *is* the decree of God.

Barth is concerned that the electing choice of the *Logos asarkos* would be a hidden choice, and this he regards as unacceptable because God has fully revealed his elective will in Jesus Christ. Barth acknowledges that the Reformed tradition has spoken of Jesus Christ as the mirror of election (*speculum electionis*), but he thinks it has done so inadequately.[21] Identifying the decree as an activity of the eternal Son leaves the ontological sphere of election ultimately unknown. On the contrary, Barth insists, 'there is nothing which is not told us concerning the meaning and direction and nature of God's will for us'.[22] Without this insight, he believes, we are left with a dangerous lack of assurance.[23] Even evangelism, he claims, is proclaiming to people what we can already be sure is true of them.[24]

---

18. Ibid., p. 50. All Greek words in quotations from Barth have been transliterated.
19. Ibid., p. 66.
20. Ibid.
21. Cf. *CD* II/2, p. 60.
22. Ibid., pp. 156–157.
23. Ibid., p. 111.
24. *CD* IV/1, pp. 58, 118.

An innovative order for the doctrine of reconciliation

Having noted the centrality of reconciliation in Christ for Barth, we now consider the ordering of his treatment of the doctrine of reconciliation. Barth is
concerned to clarify the ways in which he is innovating at this point. He therefore first sets out his understanding of the traditional order, which he sums
up as consisting of a doctrine of the person of Christ, a separate treatment
of his work and, usually, a doctrine of the two states of Christ in humiliation
and exaltation. This, he claims, is followed by a doctrine of the subjective
application of the work of Christ and discussion of the church and means by
which a person receives grace. The whole is preceded by a distinct treatment
of sin.[25]

Barth takes a different approach at each of these points. First, he fears that
the traditional separation of the person of Christ from his work leaves the discussion of Christology to be 'arbitrarily constructed'. If the two are detached,
then it will always be soteriology and ecclesiology that will gain attention at the
expense of Christology, because Christology will appear less practical: 'Is not
the Christology ultimately only so much ballast which can be jettisoned
without loss?'[26] Barth therefore thinks that he is preserving the centrality of
Jesus Christ when he orders his treatment of reconciliation within Christology,
beginning with Jesus Christ as God, then as man and then as the unity of the
two. The basic threefold pattern for Christology here, though not the soteriological content, is traditional.[27]

Secondly, Barth rejects the traditional treatment of the two states of Christ
in his humiliation (including both *exinanitio*, the act of incarnation, and *humili-
atio*, the subsequent suffering) and exaltation (*exaltatio*). Barth's particular
unease here is with the construal of the two states of Christ as two stages in
time. Instead, Barth maintains that Christ is always existent in both states in
the indivisible unity of his saving work, 'which cannot be divided into different
stages or periods of His existence, but which fills out and constitutes His existence in this twofold form'. In other words, Jesus Christ is always active in
humility and in exaltation. He is always at once brought low and lifted high.
Barth believes that this reflects the teaching of Scripture. Thus, he asks,

---

25. Ibid., pp. 123–124.

26. Ibid., p. 124.

27. Ibid., p. 126. This threefold pattern structures *CD* IV/1–3, containing chs.
     XIV–XVI. *CD* IV/1 (ch. XIV), is 'Jesus Christ, The Lord as Servant'; IV/2 (ch.
     XV), is 'Jesus Christ, The Servant as Lord', and then IV/3 (ch. XVI), is 'Jesus
     Christ, the True Witness'.

'Where and when is He not both humiliated and exalted (*der Erniedrigte und der Erhöhte*), already exalted in His humiliation, and humiliated in His exaltation?'[28]

It is important here to consider Barth's reading of Philippians 2:5–11, the text most obviously difficult for his position. Having granted that we find there the language of humiliation and exaltation, he makes this comment: 'But if there is, it is not something incidental to His being. It is the actuality of the being of Jesus Christ as very God and very man.'[29] Here we see how Barth is drawing together the two states and the two natures, seeking to identify the action (states) with the being (natures) of Jesus Christ: what Jesus Christ does is who he always is. A further distinctive is that for Barth it is Jesus Christ as God who is humiliated: 'In Him God Himself humiliated Himself (*daß Gott selbst in Ihm . . . sich selbst erniedrigte*).'[30] Berkouwer explains the implication: 'The "God Himself" in the passion of Christ does not stand in need of modification or weakening in the direction of the suffering of the Logos "according to the flesh" but is posited unreservedly as an *essentially* divine humiliation.'[31]

We might think that we find here a monophysite Christology, collapsing the distinction between the two natures of Christ, so that humiliation, proper only to man, has literally happened to the Son as God in his divine nature. This is not what Barth means. Rather, 'God humiliated Himself – not in any disloyalty but in a supreme loyalty to His divine being.'[32] Barth believes that the humiliation of the Son is suited to him because humility belongs to God the Son: 'The humility (*Die Demut*) in which He dwells and acts in Jesus Christ is not alien to Him, but proper to Him.'[33] Barth then connects the concept of humility with obedience and argues that the Son is eternally obedient to the Father. Barth is not, therefore, defining humanity as humbled, and then collapsing the divinity of Christ into his humanity so that it too is humbled. Rather, he finds humility and obedience in the heart of the Godhead. In the same way he rejects a kenotic Christology, since God does not empty himself to assume humility; a God who empties himself of himself is no longer who he is, and so cannot save.[34] Barth thinks 'that it is a difficult and even an elusive

28. Ibid., p. 133; *KD* IV/1, p. 146.

29. *CD* IV/1, p. 133.

30. Ibid., p. 134; *KD* IV/1, p. 147.

31. Berkouwer, *Triumph*, p. 301.

32. *CD* IV/1, p. 134.

33. Ibid., p. 193; *KD* IV/1, p. 210.

34. *CD* IV/1, pp. 183, 185.

thing to speak of obedience (*Gehorsam*) which takes place in God Himself', but holds that we must do so.[35]

Thirdly, Barth is convinced that the doctrine of sin cannot be a separate dogmatic *locus* apart from the doctrine of Christ. The danger of treating sin apart from Christ is the danger of natural theology: 'Who can summon us to keep a law of God which is supposed to be known to man by nature? Who can try to measure the sin of man by such a law?'[36] On the contrary, 'in the light of Jesus Christ the darkness is revealed as such'.[37] Barth's doctrine of sin is therefore developed within his threefold Christological treatment of reconciliation.

Penal substitutionary atonement

In his understanding of *Versöhnung* in the specific sense of the atoning work of the cross, Barth has no time for erroneous distortions of penal substitutionary atonement:

> We do not have here – as in the travesty in which this supreme insight and truth of the Christian faith is so often distorted – a raging indignation of God, which is ridiculous or irritating in its senselessness, against an innocent man whose patient suffering changes the temper of God, inducing in Him an indulgent sparing of all other men, so that all other men can rather shamefacedly take refuge behind his suffering, happily saved but quite unchanged in themselves.[38]

Although Barth attacks this caricature, he repeatedly expresses something that sounds like a penal substitutionary conception of the atonement. First, he is plain on the substitutionary character of the cross. This is evident in his explanation of the meaning of the verb *katallassein* (to reconcile) in 2 Corinthians 5: 'The conversion of the world to Himself took place in the form of an exchange, a substitution, which God has proposed between the world and Himself present and active in the person of Jesus Christ.'[39] Again, Barth finds the exclusive character of the experience of Christ in the Synoptic description of the Garden of Gethsemane, where he is so obviously alone.[40] For Barth,

---

35. Ibid., p. 195; *KD* IV/1, p. 213.
36. *CD* IV/1, p. 141.
37. Ibid.
38. *CD* II/1, p. 402.
39. *CD* IV/1, p. 75.
40. Ibid., p. 268.

substitution is an effective exclusive act, an act that, we might say, defines sinful man out of existence. The substitution of Christ closes the sinner out from the place of the old humanity that Christ has now occupied: 'He has finally judged sin in our place and status (*en sarki* [in the flesh], Rom. 8:3), i.e., He has done away with it as our human possibility.'[41] The powerful effect of this exclusion is based on the identity of the one who atones: because it was the Son of God who died, 'the substitution could be effectual and procure our reconciliation with the righteous God'.[42] In this way, Barth affirms a Christological construal of God's power. He finds an example of such an approach in Paul, who does not infer a general notion of omnipotence but speaks 'of the concrete omnipotence of the God who in Jesus Christ has taken the part and place of man'.[43] Barth thus refuses to follow the Idealists in their attempt to posit the divine attributes simply by extrapolating from human realities, an attempt he regards as ultimately idolatrous.[44] This Christocentric emphasis on effective, powerful exclusion provides support from the theological context for translating *Stellvertretung* as 'substitution'.[45]

Secondly, Barth states that Jesus Christ bore the judgment we merited:

> The Son of God fulfilled the righteous judgment (*das gerechte Gericht*) on us men by Himself taking our place as man and in our place undergoing the judgment under which we had passed (*an unsere Stelle das Gericht, dem wir verfallen waren, über sich selbst ergehen ließ*).[46]

Famously, Barth declares, 'it was the Judge who was judged (*es war der Richter, der da gerichtet wurde*), who let Himself be judged'.[47] This is seen, for example, in the Easter story, when 'the Judge allows Himself to be judged (*der Richter läßt sich richten*)'.[48] It is clear that the judgment in question is eschatological:

---

41. Ibid., p. 75.
42. *CD* II/1, p. 403.
43. *CD* II/2, p. 295.
44. The rejection of Idealist projections is a recurring theme of the treatment of the divine perfections in *CD* II/1.
45. Bromiley comments that he could have done so more often were it not for 'the prevailing prejudice against substitution'; see *CD* IV/1, p. vii.
46. Ibid., p. 222; *KD* IV/1, p. 244.
47. *CD* IV/1, p. 222; *KD* IV/1, p. 244. Hence the title for this section, 'The Judge Judged in Our Place'.
48. *CD* IV/1, p. 226; *KD* IV/1, p. 248.

Jesus submits to John's baptism, which is 'the sign of penitent expectation of the Judge and His *dies irae* [day of wrath]'.[49]

There is, of course, a difference between pronouncing a 'No' on sin and imposing the punishment that follows upon it. Nonetheless, Barth explicitly teaches that Jesus Christ bore the punishment for sin:

> In His doing this for us, in His taking to Himself – to fulfil all righteousness – our accusation (*Anklage*) and condemnation (*Verurteilung*) and punishment (*Strafe*), in His suffering in our place and for us, there came to pass our reconciliation with God.[50]

In another passage Barth expansively rolls together the different terms describing that which Jesus Christ bore for his people: judgment (*Gericht*), destruction (*Verderben*), non-being (*Nichtsein*), nothingness (*Nichtigkeit*) and punishment (*Strafe*).[51] Here we see the gathering of forensic terms such as *Gericht* and *Strafe* with eschatological concepts such as *Verderben* and the distinctive terminology Barth used to describe sin and evil, *das Nichtige*, 'the Nihil'.[52] As we see in this material, Barth is unashamed of speaking about the atonement as a reflexive act, an event in which God acts upon himself: 'He Himself has therefore become the object of His own severity, His own righteous condemnation and punishment in our stead.'[53]

Predestination and the atonement

For Barth it is the predestination of Christ that explains how he comes to be punished in our place. Christ bore all his suffering as the one man predestined for rejection. The predestination of Christ also explains the reflexive action of God in the atonement. As the one who is both the subject and the object of the decree of predestination, Jesus Christ is the one in whom God can act reflexively, as both the one who predestines and the one who is predestined, as both the judge and the judged. In the context of his doctrine of election,

---

49. *CD* IV/1, p. 218.

50. Ibid., p. 223; *KD* IV/1, p. 245.

51. *CD* IV/1, p. 253; *KD* IV/1, p. 278.

52. This is A. C. Cochrane's translation, which, as Herbert Hartwell notes, is to be preferred because it retains a sense of the impossibility but also the power of *das Nichtige*, a sense that alternatives such as 'nothingness' lose. See H. Hartwell, *The Theology of Karl Barth: An Introduction* (London: Gerald Duckworth, 1964), p. 149, n. 83. See below for an example of the assertion that Christ bore hell itself.

53. *CD* II/1, p. 398. Cf. *CD* II/2, p. 494.

Barth even goes so far as to speak of Jesus Christ declaring himself guilty, taking hell upon himself: 'He declared Himself guilty of the contradiction against Himself in which man was involved; . . . He tasted Himself the damnation, death and hell which ought to have been the portion of fallen man.'[54] Furthermore, the predestination of Christ explains the exclusive character of the atonement: he bears sin as the one and only man predestined to rejection: 'He elects Jesus, then, at the head and in the place of all others. The wrath of God, the judgment and the penalty, fall, then, upon Him.'[55] When the rejection has occurred, it cannot be repeated:

> Rejection cannot again become the portion or affair of man. The exchange which took place on Golgotha, when God chose as His throne the malefactor's cross, when the Son of God bore what the son of man ought to have borne, took place once and for all in fulfilment of God's eternal will, and it can never be reversed.[56]

The necessity of penal satisfaction

Barth affirms that God provides satisfaction for sin to himself through the cross: 'Because He is God He has and exercises the power as this man to suffer for us the consequence of our transgression, the wrath and penalty which necessarily fall on us, and in that way to satisfy Himself in our regard.'[57] He also endorses Anselm's 'very accurate and complete' understanding of sin as a form of debt, and of atonement as necessary debt-payment: 'Man as man is bound *Deo reddere quod debet* [to return to God what he owes]. This *debitum* [debt] consists in *rectitudo voluntatis* [uprightness of will], the subjection of his will to the will of God.'[58] Moreover, Barth affirms the necessity of punishment. Without it, if *iniustitia* (injustice) were left unpunished and God saved by mercy alone (*sola misericordia*), then *iniustitia* itself would in some sense have 'the character of a second Godhead in the face of God'.[59] Barth can even speak quite unguardedly in terms of a 'dilemma' for God between the necessity of punishment and His desire to show mercy.[60] For the dilemma to be

---

54. *CD* II/2, p. 164; cf. *KD* IV/1, p. 237.
55. *CD* II/2, p. 124; cf. p. 192.
56. Ibid., p. 167.
57. *CD* IV/1, p. 12; cf. pp. 19, 281.
58. Ibid., p. 485.
59. *CD* II/1, p. 380. On the necessity of righteous punishment, cf. *CD* II/2, p. 493.
60. *CD* II/1, pp. 400–401.

resolved, there must be punishment of some kind. Yet because the free God must be able to be faithful to himself in his mercy, the punishment will be substitutionary punishment rather than the punishment of the sinner.[61] Hence, because God is God, we find righteousness and mercy together at the cross: 'This righteousness clothed in mercy is the meaning of the fact that the Son of God took our place, that He went surety for us, so that our judgment and punishment do not have to be borne by us because they were borne by Him.'[62] This sounds very similar to some presentations of penal substitutionary atonement, but is in fact quite different. When we look more closely, we find that Barth qualifies the role of punishment in the atonement and disagrees with the classical idea of satisfaction.

A qualified role for punishment

Barth limits the place of punishment in the atonement, arguing that 'the decisive thing' is not the bearing of punishment, but the fact that Christ 'has delivered up us sinners and sin itself to destruction'.[63] When he echoes Luther in calling Jesus Christ on the cross 'the one great sinner', Barth does so to maintain the primacy of the destruction of sin over punishment: 'Not by suffering our punishment as such, but in the deliverance of sinful man and sin itself to destruction, which He accomplished when He suffered our punishment, He has on the other side blocked the source of our destruction.'[64] For Barth, the punishment of sin is a means to another, higher end, the termination of sinful man and his replacement by the new man constituted in Jesus Christ.

The unity of satisfaction and forgiveness

Given his affirmation of much of the case of Cur Deus homo, it is surprising to find Barth stating that 'our way has diverged from that of Anselm'.[65] Barth explains that he disagrees with Anselm's 'remarkable assertion that it is not worthy of God to forgive man his sin sola misericordia [by mercy alone], and therefore purely and absolutely and unconditionally'.[66] In particular, Barth questions the idea that 'divine forgiveness has to be thought of as conditioned

---

61. Ibid., p. 401.
62. Ibid.
63. CD IV/1, p. 253.
64. Ibid., p. 254.
65. Ibid., p. 486.
66. Ibid.

by a prior satisfaction for the hurt done to the divine glory, by the restitution of that which man has stolen from God'.[67]

In the passages cited earlier Barth attacks the idea of forgiveness *sola misericordia*, yet here he approves of the same idea. How can he do both? It seems that each passage is saying the same thing from a different side. In his affirmation of the need for satisfaction, Barth is insisting that an act of divine mercy must always stand together with satisfaction. In his affirmation of salvation by mercy alone, he is insisting that an act of satisfaction to divine righteousness must itself always be an act of mercy. In each case the fundamental claim is the same: satisfaction and mercy must always be held together as a single act. When Barth denies salvation by mercy alone, he is denying that mercy could exist without satisfaction. When he affirms it, he is insisting that there can be no possibility of an act of satisfaction as a necessary separate prerequisite for an act of mercy. The two must always be one. The evidence for this harmonization is the way in which Barth resists the idea of a distinct act of righteousness prior to the act of forgiveness:

> Is the incarnation of God, which is the goal of the whole sequence of Anselm's thought, really no more than the fulfilment of a prior condition which enables God to forgive in a manner worthy of Himself? Is it not itself the real accomplishment of His pure, absolute and unconditional forgiveness, His forgiveness *sola misericordia*? Is Jesus Christ only the possibility and not rather the full actuality of the grace of God?[68]

Thus, Barth denies that the incarnation is the kind of satisfaction that serves only to remove an obstacle so that the real business of forgiveness can proceed elsewhere.

Satisfaction to the love of God

In a still deeper disagreement with Anselm, Barth denies that God is the enemy of man prior to reconciliation. Paul, he insists, does not 'speak of an enmity of God against man which is removed by the atonement'.[69] Barth claims that even the wrath of God in Romans 1 'consists solely in a description of the corruption of man to which God has given him up'.[70] Again, he comments that

---

67. Ibid.
68. Ibid., p. 487.
69. Ibid., p. 74.
70. Ibid.

the thought that Christ satisfied God 'or offered satisfaction to the wrath of God . . . is quite foreign to the New Testament'.[71]

The reason Barth can speak of men deserving hell and of 'God's annihilating turning from me', while being unwilling to speak of God as man's enemy, seems to lie in his doctrine of God.[72] For Barth, it is axiomatic that we can know God only by knowing who he is in his acts: 'God is who He is in His works.'[73] Barth is not here thinking of any general works; he favours the maxim *latet periculum in generalibus* (the danger lurks in generalities), and holds that it is the specific act of God in Christ that reveals who God is.[74] There is an ongoing debate over whether Barth thinks that Christ constitutes the being of God.[75] Whether or not

---

71. Ibid., p. 253.
72. Ibid.
73. *CD* II/1, p. 260.
74. For the maxim, see e.g. *CD* II/2, p. 48.
75. McCormack finds the logical priority of act over being in Barth; see his 'Grace and Being: The Role of God's Gracious Election in Karl Barth's Theological Ontology', in J. Webster (ed.), *The Cambridge Companion to Karl Barth* (Cambridge: Cambridge University Press, 2000), pp. 97, 103. In *CD* II/1, Barth makes unequivocal statements that should warn us away from thinking that he prioritizes God's act over his being. See e.g. *CD* II/1, p. 260, where, after saying that 'God is who He is in His works', he goes on, 'He is the same even in Himself, even before and after and over His works, and without them. They are bound to Him, but He is not bound to them.' In *CD* II/1, pp. 305–306, Barth maintains that 'God as *causa prima* [first cause] cannot be both *causa* and *causatum* [that which is caused], but only *causa*' and insists that 'the divine being . . . is in need of no origination (not even an origination from itself)'. On the freedom of creation and the independence of God, see further *CD* II/1, pp. 273, 280, 311. In a later article replying to E. Chr. van Driel, McCormack answers such evidence by arguing for a development in Barth's position away from the more traditional view found up to and including *CD* II/1; see 'Seek God where He May Be Found: A Response to Edwin Chr. van Driel', *SJT* 60.1 (2007), pp. 65–66. Amazingly, McCormack even wishes to push beyond Barth's explicit position in making election determinative of the Trinity; see esp. 'Grace and Being', pp. 101–102. The debate concerning the relationship between election and divine freedom can be followed in McCormack, 'Grace and Being'; P. D. Molnar, *Divine Freedom and the Doctrine of the Immanent Trinity: In Dialogue with Karl Barth and Contemporary Theology* (London: T. & T. Clark, 2002); 'The Trinity, Election, and God's Ontological Freedom: A Response to Kevin W. Hector', *IJST* 8.3 (2006), pp. 294–306; K. W. Hector, 'God's Triunity and Self-Determination:

that is so, it is at least clear that for Barth the being of God is to be understood wholly from his act. This means that the cross reveals who God is:

> He took our place because He was God's eternal Son, because it was manifest in Him that God's eternal being is mercy, because there is nothing more real and true behind and beyond this substitution, because this substitution is the very essence of God's own being, of His divinity.[76]

Barth's assertion that 'it was manifest in Him that God's eternal being is mercy', I suggest, shows why he will not allow the idea that there is any removal of divine enmity in the atonement. God is who he is in Christ, and in Christ he is revealed as being merciful towards us, so he is always and only merciful towards us. He can have no enmity to be satisfied.

Accordingly, although Barth affirms the idea of satisfaction, it is not the divine hostility to sin that is satisfied, for God does not require retribution for sin to himself and his own justice. Rather, the divine love is satisfied by the destruction of sinful man through the cross. In a payment from the divine love to the divine love, the divine love is satisfied because God has done enough to bring human sin to an absolute end. It is the payment for sin only in the sense that love provides what it needs:

> The worst had to happen to sinful man: not out of any desire for vengeance and retribution on the part of God (*nicht aus irgend einer göttlichen Vergeltungs- und Rachsucht*), but because of the radical nature of the divine love, which could 'satisfy' (*genug tun*) itself only in the outworking of its wrath against the man of sin, only by killing him, extinguishing him, removing him. Here is the place for the doubtful concept that in the passion of Jesus Christ, in the giving up of His Son to death, God has done that which is 'satisfactory' or sufficient (*Genügende getan*) in the victorious fighting of sin to make this victory radical and total.[77]

Foonote 75 (*continued*)

    A Conversation with Karl Barth, Bruce McCormack and Paul Molnar', *IJST* 7.3 (2005), pp. 246–261; E. Chr. van Driel, 'Karl Barth on the Eternal Existence of Jesus Christ', *SJT* 60.1 (2007), pp. 45–61; McCormack, 'Seek God'.

76. *CD* II/1, p. 375.

77. *CD* IV/1, p. 254; *KD* IV/1, p. 280. D. Lauber, *Barth on the Descent into Hell: God, Atonement and the Christian Life* (Aldershot: Ashgate, 2004), p. 18, describes this as a 'significant alteration' from the earlier position in *CD* II/1. The ensuing references to II/1 will show why the alteration may not be so great.

In this way the wrath of God is an operation of his love to humankind, and not of hostility. God is not our enemy; he is implacably opposed to the sin that threatens his plan of love, and the operation of this opposition is 'wrath'. There is therefore no distinct penal operation of divine wrath not contained within the purposes of divine love. The love of God, intended by him to save, confronts those who persist against it: 'The love of God burns where they are, but as the fire of His wrath which consumes and destroys them.'[78] The reverse also holds: no act of mercy is not also and at once an act of righteousness. The more we see mercy, the more we see righteousness:

> It is where the divine love and therefore the divine grace and mercy are attested with the supreme clarity in which they are necessarily known as the meaning and intention of Scripture as a whole, where that love and grace and mercy are embodied in a unique event, i.e., in Jesus Christ, that according to the unmistakable witness of the New Testament itself they encounter us as a divine act of wrath, judgment and punishment.[79]

The rejection of an unaccompanied operation for divine righteousness is evident when Barth comments on this definition of the attribute given by the seventeenth-century Lutheran systematician Johannes Quenstedt:

> The justice of God is the perfect and immutable uprightness of the divine will requiring from the rational creature what is right and just. And it is either remunerative, by which he graces the good with rewards, or vindicative, by which he visits the evil with punishments.[80]

Barth questions the idea that God could ever act solely out of such a desire for retributive justice: 'If God in His righteousness is simply exacting, i.e., rewarding the fulfilment of His demands and punishing their non-fulfilment, how in His mercy can He take to heart the suffering of man?'[81] If God acts outside his mercy, then how is he still the God who is merciful? For Barth, an act of

---

78. *CD* IV/1, pp. 220–221.
79. *CD* II/1, p. 394.
80. My translation from ibid., p. 377: 'Iustitia Dei est summa et immutabilis voluntatis divinae rectitudo a creatura rationali quod rectum et iustum est exigens. Estque vel renumeratrix, qua bonos praemiis, vel vindicatrix, qua malos supliciis afficit.'
81. Ibid., p. 378.

justice according to Quenstedt's definition could not be an act of the God whose being was revealed at the cross.

The unity of the divine attributes in action

Barth's pairing of mercy and righteousness is a specific instance of his general understanding of the way in which the divine attributes (he prefers the term 'perfections') are to be understood as working together. Even as he distinguishes perfections of freedom from perfections of love, he insists that the two series must be neither collapsed nor separated: 'the unity of God must be understood as this unity of His love and freedom which is dynamic and, to that extent, diverse'.[82] There is no set of perfections that describes more literally the being of God than any other. There are no *attributa absoluta* (absolute attributes) that access the divine being in a way the *attributa relativa* (relative attributes) cannot; all of the absolute attributes are also relative. Barth puts it tellingly: what God is 'there in the height for us and for our sakes, here in the depths He is also in Himself'.[83] The distinction between immanent and transcendent descriptions of God has only heuristic significance.[84]

The integration of the divine perfections further illuminates the way in which Barth understands the self-satisfaction of God. The divine righteousness will never act apart from mercy, especially since both are perfections of love. Barth cannot admit the possibility of God in his justice acting simply and solely to inflict punishment on evildoers. He believes his position here combines Luther's insight that righteousness is always also mercy with Anselm's that mercy is always also righteousness. There can be no alternating between the two.[85]

This conjoined operation of divine righteousness and mercy explains why Barth can affirm the reality of the wrath of God and the constancy of reward for right and wrong: 'God does not need to yield His righteousness a single inch when He is merciful.'[86] All the requirements of righteousness are maintained at all stages because the outworking of divine love always entails the complete negation of sin. Thus, Barth's criticism of Quenstedt's formulation should not be taken as a denial of *iustitia distributiva* (distributive justice): 'The mistake of the orthodox dogmaticians was not that they held fast to this

---

82. Ibid., p. 343.
83. Ibid., p. 345.
84. Ibid.
85. Ibid., p. 380.
86. Ibid., p. 383.

concept, but that they did not follow the direction of Scripture and include and explain in their understanding of this concept the mercy of God.'[87] There is no exercise of divine righteousness that God ever intends to be separate from his mercy.

This observation leads us to the final aspect of our consideration of Barth's view of the atonement. If there is no exercise of righteousness outside the divine love, does this mean that God's love is effective for all?

The universal subjective effect of the atonement

Barth holds that the reconciling act of atonement, as God's act, 'is the most actual thing in heaven or earth. Effective by Him, it is effective as nothing else is effective.'[88] Here we touch again on Barth's denial of the Roman Catholic distinctions between different kinds of grace: there is one grace, and it is effective. The external gracious work of God in the act of Christ is not to be divided from the internal work of God in the sinner. The latter is contained within the former, and is therefore as certain as the former. For Rome to recognize the unity of grace, she 'would have to learn to trust that the genuinely subjective is already included in the true objective, and will be found in it and not elsewhere'.[89] The work of Christ is not, therefore, something external, which is then applied to the sinner, let alone something that might not be applied to the sinner. Rather, the sinner is included within the objective work of Christ:

> What He has done is not just something which applies to us and is intended for us, a proffered opportunity and possibility. In it He has actually taken us, embraced us, as it were surrounded us, seized us from behind and turned us back again to Himself.[90]

There is, therefore, no unrealized anthropological potential in the work of Christ, but the actual redefinition of all men:

> This human action and suffering has to be represented and understood as the action and, therefore, the passion of God Himself, which in its historical singularity not only has a general significance for the men of all times and places, but by which their situation has objectively been decisively changed, whether they are aware of it or not.[91]

---

87. Ibid., p. 382.
88. *CD* IV/1, p. 83.
89. Ibid., p. 87.
90. Ibid., pp. 88–89.
91. Ibid., p. 245.

Given the exclusivity of the cross, the category of condemned men is now evacuated of any content:

> The reconciliation of the world with God has taken place in Christ. And because it has taken place, and taken place in Christ, we cannot go back on it. The sphere behind it has, in a sense, become hollow and empty, a sphere which we cannot enter. The old has passed away, everything has become new.[92]

How then is it that men come to be included in Christ? For Barth the problem of the inclusion of humanity in Christ is a puzzle, principally because he is acutely aware of the existentialist prioritization of the anthropological over the Christological:

> And what do we find in R. Bultmann in our own day (*Theol of the N. T.*, E. T., 1952, I, p. 252)? 'By Christ there has been created nothing more than the possibility of *zōe*, which does, of course, become an assured actuality in those that believe.' This is the very thing which will not do.[93]

How then does 'the *Christus pro nobis tunc* [Christ for us then]' become 'the *Christus pro nobis nunc* [Christ for us now]'?[94] For Barth this problem is not merely a theoretical puzzle; it is a spiritual problem that arises from the sense that Christ can have nothing to do with sinners, a problem 'gathered up in' Peter's anxious exhortation to Jesus: 'Depart from me, for I am a sinful man, O Lord.'[95] Here is an example of what Webster has described as Barth's 'abiding sense that the difficulties which attend theological work are not solely or even primarily problems which have to do with cultural or historical or intellectual context; they are spiritual'.[96] Barth finds his answer in the inclusive resurrection of Jesus Christ from the dead. As the cross excludes all men from condemnation, so the resurrection, as the reversal of the death of the cross, is the inclusive resurrection of all men. The stronger the emphasis on effective death, the stronger the emphasis on effective life. The old world has gone, 'and in His life its own life and that of the future world is before it'.[97]

---

92. Ibid., p. 76.
93. Ibid., p. 285.
94. Ibid., p. 288.
95. Luke 5:8, cited in ibid., p. 290.
96. Webster, *Barth*, p. 171.
97. *CD* IV/1, p. 311.

The universal extent of the covenant and election

Behind Barth's view of the universal subjective effect of the atonement lies his understanding of the scope of the creation covenant. As the work of Christ is universal, so is the covenant of which it is the fulfilment.[98] Jesus Christ is the fulfilment of this universal covenant with creation, so that the 'original covenant with man' is 'the presupposition of the atonement'.[99] This means that there can be no-one outside the covenant: 'Just as there is no God but the God of the covenant, there is no man but the man of the covenant: the man who as such is destined and called to give thanks.'[100]

This universality may also be inferred in other ways. The reprobation of Christ means that there are no other people rejected. Because Jesus Christ is the one rejected man, and because his rejection satisfies the love of God, there is no space left for others to be rejected: 'God's rejection has taken its course and been fulfilled and reached its goal, with all that that involves, against this One, so that it can no longer fall on other men or be their concern.'[101] In Jesus Christ we therefore find 'the absolute subordination of the rejecting to the electing will'.[102] Thus, when Paul speaks of mercy and hardening in Romans 9, both acts are contained within the single elective act of God's will, which is a will to have mercy:

> The contradiction of *eleei* [he has mercy] and *sklērynei* [he hardens] is bracketed by this *thelei* [he wills], the one purpose of God in the election of His community. As will be stated in Rom. 11:32 with complete unambiguity, this purpose is the purpose of His mercy.[103]

Under this single elective purpose all of the acts of God are contained. The priority of election results in Barth maintaining what he terms a 'purified Supralapsarianism'.[104] The purification consists of removing any hint of a limited scope for election, while the doctrine remains supralapsarian because all of God's works are subordinate to his first intention to save all men.[105] In

---

98. Barth finds evidence for the universality of the covenant at many points within the OT; see ibid., pp. 26–34.

99. Ibid., p. 37.

100. Ibid., p. 43.

101. *CD* II/2, p. 319. Cf. *CD* II/2, pp. 450, 453, 496.

102. *CD* II/2, p. 421.

103. Ibid., p. 221.

104. Ibid., p. 142.

105. *CD* IV/1, pp. 7, 9. This pattern is clearly reflected in Barth's doctrine of creation in *CD* III.

this revision of supralapsarianism we find a reflection of Barth's prioritization of mercy:

> God's mercy and righteousness are both active in God's dealings with believers and unbelievers. But in view of the unity of the divine essence, we must at once ask whether it is possible to allocate the two attributes to different dealings of God, as though only His mercy were at work in the one case and only His righteousness in the other.[106]

Against such a possibility, Barth holds that 'predestination consists positively in *electio* [election], and does not include *reprobatio* [reprobation]'.[107]

Critique

Introduction

Several aspects of Barth's doctrine of reconciliation obviously resonate with Reformed theology. Barth accords a higher place to the Bible than his liberal predecessors; he believes in the centrality of covenant theology; he boldly affirms the effective character of divine grace and the work of Christ; he opposes those whom the Reformed have historically opposed, and he writes in a way that communicates the joy of knowing the Lord Jesus Christ. These concerns and emphases are real in his work, and the critique that follows is not meant to deny them.

However, there may be a danger in simply suggesting that one aspect of Barth's work can be enjoyed and another rejected. Such an approach presumes that his theology is divisible into wholly distinct parts, and that problems at individual points will not permeate the whole. This raises a vital question for any evaluation of Barth's mature theology: is it so consistent that it must be accepted or rejected *in toto*, or can aspects of it be preserved for us by his inconsistency? Cornelius Van Til vividly expresses the former view: 'Christianity is like an organism. Cut the tap-root of a pin-oak, and it is as good as dead even though every leaf on it is still green. Cut the heart out of a man, and he is dead even though all the members may squirm with "life" for some time.'[108] Others, such as G. C. Berkouwer, are more ready to find 'the power-

---

106. *CD* II/2, p. 16.
107. Ibid.
108. *Karl Barth and Evangelicalism* (Philadelphia: Presbyterian & Reformed, 1964), p. 28.

ful influence of the Word of God' protruding through the errors; indeed, Berkouwer describes this protrusion as 'the secret of the history of dogma' throughout the ages.[109] This is a fascinating disagreement, but its resolution lies beyond the scope of this chapter. At the most we might find hints of an answer in this one area that could suggest a line of enquiry elsewhere. We turn, then, to the specific task of developing a response to the particulars of Barth's doctrine of the atonement.[110]

The order of the doctrine of reconciliation

Barth rightly insists on the integration of Christology and soteriology, and his warning about the danger of their separation is confirmed by the witness of history. Moreover, it is hard to object to his insistence that the order of dogmatic treatment must reflect the shape of dogmatic content.

However, there are limitations. A formal separation between closely related dogmatic *loci* is unavoidable because of the imperative of heuristic utility. Barth himself mentions that separation may appear to be 'didactically useful', but he is not persuaded, because the New Testament has no distinct treatment of Christology.[111] But the same criticism could be made of Barth's own separations. Where, for example, is election treated separately from soteriology in the New Testament? Yet they are formally separate in the *Church Dogmatics*. The alternative to a formal separation of elements that are properly united would be a single strand of argument that would at every stage be so integrated as to be unfathomable to the reader. Such ultimate integration, such incomprehensible *simplicitas* (simplicity), is reserved for the God whom theology describes, and is not available to theology itself. It is proper to *theologia archetypa* (theology as it is in the mind of God himself) and unattainable by *theologia ectypa* (theology as it is among finite creatures). Further, even if two *loci* are formally separate for heuristic purposes, one can still be formulated in the light of the other, just as Barth's doctrine of reconciliation is formulated in close

---

For his critique of Barth, see esp. *The New Modernism: An Appraisal of the Theology of Barth and Brunner* (Phillipsburg: Presbyterian & Reformed, 1946); and *Christianity and Barthianism* (Philadelphia: Presbyterian & Reformed, 1962).

109. *Triumph*, p. 389. In *CD* II/1, pp. 294–296, Barth himself finds similar protrusions in some of the nineteenth-century writers he criticizes.

110. My critique will approximately follow the order of the outline, except that the centrality of Christ will be treated at the end rather than the beginning. The reasons will become apparent.

111. *CD* IV/1, p. 124.

connection with his doctrine of election. I make these points not to disagree with the integration Barth makes, but merely to demonstrate that all integration has limitations, and to suggest a more sympathetic reading of earlier historical formulations.

With the treatment of humiliation and exaltation the issues are more substantial. It is very hard to see how Barth's formulation can take full measure of the biblical data concerning the marked difference between the crucified and ascended Lord. The main difficulty with Barth's ahistorical reading is his definition of humiliation. He has drawn the eternal 'obedience' (*Gehorsam*) and 'humility' (*Demut*) of the Son so close to his incarnate 'humiliation' (*Erniedrigung*), that he has understated the shocking novelty of the incarnation. Indeed, he explicitly affirms that while the incarnation is a *novum mysterium* (new mystery) from our perspective, the divine humility means that it is not so for God. But this obscures the difference between humility and humiliation. Certainly, the Lord Jesus in humility humbled himself to humiliation, but humility and the humiliation that results from it are distinct. While God the Son is in some sense eternally 'humble' in his relationship with the Father, he is not eternally humiliated. Barth's exposition sees a small step from obedience and humility to humiliation. By contrast, Reformed theology views humiliation as a state into which the Son entered at a point in time, which then intensified until it ended decisively with his resurrection from the dead. Specifically, humiliation was the condition in which the Lord Jesus existed without the public manifestation of his glory. It was his condition when, existing in two natures perfectly united, his glory was not publicly revealed. The humiliation of the Son of God always arose from his obedience and humility, but it went beyond obedience and humility. In this sense, the earthly Christ was humiliated in a way the ascended Christ is not, and was humiliated in a way the Son certainly is not in his eternal relationship with his Father.

This clarification of the wide difference between humility and humiliation highlights the difficulty with Barth's attempt to extend the humiliation and exaltation of Jesus Christ throughout his existence and to correlate it with the two natures. Although, as we saw earlier, Barth does not formally collapse the two natures, he draws them too closely together when he reduces the step from humility to humiliation. By contrast, the historic two-stage understanding served to secure the difference between man and God because it understood the humiliation of the Son of God as happening to him in his human nature prior to his resurrection. The incarnation brought humiliation to the Son, something wholly new he experienced in this his new, human nature. The more closely Barth identifies the eternal condition of the Son with his condition as a man, the less we shall see of the new and wonderful character of the incarnation. Certainly, we must say with Barth that God was humiliated in the humiliation of Christ, but we say this with more wonder than Barth because we maintain a greater ontological distance between the humility of the eternal Son and his incarnate humiliation. This gap is bridged by the hypostatic union of the two natures, not by redefining the divine nature. We thus affirm the humiliation of God in the same way we affirm the Athanasian paradox *apathōs epathen* (he suffered impossibly) or the Virgin Mary as *Theotokos* (bearer of God). Such statements express both the reality and the wonder of the union of the two natures in one person.

Barth's reply at this point might be that the meaning of God's deity 'can be learned only from what took place in Christ'.[112] Taken as it stands, this principle is a vital one for all Christian theology. But we must affirm that the Son of God in eternity is in some respects different from what we see of his human life. For if we define who God is by an exhaustive point-for-point correspondence with the incarnate Christ, then God will end up sharing all of the attributes of man. Berkouwer presses this point, arguing that the same logic would require us to say unqualifiedly that God died as God, which Barth does not do.[113] Faced with such outcomes, all theologians, including Barth, maintain some kind of implicit or explicit criteria for distinguishing the characteristics that should be predicated of Christ's deity on the basis of his humanity from those that should not. Compassion, for example, is freely inferred, while death is not. But even with compassion there are differences, for the compassion of the eternal Son as God is not associated with the physical phenomena that accompany strong human affections. In making such distinctions we do not 'go behind' the incarnate Son; if Jesus Christ reveals that his incarnate body is created, then it is precisely by speaking of his pre-incarnate disembodied life that we take seriously the revelation of the incarnation. Likewise, if the incarnate Christ reveals that as God he is eternally glorious and not humiliated, then to project his humiliation on to his divine life is to disregard what has been revealed.

Just as Barth's doctrine of the two states of Christ is in danger of obscuring the historical character of the humiliation of the Son, so also his relocation of the doctrine of sin within the doctrine of reconciliation runs the risk of flattening the historical character of God's revelation. At one level Barth makes a very important point when he emphasizes that it is only in relation to Jesus Christ that we discover the nature of sin. This certainly follows, for example, from the parable of the wicked tenants (Matt. 21:33–44), for it is in

---

112. Ibid., p. 177.
113. *Triumph*, p. 307.

the treatment of the son that the full wickedness of the tenants is exposed. In the same parable we do, however, find a caution about pushing this point too far: before the tenants set eyes on the son and kill him, they have already killed several of the owner's servants. The history of Israel, which the parable depicts, permits and even requires us to speak of sin before we speak of the Lord Jesus Christ. As Paul argues, it is the sin of Israel under the law that silences the world (Rom. 3:19), and this sin was evident even prior to her rejection of the Son. While it is true that the rejection of the Son reveals the full depth of sin, we cannot push this Christological insight so far as to deny the place of the revelation through Israel's history.

I do not mean here to side with Reformed biblical theologians against their brother systematicians; to decide, for instance, for Johannes Coccejus and against Gisbertus Voetius. My point is simply that no systematic theology can safely argue a position that undermines the propriety of the progressive nature of revelation. Biblical theology recognizes and follows the historical order that God himself has followed in his acts and in his word, and thereby shows that there is another position between understanding a doctrine solely on the basis of the final revelation of God in Christ and constructing a natural theology. Perhaps reading the long history of Israel's sin makes a systematic theological point that cannot be made in another way. Certainly, our systematic theology may safely follow the historical pattern of fall, Israel and Christ.

Satisfaction to the love of God

Opinions are divided on the question of whether or not Barth teaches a penal substitutionary doctrine of the atonement. According to Cornelius Van Til, it is plain that 'Barth does not hold to the orthodox doctrine of the substitutionary atonement.'[114] By contrast, H. Cunliffe-Jones thinks that Barth endorses penal substitution, though he disapproves, writing of Barth's 'disastrous retrogression to the uncritical use of the penal substitutionary theory'.[115] Cunliffe-Jones is challenged by R. G. Crawford, who argues that Barth uses familiar terminology but has 'moved beyond' penal substitution.[116] B. L.

---

114. *Has Karl Barth Become Orthodox?* (Philadelphia: Presbyterian & Reformed, 1954),
     p. 171. So too F. H. Klooster, 'Karl Barth's Doctrine of Reconciliation', *WTJ* 20
     (1958), p. 183; Come, *Introduction*, p. 201; H. Blocher, 'The Sacrifice of Jesus Christ:
     The Current Theological Situation', *EuroJTh* 8.1 (1999), p. 25.
115. 'The Meaning of the Atonement Today', *Theology* 74 (1971), p. 119.
116. 'The Atonement in Karl Barth', *Theology* 74 (1971), p. 358. So too Lauber, *Descent*,
     p. 35.

McCormack takes a different view again, claiming that Barth's revised idea of satisfaction rescues the doctrine of penal substitutionary atonement:

> It was not until the twentieth century that a theologian emerged who was finally able to overcome the deficiencies in the satisfaction theory as traditionally set forth in Reformed theology and to give it a more solid foundation. That theologian was Karl Barth.[117]

Although McCormack is correct to identify Barth's redefinition of satisfaction, he underestimates the way in which it alters penal substitution beyond recognition.

Barth's redefinition of satisfaction is incompatible with the depiction of God's wrath in the New Testament. For example, he maintains that Romans 1:18 identifies the wrath of God solely with the 'corruption of man to which God has given him up', but this is not what the passage says. We do indeed find a catalogue of the effects of the divine No to sin, but these effects are the result of a disposition in God against sinful man. Paul does not say that these things constitute the sum of the wrath of God; rather, they reveal the wrath of God. Behind the action stands the hostile personal disposition of God towards sinners.[118]

The distance between Barth and Paul emerges yet more starkly in Barth's exegesis of Romans 12. Barth's repudiation of a certain conception of divine retribution constitutes a rejection of the very terms Paul himself uses in ascribing retributive intent to God:

> For the sake of this best, the worst had to happen to sinful man: not out of any desire for vengeance and retribution on the part of God (*einer göttlichen Vergeltungs- und Rachsucht*), but because of the radical nature of the divine love, which could 'satisfy'

---

117. 'For Us and For Our Salvation: Incarnation and Atonement in the Reformed Tradition', in idem, *Studies in Reformed Theology and History* 1.2 (Princeton: Princeton Theological Seminary, 1993), p. 28. J. Terry, 'The Justifying Judgement of God', *Anvil* 22.1 (2005), p. 34, agrees that Barth can strengthen penal substitution. Cf. the way in which Lauber misrepresents the tradition and then contrasts Barth with it in *Descent*, p. 19.

118. Barth has an unusual account of the revelation of the wrath of God in the gospel itself, but the issue of the nature of the wrath with which we are concerned here stands regardless of where the wrath is revealed. On the revelation of wrath in the gospel, see *CD* IV/1, pp. 392–396.

itself only in the outworking of its wrath (*ihres Zornes*) against the man of sin, only by killing him, extinguishing him, removing him.[119]

Barth here seeks to hold on to 'wrath' (*Zorn*) as the killing of sin, without positing any divine desire for 'retribution' (*Vergeltung*) that precedes it. But Paul, as translated by Luther, sees wrath as a manifestation of God's active intention to seek retribution: 'Beloved, never avenge yourselves, but leave it to the wrath of God (*dem Zorn Gottes*); for it is written: "Vengeance (*Die Rache*) is mine, I will repay (*ich will vergelten*), says the Lord"' (Rom. 12:19, Luther's 1545 translation).

According to McCormack's criticism, the problem with the traditional view of satisfaction is that it makes the incoherent claim that God is at once the friend and the enemy of man.[120] Is it possible to understand how God might simultaneously love and hate a sinner? A popular explanation attaches hatred to the sin and love to the sinner, but this fails to grasp the relationship between the two, as Alan J. Torrance argues: 'Sin is not ontologically insignificant or incidental. It denotes what we *are*, that is, our "being-in-act" and our whole orientation – our "minds." We are not essentially God's lovable friends and hostile only in our extrinsic acts.'[121] Rather, it is necessary to grasp that the sinner is loved and hated by God in different ways. The coexistence of love and hate would indeed be self-contradictory if it entailed God acting in mercy toward a sinner and condemning him at the same time and in the same manner. Such self-defeating action would be impossible. But there is no contradiction in God hating the sinner when he regards him in himself as a child of Adam, and yet loving him when he regards him as a child of God chosen in Christ. The unconverted sinner is regarded by God in this twofold way, and his status is changed in history when God unites him to Christ through faith, so that the sinner dies and a new man lives in Christ under the love of God. Adam is dead; Christ now lives. While this may involve some of the puzzles that arise in any attempt to conceive of how the eternal God relates to history, it does not entail any particular contradictions. Here again, Barth is in danger of collapsing the processes of history into a single state in which the end defines the whole. He risks so nullifying any idea of transition from God's hostility to his mercy that

---

119. Ibid., p. 254; *KD* IV/1, p. 280.
120. 'For Us', pp. 26–27.
121. 'Is Love the Essence of God?', in K. J. Vanhoozer (ed.), *Nothing Greater, Nothing Better: Theological Essays on the Love of God* (Grand Rapids: Eerdmans, 2001), p. 132, n. 33.

he undermines the historical change that takes place in God's relationship with his people.

The unity in action of the divine attributes

While Reformed theology affirms the simplicity of God and thus his unity, Barth's account of the unity of the attributes in every divine action is quite different. It is one thing to say that divine mercy and righteousness must always agree in their outworking when they are both exercised at the same time toward the same creature. This is a common Reformed affirmation, often exemplified in a Christological reading of Psalm 85:10. It is quite another thing to claim, as Barth does, that 'divine mercy necessarily precedes' righteousness. Barth eschews the picture of the divine attributes as points on the surface of a sphere, all equidistant from the centre, thereby rejecting the classical doctrine of divine simplicity.[122] Such a privileging of mercy is incompatible with the equal ultimacy of the divine attributes entailed by the classical and Reformed doctrine of God.

Barth's view of the attributes is problematic because it renders the mercy of God necessary, and thereby undermines the character of mercy as mercy and impinges on divine freedom. Barth would surely reply that he thinks that the exercise of divine mercy is indeed free because God has chosen to be the merciful God: this is the free will of the electing God. The difficulty with this claim is that it places Barth on the horns of a dilemma. On the one hand, he might say that the mercy seen in Christ reveals who God is in himself because we know that God reveals himself as he truly is. Much that Barth says points in this direction, for example: 'The mercy of God lies in His readiness to share in sympathy the distress of another, a readiness which springs from His inmost nature and stamps all His being and doing.'[123] In this case, because God in Christ is always and only merciful, God is necessarily merciful. But then his mercy is not chosen or free.[124] On the other hand, the mercy seen in

---

122. *CD* II/1, p. 376.

123. Ibid., p. 369.

124. It is interesting that McCormack grants that he cannot explain how God is free in his eternal self-determination given that he will not allow a concealed God behind God prior to the choice: 'I may not be able to explain *how* an eternal decision is free, but I know of a certainty *that* it is. I know that it is because its content is grace and grace is not grace unless it is free.' That, of course, simply begs the question. See 'Christ and the Decree: An Unsettled Question for the Reformed Churches Today', in L. Quigley (ed.), *Reformed Theology in Contemporary Perspective* (Edinburgh: Rutherford House, 2006), p. 141.

Christ may not reveal who God is in his essence, because he is indeed free to be otherwise. Other passages point in this direction: 'From all eternity God could have excluded man from this covenant. He could have delivered him up to himself and allowed him to fall.'[125] But in this case we do not know God as he is, or at least not as he might be. The balance of evidence suggests that Barth takes the former route rather than the latter. This appears particularly in his understanding of God's being in act. Barth insists that God's righteousness is always preceded by his mercy in his actions. Because God is who he is in his act in Christ, this shows us that the perfection of righteousness in God himself is always preceded by the perfection of mercy. But if this is so, then God cannot be free, either in being or act, to choose whether or not to intend mercy. Although Barth asserts God's freedom not to be merciful, his affirmations are contradicted by his understanding of the divine being and acts.

For Reformed theologians such as John Owen, the same pattern of inference applies, but it is unproblematic because it pertains to divine justice rather than mercy. The logic can be mirrored as follows. On the one hand, we might say that the righteousness seen in Christ reveals who God is in himself because we know that he reveals himself as he truly is. In this case, because God in Christ is always and only righteous, God is necessarily righteous. If that is the case, then his righteousness is not free: God cannot act without it. On the other hand, the righteousness seen in Christ may not reveal who God is in essence because he is indeed free to be otherwise, in which case we do not know God as he is, or at least as he might be. The latter conclusion is unacceptable, but the former is without difficulty, because it is not inimical to the nature of divine righteousness to be necessary, provided that the necessity is internal to God's own life.

The difficulty for Barth is that to render mercy necessary is to contradict its very nature, a problem that does not arise with justice. Paul Helm explains:

> If God has to exercise mercy as he has to exercise justice then such 'mercy' would not be mercy. For the character of mercy is such that each person who receives it is bound to say 'I have no right to what I have received. It would have been perfectly consistent with God's justice had I not received it'. And so in this respect the logical character of mercy is vastly different from that of justice.[126]

---

125. *CD* II/2, p. 166. See also *CD* IV/1, pp. 79–80.
126. 'The Logic of Limited Atonement', *SBET* 3.2 (1985), p. 50.

Some critics have concluded from this kind of argument that historic Reformed theology denies that mercy is an attribute of God at all.[127] But, among others, Owen is emphatic: 'To prove mercy to be an essential property of God, it is sufficient that he exercises it towards any: for in this very matter, that ought to be set down as a natural perfection in God which is the proper and immediate source and ground of that operation.'[128] This is more than a mere assertion. The principle here is that the universal exercise of an attribute does not arise from its naturalness to God's being, but from its nature as an individual attribute. In our examples, the universal equity that justice requires demands the kind of universal exercise that the very nature of mercy precludes. Like Barth, the Reformed can therefore affirm that God's acts reveal his being, but they can accommodate without difficulty the Scriptural testimony that he intends both mercy and hardening. Mercy does not necessarily precede in God's actions, and it therefore does not necessarily precede in his being. The divine attributes are exercised as befits their character. The Reformed can thus maintain that the God who is free to act mercifully or not is truly merciful, while Barth has undermined the nature of divine mercy.

This criticism of Barth's account of the divine attributes also shows the problem with his claim that the covenant of redemption is unnecessary because God does not need to decide to unite his mercy and his righteousness. If mercy is natural to God but is not therefore necessarily exercised, then there is space for him to decide to act mercifully in certain ways before the foundation of the world. Understanding the nature of divine mercy reopens the way to maintaining, with the Reformed, a particularist covenant of redemption.

In making this observation we find ourselves already moving from the nature of the atonement to its intended scope. The moment of transition between the two aspects is an appropriate juncture at which to demur from a criticism of Barth made by Berkouwer, with whose 'great book' I am largely in agreement.[129] Berkouwer objects to Barth's inclusive view of the cross:

---

127. For this reading of Owen and Jonathan Edwards, see J. McLeod Campbell, *The Nature of the Atonement* (London: Macmillan, 1915), p. 54.

128. J. Owen, 'A Dissertation on Divine Justice', in W. H. Goold (ed.), *The Works of John Owen*, 23 vols. (Edinburgh: Banner of Truth Trust, 1967), vol. 10, p. 581 (i.11).

129. The description is that of Barth himself, who, as a result of reading *The Triumph of Grace*, repented of his dismissive comment on the Dutch neo-Calvinists who dared to criticize Mozart as 'men of stupid, cold and stony hearts to whom we need not listen'; see *CD* III/4, p. xiii. He makes amends with the 'great book' comment in *CD* IV/2, p. xii.

The Church confesses 'not we, but He' as the *essential* element in Christ's vicarious suffering. Sometimes Barth gives the impression that he wishes to express this thought also as, for instance, when he speaks about the *exchange*. But from everything it appears that this exchange does not exclude but *includes* our extinction.[130]

For Berkouwer, this inclusive understanding means that Barth's account of substitution is 'wholly different' from that of the church.[131] But this objection is flawed. There is nothing novel in speaking inclusively of the atoning death of Christ on the basis of the doctrine of union with Christ, so long as this emphasis is held alongside affirmations of Christ's exclusive experience of eschatological punishment. Owen, for example, argues that God punishes Christ inclusively:

> The federal head and those represented by him are not considered as distinct, but as one; for although they are not one in respect of personal unity, they are, however, one, – that is, one body in mystical union, yea, *one mystical Christ*, – namely, the surety is the head, those represented by him the members; and when the head is punished, the members also are punished.[132]

The connection between penalty and inclusion is also found among the Fathers, for example Cyril of Alexandria, who writes that 'we have paid in Christ himself the penalties for the charges of sin against us'.[133]

The extent of the atonement

The difficulty with Barth's account of inclusivity is not with the idea of involvement in Christ's death, but with the universal scope of that involvement. As we have seen, one of the major implications of Barth's redefinition of divine wrath is that he cannot envisage an occasion on which God would intend only retribution against one of his enemies. Retribution might come if an enemy refuses the divine grace, but God would never intend his wrath to act apart from his

---

130. *Triumph*, p. 317.
131. Ibid. Donald G. Bloesch finds the same difference; see *Jesus is Victor! Karl Barth's Doctrine of Salvation* (Nashville: Abingdon, 1976), pp. 50–51.
132. 'Dissertation', vol. 10, p. 598 (ii.15).
133. My translation from Cyril of Alexandria, *De adoratione et cultu in spiritu et veritate*, in J. P. Migne (ed.), Patrologia graeca (Paris, 1857–), 68, p. 296 (iii.100): 'ektetikotōn hēmōn en autō tō Christō tōn eis hamartian aitiamatōn tas dikas'.

love.[134] When we are dealing with the cross, there is a sense in which Barth is right that the divine wrath can be accounted for within the divine love. God wills to punish sin in the atonement in order to spend his wrath, to remove the obstacle to the application of his love to the sinner. In this sense, the wrath of God spent on the cross is entirely framed within an intention of love for those for whom Christ died. But is it always the case that divine wrath is simply the outworking of rejected love? Does God intend the salvation of all?

We find a striking confirmation of the usefulness of reading Barth against a historic Reformed background when we compare one of his illustrations of the effect of the cross with one used by Owen. Barth seeks to show how the death of the world has been accomplished in the death of Christ, and how Christ's life reveals the future of the world:

> By way of illustration, let us suppose that the kingdom of heaven is like a king whom it has pleased to confer on someone an order. Now normally the man will be in the happy position of being able to receive the distinction. But there may be the abnormal case when because of pressing or tragic circumstances, or because he is hindered by outside forces, he is not in a position to do this. Is it not clear that in both cases the will and act of the king form a complete action, and all is well and good for the recipient even in the second and abnormal case? Has he failed to receive the order because he could not do so in person?[135]

In Barth's view, of course, the answer is a firm No. But compare with this an illustration John Owen uses against the Arminian idea of a universal, and therefore not universally effective, atonement:

> When a man hath obtained an office, or any other obtained it for him, can it be said that it is uncertain whether he shall have it or no? If it be obtained for him, is it not his in right, though perhaps not in possession? That which is impetrated or obtained by petition is his by whom it is obtained. It is to offer violence to common sense to say a thing may be a man's, or it may not be his, when it is obtained for him; for in so saying we say it is his. And so it is in the purchase made by Jesus Christ, and the good things obtained by him for all them for whom he died.[136]

---

134. So too McCormack, 'For Us', pp. 28–29.

135. *CD* IV/1, p. 312. By 'order' (*Orden*, *KD* IV/1, p. 344) Barth of course means some kind of honour, not a command.

136. 'The Death of Death in the Death of Christ', in Goold, *Works of John Owen*, vol. 10, p. 233 (ii.5).

Here, then, we find that Owen and Barth are at one in their insistence on the effectual nature of the atonement. But there is a crucial difference. For Barth alone, the 'alteration' of every man 'is not dependent upon the way in which it is regarded, upon whether it is realised and fulfilled in faith or unbelief'.[137] Barth differs from Owen, and from the Reformed tradition, in speaking of the atonement as effective in the recreation of humanity apart from faith in Christ. This difference takes us inevitably to the issue of Barth's universalism. In one sense this issue is the province of those investigating his eschatology, but at the level of its basis in reconciliation it falls within the bounds of our discussion here.

It is clear that Barth is not formally a universalist, since he believes we cannot bind the freedom of God by teaching the *apokatastasis* (restoration).[138] Nonetheless, he speaks strongly of sin as having 'no possibility – we cannot escape this difficult formula – except that of the absolutely impossible (*schlechthin Unmöglichen*)', and of being 'a definite possibility even if it is only the impossible possibility (*unmöglichen Möglichkeit*)'.[139] Barth's construction of an impossible possibility cannot be thought simply to preserve the vital insight that, in the light of God's perfect truth, abundant goodness and certain victory over his enemies, sin is nonsensical. For he describes sin not just as irrational but also as an 'ontological impossibility (*ontologische Unmöglichkeit*)'.[140] For Barth, sin is a failed refutation of our true humanity. He gives a graphic description of the sinner's impossible self-contradiction: 'All his mistakes and confusions and sins are only like waves beating against the immovable rock of his own most proper being and to his sorrow necessarily breaking and dashing themselves to pieces against this rock.'[141] Barth speaks of sin as 'neither a creature nor itself a creator'.[142] He seems to echo here the classical language of sin as *privatio boni* (privatation of the good), as self-annihilative *non ens* (non-being), but he actually holds that the view of sin as mere absence of the good fails to express its enslaving power and the way in which it actively opposes true reality.

The main difficulty here, which has often been noted before, is the tension

137. *CD* IV/1, p. 312.
138. E.g. *CD* II/2, pp. 417–419; *CD* II/2, pp. 422–423.
139. *CD* IV/1, p. 410; *KD* IV/1, p. 454; *CD* II/1, p. 503; *KD* II/1, p. 566.
140. *CD* III/2, p. 136; *KD* III/2, p. 162; cf. Berkouwer, *Triumph*, pp. 215–234. Barth confirms that he means more than the incomprehensibility of sin in his comments on Berkouwer's book; see *CD* IV/3.1, p. 176.
141. *CD* IV/1, p. 91. On the futility of the attempt, cf. *CD* II/2, pp. 316, 346, 349.
142. *CD* IV/1, p. 140; cf. *CD* II/2, p. 295.

between Barth's statements about the effectiveness of Christ's work for all and his insistence on the possibility of a final No to God. Barth himself recognizes that as we consider the cross and resurrection, 'theological consistency' might incline us to universalism, but he allows it only as something for which we may hope and pray, not something on which we may count.[143] I say 'only', but we must take seriously the fact that an emphasis on the hope of universal salvation recurs frequently in Barth. Moreover, Barth cannot deny the demands of consistency by locating the effectiveness of Christ's work in mere possibility, or even in its objective effect apart from its subjective application by faith.[144] We have seen how he enunciates with emphasis his conviction that the outworking of the atonement for individuals is not merely a possibility dependent on a further subjective act. It is this insistence that invites scrutiny. As Berkouwer puts it, 'the asking of the apokatastasis question is not illegitimate but is warranted by the simple fact of taking Barth seriously'.[145]

As we stare at this puzzle, Barth's doctrine of the atonement begins to unravel. The problem can be put very simply: either Christ's work is effective for all, and all will be saved, or it is effective only for some, and only they will be saved. Neither outcome is acceptable to Barth, but one or the other must follow from what he writes. It is impossible for Christ's work to be effective for all in Barth's specific sense and yet for any of them to perish. If someone perishes, then the effectiveness of the work must either be redefined, or else it must be limited to a particular group, the elect, as in historic Reformed theology. Given that any redefinition that allowed some to perish would deny the efficacy and sufficiency of grace, the Reformed doctrine of particular redemption is the only alternative. Here lies one of the great curiosities of Barth's theology: he is at one with the Reformed on the effectiveness of the atonement, but he has departed from them on the extent of the divine intention. He is quite clear that the 'grim doctrine' of particular redemption must be rejected.[146] This leaves Barth in an impossible position, maintaining two contradictory claims: that Christ died effectually for all, and that we cannot be sure that all will be saved.[147]

---

143. *CD* IV/3.1, pp. 477–478; cf. *CD* II/2, p. 296.

144. The attempt is made e.g. in J. D. Bettis, 'Is Karl Barth a Universalist?', *SJT* 20 (1967), pp. 435–436.

145. *Triumph*, p. 112.

146. *CD* IV/1, p. 57.

147. O. D. Crisp, 'On Barth's Denial of Universalism', *Them* 29.1 (2003), pp. 18–29, gives a characteristically svelte statement of the dilemma and presses it home ruthlessly.

Many respond at this point that the Reformed, driven by a demand for logical coherence, are seeking to go where the Bible does not go. Sometimes this response appears to be a denial of the need for logic in theological reasoning, but such an extreme position is unsustainable. If such a deep aporia as Barth's is tolerable, then all meaningful speech ought to cease. The very discussion in which we are engaged is rendered impossible if we can happily abandon the law of non-contradiction. If someone defends Barth and disagrees with my criticism by attacking its presupposition of logic, then I may simply reply that I maintain my criticism and yet still agree with them. We can, by definition, no longer contradict one another. Discourse is dead.[148] This is not to deny that there are many things mysterious to the Christian, but mystery is different from flat contradiction. Mystery requires our humility, but contradiction, a quite different thing, would preclude thought.[149]

The more sophisticated form of this criticism does not reject logic itself but the particular form of logic used by Barth's critics. For example, James B. Torrance, writing on the issue of the extent of the atonement, attacks the use of the 'logic of Aristotle' with its dichotomy of 'actuality' and 'possibility', favouring 'the logic of the incarnation'.[150] Thomas F. Torrance argues that the choice pressed on Barth between universalism and particular redemption arises only if we adhere to what he terms the 'Latin heresy' with its Aristotelian 'notion of external logico-causal connections'.[151] Similarly, George Hunsinger rejects charges against the coherence of Barth's position on divine sovereignty and human freedom that are 'based on a neutral conception of formal logic'.[152] He holds that the relation between objective grace and its subjective effect in Barth should be viewed as shrouded in the mysterious and miraculous activity of the Spirit, which cannot be analysed as if it were part of a common human category.[153] In the end, 'theology must content itself with description and resist the temptation to explanation'.[154] In the background here is the way in which

---

148. For this point, see Helm, 'Logic', p. 54.
149. This crude form of the objection occurs more in verbal than written debate; writers are normally more cautious than to countenance a dismissal of all logic.
150. 'The Incarnation and "Limited Atonement"', *EQ* 55 (1983), pp. 84, 86.
151. *Karl Barth: Biblical and Evangelical Theologian* (Edinburgh: T. & T. Clark, 1990), p. 237.
152. *How to Read Karl Barth: The Shape of His Theology* (New York: Oxford University Press, 1991), p. 223.
153. Ibid., ch. 7.
154. Ibid., p. 111. Jeannine Michele Graham follows T. F. Torrance and Hunsinger at this point; see her *Representation and Substitution in the Atonement Theologies of Dorothee*

Barth himself questions the idea of causation, maintaining in his discussion of the divine *concursus* (concurrence) that 'we have to drop the ordinary but harmful conception of cause, operation and effect' in order to take it up again without 'what are at root godless notions of causality'.[155]

These responses, while more qualified than a total rejection of logic or causation, are unsuccessful. The difficulty with each of them is that, like the rejection of logic *tout court*, they reject too much. It is no uniquely Aristotelian species of argument that holds that the atonement either is or is not effective. It is no esoteric notion of causal connection which insists that if Christ's death causes salvation, then salvation must occur. And it is no recondite tenet of formal logic which requires either that all are redeemed or that they are not. In each case, only the thinnest notion of logic or causation need be accepted to undermine Barth's position. So long as we allow the idea that there is something that either does or does not effectively bring about something else, then Barth faces his dilemma. We need only to grant the reality of the alternatives that the work of Christ either is or is not the effective cause of salvation for the dilemma to arise. This is hardly a major capitulation to a looming and sinister system alien to the gospel, let alone, *pace* Torrance, some kind of heresy. If we reject even this minimal notion of causation, then other crucial causal relations dissolve. In particular, if we follow Hunsinger and refuse to speak of effective causation because we speak of the work of the Holy Spirit, then we can never meaningfully ascribe the cause of our salvation to God and praise him for it. It is true that we can never understand the details of how the Holy Spirit works, but the exclusion of causal connections dismantles reality itself, including the realities of praise that the Bible attests. The idea that God is the efficient cause of salvation is not an alien principle: it is something Scripture itself tells us.

More pointedly, Barth cannot evade the pressure of the contradiction by rejecting the use of logical consequence or effective causation, because he himself uses such categories. We find an example of this in his criticism of the Lutheran denial of the sovereignty of grace. Barth describes the Lutheran doctrine of foreknown faith (*praevisa fides*) as it was propounded in the tradition of the Formula of Concord: election is based on God's foreknowledge of 'the fact of the work of Christ, and the fact of faith directed towards that work'.[156] Barth

---

Sölle, John Macquarrie, and Karl Barth, American University Studies, 7.230 (New York: Peter Lang, 2005), pp. 381–385.

155. *CD* III/3, p. 118. This form of the response is also found in Hunsinger, who cites this passage from Barth in *How to Read*, p. 200.

156. *CD* II/2, p. 71.

argues that this position actually resolves into Arminianism, binding God to what he foresees others doing: 'at this point, in spite of all other differences, in spite of its intended and avowed anti-Pelagianism, the Lutheran teaching occupies common ground with the Arminian doctrine'.[157] Barth explains the Lutheran view that even the *praevisa fides* must be based on the free decision of God, but nonetheless insists that the Lutherans are caught in a 'dangerous dilemma'. If we take seriously their insistence on the free grace of God, their position will reduce to the Calvinist *decretum absolutum* (absolute decree). But if we give full weight to their emphasis on the human response in conditioning the divine will, 'we shall avoid "Absolutism," but what about Pelagianism?'[158]

> The deduction may not be explicit and it may be involuntary, but is it not inevitable that God knows from all eternity that in certain men there will not be any opposition, and that because He knows these men He elects them? The deduction was denied, but it could hardly be evaded, and it was on account of this undeclared deduction that the Calvinists decisively rejected the tenet of *praevisa fides*, and with it the whole Lutheran doctrine of predestination.[159]

Barth here sounds exactly like his own critics. And since he rejects the Lutheran position because of its logical consequences, he can hardly evade such criticisms made on the basis of his own statements.

Barth's own 'dangerous dilemma' can be put simply. If we take seriously his insistence that Christ died effectively for all, his position will reduce to universalism. But if we give full weight to his emphasis on the impossible possibility of final rejection, we shall avoid universalism, but what about an ineffectual atonement? The deductions may not be explicit and they may be involuntary, but is not one of them inevitable? The deductions are denied, but they can hardly be evaded, and it is on account of these undeclared deductions that we must reject the Barthian doctrine of the atonement. Barth has tied himself in a knot, whereas the Reformed tradition avoided this problem by maintaining a particular scope for the intention of the atonement.[160]

---

157. Ibid., p. 73.

158. Ibid., p. 74.

159. Ibid.

160. It is important to remember that the Reformed hold to an infinite value for the blood of Christ on the basis of a Chalcedonian Christology, while also maintaining that the intended application of the atonement is limited. See e.g. Owen, 'Death of Death', vol. 10, p. 295 (iv.1), on the sufficiency of the cross to redeem even a plurality of worlds.

In view of Barth's professed desire to teach only what the Scriptures teach, the obvious counter to the Reformed view of particular redemption is that it does not and cannot comport with the abundant biblical data alleged in support of a universal atonement. Thus, the argument runs, Barth is saying what the Bible requires him to say and living patiently with a tension evinced by Scripture itself. The issues raised by this claim are obviously beyond the scope of the discussion here, for they cover the exegesis of many biblical texts.[161] For Barth, however, the key move is not exegetical but hermeneutical. As we saw earlier, Barth speaks of 'the divine love' and 'the divine grace and mercy' as 'the meaning and intention of Scripture as a whole'.[162] On this presuppositional basis he then reads all biblical passages with the conviction 'that the Word of God is the content of the Bible', and that this Word of God 'forms the content of Scripture'.[163] The forcefulness with which this hermeneutic operates in Barth's theology is deeply problematic, since it serves to neuter the force of passages such as Romans 9 which challenge his view that mercy always precedes rejection. Barth himself warns that the danger lies in generalities; this caution must be applied to his own hermeneutical method that overwhelms uncomfortable exegetical particularities.

To substantiate this criticism of Barth's method, it must be shown that he misreads and universalizes one strand of the biblical portrayal of Jesus Christ at the expense of others. This is my claim: not that it is wrong to hold that Jesus Christ must determine our knowledge of God, but that the Jesus Christ who does so must be the Jesus Christ who is described in the full breadth of Scripture, not the Jesus Christ of a single strand that has assumed the role of an abstracted principle. As we have seen, Barth sought to avoid this embrace of principle at all costs, but in my judgment he failed. This raises another question, the solution of which lies beyond the scope of this essay. I offer, therefore, one example of an exegetical argument which begins

---

161. Graham rightly identifies the importance of the exegetical endeavour at this juncture, but she appeals hastily to the biblical use of the word 'all' to prove a universal intent for the atonement; see *Representation and Substitution*, p. 381. Such appeals presume what must be proved, that 'all' means every individual without exception, when there is significant biblical evidence that the word cannot always be construed as exhaustive (e.g. Acts 1:1, esp. when read with John 21:25; Acts 22:15; Rom. 5:18). Without endorsing every moment of Owen's exegesis, there are good examples of a more careful contextual approach in bk. 4 of 'Death of Death'.

162. *CD* II/1, p. 394.

163. *CD* II/2, p. 152.

to suggest that Barth has a mistaken and abstracted picture of Jesus Christ.

Barth believes that Jesus Christ is God's Yes to all men. This language comes from Paul, in 2 Corinthians 1:19–20: 'For the Son of God, Jesus Christ, whom we preached among you, Silvanus and Timothy and I, was not Yes and No; but in him it is always Yes. For all the promises of God find their Yes in him,' RSV. The echo of this passage in the use of the terms *Ja* and *Nein* is one of the motifs of Barth's writing. Most importantly, he cites it at the start of his treatment of election and uses it to attack the Reformed idea of reprobation. For Barth, predestination is solely the good news of God's Yes to all humankind. He grants that there is a shadow cast by the gospel in that it cannot be preached without mentioning the No, but the No is always utterly subordinate to the purpose of the Yes: 'The Yes cannot be heard unless the No is also heard. But the No is said for the sake of the Yes and not for its own sake. In substance, therefore, the first and last word is Yes and not No.'[164]

Barth continues with the image of the shadow and argues that the doctrine of predestination itself has come under a shadow he is determined to disperse: 'In the light of this election the whole of the Gospel is light. Yes is said here, and all the promises of God are Yea and Amen (2 Cor. 1:20). Confirmation and comfort and help are promised us at this point, and they are promised us at every point.'[165] The difficulty with this pivotal argument is that Barth misreads what Paul says. Paul does not say that the intention of God for all humanity is only ever Yes. He says that Jesus Christ is Yes to all the promises of God. It is one thing to affirm that the gospel is the positive fulfilment of all the promises of God; it is quite another to say that God only ever intends his Yes, and never his No, to the whole human race. To his people the promises of God are always words of confirmation and comfort and help, even when they warn. But although Paul says here that the gospel is for the world, he does not say that God intends the salvation of every individual, including those outside Christ. This is clear from the scope of the promises in view. The great promises given to Israel, especially in the person of Abram, are not promises to every human individual. Certainly, Israel has a mission to the nations, but there is a considerable difference between a promise of the salvation of nations, and a promise of an intended salvation for every individual within every nation. Paul speaks of the former, but Barth repeatedly uses his language to maintain the latter. This use of the promise is further undermined when we recall the promised fate of Abram's enemies: '[H]im who curses you I will curse' (Gen. 12:3, RSV).

---

164. Ibid., p. 13.
165. Ibid., p. 14.

Conclusion

Measured against the background of historic liberalism, there are welcome themes in Karl Barth's soteriology. Nonetheless, a single problem emerges at several points: the weakening of any emphasis on history or eternity. Barth displaces history in several ways. The historical humiliation of Christ is lost to a Christology focused solely on the two natures, the progressive revelation of sin is excluded in favour of a final revelation in Christ, and mercy is rendered unmerciful by absolutizing the single divine Yes in Christ at the expense of historical enmity to the sinner. This emphasis on the effective Yes also implies a universal salvation that questions the place of the history of human sin.

Similarly, eternity is diminished when Barth rejects the covenant of redemption on the grounds that it locates election in the *Logos asarkos*, arguing instead that the incarnate Christ alone constitutes the decree of God. It is true that in his incarnate life Christ echoes his eternal electing will, but to speak of the will of the *Logos asarkos* does not entail bypassing the incarnation. As we saw earlier, if the incarnate Christ reveals something of the work of the eternal Son prior to the incarnation, then we do no honour to the revelation of the incarnation by refusing to speak of him as he has spoken of himself. We are not faced with a choice between speaking *ex nihilo* of the eternal Son or speaking only of the incarnate Christ: we may instead speak of the covenant of the eternal Son with the Father revealed by the Son in his incarnation. Nor will Barth's rejection of an electing decree in eternity rescue him from the pastoral problem of uncertainty. So long as he admits the possibility, albeit the impossible possibility, that some may not be saved, there is room for someone to fear that this will be his end. As Berkouwer argues, the uncertainty of the *decretum absolutum* Barth thought he had removed 'returns unavoidably at another point, namely, in the ontological impossibility of sin and unbelief and in the rejection of the apokatastasis'.[166]

The criticism that Barth displaces eternity and history might be put another way, using the image of three spaces.[167] 'Thirdspace' denotes the space of human history, and 'secondspace' the inner divine life in eternity. 'Firstspace' is the space occupied by the God-man Jesus Christ. This space has priority: the incarnate Christ displaces divine eternity and the unfolding realities of

---

166. *Triumph*, p. 287.

167. This image was suggested to me by Barth's analogy for the exclusion of the old humanity from an empty 'sphere (*der Raum*)'; see *CD* IV/1, p. 76; *KD* IV/1, p. 81. I have borrowed the terminology (but not the content) of three spaces from human geography via my colleague Matthew Sleeman.

human history. In critiquing Barth's theology it is vital to remember that he has three spaces and not just two. When he seems to downplay the significance of thirdspace, he does not therefore automatically elevate secondspace, or vice versa. Rather, he consistently elevates firstspace. Always, Barth emphasizes that we must understand the reality of the God-man Jesus Christ to be the *primum quid* (first thing). This is what may safely be called the Christomonism of Barth: not a denial of eternity or of human history, but an utter displacement of them by the all-determining incarnate Yes of God.

It might be said in defence of Barth that Jesus Christ the *primum quid* is not really a distinctive *quid* at all, because he is the perfect combination of eternity and history: as the God-man he is in fact God and man, eternity and history, united in one person.[168] Thus, it might be argued that Barth seeks to secure both in his affirmation of the two natures. Indeed, Barth himself replied to Berkouwer's charge that he denied history by pointing to his emphasis on Jesus Christ: 'To say "Jesus" is necessarily to say "history," His history, the history in which He is what He is and does what he does.'[169] But the way in which Barth deploys his conception of Christ shows that it excludes eternity and history: time after time Barth's Christ displaces eternity, even the eternity of the Son, and history, even the history of Christ's passion. We have repeatedly seen that, in the end, Barth regards eternity and history as functionally irrelevant for Christian theology. In effect if not in theory, Barth's Christ, the Christ who intends only Yes, negates both time and eternity, and thus jeopardizes the properties of both natures. For Barth's Christ is at decisive moments an abstracted and enforced principle rather than the Christ of the Scriptures.[170]

© Garry J. Williams, 2008

---

168. Hunsinger, *How to Read*, ch. 7, explores the way in which Barth's view of divine and human agency is patterned on the Chalcedonian formula.

169. *CD* IV/3.1, p. 179.

170. On the idea that Barth has replaced Christ with a principle, see C. Brown, *Karl Barth and the Christian Message* (London: Tyndale, 1967), pp. 138–139.

I am very grateful to my research assistants Steve Jeffery and Tom Watts for their contribution to preparing the final draft of this chapter for publication.

9. KARL BARTH AND THE VISIBILITY OF GOD

Paul Helm

Karl Barth held that *God freely reveals himself and that this revelation of himself is solely and exhaustively in Jesus Christ.* According to him this is the result of God's 'primal and basic decision'

> in which He wills to be and actually is God, in the mystery of what takes place from and to all eternity within Himself, within His triune being, God is none other than the One who in His Son or Word elects Himself, and in and with Himself elects His people.[1]

This is Barth's doctrine of the *visibility* of God. This chapter endeavours to examine this and similarly worded claims in Barth, to see, in the first place, what he believed such statements entail and what they exclude or are incompatible with. Barth held that in working out the implications of such statements Christian theology comes into its own, because at all points it is explicitly and immediately connected with Christ's person and work, and that the appreciation of this fact is something of a novel discovery, an 'innovation' in Christian theology.[2] The italicized words above, in the first paragraph,

---

1. *CD* II/2, p. 76; see also pp. 115, 158. In this chapter we shall chiefly consider material from *CD* II/2, but also from sections of *CD* IV/1.

2. *CD* II/2, p. 77.

thus embody a theological claim of some magnitude. A corollary of the claim, according to Barth, is that the tradition, lacking this insight, espouses the idea of a 'hidden' God, a God who is not exhaustively revealed in Jesus Christ, and who is therefore not fully the Christian God. It follows that those who have failed to appreciate the importance of divine visibility – I shall refer to them in this chapter as 'the tradition' – have a radically defective view of God. In offering what I hope will be a careful and sympathetic account of Barth's views, my principal aim is to examine the cogency and coherence of Barth's proposal against the tradition he critiques. The conclusions are somewhat paradoxical: it turns out, on each of two plausible readings of what he says, that Barth is himself a part of the tradition he believes he has supplanted.

Barth's critique of God's 'hiddenness' and his affirmation of his visibility are chiefly to be found in his treatment of election and of the person of Christ.[3] We shall consider these in order. Finally, we shall consider what Barth has to say about certainty and scepticism about God's salvific intentions, something that preoccupies him throughout his criticisms of divine hiddenness.

Election

Election is basic to Barth's theology. It is 'the sum of the Gospel'.[4] Election is God's election of himself in Jesus Christ, and this for Barth conditions the entire character of Christian theology. More strongly, not only is election basic, but so is reprobation, although not in an identical way. For it is God's reprobation of himself in Jesus Christ that also contributes crucially to theology's Christian character. Jesus Christ is the eternally reprobate one, just as he is the eternally elect one. He embodies both grace and judgment, divine mercy and

---

3. Barth also deals with the theme of 'hiddenness' in *CD* II/1 (§27, pp. 179–203). But there the word is used in an epistemic sense. It concerns the mode of God's revelation. Barth's point is that we have no natural capacity to know God. Such knowledge cannot be identified with any human cognitive process or its result. So God comes to us in a way that is discontinuous with our normal cognitive powers. This 'hiddenness' does not signal a general agnosticism about God, and it is not in any way at odds with the subject of this chapter. 'In this revelation, in Jesus Christ, the hidden God has indeed made himself apprehensible' (ibid., p. 199).

4. *CD* II/2, p. 12.

divine wrath. About the God who thus elects and reprobates Jesus Christ, Barth has this sort of thing to say:

> The Subject of the election, of this election, the Subject with which the Christian doctrine of election must reckon, is not in the least a 'God in general', as he may be conceived and systematically constructed from the standpoint of sovereignty, of omnipotence, of a first cause, of absolute necessity. It is always unconditioned thinking which undertakes to construct such a 'God in general', and (notwithstanding all the theoretical protestation against *potentia absoluta* [absolute power]) the result of such unconditioned thinking must always be an unconditioned God, a God who is free *in abstracto* [in the abstract] . . . the true God is the One whose freedom and love have nothing to do with abstract absoluteness or naked sovereignty, but who in His love and freedom has determined and limited Himself to be God in particular and not in general, and only as such to be omnipotent and sovereign and the possessor of all other perfections.[5]

And as regards reprobation:

> We are no longer free, then, to think of God's eternal election as bifurcating into a rightward and a leftward election. There is a leftward election. But God willed that the object of this election should be Himself and not man. God removed from man and took upon Himself the burden of the evil which unavoidably threatened and actually achieved and exercised dominion in the world that He had ordained as the theatre of His glory. God removed from man and took upon Himself the suffering which resulted from this dominion, including the condemnation of sinful man.[6]

So we must not think of God firstly or chiefly as a sovereign ruler, not even as a wise and faithful sovereign ruler, and of divine election as one activity of that rule, subordinated to it.[7] Otherwise, we are landed with a God whose providence and predestination are hidden.[8] We must begin with true, concrete deity, not a God 'in general',[9] not deity *in abstracto*.[10] What an 'abstract' God or a 'God in general' is is not immediately clear, but I think Barth means a God whose

---

5. Ibid., p. 49.
6. Ibid., p. 172.
7. Ibid., p. 50.
8. Ibid., p. 51.
9. Ibid., p. 49.
10. Ibid., pp. 44–45.

character does not specify his salvific activities. It is only through the character of divine election that the character of God is fully revealed, and not (rather surprisingly) the other way around.

> It is undoubtedly the case . . . that the election does in some sense denote the basis of all the relationships between God and man, between God in His very earliest movement towards man and man in his very earliest determination by this divine movement. It is in the decision in favour of this movement, in God's self-determination and the resultant determination of man, in the basic relationship which is enclosed and fulfilled within Himself, that God is who He is. The primal relationship belongs, therefore, to the doctrine of God.[11]

So God is abstract, a 'God in general' if and only if he could have had salvific relationships with humankind other than those he has in fact had. Further, the election of Jesus Christ is not the appointment of a mere executor of a divine decree. He is the subject or agent of election. He is elected, but in the person of Jesus Christ God also elects himself.

> As we have to do with Jesus Christ, we have to do with the electing God. For election is obviously the first and basic and decisive thing which we have always to say concerning this revelation, this activity, this presence of God in the world, and therefore concerning the decree and the eternal self-determination of God which bursts through and is manifested at this point.[12]

It is for this reason that predestination cannot for Barth be a part of providence: it is the whole of providence. For if it were a part of providence then God would be a God 'in general' and election merely one function of God's general relationship with the world.[13]

Is God the most perfect being? Barth answers yes. But his perfections are not the set of Anselmic 'abstract' perfections, a 'God in general' but the concrete perfections of a God who is *this* God, the God and Father of our Lord Jesus Christ. Any divine decree issues, naturally enough, in a limitation of God. But this is not Barth's point. Rather, there is only one limitation that 'befits' God. Nevertheless, we shall see that Barth regards such a limitation as the free determination of God, and so gets himself into trouble.

---

11. Ibid., p. 52.
12. Ibid., p. 54.
13. Ibid., p. 78.

A hidden God?

One might think that Augustine and the Reformers' insistence that election is *in Christ* is Barth's point. For theirs is a view of election that is not 'general', their God is not abstract, for the electing God is the God and Father of our Lord Jesus Christ. But Barth demurs:

> Our thesis is that God's eternal will is the election of Jesus Christ. At this point we part company with all previous interpretations of the doctrine of predestination. In these the Subject and object of predestination (the electing God and the elected man) are determined ultimately by the fact that both quantities are treated as unknown.[14]

Furthermore:

> In this matter of election are we noetically to hold by Christ and Christ alone because critically there is no election and no electing God outside Him? Or is it rather the case that we are to understand its assertion merely as an impressively stated pastoral rule, a practical direction regarding the attitude which, *rebus sic stantibus* [as things stand], we ought to adopt toward this matter if we are not to be plunged into doubt or despair?[15]

We are not to consider Christ as the mirror of God's election (as Calvin put it) because this is good pastoral practice to do so but because he *is* God's election.

We see here what Barth means by election being basic.[16] Putting the point in the aseptic language of logic, it means that there is a broadly logically necessary and sufficient connection between who God is and his decision of election in Christ. God is the God who reveals *himself* in Christ. So it appears that God in his self-determination acts so as to ensure, as a matter of logic, that he is the elector of Jesus Christ. That gives God his identity. So when, for Barth, God reveals himself, it *must be* this revelation in Jesus Christ that constitutes God's character. That is the significance of Barth's remark on pastoral guidance. For him, only a fully visible, revealed God can have the sorts of pastoral consequences that are desirable and that according to Barth, Calvin's doctrine of predestination and election does not deliver on account of the alleged 'hiddenness' of his God. Barth's version of election in Christ has these

---

14. Ibid., p. 146.
15. Ibid., p. 63.
16. Ibid., p. 77.

benign pastoral consequences because, as he claims, God's hiddenness is fully eliminated.[17]

> Is it the case, then, that in the divine election as such we have to do ultimately, not with a divine decision made in Jesus Christ, but with one which is independent of Jesus Christ and only executed by Him? Is it the case that that decision made in Jesus Christ by which we must hold fast is, in fact, only another and a later and subordinate decision, while the first and true decision of election is to be sought – or if we follow the pastoral direction had better not be sought – in the mystery of the self-existent being of God, and of a decree made in the absolute freedom of the divine being?
>   If in any sense we are forced to accept this second interpretation, it is inevitable that there should be tension between the theological truth and the pastoral direction which would have us hold fast by Christ. And in this tension it is the latter which will feel the strain the more seriously. It is only those who accidentally have not experienced or suspected the existence of the hidden truth who can really be satisfied with the advice simply to hold fast by the incarnate Son of God and the Word and Spirit of God and not enquire concerning the hidden will of the Father and of the eternal Godhead.[18]

But as we shall see, matters do not work out for Barth straightforwardly because of the tangles he gets into over divine freedom.

We see another side of this in Barth's critique of the doctrine of double predestination. As already noted, for Barth, Christ is both the elect one and the reprobate one. Yet these two characterizations are not to be understood symmetrically, or in such a way that one neutralizes the other. Rather as the elect one Christ triumphs over his own reprobation so that no others suffer the fate of being reprobate.

> For the only knowledge which we have of man's foreordination to evil and death is in the form in which God of His great mercy accepted it as His own portion and burden, removing it from us and refusing to let it be our foreordination in any form. That removing and refusing took place in Jesus Christ.[19]

This is in sharp contrast to the tradition, for whom 'the elect' and 'the reprobate' constitute two exclusive classes of people which together are exhaustive of the human race.

---

17. Ibid., p. 66.
18. Ibid., p. 64.
19. Ibid., p. 172.

What is interesting and at first sight puzzling about Barth's method is how a priori it is. One wants to ask, where is Scripture in all this? What biblical data has the tradition overlooked? If the Christ who is the subject of election is, according to Barth, a universalistic Christ, then what has happened to the sharply particularistic Christ of the Gospels? (e.g. Matt. 25:33; 28:32–33; Luke 24:40).[20] But on further reflection this a priori approach is in fact inevitable. For Scripture is de facto, informing us of what is the case, of what God has in fact done and revealed to us. The question of what God might have done but hasn't, or whether God had to do what he did, is rarely if ever considered there. By contrast, Barth is concerned to go back to first principles, to the basics, and to argue what must be the case. He is in effect asking and attempting to answer the question 'What basic character must theology have to be Christian theology?' In a different context, one that had greater regard for the very words of Scripture in determining doctrine, such an approach would have been regarded as purely speculative.

If there were a contingent, merely accidental, connection between God and our election in Christ, it would follow according to Barth that the fact of election in Christ could perform only an epistemic role, and a poor one at that. This is because our relation to Christ could be probabalistically related only to God's character; it would not entail that God has that character. Following Calvin's advice to regard Christ as the mirror of election could at best turn our attention away from the abyss of God's hiddenness, distracting us from the contemplation of God's 'left hand'. In these circumstances it seems that belief in our election in Christ would not entail our election, for such an election is contingent if (according to Barth) the result of a *decretum absolutum* (absolute decree), a decision apart from Christ, the will of a hidden God, and our belief in our election in Christ may turn out to be false. Our relationship to Christ would merely provide us with a means, perhaps the only means, God has provided for satisfying ourselves about our own election, a 'pastoral rule' that is inherently unsatisfactory. In these circumstances there would be a merely contingent relation between God and our election in Christ, for God could have acted otherwise, and might in fact have done so. But then who is this God who could have acted otherwise? Barth's answer: he is a hidden God.

---

20. Whether or not Barth is a universalist has been debated; see J. Colwell, 'The Contemporaneity of the Divine Decision: Reflections on Barth's Denials of "Universalism"', in N. M. de S. Cameron (ed.), *Universalism and the Doctrine of Hell* (Carlisle: Paternoster, 1992), pp. 139–160. Cf. O. D. Crisp, 'On Barth's Denial of Universalism', *Them* 29.1 (2003), pp. 18–29.

The thought of the election becomes necessarily the thought of the will and decision of God which are hidden somewhere in the height or depths behind Jesus Christ and behind God's revelation. The first and last question in respect of the relationship between God and man brings us face to face with a God who is above and beyond Jesus Christ and with a relationship which is independent of Jesus Christ. How, then, can we attain to any sure knowledge of God or ourselves? How, then, can we have any sure knowledge of this relationship? How can we be certain that it is good to be so fully in the hands of God as we are proclaimed to be when we assert that God elects?[21]

Our thesis is that God's eternal will is the election of Jesus Christ. At this point we part company with all previous interpretations of the doctrine of predestination. In these the Subject and object of predestination (the electing God and elected man) are determined ultimately by the fact that both quantities are treated as unknown. We may say that the electing God is a supreme being who disposes freely according to his own omnipotence, righteousness and mercy. We may say that to Him may be ascribed the lordship over all things, and above all the absolute right and absolute power to determine the destiny of man. But when we say that, then ultimately and fundamentally the electing God is an unknown quantity.[22]

Let us think a little more about what Barth means or might mean by 'the hiddenness of God'. He certainly does not mean that on the traditional view God is an unknowable *substratum*, or at best an abstract divine substance, as has been alleged was Augustine's view.[23] For even as 'hidden', God is 'omnipotence, righteousness and mercy'. We can also see that the hiddenness of God for Barth is not a matter of degree. For the God of 'omnipotence, righteousness and mercy' is clearly not a *totally* hidden God. Yet Barth's contrast between the 'abstract' and the 'particular' is not altogether clear. For clearly a God who is understood in terms of the possession of 'abstract' powers in the Barthian sense is not himself abstract. Anselm's Most Perfect Being, the sum of all perfections, is concrete, unique. But he is, nevertheless, for Barth, a 'God in general' because his nature is insufficiently specified in explicitly Christian, salvific terms. Hiddenness, the absence of particularity, has to do with the

---

21. *CD* II/2, p. 64.

22. Ibid., p. 146; see also p. 65. According to Barth, the Reformation, with its Christological understanding of election, was right in intention but not in execution. See ibid., p. 76, for a summary of this view.

23. C. Gunton, *The Promise of Trinitarian Theology* (Edinburgh: T. & T. Clark, 1991), p. 54.

character of God's decree or decision. But God is hidden, not fully revealed as the God he is, if he is not exhaustively revealed in Christ. Then he remains a God 'in general'. For in this case there is, apart from his revelation in Christ, a remainder, something over. If it is conceivable that God could have acted in some other way, decreed some other states of affairs than those he has in fact decreed, then God would be hidden. If God *makes himself* a particular God, no longer hidden, by the primal decision that he takes, his decision to be our God in Jesus Christ, then he is no longer a hidden God. This brings us to the character of God's decision, his freedom.

The freedom of God

The Christian tradition has maintained, by and large, that God does have such freedom, freedom to decree between alternatives.[24] Free to create or not to create. Free to create and not to redeem. Such freedom has generally been upheld, even if sometimes in a qualified way. It has been argued, for example by Aquinas, according to Norman Kretzmann,[25] that though God in his overflowing generosity and benevolence must create *some* world, he need not have created *this* world. But even on this view God is free to choose between alternatives. To deny such freedom of choice to God is generally believed to take one in the direction of pantheism, or of panentheism, to the idea that the world is a natural extension of God in some sense 'contained' within him.

Barth stoutly upholds the freedom of God, repeatedly stressing his 'free, subjective self-determination, the primal act of lordship over everything else'.[26]

> The eternal God was not under an obligation to man to be in Himself the God whose nature and property it is to bear this name. That He is, in fact, such a God is grace, something which is not merited by man but can only be given to him. And that God is gracious, that in assuming this name He gives Himself to the man who has not merited it, is His election, His free decree. It is the divine election of grace. In a free act of determination God has ordained concerning Himself: He has determined Himself.[27]

---

24. W. Rowe, *Can God be Free?* (Oxford: Clarendon, 2004).

25. *The Metaphysics of Creation: Aquinas's Natural Theology in Summa Contra Gentiles II* (Oxford: Clarendon, 1999), ch. 4.

26. *CD* II/2, p. 100.

27. Ibid., p. 101.

There are two separate issues here. It may be granted, with Barth, that God is free in the sense that he is under no obligation to do what he does. But could he have done other than he did? On Barth's view of God's visibility it does not seem to be possible. For if God could have done other than he has done, then there is a 'remainder', a hiddenness. Yet to say that God is not free would be to go against almost the entire tradition. So my questions are, 'How can God both be free in what he does, and yet not remain a "hidden" God? How can God determine himself? Who is the God who determines himself? What character does he have? Is he, for all Barth's protestations to the contrary, a God in general? What is the character of this free decree or decision or self-determination?'

While upholding divine freedom, Barth nevertheless seems to tell two contrasting stories about it. According to the main story, he has a rather unusual sense of 'freedom' as this applies to God. The highest form of freedom, and thus the only form possible for God, is not the freedom between alternative courses of action, nor even the freedom to be oneself, free of all external constraints or conditions, but the freedom (unconstrained by any external impediments) to decide to be *this* God. As Barth says:

> Even if the concept freedom is filled out by that of love, it makes no essential difference, unless by both concepts we understand the one decisive thing: that the true God is the One whose freedom and love have nothing to do with abstract absoluteness or naked sovereignty, but who in His love and freedom has determined and limited himself to be God in particular and not in general, and only as such to be omnipotent and sovereign and the possessor of all other perfections.[28]

> [W]e maintain of God that in Himself, in the primal and basic decision in which He wills to be and actually is God, in the mystery of what takes place from and to all eternity within Himself, with His triune being, God is none other than the One who in His Son or Word elects Himself, and in and with Himself elects his people. In so far as God not only is love, but loves, in the act of love which determines His whole being God elects. And in so far as this act of love is an election, it is at the same time and as such the act of His freedom.[29]

Note here Barth's reference to the mysterious character of God's eternal decision. But it is not as if, in using such expressions, he intends 'hiddenness' to return by the back door. Rather, as he puts it elsewhere:

---

28. Ibid., p. 49.
29. Ibid., p. 76.

We have to do with this mystery too – the mystery of God, and the mystery of man which arises as man is caught up by the eternal will of God into God's own mystery. But what matters here is really the nature of this one and twofold mystery, whether it is incomprehensible light or incomprehensible darkness.[30]

God's mystery is the mystery of incomprehensible light. Nevertheless, the question remains, *who* is this God who elects himself? Is he not a hidden God? If Barth replies, this God is Father, Son and Holy Sprit, the tradition agrees. If he says, this God is *behind* or *before* his trinitarian self, he seems to commit himself to an exaggerated form of 'hiddenness', one not endorsed by the tradition, and one that is incoherent. Let us call this the *self-constituting* view of God's freedom.

Bruce L. McCormack, who favours this interpretation of what Barth means by divine freedom, is emphatic that God's election of Jesus Christ is in some sense 'constitutive' of God's being.[31]

> The *decision* for the covenant of grace is the ground of God's triunity and, therefore, of the eternal generation of the Son and of the eternal procession of the Holy Spirit from Father and Son. In other words, the works of God *ad intra* (the trinitarian processions) find their ground in the *first* of the works of God *ad extra* [election]. And that also means that eternal generation and eternal procession are willed by God; they are not natural to him if 'natural' is taken to mean a determination of being fixed in advance of all actions and relations.[32]

And again:

> God is so much the Lord that he is sovereign even over his own being. In a primal decision, God assigned to himself the being he would have for all eternity. That which is truly 'essential' to him – that is to say, that which constitutes the self-identical element in the livingness of God – consists finally in a *decision* whose content is the covenant of grace.[33]

---

30. Ibid., p. 146.

31. 'Grace and Being: The Role of God's Gracious Election in Karl Barth's Theological Ontology', in J. Webster (ed.), *The Cambridge Companion to Karl Barth* (Cambridge: Cambridge University Press, 2000), p. 100.

32. Ibid., p. 103.

33. 'Christ and the Decree: An Unsettled Question for the Reformed Churches Today', in L. Quigley (ed.), *Reformed Theology in Contemporary Perspective* (Edinburgh:

At the very least, this concept of freedom, which leads McCormack to say that for Barth the incarnation is constitutive of God's being, and which in fact seems to entail that everything that occurs is constitutive of that being, certainly imperils the distinction between the immanent and economic trinities. Yet it does not follow that God is not in some sense both immanent and economic, understood as free to be trinitarian or not. But can McCormack seriously be proposing this? Could God have chosen *not* to be trinitarian? Only a moment or two's reflection is needed to realize how nonsensical this is. It is like supposing that I could have chosen to have the mind of a bat.

In the sentences 'God decides to be trinitarian' and 'God is sovereign even over his own being' *who* is this God who decides and who possessed such sovereignty? Despite Barth's pains to eliminate every vestige of a 'hidden' God, the idea here returns with a vengeance, at least on McCormack's understanding. For Barth is positing a God who assigns himself a being, or a character. Does this mean that God does not already have a character? Barth's God freely gives himself the character of redeemer together with all that is necessary for having such a character. Who is this God who so acts? It is no good saying, with McCormack, that for Barth '"essence" is given in the act of electing, and is, in fact, constituted by that eternal act'.[34] For necessarily, actions have agents. The act of electing must be the action of someone; it cannot be an act of no-one that, upon its occurrence, constitutes the agent as a someone. At the very least such a someone is deeply 'hidden'. But in fact this interpretation looks to be quite nonsensical, as is the idea that God might choose his own essence. On this interpretation Barth's view literally makes no sense. At its centre is not so much divine hiddenness as a black hole of incoherence.[35]

McCormack offers the following reply to this objection:

> Critics will no doubt wish to ask whether it is even coherent to speak of God as assigning to himself his own being. Without a subject, there can be no act. If God did

---

Footnote 33 (*continued*)
      Rutherford House, 2006), p. 139. Although published in 2006, this paper was
      presented to the Rutherford House Dogmatics Conference in 1997.
34. 'Grace and Being', p. 99.
35. It won't do either to have recourse to 'God's being is in his becoming'. Such talk,
      reminiscent of Hegel, defines God dynamically. It is one thing for God to be
      defined in such a way, but quite another to say that God decides what God he is
      to be. The God he decides to be is clearly not a matter of definition, but of his
      (supposed) decision.

not exist above and prior to the decision, surely there would be no Subject to make it. Such an objection sounds very compelling until we realize that the very form of the question temporalizes the decree – and that is a problem that has dogged the doctrine of predestination throughout the centuries. It introduces into God a 'before' and an 'after' so that what we have, in effect, is a God before the decree and a God after the decree. Where this occurs, it is no longer possible to think of the decree as eternal.[36]

But this won't do. At the heart of McCormack's exposition of Barth there is confusion over time and eternity. To start with, it is McCormack (and Barth) who countenance a 'before' and 'after' in the discussion: 'before' there is God who is sovereign over his own being, and 'after' there is the God whom he freely decides to be.[37] But the traditional understanding of predestination does not temporal- ize the decree either, but, in recognizing that the decree is eternal, orders its various elements logically. So McCormack's remark that 'if the decree is eternal (and it is) then there can be no God hidden behind the veil of the decree' must apply equally to the traditional view as well. If on that view the decree is eternal, as it is, then (by McCormack's argument) nothing is veiled. McCormack's reply is a red herring. The deep incoherence of the self-constituting view remains.

In a more recent piece,[38] McCormack digs himself more deeply into this particular interpretation of Barth. He proposes five logical consequences from the fact, as he believes it to be, that Barth made Jesus Christ (rather than the 'eternal Logos') to be the electing God. In the course of elucidating these he commits Barth to the following propositions:

1. There is an eternal act in which God gives to himself his own being as Father, Son and Holy Spirit. This eternal act is the same one in which he chooses to be in the covenant of grace with human beings.[39]
2. What is natural and necessary in God is itself a consequence of the one act of self-determination.[40]

---

36. 'Christ and the Decree', pp. 140–141.
37. This comes out explicitly in 'Grace and Being': 'What is the logical relation of God's gracious election to the triunity of God? We are not asking here about a chronological relation. Election is an eternal decision and as such resists our attempts to temporalize it' (p. 101).
38. 'Seek God where He May Be Found: A Response to Edwin Chr. van Driel', *SJT* 60.1 (2007), pp. 62–79.
39. Ibid., p. 66
40. Ibid.

3. It is necessary to distinguish between what God is necessarily and naturally (an act of self-affirmation) distinct from any subsequent act of self-determination. How God's being is structured is a function of his own eternal will and decision.[41]

4. 'While it is true that there is no act (or decision) without a subject,' he says, 'the identity of that subject may not be distinguished from the identity of God as constituted in the event in which God chooses to be God "for us" – because the being of the subject may not be distinguished finally from the act in which its being is given'.[42]

The problem with this interpretation of Barth remains, though it is now somewhat more apparent. Besides a general problem of comprehending some of McCormack's prose,[43] there is an obvious problem with points 1 and 2. It emerges that there is a divine act of self-*affirmation* and a divine act of self-*determination*, and that these are distinct types of act. Given the nomenclature, one might think that what God is necessarily and naturally he is beyond any of his acts, prior to them, and that what he is necessarily and naturally gives rise to what he does. But apparently not; for what is natural and necessary is, according to McCormack, a *consequence* of the one act of self-determination. What God self-determines are those features that are natural and necessary. So the question I posed earlier becomes more sharply focused: who then is the agent of this primal act of self-determination?

Moving to points 3 and 4, which are in effect McCormack's attempt at an answer to our question, his remarks succeed only in adding further support to my own argument that on this interpretation of Barth, and the difficulties it engenders, the divine freedom is jeopardized. For it appears that God's being (what God is) is to be understood retrospectively. His being is what he has, contingently and as a matter of fact, decided to do. But if this is meant seriously, then what God does contingently establishes what he is essentially. He

---

41. Ibid., p. 67.

42. Ibid.

43. E.g. 'The only thing that is absolutely necessary for God is existence itself but such a consideration may not be abstracted from the decision in which God gives to himself his own being – and then played against that which is contingently necessary for him . . . What God cannot do precisely in the one eternal event in which he gives himself his own being is something that can only be thought about in the light of what he decided, in fact, to do and to be' (McCormack, 'Seek God', p. 67).

is what, as it turns out, he does. But of course, as a solution to the difficulty of divine freedom, this won't do either.

However, while the self-constituting view is undoubtedly the main thrust of Barth's view of freedom, there is another aspect to it, perhaps (as Barth himself might call it) a 'shadow', but real for all that. For example, in discussing the idea of double predestination, and his opposition to the traditional idea of reprobation, he says:

> But the emphatic nature of our opposition does not derive from any preconceived idea that the love of God prevents His equal willing of both [blessedness and perdition], thus excluding any such symmetrical understanding of double predestination. What right have we to tell God that in His love, which is certainly quite different from ours, He cannot equally seriously, and from the very beginning, from all eternity, condemn as well as acquit, kill as well as make alive, reject as well as elect? Even today we must still defend the older doctrine against this kind of objection.[44]

Or consider this

> From all eternity God could have excluded man from this covenant. He could have delivered him up to himself, and allowed him to fall. He could have refused to will him at all. He could have avoided the compromising of His freedom by not willing to create him. He could have remained satisfied with Himself and with the impassible glory and blessedness of His own inner life. But He did not do so. He elected man as a covenant-partner. In His Son He elected Himself as the covenant-partner of man.[45]

Without here going into the question of predestination, but simply considering what implication these words have for Barth's understanding of divine freedom, it seems clear that if this is true, God could have willed a different order of things than the one he in fact ordained. He cannot now ordain it, of course, but 'from the very beginning, from eternity' he could have. This is an instance of the freedom to choose between alternatives.

Such passages strongly suggest a second story, another view of divine freedom, that God is free in that he may choose man as his covenant partner or refrain from doing so. Paul D. Molnar is attracted to this interpretation, maintaining that according to Barth, God has freedom in the sense that he has

---

44. *CD* II/2, p. 171.
45. Ibid., p. 166.

alternatives of which the actual world is but one.[46] Divine freedom, he says, is for Barth 'the basis for human freedom and for human self-determination'.[47] Without it, human freedom would be dissolved and theology would collapse into anthropology.[48] And he thinks, with some justification, that if the sense of divine freedom here is not the freedom to do otherwise, then the distinction between the immanent and economic Trinities is put in peril. 'For Barth, God exists eternally as the Father, Son and Holy Spirit and would so exist even if there had been no creation, reconciliation or redemption.'[49]

> Barth insisted that the Trinity exists eternally in its own right and thus even the electing God is not subject to any necessities, especially a necessity that would suggest that the ground of his triunity is the covenant of grace. It is exactly the other way around. The covenant of grace is a covenant of grace because it expresses the free overflow of God's eternal love that takes place in pre-temporal eternity as the Father begets the Son in the unity of the Holy Spirit. None of this is subject to a principle of love, and God's being is not the result of his will. Rather his will to elect expresses his freedom to be God in a new way as God for us. It expresses the fact that . . . God is Lord of his inner life as well as of his actions *ad extra* [outside himself]. But none of this is required by his essence, and his essence most certainly is not contingent upon his works *ad extra*.[50]

There is some obscurity here, suggesting that Molnar has not altogether extricated himself from the nonsense of God choosing to be trinitarian. Molnar seems to think of the covenant of grace as being integral to the Father's eternal begetting of the Son, thus wobbling back in the direction of McCormack's view. But if the establishing of the covenant of grace is integral to or intrinsic to the begetting of the Son, part of the package, then if God is necessarily trinitarian, and if the covenant is intrinsic to the begetting of the Son, then the distinction between the immanent and the economic Trinity collapses. How then could God be Lord of his inner life? For if God is Lord of his inner life, then it would seem that that life, what God willed or chose, could have taken another direction from the one it in fact did take. I shall assume Molnar has some way of understanding his words that preserves his earlier

---

46. *Divine Freedom and the Doctrine of the Immanent Trinity* (London: T. & T. Clark, 2002).

47. Ibid., p. 62.

48. Ibid., p. 64.

49. Ibid., p. 63.

50. Ibid.

point about God's freedom to do otherwise, though it is unclear what this understanding might be. Let us call this the *alternative choice* view of freedom.

Whatever Molnar's final position is, it seems clear that according to certain passages in Barth, God could have done otherwise than he did, and so is in that sense free to have decreed an alternative state of affairs – though Barth may prefer to reserve the term 'free' for some other feature of divine activity. But if God is 'free' in the sense that he could have done otherwise than he has in fact done, then there is also a 'hiddenness' to him. Perhaps not as radical a hiddenness as on the constitutive view of divine freedom, but hiddenness for all that. Maybe we should here distinguish between an *actual* hiddenness and a *potential* hiddenness. Then Barth's words here may imply a potential hiddenness, one he thinks ought not to trouble us now, for it now for ever remains an unactualized possibility, rather than the actual hiddenness entailed by the traditional view of double predestination, which issues from a *decretum absolutum*, which (he thinks) must trouble us now. Yet it is unclear he is entitled to say this. If he criticizes the tradition for allowing that hiddenness possibly implies caprice, may he not also have to allow for caprice?

Clouding the debate about what exactly Barth means by divine freedom are some misunderstandings about the idea of divine freedom, at least as the tradition understood it. Molnar holds (without offering any argument) that if God's 'decision' is eternal, then it is a matter of logical necessity and so not free. He writes, 'But if God's election has always taken place, how then can it be construed as a decision; does it not then become a necessity (a logical necessity at that), that is, the very opposite of what Barth intended with his doctrine of the immanent Trinity?'[51] But this is not so. On the traditional view God's eternal decision might not have been; it is not part of his nature.[52] So the choice is not between a God who is (in some sense) in time, whose decisions are events in time, so preserving the distinction between the economic and immanent trinities, or a God whose decision is timelessly eternal and so part of his nature, placing the distinction between the economic and immanent

---

51. Ibid., p. 62.

52. For discussion of this point, see e.g. P. Helm, *Eternal God* (Oxford: Clarendon, 1988), ch. 10. Aquinas e.g. argues that God (who according to him is timelessly eternal) could have created a world that has always been. He thinks that he did not, but that he could have; see 'On the Eternity of the World', in T. Aquinas, *Selected Writings*, trans. R. McInerny (London: Penguin, 1998), p. 712. For further discussion, see N. Kretzman, 'Ockham and the Creation of the Beginningless World', *Franciscan Studies* 45 (1985), pp. 1–31.

Trinities in peril. There is a third option: a God whose decision is timelessly eternal but nevertheless might have been other than it is, so preserving divine eternity, divine freedom and the distinction between the two senses of 'Trinity'.

So on either view, the self-constituting view of divine freedom (favoured by McCormack) or the alternative-choice view (favoured by Molnar), Barth remains committed to some version or other of divine 'hiddenness'. On the first interpretation there is the problem of who the God is who eternally decides to be the God and Father of our Lord Jesus Christ, while on the second interpretation God is hidden because his gracious decision to take us as his covenant partners is not the only possible decision for him.

The person of Christ

Barth's critique of hiddenness in his treatment of election is reinforced by what he has to say regarding the person of Christ and particularly by his negative remarks about the *extra Calvinisticum* (see below for definition). Here Barth is in explicit dialogue with Calvin. There can be no real debate about Calvin's view. According to Calvin, the Logos remains *asarkos*, 'without flesh' (though Calvin does not use this term), even while he is incarnate, and a fortiori he is *asarkos* prior to the incarnation. This follows from Calvin's commitment to what has come to be known as the *extra Calvinisticum*, the view that in the incarnation God the Son, being *autotheos* (God himself), retained all essential divine properties, including immensity and omnipresence, and therefore could not be confined within the limits of a human person. It is disputed whether this view is unique to Calvin. In an excellent study, *Calvin's Catholic Christology*,[53] E. David Willis shows that the *extra Calvinisticum* might equally well be called the *extra Patristicum* or the *extra Catholicum*, citing statements of it (or of its equivalent) from a host of Christian writers from Athanasius to Aquinas. So, at least on the strength of this evidence, the position I shall discuss represents an important strand of the tradition.

In the *Institutes* John Calvin refers explicitly to the *extra* in two places. First, in his discussion of the incarnation in Book. 2:

> They thrust upon us as something absurd the fact that if the Word of God became flesh, then he was confined within the narrow prison of an earthly body. This is mere

---

53. Leiden: E. J. Brill, 1966.

impudence! For even if the Word in his immeasurable essence united with the nature of man into one person, we do not imagine that he was confined therein. Here is something marvellous: the Son of God descended from heaven in such a way that, without leaving heaven, he willed to be borne in the virgin's womb, to go about the earth, and to hang upon the cross; yet he continuously filled the world as he had done from the beginning![54]

And, secondly, in his discussion of the nature of the Lord's Supper:

But some are carried away with such contentiousness as to say that because of the natures joined in Christ, wherever Christ's divinity is, there also is his flesh, which cannot be separated from it . . . But from Scripture we plainly infer that the one person of Christ so consists of two natures that each nevertheless retains unimpaired its own distinctive character . . . Surely, when the Lord of glory is said to be crucified [1 Cor. 2:8], Paul does not mean that he suffered anything in his divinity, but he says this because the same Christ, who was cast down and despised, and suffered in the flesh, was God and Lord of glory. In this way he was also Son of man in heaven [John 3:13], for the very same Christ, who, according to the flesh, dwelt as Son of man on earth, was God in heaven. In this manner, he is said to have descended to that place according to his divinity, not because divinity left heaven to hide itself in the prison house of the body, but because even though it filled all things, still in Christ's very humanity it dwelt bodily [Col. 2:9], that is, by nature, and in a certain ineffable way. There is a commonplace distinction of the schools to which I am not ashamed to refer: although the whole Christ is everywhere, still the whole of that which is in him is not everywhere. And would that the Schoolmen themselves had honestly weighed the force of this statement. For thus would the absurd fiction of Christ's carnal presence have been obviated.[55]

This is what Barth says about the *extra Calvinisticum*:

We may concede that there is something unsatisfactory about the theory [of the *extra Calvinisticum*], in that right up to our own day it has led to fatal speculation about the being and work of the *logos asarkos*, or a God whom we think we can know elsewhere, and whose divine being we can define from elsewhere than in and from the contemplation of His presence and activity as the Word made flesh.[56]

54. *Institutes of the Christian Religion*, trans. F. L. Battles (London: SCM., 1966), 2.13.4.
55. Ibid. 4.17.30. For further discussion, see P. Helm, *John Calvin's Ideas* (Oxford: Oxford University Press, 2004), ch. 3.
56. *CD* IV/I, p. 181.

This is the same point as earlier, though now expressed as an aspect of Christology. Earlier, a God who is 'behind' his decree is hidden; here, the Logos considered *asarkos*, apart from incarnation in Jesus Christ, is hidden. A *Logos asarkos* entails a hidden God, indeed, he *is* a hidden God. Barth suggests a connection between what he takes to be Calvin's position and something he calls 'fatal speculation', because it entails a God whose being we can 'define' (note Barth's word) apart from the incarnation.

> Is it the case that . . . while Christ is indeed the medium and instrument of the divine activity at the basis of the election, and to that extent He is the revelation of the election by which factually we must hold fast, yet the electing God Himself is not Christ but God the Father, or the triune God, in a decision which precedes the being and will and word of Christ, a hidden God, who as such made, as it were, the actual resolve and decree to save such and such men and to bring them to blessedness, and then later made, as it were, the formal or technical decree and resolve to call the elect and to bring them to that end by means of His Son, by means of His Word and Spirit?[57]

Note however that according to Molnar:

> [Barth] rejected a *logos asarkos* in his doctrine of creation if it implies a 'formless Christ' or a 'Christ-principle' rather than Jesus who was with God as the Word before the world existed; he rejected it in connection with reconciliation if it meant a retreat to an idea of God behind the God revealed in Christ; but he still insisted it had a proper role to play in the doctrine of the Trinity and in Christology, describing it as 'indispensable for dogmatic enquiry and presentation.'[58]

While Barth's exact position on the propriety and role of the idea of *Logos asarkos* may not be altogether clear, nevertheless its main thrust is evident. It opens the door to a consideration of the Logos apart from incarnation and redemption.

Incidentally, if by his remark about 'heights or depths behind Jesus Christ' Barth is intending to characterize the traditional position, it is obviously a misstatement. It is fundamental to the tradition that Jesus Christ is not simply an executor of the Father's will, but as the Logos he fully participates in it. As is seen in this quotation from Calvin's commentary on Hebrews 1:3:

---

57. *CD* II/2, p. 64.
58. *Divine Freedom*, p. 71, quoting from *CD* III/1, p. 54. He also cites *CD* IV/1, pp. 168ff., and *CD* III/2, pp. 65–66, 147–148.

When you hear that the Son is the glory of the Father's glory, bear in mind that the glory of the Father is invisible to you until it shines forth in Christ: and that he is called the very image of His substance because the majesty of the Father is hidden, until it shows itself as impressed on His image.[59]

Calvin asserts the closest possible concurrence between the Father and the Son in the work of our redemption, as when he says the following:

But, as many as were at last incorporated into the body of Christ were God's sheep. As Christ Himself testifies (Jn. 10.16), though formerly wandering sheep and outside the fold. Meantime, though they did not know it, the shepherd knew them, according to that eternal predestination by which He chose His own before the foundation of the world, as Augustine rightly declares.[60]

So who is the agent, or to use Barth's term, the 'Subject' of predestination, according to Calvin here? Not the Father, or at least not the Father in distinction from the Son, a God 'elsewhere'. The Son himself, the shepherd, chose his own before the foundation of the world. He is the agent of election, he eternally chose his own and as a good shepherd laid down his life for the sheep. But not in a way that separates him one smidgen from the Father. So although the Father is in certain important respects 'hidden', in these equally important respects he is most clearly visible. So Barth's appreciation of the tradition is somewhat exaggerated, as is the contrast between his own success at eliminating 'hiddenness' and the tradition's failure to do so.

Are these statements of Calvin's references only to the economy, as McCormack thinks they are?[61] Perhaps they are, or are partly. But my points are rather different. First, that there is a clear sense in which, in the economy, the Son is not subordinated to the Father. The work his Father had given him

---

59. *Calvin's New Testament Commentaries*, ed. D. W. Torrance and T. F. Torrance, 12 vols. (Grand Rapids: Eerdmans, 1959–72), vol. 12, p. 8.

60. *Concerning the Eternal Predestination of God* (1552), trans. with an introduction by J. K. S. Reid (London: James Clarke, 1961), p. 150; cf. p. 127. See also his commentary on John 13:18, *Calvin's New Testament Commentaries*, vol. 5, p. 62. Such an understanding of the relation of the Son to the Father in the economy is fundamental to 'covenant theology'. For more on Calvin's view of God's visibility, see R. C. Zachman, *John Calvin as Teacher, Pastor and Theologian* (Grand Rapids: Baker, 2006), pp. 213–215.

61. 'Christ and the Decree', p. 134.

to do is also the work he has given himself to do. Further, in respect of hiddenness and visibility, whatever is true of the Father is true of the Son. If the Father is to some degree hidden, then so is the Son, in precisely the same way; if the Father is to some degree visible, then so is the Son, in precisely the same way. They operate in parallel and are to that degree the same. McCormack's alterative reading is incoherent. Besides, it is pure speculation to suppose that in their hiddenness the Father and the Son are capable of adopting altogether different characters; to be malign, or capricious, for example. Or to suppose that, in virtue of a residual hiddenness, in the economy the Son could have failed to have cooperated with the Father.

If the Logos chose his own, how could he fail to collaborate with the Father? In his anxiety to carry the Christological character of election through theologically (as he puts it[62]) Barth is sometimes guilty of non sequiturs. His point (made contra Heinrich Bullinger and the Helvetic Confession) is not proved by noting that 'in John's Gospel the electing Father and the electing Son are one and the same'.[63] For that fact is well understood by the tradition. It does not follow from this, however, that there is no hiddenness in God, both Father and Son. The *en autō* (in him) of Ephesians 1:4 or the *houtos* (he) of John 1:2 are not decisively in his favour, as Barth claims. For they are quite consistent with, for example, Calvin's view that they refer to the participation of the Logos in the eternal counsel of redemption. These Scriptural points raised by Barth can be appropriated also by Calvin and the traditional understanding of *in Christo* (in Christ). But what about other data not alluded to by Barth? What about the biblical data on particularism, or on reprobation? Barth makes no attempt to appropriate these data, and it is doubtful that he could do so consistently.

Certainty and uncertainty

We turn, finally, to consider some epistemological aspects of Barth's view. We have noted that throughout his discussion of election Barth is concerned with the pastoral problem of uncertainty, with the lack of assurance about election, and with the way in which he believes such uncertainty is entailed by and promoted by the idea of God's hiddenness, and especially by the *decretum absolutum* of John Calvin. One of the themes in Barth's critique of the tradition,

---

62. *CD* II/2, p. 65.
63. Ibid.

particularly of Calvin, is that grounding election in the *decretum absolutum* entails radical scepticism and uncertainty about one's own standing. 'The electing God of Calvin is a *Deus nudus absconditus* [a hidden God].'[64] If this is so, how can a person be certain he is saved? What evidence ought a person to look for to ground such a belief? Barth's answer is, only a metaphysical state of affairs that by the universality of its scope guarantees our salvation even were we to doubt it. Perhaps it is not too much to say that it is the need to free people from such uncertainty that motivates Barth's exposition.[65]

In a classic passage in the *Institutes* Calvin asserts that Jesus Christ is the mirror of our election. He explicitly guards himself against the charge that the particularism of eternal election must lead to speculation and uncertainty as to whether we are among the elect. We must not endeavour to reason a priori from the doctrine of election. That way we shall find 'no end, in wand'ring mazes lost'.[66] Rather to avoid self-deception we must reason a posteriori from our communion with Christ.

> But if we have been chosen in him, we shall not find assurance of our election in ourselves; and not even in God the Father, if we conceive him as severed from his Son. Christ, then, is the mirror wherein we must, and without self-deception may, contemplate our own election. For since it is into his body the Father has destined those to be engrafted whom he has willed from eternity to be his own, that he may hold as sons all whom he acknowledges to be among his members, we have a sufficiently clear and firm testimony that we have been inscribed in the book of life [cf. Rev. 21:27] if we are in communion with Christ.[67]

Barth demurs:

> They [the Reformers] did state that Jesus Christ is for us the *lumen* or *speculum electionis* [the light or mirror of election]. But they thought it sufficient to base this belief upon the reference to Jesus Christ as the first of the elect according to His human nature. They restrict themselves to this basis with the same exclusiveness as Thomas. They missed the fact that this basis is quite insufficient to explain the *en autō* of Eph. 1.4. And they also missed the fact that to establish the certainty of a belief in our own salvation it is not sufficient merely to say that in respect of our election we must

---

64. Ibid., p. 111.
65. Ibid., p. 107; see also pp. 110–111, 115–116.
66. J. Milton, *Paradise Lost*, 2.561.
67. *Institutes* 3.24.5.

cleave only to Jesus Christ on the ground that He must be regarded as the first of the elect, the Head of all others, the means chosen by the electing God for the execution of that which He determined concerning those elected by Him. A statement of this kind will hardly serve even as a truly effective or penetrating pastoral admonition. For when we tackle that question which is no mere quibble, but decisive for each of us, the question whether we ourselves belong to those who profit by what God has ordained to be of benefit to His elect in and through the means which He first elected, in other words, whether we ourselves are of the number of the elect, what is the value of an answer of this type? If in regard to the decisive factor, the election itself, or the electing God, we cannot fix our gaze and keep it fixed on Jesus Christ, because the electing God is not identical with Christ but behind and above Him, because in the beginning with God we have to reckon with someone or something other than the *houtos* of John 1.2, a decision of the divine good pleasure quite unrelated to and not determined by Him, what useful purpose can such an answer serve?[68]

Does Barth understand Calvin at this point? He seems to think that Calvin's mirror is simply a strategy, a pastoral rule for changing the subject from the *decretum absolutum* to Christ. He says:

> The christological reference was warmly and impressively made [at the time of
> the Reformation], but it is left standing in the air. It cannot be carried through
> theologically, and for this reason. It does forbid in practice any glancing away at an
> absolute decree of God, i.e., a decree which is different from the eternal saving
> decision of God as made in Jesus Christ. Yet it does not exclude any such glancing
> away in theory, but more or less expressly permits it.[69]

But this is not so. According to Calvin, no-one *can* knowingly be in communion with Christ and yet have any possible grounds for doubting his election. No-one *can* know of his election without being in communion with Christ. So no-one *can* have any reason to 'glance' at an absolute decree. How could they do it? By such a glance what could they possibly see that looking to Christ would not reveal? Calvin's point is a logical one, and thus a point of principle. It is not merely pragmatic or pedagogic.

In Barth's consideration of assurance there is a confusion between or at least a conflation of two distinct issues. He seems at times to think that mere

---

68. *CD* II/2, p. 110.
69. Ibid., p. 65.

hiddenness entails uncertainty,[70] at other times that it is the particularity of the traditional conception of election that ensures uncertainty. And of course, as a matter of fact the tradition (from the New Testament, from Augustine, through Anselm and Aquinas, to Calvin and Luther) *has* maintained that God's salvific intentions are particular and not universal.[71] This has led to the question 'How may a person be certain he or she is saved, and gain assurance?' This is the uncertainty Barth is concerned about, together with the mistaken theological grounds that, he claims, give rise to this question. But he fails to see that there is no logical connection between the hiddenness doctrine and a lack of certainty. For let us suppose what has been called 'Augustinian universalism'.[72] Suppose it were held that the Christian message is that by his grace God has redeemed everyone through Jesus Christ. Further, suppose this fact were universally known and believed. Then the grounds for doubt or uncertainty as to whether or not I am elected would have been decisively removed. There would no non-saving 'remainder' in God, the class of the reprobate would have no members and there would be no possibility of being a reprobate. Yet this state of affairs would not satisfy Barth's most basic worry. For if such Augustinian universalism stemmed from an absolute decree of God, a decree that could have been other than it is had God so willed it, then on Barth's account God would remain hidden, a 'God in general'. For about such Augustinian universalism, stemming as it does from the divine decree, there is some 'remainder', and so God remains the 'hidden' God. And Barth holds that hiddenness as such (or more properly, belief in hiddenness) must entail uncertainty. Nevertheless, one might argue that had the Christian tradition seen things differently, if universalism rather than particularism had been the default position, then most if not all of Barth's worries about doubt and uncertainty would have been settled without the need to have recourse to his theological innovations regarding the nature of God.[73] For Barth it is not the supposed divine hiddenness that allegedly engenders uncertainty but the particularism of the tradition, though it is not clear that he sees this.

In order to remove uncertainty about our election in the Barthian manner

---

70. Ibid., p. 63.

71. For a brief account of the evidence for this, see P. Helm, 'Classical Calvinist Doctrine of God', in B. Ware (ed.), *Perspectives on the Doctrine of God: Four Views* (Nashville: Broadman & Holman, forthcoming).

72. For an interesting discussion of this possibility, see O. D. Crisp, 'Augustinian Universalism', *International Journal for Philosophy of Religion* 53 (2003), pp. 127–145.

73. *CD* II/2, p. 77.

not only has Barth's own proposal to be cogent, and to be grounded in Scripture, but a person who seeks the removal of doubt as to his destiny must *believe* both that Barth's account is cogent and that it is a better account of the biblical data than any rival. It seems a tall order to expect everyone concerned about their eternal state to ingest the abstruse doctrine of God presented in the pages of the *Church Dogmatics*, a doctrine about which, as we have seen, even seasoned Barth scholars may have reasonably argued differences of opinion. More seriously perhaps, can we be assured that the Jesus Christ who is the subject of election – Barth's Jesus Christ – is the true Jesus Christ and that the particularistic Jesus of the Gospels is a false or deviant Christ? May not our uncertainty on this point also have adverse pastoral consequences? And how does Barth's doctrine of universal election safeguard assurance, given God's hidden, primal decision to be a Saviour God? The question of certainty and uncertainty with regard to a person's eternal destiny cannot be solved by fiat or by a piece of theological creativity. The ultimate test for whether this is legitimate, well-grounded assurance with regard to a person's relation to Christ can only be settled by reference to the biblical testimony to Christ, including Christ's own words on the matter. At the very least, to enjoy the certainty Barth aspires to, then what Barth holds with respect to election in Christ must not only be true, but a person must strongly believe it is true.

Conclusion

In my examination of Barth's visibility doctrine several things have emerged. On two plausible readings of his view of the freeness of divine election, Barth is himself committed to a 'hidden' God. On one of these readings, the more radical, in which Barth ties himself in knots over the idea of divine freedom, God is deeply and totally hidden behind his free 'primal decision'. On the second, less radical view, in which God freely chooses to have us as his covenant partners, he is partly hidden, since this choice could have been otherwise. The common factor in these two readings is Barth's understanding of divine freedom, which is at best highly ambiguous, and at worst incoherent. These conclusions are reinforced by Barth's remarks on the *Logos asarkos*. So despite his lengthy, tortuous discussion, Barth does not escape postulating a hidden God. Further, Barth's claims for the originality of his 'innovation', and the need for it, must be judged against the backdrop of an exaggerated understanding about 'hiddenness' in the tradition, particularly his misunderstanding of John Calvin's view of election. Finally, Barth's concerns about pastoral direction regarding personal assurance arise out of a confusion between the hiddenness doctrine he is ostensibly combating and the particularism of the traditional doctrine of election.[74]

---

74. I am grateful to Oliver Crisp, John Colwell and the editors for help with earlier versions of this chapter.

10. KARL BARTH AND JONATHAN EDWARDS ON REPROBATION (AND HELL)

Oliver D. Crisp

> Of making many books there is no end, and much study is wearisome to the flesh.
>
> (Eccl. 12:12, NKJV)

The sage words of Qoheleth are particularly apt when beginning yet another discussion of Barth's work that touches upon his doctrine of election and, hence – as we shall see presently – of reprobation too. Much has been written on Barth's doctrine of election: perhaps, too much. Or rather, perhaps too little that does anything more than trot out one of two well-worn construals of Barth's doctrine. On the one hand, there are those who claim Barth's account of election yields some version of necessary universalism, which, for present purposes, is the doctrine according to which all human beings will inevitably be saved through the work of Christ; it is not possible, given divine ordination, that any of humanity will finally be lost in hell. On the other hand, there are those adamant that Barth's doctrine of election yields no such conclusion. Although his is an optimistic account of election that leads us to hope for the salvation of all, it does not promise the salvation of all: nothing in Barth's account *entails* universalism, so it is said. And (the *coup de grace*) Barth himself denies that his doctrine of election is universalistic. If we take him seriously in this regard, we should interpret what he does say about the matter in line with these explicitly non-universalistic statements.

I have no desire in this chapter merely to add to the seemingly endless iterations of these two views on Barth's doctrine of election.[1] However, in the recent literature Stephen R. Holmes has made the interesting and controversial claim that Barth's doctrine of election actually yields a more satisfying account of reprobation, and of hell, than that offered by his Reformed forebears because, unlike a number of classical Reformed theologians, Barth had a theological account of the 'No' (to use Barth's language) as it is pronounced in Jesus Christ. Thus, Holmes:

> Calvin, and the tradition that came after him, had almost nothing theological to say about the reprobate; Barth, by contrast offers a long and richly theological account of God's 'No' as it is pronounced in Jesus Christ. Is it not then fair to say that, in contrast to Calvin and the tradition, Barth had a doctrine of reprobation?[2]

In this chapter I want to argue that this is not, in fact, a fair assessment of the matter. Although Holmes is right to point to the theological richness of Barth's doctrine of election (and reprobation), he is wrong to claim that Calvin and the tradition that followed in his footsteps 'had almost nothing theological' to say about the reprobate. He is also mistaken if he thinks that, taken just as it is given in the *Church Dogmatics*, Barth's account of reprobation (and hell) is 'more theologically satisfying' than the sort of view expressed by most other classical Reformed theologians on this matter. In fact, precisely the opposite is true of Barth's doctrine of reprobation. What Barth tells us about the nature of God's electing (and reprobating) act can mean only one of two things: that his account is a species of necessary universalism after all, in which case no mere human is finally cut off from the presence of God in hell; or, that Barth's account is inconsistent and the different strands of his thinking on this matter do not form a coherent whole.

This does not mean Barth's doctrine of election is without merit, however.

---

1. I have contributed my own views on this matter previously. See O. D. Crisp, 'On Barth's Denial of Universalism', *Them* 29 (2003), pp. 18–29; and 'On the Letter and Spirit of Karl Barth's doctrine of Election: A Reply to O'Neil', *EQ* 79.1 (2007), pp. 53–67. The two views on Barth's doctrine of election are given fuller exposition there, with accompanying citations from the literature.
2. *Listening to the Past: The Place of Tradition in Theology* (Grand Rapids: Baker Academic; Carlisle: Paternoster, 2002), p. 134. Compare idem, *God of Grace and God of Glory: An Account of the Theology of Jonathan Edwards* (Edinburgh: T. & T. Clark, 2000), chs. 6–7. My criticisms of Holmes are offered in a friendly spirit. Dr Holmes is, to my mind, one of the most able historical theologians at work today.

I have argued elsewhere that Barth's doctrine of election, though internally disordered, is best understood as the story of a great raconteur. It is full of big ideas and bold suggestions, which, if one analyses them too closely, do not hang together. But, if we step back and look at the bold suggestions themselves, we would find several competing accounts of divine election and reprobation in Barth's work. These different descriptions of the doctrine are nevertheless theologically interesting, even provocative, reports on election.[3]

The argument proceeds as follows. First, I shall offer a short recapitulation of Barth's doctrine of election, focusing on the matter of reprobation and the doctrine of hell. Then, in a second section, I shall compare Barth's account of hell with that of another great Reformed divine, Jonathan Edwards (1703–58). I choose Edwards as my interlocutor, rather than John Calvin or some other eminent Reformed theologian who defends a more traditional account of reprobation and hell, for several reasons.[4] First, Edwards thought about eschatology with great care and intellectual rigour. Second, he is well known as an exponent of a robust or 'traditional' doctrine of hell,[5] although, as Holmes points out, Edwards's published corpus makes much less reference to hell than popular reporting would suggest.[6] And third, the relationship between Edwards and Barth on reprobation has been scrutinized in the recent literature by Holmes, in some of his own work on this matter.[7] This, as we shall see, has a bearing upon Holmes's claim about the theological superiority of Barth's doctrine of reprobation. A third section offers a critical assessment of Edwards and Barth on

---

3. Cf. Crisp, 'On the Letter and Spirit', pp. 66–67.

4. Of course, there are other eminent divines who are not Reformed in their theology, but who defend a traditional account of hell. However, I am particularly interested in the relationship between Barth and earlier theologians in his own Reformed tradition in this regard. For reasons of space I shall not address the wider question of Barth's relationship to other traditionalist accounts of reprobation and hell, though this is also an interesting theological question.

5. There has been some interest in Edwards's views on this matter. For two recent treatments, see the chapters by Jonathan Kvanvig and William Wainwright in P. Helm and O. D. Crisp (eds.), *Jonathan Edwards: Philosophical Theologian* (Aldershot: Ashgate, 2003). There is also relevant material in N. Fiering, *Jonathan Edwards's Moral Thought in its British Context* (Eugene, Oreg.: Wipf & Stock, 2006 [1981]).

6. *God of Grace*, p. 216. See also idem, 'The Justice of Hell in the Display of God's Glory in the Thought of Jonathan Edwards', *ProEccl* 9 (2000), p. 392, n. 19.

7. In fact, Holmes suggests that there are similar structural problems in the theologies of both Calvin and Edwards on the doctrine of reprobation. See *God of Grace*, p. 264.

reprobation and hell. In the final part of the chapter, I return to Holmes's assessment of Barth and the Reformed tradition on reprobation, with two issues in mind: does Holmes give us a fair account of the merits of Barth's view versus those of the Reformed tradition? And, does Holmes fairly represent the differences between Barth and Edwards in particular, on this matter? In both instances, I shall conclude that Holmes's assessment is wanting. Barth's account is not superior to exponents of a traditional doctrine of hell like Edwards if we take Barth at face value, as he expounds his position in the *Church Dogmatics*. And this, I suggest, is how we must take Barth on pain of misconstruing or misrepresenting what he does say on this important theological topic. Consequently, and *pace* Holmes, I conclude that Barth's doctrine of reprobation and of hell – what we might call the 'dark side' of his doctrine of election – is not an improvement upon the traditional doctrine espoused by Reformed thinkers like Edwards.

Barth on election and reprobation

Barth's views on reprobation are of a piece with his views on election. Or, to put the same point rather differently, Barth's account of reprobation is one part of his doctrine of election as outlined in *CD* II/2 in particular. He has no account of reprobation apart from what he says about election. An assessment of what he has to say on reprobation requires us to take this into account. What, then, does Barth say about these matters? Put in barest outline, his position can be expressed in the following fashion (this 'story' comports with what Barth says in *CD* II/2).[8]

First, we must consider the matter of the divine decrees, that is, the (logical) sequence of divine ordinances present in the divine mind logically prior to any creative action on his part. As is well known, Barth is a supralapsarian with respect to the ordering of the decrees.[9] That is, he thinks God

---

8. Barth changed his mind about the nature of election (and reprobation) in significant respects in the course of his career. In his *Göttingen Dogmatics*, written at the beginning of his academic career, he seems to take for granted something much more like the traditional Reformed view of election. Recently, Suzanne McDonald has argued that this more traditional account of election also informs aspects of earlier portions of *Church Dogmatics*, esp. I/1; see 'Barth's "Other" Doctrine of Election in the *Church Dogmatics*', *IJST* 9.2 (2007), pp. 134–147.

9. Barth's views can be found in *CD* II/2, pp. 127–144, and correspond to what is said above. But the distinction between supralapsarianism and infralapsarianism

lays out his plans concerning the final destiny of human beings logically prior to his decision to permit the fall (hence *supra-lapsus*). However, unlike those among his Reformed forebears who took a supralapsarian position and aligned themselves with the doctrine of double predestination, Barth does not think that at the very logical 'moment' at which God ordains the final end for which humankind is destined there is a fork in the divine decrees, with some of humanity being elected to eternal life, and the rest being reprobated such that they are eventually damned to hell.[10] Barth inverts this 'double decree', so that both election and reprobation have one single subject (in the first instance), namely Christ. Thus, Barth says, God elects Jesus Christ, the elect one:

> Jesus Christ, then, is not merely one of the elect but *the* elect of God. From the very beginning (from eternity itself), as elected man He does not stand alongside the rest of the elect, but before and above them as the One who is originally and properly the Elect. From the very beginning (from eternity itself), there are no other elect together with or apart from Him, but, as Eph. 1.4 tells us, only 'in' Him . . . 'In Him' means in His person, in His will, in His own divine choice, in the basic decision of God which He fulfils over against every man.[11]

Footnote 9 (*continued*)

　　is a difficult and arcane one not easily parsed out, as Alvin Plantinga has recently pointed out. See his 'Supralapsarianism, or "O Felix Culpa"', in P. van Inwagen (ed.), *Christian Faith and the Problem of Evil* (Grand Rapids: Eerdmans, 2004), pp. 1–25.

10.　Conceivably, a Reformed theologian could argue that God's decree in election consists in a positive decree to save some, but does not include a 'positive' decree to reprobate others. One might think that reprobation is not decreed by God, but is a consequence of human sin such that particular humans damn themselves by their actions and God permits this state of affairs to occur. In which case, reprobation would be a decree to permit some fallen human beings to damn themselves, rather than a 'positive' decree whereby God ordains that some will be damned. This distinction is a fine one, and depends on some number of fallen humanity having the capacity to damn themselves, and God concurring with this in his decree to permit this, rather than God being the sole agent in reprobation. Whether or not Reformed theologians are able to make good on this claim (where such theologians reject the idea that God 'positively' decrees the reprobation of some number of fallen humanity) is beyond the scope of this chapter.

11.　*CD* II/2, pp. 116–117.

God also reprobates Jesus Christ, who, in addition to being the elect one is also the reprobate one. For this reason, Barth can say of Christ that 'He is the Rejected, as and because he is the Elect. In view of His election, there is no other rejected but Himself. It is just for the sake of the election of all the rejected that He stands in solitude over against them all.'[12]

Second, all humanity apart from Christ are somehow incorporated, or co-opted into this divine act of election and reprobation (see *CD* II/2 §34). Thus, all humanity apart from Christ is somehow derivatively elect as a consequence of being incorporated into the election (and reprobation) of Jesus Christ. Moreover, and third, this derivative election, like the election of Jesus Christ, is irrevocable and effectual: all humanity apart from Christ is derivatively elect because of the election of Christ. This means that Christ's work is not just *sufficient* for the salvation of all humanity: it is *efficient* for the salvation of all humanity. No human being is outside the ambit of divine election, such that no human being can be, as it were, derivatively reprobate. The work of Christ as the one elect and reprobate in my place, what Barth memorably describes as 'the Judge Judged in our place', means that the very idea that any human being apart from Christ could now be reprobate is an 'impossible possibility', meaning, in this context, an outcome that is inconceivable.[13]

Thus far Barth's account of the election of Jesus Christ appears to have the consequence that, necessarily, all humanity are saved because all humanity is incorporated into the election of Christ and this divine decree is certain and irrevocable. Notice that this does not mean Barth has no account of divine reprobation. In fact, he has a robust, if eccentric, doctrine of reprobation, because he avers that Christ is the one who is reprobated according to the divine decree in election. But this does seem to mean that the only person who suffers reprobation and who might, as a consequence of this, be a candidate for punishment in hell, is Christ. In which case, no human being apart from Christ is reprobate. You and I are somehow incorporated into Christ's election, and our sin is somehow laid upon him so that he is reprobate instead of

---

12. Ibid., p. 353.

13. See e.g. the strong language of *CD* II/2, p. 319, where Barth tells us that Christ alone takes upon himself rejection and that such rejection, that is, reprobation, cannot be visited upon any human being other than Christ because he has already suffered in place of every other human being. Final rejection 'is the very goal which the godless cannot reach, because it has already been taken away by the eternally decreed offering of the Son of God to suffer in place of the godless, and cannot any longer be their goal'.

us. But only Christ suffers as one rejected by God the Father. Indeed, it is because Christ has done this that no human being can now be cut off from relationship to God. We are reconciled to the Father through Christ as the elect one. This means that the *ordo salutis* (order of salvation) has to do with coming to understand what has already been done by Christ on our behalf, rather than repenting and turning to Christ, the way of thinking about the *ordo salutis* familiar from Reformation and post-Reformation Reformed writers. We might put it like this: on Barth's way of thinking, coming to faith is about realizing that one is already numbered among those saved because of the election of Christ. It does not require some forensic and/or moral change in my status before God, because that forensic and/or moral change has already been brought about by the work of Christ, the elect and reprobate one. What is required in conversion is an epistemic change, that is, a coming to realize something about my forensic and/or moral status before God that I did not previously understand. It is rather like someone who develops an interest in painting, and who yearns to be admitted to the Royal Academy of Art, discovering – to his astonishment! – that he has already been elected to that prestigious body, by some kind benefactors.[14]

The story outlined thus far is not without its problems. For one thing, it is difficult to know what to make of the idea that God incarnate is the only human being reprobated by God the Father. How can one of the persons of the divine Trinity be reprobate – that is, cast off by God, according to his eternal decree? Surely, if a person is numbered among the reprobate, he is cut off from the blessings of God and bound for perdition in hell. Barth accedes to this. But he also claims that Christ is the elect one too. Yet, if anything, this makes matters even more difficult. How can a person cut off from God by irrevocable and unchanging divine decree also be the subject of God's election (and this, presuming it makes sense to talk of one of the persons of the divine Trinity being the subject of divine election)? We might even ask how it is that, if Christ is elect and reprobate, his reprobation does not prevail over his

---

14. Cf. the thesis of *CD* II/2, §35, p. 306, which includes the following: 'The man who is isolated over against God is as such rejected by God. But to be this man can only be by the godless man's own choice. The witness of the community of God to every individual man consists in this: that this choice of the godless man is void; that he belongs eternally to Jesus Christ and therefore is not rejected, but elected by God in Jesus Christ; that the rejection which he deserves on account of his perverse choice is borne and cancelled out by Jesus Christ; and that he is appointed to eternal life with God on the basis of the righteous, divine decision.'

election, such that he and we are at the last eternally rejected, rather than eternally elected.[15]

These matters are not easily settled. It is not just that it is difficult to make sense of these notions, although that is a serious concern. It is the prospect that no sense can be made of them; that to suggest God incarnate is the subject of a divine decree that has two aspects, reprobation and election, is to suggest something simply inconceivable given other orthodox theological commitments. To see the force of this criticism, consider an analogy. If I were to have my leg removed and incinerated in an oven, thereafter I would be without my leg, and with no prospect of having it returned to me whole and intact, to be reattached to my body. Yet, on Barth's way of thinking, something like this does happen to the divine Trinity. For, on his account, the second person of the Trinity is reprobate and elect. But that is to say the second person of the Trinity, who is himself one of the 'modes' of the divine being, according to Barth, is somehow cut off from God, because he is reprobate. Yet he is also chosen (by the Father, another of the divine modes) to be the one elect human being. Stranger still, it is because of this divine act of election that all the rest of humanity may be saved by being somehow incorporated into the election of Christ. This last aspect of Barth's doctrine is rather like having my daughter's details on my passport as I pass through customs (where she has no separate passport). My child is allowed to pass into the country of destination because she is 'incorporated' into my passport for the purposes of travelling from one country to the other. In a similar fashion, I am somehow able to pass from death to life because of the election and reprobation of Christ on my behalf. I am, as it were, incorporated into the election of Christ and may 'pass' from death to life on his 'ticket'.

But aside from problems with the notion of Christ being both the elect and reprobate one, Barth's account appears to be internally disordered. As well as affirming that all humanity are derivatively elect in Christ, and that this derivative election is irrevocable such that no mere humans can be reprobate any longer, or do anything to 'step outside' their derivative election (on account of

---

15. It might be thought that Barth is committed only to the notion that God incarnate is reprobate, not the second person of the Trinity, in abstraction, as it were, from the incarnation. But this makes about as much sense as claiming, 'it is the human nature of Christ that brings about salvation, not his divine nature'. If we think this statement is false (which, on catholic Christology, it must be), how is this different from saying that Christ's human nature alone might be reprobate, without any involvement of his divine nature?

Christ's work as the reprobate and elect one), Barth also says things elsewhere in the *Church Dogmatics* like this:

> [I]f he [the believer] believes in Him [Christ], he knows and grasps his own righteousness as one which is alien to him, as the righteousness of this other, who is justified man in his place, for him. He will miss his own righteousness, he will fall from it, if he thinks he can and should know and grasp and realise it in his own acts and achievements, or in his faith and the result of it. He will be jeopardising, indeed he will already have lost, the forgiveness of his sins, his life as a child of God, his hope of eternal life, if he ever thinks he can and should seek and find these things anywhere but at the place where as the act and work of God they are real as the forgiveness of his sins, as his divine sonship, as his hope, anywhere but in the one Jesus Christ.[16]

The problem is that this sounds much more conditional than some of the earlier remarks in *CD* II/2. Perhaps Barth means that all humanity is derivatively elect in Christ, that this act of derivative election is certain and irrevocable, but that, through an act of will, you and I may 'opt out' of our elect status, thereby damning ourselves. This may reflect the distinction, found in much classical Reformed theology, between reprobation, which depends on the divine decree, and damnation, which is a consequence of human action. I damn myself by my own actions, one might think, although God ordains that I am reprobate. And, in a similar vein, perhaps Barth means to say that God derivatively elects you and me, but we may damn ourselves by opting out of that arrangement by an act of free will. The problem with this reading of Barth is that what he says about the nature of our derivative election in parts of *CD* II/2 sounds much stronger than this. The weaker, more conditional, reading of Barth requires that you and I can exercise significantly free choices in certain moral decisions, where I could have chosen to act other than I did. But such a libertarian account of free choice seems at odds with what Barth says in those passages that stress the supralapsarian decision to elect Christ and all humanity in Christ, and which imply that this determines my final destiny. In these stronger passages in *CD* II/2 what Barth says sounds much more like a version of theological compatibilism, the doctrine according to which divine predestination is compatible with human free will.

So it seems there are difficulties with Barth's account. If we take what he says about the nature of election seriously, it raises grave questions about how

---

16. *CD* IV/1, p. 631.

Christ can be both the elect and reprobate one. And, taken together with other things he says in *Church Dogmatics*, it seems that Barth oscillates between what I have called the 'strong' version of his doctrine, according to which God predestines the salvation of all 'in' Christ irrevocably, and the 'weaker' doctrine, whereby my status as one of the derivatively elect is dependent on my not opting out of this state by an act of free will. Taken as a whole, Barth's doctrine seems to be neither consistent, nor coherent.

Edwards on reprobation and hell

We come to Edwards's account of reprobation and hell. Here the question before us is whether the internal logic of Edwards's view fairs any better than that of Barth. It seems to me that it does, with certain qualifications. Edwards's views must be gleaned from a number of different places in his somewhat diffuse body of work. When we lay these side by side we find that there are several different aspects to Edwards's position. We shall consider three strands of reasoning central to Edwards's case. These comprise (1) an argument for the conclusion that all sin is against God, (2) an argument from the infinite value of God to the conclusion that all human sinners deserve an infinite punishment in hell, and (3) a teleological argument about the reasons why God must display his divine retributive justice in the punishment of some human sinners in the created order.

Recently, Jonathan L. Kvanvig has stated that 'Edwards gives the most complete and detailed defence found in the literature, of the claim that all sin is against God.'[17] Kvanvig is certainly right to suggest that Edwards thought about this problem with a great deal of care. One place in which Edwards rehearses this argument is in his dissertation 'The Nature of True Virtue'.[18] In the first two chapters of that work, Edwards makes several claims that are

---

17. 'Jonathan Edwards on Hell', in P. Helm and O. D. Crisp (eds.), *Jonathan Edwards: Philosophical Theologian* (Aldershot: Ashgate, 2003), pp. 1–11. Holmes has dealt with these matters in two articles, 'The Justice of Hell', and 'Everlasting Punishment and the Goodness of God: Some Contributions to the Current Debate from Jonathan Edwards', *Philosophia Christi* 8 (2006), pp. 327–342.
18. This is one of Edwards's 'Two Dissertations', the other being 'The End of Creation', which Edwards intended to be read prior to 'True Virtue'. Both can be found in P. Ramsey (ed.), *Ethical Writings: The Works of Jonathan Edwards*, vol. 8 (New Haven: Yale University Press, 1989).

important for the present concern. First, he makes an ontological claim that God is the greatest and most perfect being, and may be identified with 'being in general'. Second, he says that truly virtuous actions are somehow in accordance with 'being in general', that is, they are actions where pleasing God, or acting in a way consistent with God's moral law, is at least one of the aims of such actions. Third, and following on the heels of the previous point, Edwards maintains that those who act in accordance with 'private systems' or for the benefit of 'particular persons', as a small fraction of the totality of being rather than 'being in general' (i.e. God), do not manifest true virtue.

The idea here seems to be that God and 'being in general' are inextricably linked (perhaps identical) coupled with the notion that an action is virtuous only if it is motivated by God as 'being in general'. As Kvanvig puts it, 'because God must be central to virtuous behaviour in this way, the central failure in sinful behaviour is a failure to involve God in one's motivations, and hence to sin against God'.[19] This means that any putative 'good' act that has as its object something other than God as its final end (e.g. helping someone cross a road because *I feel like it*) must be sinful in Edwards's eyes. If this is right, then he is making a point about action in general, and what makes such actions sinful, rather than considering manifestly sinful actions only (like murder). On the matter of particular sinful acts, Edwards says that all sin aimed at something other than God – things like 'private systems' or 'particular individuals', such as sins against my brother or a community or a nation – turns out to be sin against God, as 'being in general'. Thus, on Edwards's way of thinking, putatively 'good' acts not aimed at God turn out to be sinful and, in addition, all sinful acts turn out to be sins against God (at least indirectly).

But why believe that? Suppose a child in the same class as my son hits my son at lunchtime, intending to hurt him. Does this little boy thereby commit a sin against me? Not obviously, we might think. I may be upset and offended by such action, but usually we consider intentionality an important factor in judging who it is that is sinned against in such actions. The boy intended to hurt my son; he did not intend to hurt me. He may not even know that my son has a father still living, still less intend to sin against me by sinning against my son. Yet Edwards would have us believe that the little boy's action is a sin not only against my son but against God because all sin is sin against God. Odder still, on Edwards's view, helping an old lady across the road simply because I feel like it is sinful because I have not been cognizant of God in performing the actions I do.

---

19. 'Jonathan Edwards on Hell', p. 5.

One way to make sense of this would be to argue that the relationship between the Creator and his creatures is such an intimate one that any sin committed by one creature against another is also and additionally an indirect sin against the creator of that creature. Consider the person who shouts at a monarchist 'I hate all monarchists! Long live the Republic!' We might think that the expression of such sentiments is offensive not only to the poor monarchist, but also to the monarch, whose reign is being impugned. And we might think that part of the reason for this offence is derived from the fact that the anti-monarchist has a duty to serve his prince, not to seek to overthrow or undermine him. The problem with such examples, like the one of my son and the school bully, is that the relationship between the Creator and the creature in view here is much more intimate than these examples suggest. Edwards's thinking presumes God is not merely a divine parent, but the agent that maintains us in being at each moment of our existence, without whose providential care we would cease to exist.[20] Coupled with his strong views about what counts as virtuous action, and what does not, this aspect of Edwards's thinking requires some hard swallowing.

We come to Edwards's argument from the infinity of God to the conclusion that all human sinners deserve an infinite punishment in hell. In his miscellaneous remarks on *Satisfaction for Sin*, Edwards observes,

> it is requisite that God should punish all sin with infinite punishment; because all sin, as it is against God, is infinitely heinous, and has infinite demerit, is justly infinitely hateful to him, and so stirs up infinite abhorrence and indignation in him. Therefore, by what was before granted, it is requisite that God should punish it, unless there be something in some measure to balance this desert; either some answerable repentance and sorrow for it, or some other compensation.[21]

Assume that all sin is against God (at least indirectly). Then, says Edwards, all sin, because it is against God has an infinite heinousness, presumably because

---

20. Even this does not do Edwards's thinking justice, because Edwards thinks God continuously creates the world at each moment of its existence (denying the doctrine of the divine conservation of the world in being), and he also thinks that God is the sole agent in creation – which leads him to espouse occasionalism. See Crisp, 'How "Occasional" Was Edwards's Occasionalism?', in Helm and Crisp, *Jonathan Edwards*, pp. 61–77.

21. From E. Hickman (ed.), *The Works of Jonathan Edwards*, vol. 2 (Edinburgh: Banner of Truth, 1974 [1834]), p. 565.

it is a sin committed against a being of infinite worth and honour. Such sin is worthy of an infinite punishment in hell because an infinitely heinous sin has or generates an infinite demerit. And only some 'answerable compensation' for this sin can balance off its disvalue, if it is not to lead to an infinite punishment in hell. Since it is an *infinite* disvalue, an infinitely valuable compensation must be offered in its stead. And compensation of such value can be found in the work of Christ for sinners.

Laying to one side the question of the precise value accruing to the work of Christ, we might want to take issue with Edwards's characterization of all sin (however apparently trivial to us) as worthy of an infinite punishment in hell in virtue of having an infinite demerit on account of being a sin against a being of infinite worth and honour. This has several peculiar consequences. One consequence of this view is that sin against God has infinite consequences because of the worth of God, such that all sin is worthy of an infinite punishment. But this means that mass murder and telling a lie both generate a punishment that is infinite. And this seems very odd indeed. Another consequence, closely related to these, is that sin against God has a qualitatively different disvalue when compared to sin against any other being (although, of course, on Edwards's view, all sin is at least indirectly a sin against God).

Let us consider each of these problems. Edwards's argument depends on the notion that the worth of the being against which one sins is of primary interest in determining the punishment due for sin. But, without further qualification, this seems false. If I slap Madonna and also slap Mother Teresa, is my slapping Mother Teresa somehow a worse crime than the slapping of Madonna?[22] One might think it is, because Mother Teresa is a woman of great sanctity, whereas Madonna is not. But how is that morally relevant in judging the two cases? It might be thought that the only morally relevant issue is that I have assaulted two human beings I ought not to have, not that I have assaulted one saintly person and one less-saintly person.

Perhaps an Edwardsian could respond by saying that even if this is true in the case of crimes committed against beings of the same kind, like *human* persons (be they saints or sinners), this does not necessarily obtain in the case of sins committed against a being of a different order (e.g. a *divine* person). All Edwards needs for his argument to have purchase is the notion that crimes against the Creator carry a different order of moral seriousness than crimes committed against other creatures. This seems plausible. The dignity of the

---

22. The reasoning here draws upon the 'three slappers' argument in Marilyn McCord Adams's article 'Hell and the God of Justice', *RelS* 11 (1975), pp. 433–447.

divine being may be of a different moral order of magnitude from the dignity of any creature, such that a crime committed against such a divine person is significantly more grave or heinous.

Yet even if we grant this, the fact that all sin generates an infinite demerit seems strange. But consider again the Edwardsian position. If any offence against a divine being is an offence against a being of infinite worth and value, then – it would seem – any crime against such a being generates an infinite disvalue. It is a crime against a being of a different order of value than any created being. Nevertheless, the way in which blasphemers and murderers are punished in hell might be different in a way that is morally relevant. Suppose that for every moment spent in hell the blasphemer is punished by receiving a pinprick of pain in his body, whereas the murderer suffers pain equivalent to a large electric shock. One might reason that if each of these individuals is going to suffer an infinite amount of punishment, then in the end they will have suffered equal amounts of pain – and this is what seems odd about the Edwardsian notion of infinite punishment for all sin. Even if we concede this, one might prefer the pinprick to the electric shock at every moment of one's continued existence in hell, because at any given moment of my conscious experience in hell I would be enduring less pain if I suffered the pinprick than I would if I suffered the electric shock (although, by hypothesis, both would end up enduring the same amount of pain if the punishment is an infinite one[23]). This goes some way to alleviating the counter-intuitivity of this aspect of Edwards's thinking; but it does not go all the way towards doing so.

The third aspect of Edwards's reasoning has to do with a teleological argument about the reasons why God must display his divine retributive justice in the punishment of some human sinners in the created order. Edwards, like

---

23. Here I shall not enter into the problem of actual infinites, nor of the sort of infinity in view (e.g. 'countable' or 'uncountable', i.e. whether the infinite series in question can be put in a one-to-one correspondence with the set of natural numbers or not). Of course, if punishment in hell is a case of a potential, rather than actual, infinite, that is a temporal series which never ends, but that is not, strictly speaking, infinite (because there is always a finite number of temporal moments in the series, however massive, and adding one more temporal moment to the series yields only a larger finite number of such moments), then it turns out that the punishment for the murderer and the blasphemer are unequal, though the punishment has the same duration in each case – which would make matters slightly easier for the Edwardsian in one respect, although, of course, it would also raise problems with the notion of an infinite punishment.

most classical divines, thinks that divine retribution is an essential component of divine justice. Among other things, this means that there must be a fit between crime and punishment. In addition, Edwards does not think that God *may* punish such sin, but that he may not. He thinks that God *must* punish such sin because it is in the nature of God to act in accordance with his retributive justice when it comes to sin.[24] The sin of some sinners will be expiated in the person of Christ, whose work on their behalf means they are no longer held culpable for their sin. But Edwards also thinks that God must display the glory of his retributive justice in the created order as well as his mercy and grace through the work of Christ (i.e. he holds to something like the following: *necessarily, any created theatre of divine glory must be one in which all aspects of that glory are manifested*). And he takes this to mean some number of fallen humanity must suffer the infinite punishment in hell due for their sin. It is, we might think, in the nature of God to display his glory in his creation, and it is in the nature of such a display of divine glory that God's justice and mercy are both made manifest, in order that God's holy character is vindicated before his creatures. Thus, God's punishment of some sinners in hell is part-and-parcel of his self-glorification, which Edwards believes is the ultimate end of all God's works.

Is Barth's account preferable to Edwards's account?

Having outlined some of the central aspects of the accounts of reprobation given by Barth and reprobation and hell in Edwards, we are now in a position to evaluate which of the two is preferable. (Of course, it may be that neither is preferable, or that some other account is better than either – but we shall restrict ourselves to consideration of whether one of the two accounts offered here is preferable to the other.)

In his account of Edwards's theology, Holmes suggests that one major problem with the Edwardsian doctrine of reprobation is that it means human beings are separated into two classes, the elect and the reprobate. This is a problem because it means that there are two orders of humanity in the mind of God. One order is elect and bound for life in heaven and union with God.

---

24. Not all Reformed divines agreed with Edwards on this matter. For instance, the young John Owen thought God may, but not must, punish sin. For discussion of this, see C. R. Trueman, *The Claims of Truth: John Owen's Trinitarian Theology* (Carlisle: Paternoster, 1997).

The other is reprobate and bound for everlasting perdition – and God creates such human beings with this end in mind. Thus, Holmes:

> On the basis of the gospel story we simply cannot accept that God glorifies Himself in two equal and opposite ways, in the display of His justice and the display of His grace. In speaking of the Father of Jesus Christ, we cannot speak of God's freedom without immediately also speaking of His love . . . To speak only of 'grace', 'mercy' and 'freedom', as Edwards does, leads inevitably to the double decree and the vision of God creating some people only to torture them for all eternity in unimaginable ways.[25]

Holmes goes on to spell out the nature of his complaint against Edwards and those Calvinists who adhere to a doctrine of double predestination, the doctrine according to which God ordains the reprobation of those humans he does not ordain for election. Holmes says the Calvinistic doctrine held by both Calvin and Edwards means the elect, those united to Christ through his work of salvation, are eternally secure as the objects of God's grace. By contrast, the reprobate are 'separated from Christ by "a great gulf fixed", and so any goodness, religious practice, or apparent faith on their part [is] worthless. This is true of Calvin, and true of Edwards. It is not true of Barth.'[26]

To this must be added several comments in his later treatment of Barth's doctrine of reprobation and the doctrine of reprobation in the Reformed tradition, in his book on historical theology entitled *Listening to the Past*. There Holmes says Barth's account of reprobation teaches us two things the traditional Reformed account favoured by the likes of Calvin or Edwards, does not. These are (1) that we must talk of those 'outside the Church' in a way that 'links' them in 'powerful ways' to the name of Jesus Christ, and (2) that any account of hell must somehow be connected 'with Jesus Christ'.[27]

But what exactly is the problem Holmes perceives in the traditional Reformed account of reprobation? He says that Barth's doctrine of election is innovative because Barth wants to make reprobation *part of the gospel*. For on Barth's account, it is Christ who is reprobate, not fallen human beings.[28]

---

25. *God of Grace*, p. 239.

26. Ibid., p. 265.

27. *Listening to the Past*, p. 134.

28. 'I do not think it has been sufficiently recognised that this [namely, Barth's account of election] is only decisively innovative with regard to reprobation; in the case of election it merely sets on a sounder systematic base the things the tradition has always been trying to say' (ibid).

Holmes also says he believes the traditional Reformed doctrine removes 'hell from any essential connection to the major themes of Christian theology', which, Holmes thinks 'was mistaken' because 'a more adequate account of the decree may offer a way of giving a theological account of perdition that is not strange and disconnected, but woven into the central themes and stories of Christian theology'.[29]

Let us take stock. There seem to be three main issues that lie behind what Holmes says in these different passages. These are as follows.

1. The traditional Reformed account of reprobation means God creates some human beings for reprobation and hell. But this has unacceptable theological consequences, for example that it makes God a divine tyrant, who creates some people only to torture them forever for his own greater glory.

2. On this traditional Reformed account of reprobation and hell there is no connection between reprobation and Christ, whereas there is a connection between election and Christ. But this is also theologically unacceptable because any adequate account of election must also show how reprobation is connected to Christ. (The same applies to any theological account of those outside the church, according to Holmes.)

3. Barth's account of the election and reprobation of Christ succeeds where the Reformed account does not, precisely because he links reprobation with Christ (the reprobate one) and brings reprobation within the orbit of Christology.

The problem with Holmes's three complaints should be clear, given the foregoing treatment of Barth and Edwards in the first two sections of this chapter. The first complaint is simply a consequence of the traditional Reformed account of reprobation. That is, the doctrine of double predestination entails that God creates a certain number of human beings that will suffer an infinite punishment in hell. It is also true that theologians like Edwards have not been slow to capitalize on the idea that those in hell will suffer terrible torments while the elect watch with approval from the vantage of heaven – in fact, Edwards thinks that the righteous will contemplate the end of the wicked as a means to further glorify the God whose just punishment is being served upon those in hell.[30]

Two things can be said about this. The first, picked up by Holmes himself, is that the traditional doctrine of hell seems terrible to our modern ears

29. Ibid., p. 135. Cf. Holmes, 'Justice of Hell', pp. 402–403, for similar sentiments.
30. See Edwards's sermon 'The End of the Wicked Contemplated by the Righteous', in Hickman, *Works of Jonathan Edwards*, vol. 2, pp. 207–212.

because it is out of step with our modern intuitions about how God should behave.[31] But our intuitions about these matters are hardly a reliable guide, given what Scripture says about the noetic effects of sin. To put it another way, the fact that an infinite punishment for sin seems an appalling, even disproportionate, punishment to contemporary human beings does not necessarily mean it is an appalling, disproportionate punishment. It may be that this is simply testimony to our failure to take with sufficient seriousness the idea of sinning against a being of infinite beauty and value. The second thing to say is that even if one opts for a traditional Reformed account of the punishment of sin in hell, this does not commit one to a particular thesis about the *nature* of that punishment. Edwards's picture of the end of the wicked contemplated by the righteous is certainly one traditional image. But it is an *image*. For all we know, the punishment of those in hell will take a very different form from that Edwards preached on.

Holmes's second complaint is difficult to square with traditional Reformed theology. It is true that, according to the traditional Reformed account, the reprobate have no connection to the saving work of Christ, whereas the elect do. But from this it does not follow that on the traditional Reformed account the reprobate have no connection to Christ. For presumably, the reprobate exist because of the agency of Christ (John 1:3) and are sustained by the triune God if one takes seriously the principle, endorsed by all traditional Reformed theologians, that *opera trinitatis ad extra sunt indivisa* (the external works of the Trinity are indivisible). The work of the Father in creating and sustaining the world are also the actions of the Son and Spirit who are perichoretically united with the Father in all he does. But this is simply catholic doctrine. No traditional Reformed theologian would deny this. And from this it follows that the act of reprobation is an act of the Triune God, since the act of reprobation is a work of God *ad extra* (to the outside). It can hardly be a work of God *ad intra* (to the inside, or 'internal to' God), since the divine decrees concern God's intention in creating, not some putative relation between the divine persons in their hidden divine life. So, given other commitments of Reformed theology, like a robust doctrine of the Trinity, it is simply false to say there is no connection between the reprobate and Christ on the Reformed account. Christ as the agent through whom all things were made is present, as is Christ the one present in the act of sustaining the cosmos (including the reprobate) and Christ the one who comes to judge the living and the dead. The traditional Reformed account of these matters is robustly Christological. It is just that the

---

31. *Listening to the Past*, p. 135.

Christology concerned has to do with aspects of the work of the second person of the Trinity apart from his work of redemption.[32] But this can hardly be a shortcoming of the Reformed view if the work of Christ is applicable only to those for whom Christ died, namely the elect (and the elect are some fraction of humanity less than the total number of humans). So, what Holmes's criticism amounts to is this: the Reformed conceived of the nature of the relation between Christ and the reprobate in a different way than did Barth. But, once again, this is bound to be the case given the logic of the Reformed position, over and against that of Barth.

What of Holmes's third complaint? This was that Barth's account of the election and reprobation of Christ succeeds where the Reformed account does not, precisely because he links reprobation with Christ (the Reprobate One) and brings reprobation within the orbit of Christology. But from what we have seen of Barth's position, what Barth actually says about the nature of reprobation is not preferable to the traditional Reformed account because Barth's position is incoherent. Nor is it clear how Christ can be the one who is reprobate (or elect for that matter). One could take Barth's doctrine in the direction of universalism if we ignore some of the things he says about the nature of derivative election 'in' Christ. This would mean there are no human beings who will finally end up in hell. All are derivatively elect; none is derivatively reprobate, and this would mean Barth's doctrine does make reprobation 'part of the gospel' in the sense that it would mean all humanity are finally elect because of the work of Christ (in becoming vicariously reprobate 'for us'). But the price of this construal of Barth's doctrine will be too high for most, including Barth himself. But if we think of Barth as someone who believed not all would be finally saved, or who held that this was possible, then it is difficult to see how Barth's account does link reprobation with Christ for such persons. In fact, it is difficult to know what to make of such an 'impossible possibility'.

---

32. Cf. Calvin on John 17:2: 'Now, Christ does not say that he has been placed in command of the whole world to bestow life indiscriminately. But he restricts this grace to those given to him. But how were they given? For the Father has also subjected to him the reprobate. I reply: Only the elect belong to his own flock, which he guards as a shepherd. Hence the kingdom of Christ extends to all men, but it is saving only to the elect who follow the Shepherd's voice with willing obedience. He forcibly compels others to obey him, until at last he utterly destroys them with his iron rod' (*Calvin's New Testament Commentaries*, ed. D. W. Torrance and T. F. Torrance, 12 vols. [Grand Rapids: Eerdmans, 1959–72], vol. 5, p. 136).

How could a human being who is elect-in-Christ become reprobate, since Christ has already taken upon himself our reprobation and paid the price necessary to expiate that sin (according to Barth)? As we have already seen, we could read parts of what Barth says in *Church Dogmatics* to mean that my derivative election is secure provided I do not 'opt out' of that elect state, and choose to reject Christ. The problem with this is that it flatly contradicts other things Barth says about the inexorable nature of our derivative election in Christ. And if we lay that aside for the sake of argument, then we are left with a doctrine of election that sounds very different to the tenor of Barth's account in *CD* II/2, where my derivative election is conditional upon my not rejecting Christ's salvific act on my behalf. This might be a doctrine of election that is Christological in the sense Holmes intends, but it is a doctrine of a very different order from that most Barth-scholars have found in Barth's writings.

So it seems that Holmes's three complaints against the Reformed doctrine of reprobation over and against Barth's doctrine are either trivially true given a traditional Reformed doctrine of double predestination, or wide of the mark. There may be problems with the traditional Reformed account. Holmes is right to point out that increasing numbers of contemporary theologians find the traditional Reformed doctrine unpalatable. But one must have a good theological reason for rejecting a position the main theological structures of which are common to almost all catholic theologians in the tradition, including such luminaries as Augustine, Anselm and Aquinas. Holmes offers no such theological argument. His appeal to Barth as an alternative depends on a rather selective reading of the Reformed account that brackets out important theological commitments that have a bearing on the doctrine of reprobation, like the *opera trinitatis ad extra sunt indivisa* principle. Barth's Christological account of election is not an improvement on this, because his alternative, though suggestive, makes incomplete sense as it stands.

Postscript

Another, nineteenth-century, Holmes, once made the famous remark 'When you have eliminated the impossible, whatever remains, *however improbable*, must be the truth.'[33] We have seen that, given what Barth himself says about the

---

33. Sherlock Holmes, in A. C. Doyle's *The Sign of Four* (London: Penguin, 2001), ch. 6.

doctrine of election, his account does not represent a more theologically satisfying understanding of this doctrine in general, and reprobation and damnation in particular, than is offered in traditional Reformed theology (represented
in this chapter by Edwards).

Although Edwards, like Barth, had a fertile and original mind and exhibited
bold and unusual ways of thinking about various theological *loci*, unlike Barth,
Edwards remained within the bounds of traditional Reformed thinking on this
matter. He thought there was a hell, and that God really did reprobate some
people for his own greater glory. What is more, he did not think that, in the
final analysis, God would bring about the salvation of all humanity, whether in
this life or the next. For, according to Edwards, the last great end of all things
is the glorification of God – and this act of divine self-glorification must
include the reprobation of some number of fallen humanity for both God's
justice and mercy to be displayed in the created order.

Nevertheless, what Edwards and his Reformed compatriots fail to see,
and what Barth's account does hint at, is that God might bring about his
plans, including the display of his justice in the reprobation of some fallen
humans, by reprobating only one human being. Divine justice is meted out
on Barth's account, and reprobation does occur. But it occurs only in one
human, the God-man, for the purposes of salvation. Barth drew the conclusion that the scope of this salvation is certain and unchangeable: no-one
can now be outside the bounds of God's election, and the rejection of one's
derivatively elect status is an 'impossible possibility'. Yet, somehow, some
human beings can, and perhaps do (finally?) reject Christ. Earlier, I suggested that this account of election is problematic because it means Christ
is the reprobate one, and God cannot reprobate himself. Furthermore,
someone who is reprobate is not in a position to act on behalf of fallen
humanity because God has rejected him. However, an objection to the traditional Reformed account of election could be had using Barth's position
as a point of departure. This objection turns on whether God could have
reprobated only one human being *and* thereby satisfied his divine retributive
justice. Barth thinks God does do this, reprobating the God-man. But,
assuming that Christ cannot be reprobate (because he is God incarnate, and
because this would render him incapable of acting as a saviour), it is still possible for God to reprobate one other human being, like you or me. Then
divine wrath and mercy would truly have met and the result would have been
the salvation of all humanity, bar the one rejected. The fact that Reformed
theologians, in keeping with orthodox Christian theology more generally,
have denied this conclusion raises a serious theological conundrum, which
has to do with why God has not brought about the salvation of all human-

ity (bar one) if he was able to, according to the logic of a traditional Reformed or Augustinian account of election and reprobation. But there is a way out of this problem for theologians like Edwards.[34] This involves adding a premise to the argument for double predestination, to the effect that 'there is a need for the display of both God's grace and mercy and his wrath and justice in his created order *for some number of deserving humanity*'. If, for some reason, God must display his retributive justice in the reprobation of some fraction of fallen humanity (greater than a solitary individual), then at least some of the force of a Barthian, or Barth-inspired, counter-attack on this position is absorbed by the Edwardsian, or more broadly, Reformed argument, after all.

It will seem improbable to many Barth scholars that what Barth says about the nature of the doctrine of election (and reprobation) is *less* theologically satisfying than the traditional Reformed doctrine of the double decree – after all, Barth sought to overthrow this very notion with his own reconceptualizing of the doctrine, which is supposed to be an improvement on the old, Reformed thinking about reprobation and damnation. The results are indeed bold and provocative, as expressed in the *Church Dogmatics*. But they cannot be considered a success, if, in academic discourse, a sine qua non of any successful (and, for that matter, truthful or even possibly true) doctrine is that it is expressed in such a way that, *taken as a whole*, it makes complete sense. Yet, as I have been labouring to explain here, Barth's doctrine of election, unlike Edwards's doctrine, is not coherent when taken as a whole. It might be construed as a species of universalism (if we privilege certain things Barth says and ignore others). But for many (Barth included) that was not the conclusion he was hoping for. For this reason, Stephen Holmes's account of the merits of Barth's view versus those of the Reformed tradition is wide of the mark. He is unable to make good on his initial claim, which was that Barth's account is theologically preferable because it is superior to other, traditional Reformed accounts of reprobation. Furthermore, Holmes's representation of the differences between Barth and Edwards, in particular in this matter of reprobation, is also mistaken. Edwards's account is not problem-free, but the difficulties facing his doctrine do not arise because it is internally disordered, or because Edwards appears to be in two minds about the doctrine he wants to defend. But both of these things are true of Barth's doctrine of reprobation. His account is disordered and he does appear to say different things at different times about the

---

34. For a more detailed account of this 'way out', see O. D. Crisp, 'Is Universalism a Problem for Particularists?', forthcoming in *SJT*.

nature of reprobation in *Church Dogmatics*.[35] Of course, this does not necessarily mean that Edwards, Calvin or any other Reformed divine before Barth
had the *right* account of reprobation. That would have to be argued for and I
have offered no such argument here. But given what we have considered, it
does mean that Barth's version of the divine 'No' in reprobation is not preferable to the traditional Reformed doctrine he sought to overthrow.[36]

© Oliver D. Crisp, 2008

---

35. This point is underlined by McDonald's article 'Barth's "Other" Doctrine of
    Election'.
36. I am grateful to Paul Helm, David Gibson, Steve Holmes and Sebastian Rehnman
    for comments on a previous draft of this chapter. Thanks also to Rob Price for
    help in chasing references.

11. 'CHURCH' DOGMATICS: KARL BARTH AS ECCLESIAL THEOLOGIAN

Donald Macleod

Next to the publication of the first edition of his *Commentary on Romans* in 1919 the key moment in Karl Barth's theological career came in 1931. Faced with the task of preparing a second edition of the first volume of his *Christian Dogmatics*[1] he found himself in a dilemma: 'I could still say what I had said. I wanted to do so. But I could not do it in the same way. What option did I have but to begin again from the beginning, saying the same thing, but in a different way?'[2] The result was that the second edition of *Christian Dogmatics* never appeared. Instead, work began on the *Church Dogmatics*, and the first part-volume was published in 1932.[3]

This new beginning was clearly no sudden development. Barth had been schooled in classic German Liberalism, but his faith in the Kant-Schleiermacher-Hermann synthesis had been swept away many years previously, not least by the action of the ninety-three German intellectuals who on 3 October 1914 issued 'a terrible manifesto' associating themselves with the war policy of the Kaiser.

---

1. *Prolegomena zur christlichen Dogmatik* (Zurich: Evangelischer Verlag, 1928).
2. E. Busch, *Karl Barth: His Life from Letters and Autobiographical Texts*, trans. J. Bowden (Eugene, Oreg.: Wipf & Stock, 2005), pp. 209–210.
3. The authorized English translation by G. T. Thomson, *Church Dogmatics* I/1, *The Doctrine of the Word of God*, was published in 1936 (Edinburgh: T. & T. Clark).

Among the signatories were virtually all of Barth's most revered teachers. 'It was like the twilight of the gods', Barth recalled, 'when I saw the reaction of Harnack, Hermann, Rade, Eucken and company to the new situation.'[4] In Barth's eyes, the religion and scholarship of his theological masters was hopelessly compromised by their failure in the face of the ideology of war: 'a whole world of exegesis, ethics, dogmatics and preaching, which I had hitherto held to be trustworthy, was shaken to the foundations, and with it, all the other writings of the German theologians'.[5]

Even before this, however, Barth had found himself in a predicament as a preacher. The problem was not the technical one, '*How* should he preach?' It was a matter of basic content. From 1911 to 1921 he was the pastor of the semi-industrialized Alpine parish of Safenwil, and his principal task, as he saw it, was the Sunday sermon. But what could he say? He had no right to speak to the congregation about human religious experiences. He had to bring a decisive word of divine revelation: not a human word, but 'the divine word of revelation directed *to* man'.[6]

By the time a second, thoroughly revised, edition of his *Commentary on Romans* appeared in 1922, Barth had been appointed a professor of theology at Göttingen, and as he wrestled with the task of preparing his lectures, Heppe's *Reformed Dogmatics* fell into his hands.[7] Barth now found himself becoming more and more open to Protestant orthodoxy: critical, but willing to learn, to the consternation of his theological associates, who 'could only shake their heads at this remarkable change of direction'.[8] He also developed a positive interest in the early Fathers and in Catholic Scholasticism. All the while, however, he 'kept returning from every angle to the situation of the pastor in the pulpit'.[9] He was still trying to answer the question that had so

---

4. Busch, *Karl Barth*, p. 81.
5. Ibid.
6. Ibid., p. 150. According to Timothy George, 'This tension between the preacher's duty to speak for God, on behalf of God, and the enormous presumption, indeed the impossibility, of doing so is at the very root of Barth's theological discovery' ('Running Like a Herald to Deliver the Message: Barth on the Church and Sacraments', in Sung Wook Chung [ed.], *Karl Barth and Evangelical Theology* [Carlisle: Paternoster, 2006], p. 192).
7. H. Heppe, *Reformed Dogmatics Set out and Illustrated from the Sources*, rev. and ed. E. Bizer, trans. G. T. Thomson (London: George Allen & Unwin, 1950; repr. Grand Rapids: Baker, 1978).
8. Busch, *Karl Barth*, p. 154.
9. Ibid.

troubled him during his pastorate in Safenwil: what should be stated and heard in Christian preaching today?

Fresh start

Much of this was already reflected in the first volume of *Christian Dogmatics*. Why then, when the time came for a second edition, did he abandon the original project and start all over again? And why, above all, the change of title?

The reasons are set forth in the foreword to the first volume of *Church Dogmatics*, and, somewhat more personally, in Eberhard Busch's account of Barth's life. Prominent among them was Barth's determination to exclude anything and everything that might have seemed to give theology 'a basis, a support or even a justification in terms of existentialist philosophy'. He clearly thought that even in the *Christian Dogmatics* he was hindered by 'the eggshells of a philosophical system'. Now he hoped to speak 'more freely', even though, paradoxically, he would henceforth speak 'in accordance with the church's belief'.[10] Against the background of the Enlightenment, this represents a curious reversal of roles. Philosophy is no longer freedom, but bondage; orthodoxy no longer bondage, but freedom.

Another reason for Barth's change of direction was that he was now turning his back definitively on the historical perspective of his former teacher, Adolph Harnack. Harnack had portrayed the history of dogma as the story of the betrayal of the primitive gospel and its replacement by a Hellenized form of Christianity. If this was so, then the whole of Christian thought between the Apostolic Fathers and Schleiermacher was irrelevant to the question 'What is Christianity?' and, by implication, irrelevant to dogmatics. The Greek and Latin Fathers, the Scholastics, the Reformers and the Lutheran and Calvinist dogmaticians of the seventeenth century were all, according to Harnack, fatally tainted with Greek metaphysics.

During his time as a student in Berlin, Barth had heard from Harnack's own lips the argument that 'the dogma of the early period was the self-expression of the Greek spirit in the sphere of the gospel',[11] and he had accepted his great

---

10. Ibid., p. 211.

11. Ibid., p. 39. Cf. Adolph Harnack's own words in *History of Dogma*, 3rd ed., trans. N. Buchanan (New York: Dover, 1961), vol. 1, p. 17: 'Dogma in its conception and development is the work of the Greek spirit on the soil of the Gospel.'

teacher's ideas unreservedly. By the time he came to write the foreword to the first volume of the *Church Dogmatics*, however, he had repudiated them. The very concept of dogmatics, and even the concept of the canon, were 'church' concepts, and as such part of the history from which Harnack and his school demanded we should distance ourselves. This, in Barth's view, would be fatal to dogmatics, because the finest and most interesting problems in Christian theology begin at the very point where, according to Harnack, 'we should have to stop thinking because of the fable of "unprofitable Scholasticism" or the catchword about "the Greek thought of the Fathers"'.[12] This is tantamount to saying that if we proscribe the questions raised in the allegedly Hellenized 'history of dogma' we shall have no questions left, and theology will be bereft of an agenda. Barth is now insisting, over against Ritschl, Hermann and Harnack, that theology can flourish only in constant, if critical, discussion with the centuries of ecclesiastical tradition.

And it is precisely here that we find the third and main reason for Barth's change of direction: his developing perception of the relation between dogmatics and the church. He admitted that in calling his first attempt *Christian Dogmatics*, he had been guilty of a 'light-hearted use' of the word 'Christian'. There was nothing light-hearted about his use of the word 'Church'. It was the result of sustained, sharply focused reflection on the task of dogmatics, the nature of the church and the essence of Christianity.

The church is the subject of dogmatics

This reflection bred the conclusion, first of all, that the church is *the subject* of dogmatics. This point is made forcibly in *Dogmatics in Outline*:

> [It] is no limitation and no vilification of the concept of dogmatics as a science that the subject of this science is the Church. It is the place, the community, charged with the object and activity with which dogmatics is concerned – namely, the proclamation of the Gospel. By calling the Church the subject of dogmatics we mean that where dogmatics is pursued, whether by pupil or by teacher, we find ourselves in the sphere of the Church. The man who seeks to occupy himself with dogmatics and deliberately puts himself outside the Church would have to reckon with the fact that for him the object of dogmatics would be alien, and should not be surprised if after the first steps he could not find his bearings, or even did damage. Even in dogmatics

---

12. *CD* I/1, p. xi.

familiarity with the subject must be there, and this really means familiarity with the life of the Church.[13]

One implication of this was that for Barth dogmatics was not a 'free science', but one that has as its substratum the kind of spiritual experience and perception reported by such men as Luther and Anselm. This is no warrant, however, for reverting to the practice of Schleiermacher, where theology becomes anthropology and where the propositions of dogmatics merely describe the human condition and articulate human piety. The object of theology lies outside the church, in the same way as the object of any science lies outside the observer. Here it is true both that the church is *but* the observer and that the church *is* the observer; and while theology must not become subjective, the subjective state of the theologian is nevertheless important. Church Dogmatics must be a *theologia regenitorum* (a theology of the born again): 'Faith, rebirth, conversion, "existential thinking" (i.e., thinking that proceeds on the basis of existential perplexity) is indeed the indispensable prerequisite for dogmatic work.'[14] Precisely because dogmatics is conducted by the church and within the church, its task, according to Barth, is to criticize and review the church's language about God. In this connection he returns repeatedly to article 7 of the Augsburg Confession, which defines the church as the congregation of saints, in which 'the Gospel is rightly taught and the sacraments rightly administered' (*in qua Evangelium recte docetur, et recte administrantur sacramenta*). This *recte* (rightly) is the preoccupation of dogmatics: 'Dogmatics is the science in which the Church, in accordance with the state of its knowledge at different times, takes account of the content of its proclamation critically, that is, by the standard of Holy Scripture and under the guidance of its Confessions.'[15] This presupposes, of course, that the church does actually engage in proclamation: 'There would be no dogmatics and there would perhaps be no theology at all, unless the Church's task consisted centrally in the proclamation of the Gospel.' It is precisely because this *is* her task that the church charges dogmatics with the responsibility of answering the question '*What* are we to think and say?'[16]

---

13. K. Barth, *Dogmatics in Outline*, trans. G. T. Thomson (London: SCM, 1949), pp. 9–10.
14. *CD* I/1, p. 22.
15. *Dogmatics in Outline*, p. 9.
16. Ibid., p. 12.

By what criterion?

Here lurks the fundamental issue in Barth's ecclesial theology. By what criterion does dogmatics judge the church's proclamation? At first sight Barth
seems to speak with crystal clarity on this question. Dogmatics judges the
church's proclamation 'by the standard of Holy Scripture and under the guidance of its Confessions'. Yet it eventually becomes plain that Barth has no
compunction about operating independently of the creeds, and even in contradiction of them. We shall also have to ask whether he does not show similar
independence in relation to the Scriptures themselves, striking out where they
do not lead and leaving a very strong impression that he does not feel bound
to regard every prophetic or apostolic declaration as normative.

It is in the light of the theologian's role as critic that Barth proceeds to lay
down that church proclamation is the *material* of dogmatics.[17] The 'material'
here is the material that dogmatics criticizes, and it is from this point of view
that proclamation is the presupposition of theology. Precisely because the
church's language claims to be the word of God it must be measured *by* the
word of God, and such measurement is the task of dogmatics, which starts
out with 'criticisms of yesterday's proclamation'.[18]

Yet, the criticism engaged in by dogmatics is not to be confined to proclamation. The church's social work, worship, education, youth work, ecumenical relations and the relations between church and society must all come under
theological scrutiny; and the same is true of what Barth regards as the non-
proclamatory elements in the church's God-talk, for example her hymns and
prayers. Barth is fully aware that such theological scrutiny may not always be
to the taste of modern ecclesiastics. There are 'vigorously practical men' who
boast that they live 'quite untheologically'.[19] But Barth asks what these practical men do. They talk and they preach and they write! Is their right to do so
to be unquestioned? And is what they say to be unquestioned? If it is, and if
we are to yield to this demand for 'quite untheological thought and language',
we will merely be conceding the freedom to babble heresy: and there is no
room in the church for such freedom.[20]

At the same time, Barth insists that theology as such cannot claim to be
proclamation: 'The central thing to be proclaimed we may not and cannot

---

17. *CD* I/1, p. 51.
18. Ibid., pp. 86–87.
19. Ibid., p. 85.
20. Ibid., p. 86.

expect to hear from dogmatics.' Its role is merely to serve as a balustrade to prevent the proclamation from falling into the abyss. But this is rendered slightly curious by the fact that Barth's *Dogmatics* shows little sign of engaging with the church's proclamation, as distinct from the church's theology. If we were to take his methodological statements at face value, we would expect him to devote a substantial amount of attention to the church's proclamatory, homiletical literature. Here, after all, is 'yesterday's proclamation', which it is the alleged task of dogmatics to criticize. What we find, instead, is that Barth is engaging with the church's theology as represented particularly by the Fathers, the Schoolmen, the Reformers and the seventeenth-century dogmaticians. Of course, as Barth concedes, crossings of the boundary between dogmatics and proclamation are inevitable. But it is still curious, granted his starting point, that he conducts his dialogues with such figures as Augustine, Anselm, Aquinas, Lombard, Luther, Calvin, Turretin and Wollebius. Even when he does engage (as he does, and most effectively) in criticism of the contemporary 'pulpit', his dialogue partners are Schleiermacher, Ritschl, Harnack, Hermann and Bultmann. All of these men preached, but they were not primarily preachers. They were scholars and theologians, and by directing his critique of the church's proclamation at such targets Barth is conceding that the line between dogmatics and proclamation is a very thin one. The theology of Schleiermacher and Hermann was not merely the presupposition of the pre-war German pulpit; it was its actual message. By contrast, Barth's engagement with 'proclamation' as distinct from dogmatics is minimal. Helmut Thielicke, by contrast, could write the fascinating volume *Encounter with Spurgeon*.[21] It is hard to imagine Barth doing the same. His conversations are with Anselm, Thomas, Calvin and Schleiermacher.

The critical attitude and church proclamation

Once we define dogmatics as critique of the church's proclamation, we encounter an inevitable tension between the critical mindset of the scholar and the believing attitude of the churchman. Barth himself quotes from Paul Althaus to this precise effect, highlighting the potential conflict between the 'critical attitude' and 'church proclamation'.[22] Both of these are equally necessary to the theologian, but they appear mutually to endanger each other. To the

---

21. Trans. J. W. Doberstein (Cambridge: Cambridge University Press, 1964).
22. *CD* I/1, p. 23.

extent that dogmatics is a 'science' the theologian must prosecute his work in
association with the other academic disciplines, and the church must conduct
her self-test by the human application of human means.[23] But the dogmatician's church connection already means that he or she is already committed in
faith (though not *implicit* faith) to the church's teaching. To what extent does
this leave us free to criticize? The point of Althaus's remark is sharpened by
the observation of Robert Jenson that the slogan of the Enlightenment ('one
made definitive for the movement by its perfecter, Immanuel Kant') was the
intellectual policy of 'critique': the suspicion of all appearances of truth.[24]
Does Barth's principial espousal of criticism mean that dogmatics must live
within this culture of suspicion? And if so, does this mean that in dogmatics
it is faith itself that is being critical? Or, on the contrary, is dogmatics being
critical of faith?

Barth's way out of this would be to accept, along with Reformed orthodoxy, that no science can give 'scientific proof' of its own axioms.[25] To this
extent, all science is based on presupposition. The presuppositions of
Christian theology are, first, that God *is* and, secondly, that he has *revealed*
himself in his word, holy Scripture. These are certain to faith, the one
through the God-implanted *sensus deitatis* (awareness of deity), the other
through the *testimonium internum Spiritus Sancti* (the inward testimony of the
Holy Spirit). The scientific procedure (Christian dogmatics) stands on the
foundation of these presuppositions. Theology can reflect on these presuppositions, but it cannot prove them, since that would imply asking the theologian to stand on an alien, non-theological foundation in order to prove his
own presuppositions. The scientific nature of dogmatics appears, not in its
ability to 'prove' its first principles (even the scientist cannot 'prove' his own
existence), but in the consistency and thoroughness with which it applies its
own criteria. By the same token, the theologian is showing an appropriately

---

23. Ibid., p. 22.
24. 'Karl Barth', in D. F. Ford (ed.), *The Modern Theologians*, 2nd ed. (Oxford: Blackwell,
     1997), p. 23.
25. See e.g. H. Bavinck, *Reformed Dogmatics*, vol. 1, ed. J. Bolt, trans. J. Vriend (Grand
     Rapids: Baker, 2003), pp. 207–214, 561–600. Bavinck argues (p. 209) that 'There is
     indeed no room for a philosophical theory of fundamental principles that must
     first lay the foundation for the study of theology and has the right to justify this
     pursuit. If dogmatics or theology in general did not, like other disciplines, have its
     own fundamental principles (*principia*), it could not lay claim to the name of being
     "a science concerning God".'

critical attitude, not when he is sceptical towards his own canon, but when he refuses to accept anything as true till it is proven from that canon, holy Scripture, the *principium cognoscendi* (principle of knowledge) of his own scientific discipline.

Here is a route to a viable accord between the 'critical attitude' and 'church proclamation'. Barth, however, cannot go down this road. Nor can he claim that his scepticism is simply that of the Bereans, who searched the Scriptures to check whether what Paul said was true (Acts 17:11), though there are certainly statements in *Church Dogmatics* and elsewhere which would suggest that this is indeed the line he is pursuing. He quite rightly rejects the notion of the infallibility of the church. Our task cannot be merely to repeat what has been prescribed in ancient or modern times by a church authority.[26] In accordance with this, Barth also lays down that no creed or confession, whether of the Reformation or of our own day, can claim the respect of the church in the same degree that Scripture in its uniqueness deserves it. Dogmatics, therefore, has to measure the church's proclamation by the standard of the holy Scriptures, the Old and New Testaments.[27]

Taken at face value, this means that Scripture is the norm by which dogmatics regulates itself and by which it tests the proclamation of the church. Yet there are clear signs that the 'critique' also extends to Scripture itself, and this becomes particularly clear in Barth's chapter on 'Scripture as the Word of God',[28] where he argues not only that the Bible is vulnerable to criticism, but that its capacity for error is by no means confined to minor factual detail, dubious chronology or outmoded cosmogony, but extends even to its religious and theological content. The reason for this is that its authors speak as fallible, erring men like ourselves. Their word, therefore, can be read and assessed as a purely human word and

> subjected to all kinds of immanent criticism, not only in respect of its philosophical, historical and ethical content, but even of its religious and theological content. We can establish lacunae, inconsistencies and over-emphases. We may be alienated by a figure like Moses. We may quarrel with James or with Paul. We may have to admit that we can make little or nothing of large tracts of the Bible, as is often the case with the records of other men. We can take offence at the Bible.[29]

---

26. *Dogmatics in Outline*, p. 10.
27. Ibid., p. 13.
28. *CD* I/2, pp. 473–537.
29. Ibid., p. 507.

This is not the place for an analysis of Barth's doctrine of Scripture (see ch. 6 in this volume). Suffice it to say that whatever the commitment to *church* dogmatics, this attitude to Scripture has not been worked out 'in the sphere of the Church'.[30] Instead, the Christian theologian has stood outside his own theology to criticize his own canon. The issue here is not inerrancy or some mechanical theory of inspiration. The issue is canonicity: the competence of Scripture as Supreme Judge in all matters theological. If Barth is correct, not only can the church err; Scripture can err. A theological statement may be biblical, and yet wrong. Nor is this some mere inconsistency in Barth's system; it flows from its heart, from the belief that the unity between Scripture and the word of God is not a fact, but an event. There can be no direct identification of revelation and the Bible, such as would entitle us to say that Scripture *is* the word of God. We can say only that it becomes or may become the word of God; and this is entirely a matter of the divine freedom.[31]

All this leads to one clear conclusion: *Paulus dixit* (Paul has spoken) and *Deus dixit* (God has spoken) are two different things.[32] This is why we can 'quarrel with Paul', as noted above (raising the interesting conundrum whether it is appropriate to quarrel with him *after* his word becomes the word of God, or only before). If this is true, then someone superior to an apostle, and something more authoritative than Scripture, is sitting in judgment on the theological content of the Bible itself. We may, in other words, appeal against a ruling of the Supreme Judge, a radical departure from *church* dogmatics.

It is hardly surprising, in the light of this, that Barth is prepared to stand in judgment over the church's creeds. These ancient symbols do indeed have an authority that must be taken seriously, as have the Reformed confessions and the early fathers, and Barth was indeed resolved to continue in 'the Reformation line'. But he could not become an orthodox Calvinist. Even less

---

30. See the article 'The Church Doctrine of Inspiration', in B. B. Warfield, *The Inspiration and Authority of the Bible* (Philadelphia: Presbyterian & Reformed, 1948). Warfield refers to what he calls 'this well-defined, aboriginal, stable doctrine of the church' and argues (p. 107) that 'this attitude of entire trust in every word of the Scriptures has been characteristic of the people of God from the very foundation of the church. Christendom has always reposed upon the belief that the utterances of this book are properly oracles of God.' It is precisely this 'church' doctrine that Barth repudiates: 'we have to resist and reject the 17th century doctrine of inspiration as false doctrine' (*CD* I/2, p. 525).

31. *CD* I/1, p. 127.

32. Ibid., p. 127.

could he support Lutheran confessionalism.[33] And even though he wanted to write a *church* dogmatics, he could not write in the tradition of any confession. In accordance with this, he would deliver his 1937/1938 Gifford Lectures 'connected to' the Scots Confession,[34] but he would not bind himself to a historical analysis of the text or commit himself to expounding its original meaning. Instead, he would try to work out how he must 'respond' to it. In the same way, he would discover Heppe's *Reformed Dogmatics*, and record his pleasure at finding himself 'in the sphere of the Church' and at discovering 'a dogmatics which had both form and substance', but he was also clear that 'a return to this orthodoxy (to stick to it and to do the same sort of thing) was impossible. For even in that early period the "bane of Israel" which hitherto I had met in its neo-Protestant form was already in evidence and was making itself felt.'[35] This probably explains, too, why, though on every issue he would consult John Calvin, he would seldom follow him.[36] And what was true of his attitude to the Reformed tradition was equally true in relation to all others. At best, he was willing to learn; invariably he was critical (he himself would add, 'in an exalted sense of the word').[37] Furthermore, not only was he unwilling to produce theology in the tradition of any one confession; he was also incapable of abiding by their consensus, and even of showing any strong loyalty to the famed principle of Vincent of Lerins that we should hold to what has been believed 'everywhere, in every place and by everyone' (*quod ubique, quod semper, quod ab omnibus*). *Church Dogmatics* shows abundant evidence of massive and meticulous research, but in the last analysis the author is a theological loner in a sense that Augustine and Calvin were not.

The result, from the viewpoint of the history of Christian dogma, is a theological smorgasbord. Authorities are consulted, criticized and responded to, but the outcome is always the same: Barth picks and chooses; or, to change the metaphor, the great authorities of the past, however illustrious, become mere

---

33. Busch, *Karl Barth*, p. 211.
34. *The Knowledge of God and the Service of God according to the Teaching of the Reformation*, trans. J. L. M. Haire and I. Henderson (London: Hodder & Stoughton, 1938), p 10.
35. Busch, *Karl Barth*, p. 154.
36. See further Sung Wook Chung, *Admiration and Challenge: Karl Barth's Theological Relationship with John Calvin* (New York: Peter Lang, 2002). He regards Barth's relationship with Calvin as 'ambivalent' and concludes that he follows the Reformer only when he hopes to gain support from Calvin to prop up his own arguments (p. 170).
37. Busch, *Karl Barth*, p. 210.

springboards for his own thought and conclusions. He holds firmly by the great gospel miracles of the Apostles' Creed: the virgin birth and the empty tomb. He endorses the *homoousion* and, in association with it, the *theotokos*.[38] He stands with the church on Chalcedon, the hypostatic union and even the concepts of *anhypostasia* and *enhypostasia*. And he writes with unsurpassed eloquence on the doctrine of vicarious atonement ('The Judge Judged in our Place').[39]

But on a wide range of key issues he simply goes his own way. On natural theology, he distances himself not only from Aquinas, but from Calvin.[40] On the Trinity, he declares that while he does not wish to outlaw outright the concept of 'person' or withdraw it altogether from circulation, he can use it only as 'a practical abbreviation and as a reminder of the historical continuity of the problem'.[41] On crucial Reformation issues such as the relation of law and gospel, nature and grace, he found it impossible to follow either Luther or Calvin, and deemed it necessary to construe them 'more exactly and thus differently from the patterns which I found in the sixteenth century'.[42] On the doctrine of baptism, he distanced himself from Fathers, Scholastics and Reformers alike, and chose, essentially, the position of the Anabaptists, describing infant baptism as 'a practice which has pushed its way into the Church *force majeure* and in which the character of baptism both as obedience and response is so obscured as to be virtually unrecognisable'.[43] On the doctrine of election he strikes out in defiance of Augustine and Calvin (and St Paul?) and boldly goes where no man has gone before.[44] And in espousing the

---

38. *CD* I/2, p. 137. Note: *homoousios* = 'of the same substance'; *theotokos* = 'the one who gives birth to God'.
39. *CD* IV/1, pp. 211–283.
40. While arguing that 'the revival of the gospel by Luther and Calvin 'consisted in their desire to see both the church and human salvation founded on the Word of God alone, on God's revelation in Jesus Christ', Barth nevertheless has to concede not only that Calvin sometimes made 'a guarded and conditional use of the possibility of "Natural Theology"' (as in the opening chapters of the *Institutes*), but also that he 'occasionally' made 'an unguarded and unconditional use of it' (*Knowledge of God*, pp. 8–9).
41. *CD* I/1, p. 412.
42. Busch, *Karl Barth*, p. 211.
43. *CD* IV/4, p. 195. While Barth reaches the conclusions of the Anabaptists, he does not, of course, use their form of argument, namely the absence of explicit New Testament warrant for infant baptism.
44. *CD* II/2, pp. 3–506. 'We cannot', he writes, 'be too soon, or too radical, in the opposition which we must offer to the classical tradition' (ibid., p. 13). He follows

idea of the fallen humanity of Christ he goes where none but a few eccentrics have gone before.[45]

Even Scripture itself seems to have been more of a springboard than a source or norm, as if Barth were more interested in what it suggested to him than in what it actually said, an almost impressionistic theology. 'In dogmatics', he wrote, 'it can never be a question of the mere combination, repetition and summary of biblical doctrine.'[46] Theology does not merely enquire what apostles and prophets have said; its business is with 'what we ourselves must say on the basis of the Apostles and Prophets'.[47] And here, as so often, he claims the support of Calvin, suggesting that though the *Institutio* was interwoven with exegesis, its aim was 'to direct Christian thought and language to its own responsibility in the present'.[48]

It is true, of course, that the task of the dogmatician is not complete with exegesis, any more than it is with biblical or historical theology. Barth's own *Church Dogmatics* clearly illustrates this: the sections in small print would not constitute a dogmatics by themselves. Nevertheless, there is surely no tension between exegesis and theology, or between dogmatics and biblical or

---

this with the comment 'there is a movement away from the biblical testimony even in Augustine' (p. 16).

45. Barth's views on the *sarx* (flesh) assumed by Christ are set forth in *CD* I/2, pp. 151–155. He is fully aware that he is diverging from Luther, Calvin and the Leiden Synposis. His main predecessor in advocating this doctrine was Edward Irving, a Church of Scotland minister who was deposed for heresy in 1833. Barth, however, does not appear to have read Irving for himself. His knowledge is second-hand, gained from H. R. Mackintosh, *The Doctrine of the Person of Christ* (Edinburgh: T. & T. Clark, 1931), p. 277. See further D. Macleod, 'The Doctrine of the Incarnation in Scottish Theology', *SBET* 9 (1991), pp. 40–50.

46. *CD* I/1, p. 6.

47. Ibid., p. 16.

48. Ibid., p. 17. It is arguable that Calvin's aim was the reverse: to lay a foundation for exegesis. See e.g. his preface to the 1559 edition of the *Institutes*, where he makes plain that the purpose of 'this work of ours' was to serve the commentaries by dispensing with the 'need to undertake long doctrinal discussions, and to digress into commonplaces'. He writes, 'it has been my purpose in this labor to prepare and instruct candidates in sacred theology for the reading of the divine Word in order that they may be able both to have easy access to it and to advance without stumbling' (J. Calvin, *Institutes of the Christian Religion*, trans. F. L. Battles, ed. J. T. McNeill, [Louisville: Westminster John Knox, 1960], vol. 1, p. 4).

historical theology. Was it not Calvin's concern, and should it not be ours, to say what the apostles and the prophets said, but to say it in the language of our own day and in application to our own situation?

It is Barth's concern to *speak on the basis* of biblical doctrine rather than to *summarize* it that explains his espousal of such ideas as the fallenness of Christ's humanity. There is no explicit warrant for such a notion in the text of Scripture. Indeed, Paul seems to go out of his way to avoid even suggesting it, when he chooses his words so carefully in Romans 8:3, speaking of Christ as coming 'in the likeness of flesh of sin'. At best, the idea of the Lord's fallenness can be defended only as an alleged development either from the incarnation itself or from such facts as Christ's temptability and his dependence on the Holy Spirit, or from the principle that the 'un-assumed is the unhealed'.[49] But the links are tortuous, and fragile.

The same is true of Barth's doctrine of election, involving both universal election and universal reprobation. This doctrine seems, like the Marian dogmas of Roman Catholicism, to owe all its plausibility to its link with some original idea. What Barth did, in fact, was to lift it out of its original setting in the *ordo salutis*, 'order of salvation' (where it was connected to effectual calling and the new birth), and place it instead in Christology,[50] arguing that since human nature was elect in Christ (in the incarnation) all humans are elect in Christ; and since human nature was reprobate in Christ (at Golgotha) all humans are reprobate in Christ.[51] But why, if all humans are elect, do all not,

---

49. '[T]here must be no weakening or obscuring of the saving truth that the nature which God assumed in Christ is identical with our Nature as we see it in the light of the Fall. If it were otherwise, how could Christ be really like us?' (*CD* I/2, p. 153).

50. Cf. Berkouwer's remark on Barth's doctrine: 'In the doctrine of election everything depends on the relationship between predestination and Christology' (G. C. Berkouwer, *The Triumph of Grace in the Theology of Karl Barth*, trans. H. R. Boer [London: Paternoster, 1956], p. 103).

51. 'In Jesus Christ God in His free grace determines Himself for sinful man and sinful man for Himself. He therefore takes upon Himself the rejection of man with all its consequences, and elects man to participation in His own glory.' This appears to involve the further idea that the hypostatic union is itself the atonement: the 'being' of Christ is his atoning 'activity', and to separate the 'being' from the 'activity' is Nestorianism; see T. F. Torrance, *Karl Barth: Biblical and Evangelical Theologian* (Edinburgh: T. & T. Clark, 1990), p. 237.

KARL BARTH AS ECCLESIAL THEOLOGIAN

in Calvin's terms, 'receive the grace of Christ'; and why, if all are reprobate, do any receive the grace of Christ?

Barth's supporters have justified him on the ground that in this doctrine of predestination the whole doctrine of God is at stake, because the predestinarianism of Augustine and Calvin (the *church* doctrine) makes grace *accidental*.[52] But the whole force of this argument depends on word selection. What if, in place of *accidental*, we speak of *optional*? This does not mean that it is optional with God whether or not to be gracious. That in itself can never be a matter simply of the divine freedom: certainly not a matter of the liberty of alternative choice, as if God had the freedom to choose either to be, or not to be, gracious. But it is certainly optional with God how his grace will be exercised.[53] Indeed, to argue that God has no option but to be symmetrically gracious to all is to argue that we have a right to grace; and that is to collapse grace into justice. Over against that, Scripture consistently portrays grace as a matter of sheer divine sovereignty, even to the extent that side by side with election there is always a passing-by (a preterition). The fallen human race is chosen; the apostate angels are not. Israel is chosen; the nations are not. Jacob is chosen; Esau is not. This is not to argue for a symmetrical double predestination, in which both salvation and perdition are related equally and in the same sense

---

52. See B. L. McCormack's chapter 'Calvin and the Decree', in L. Quigley (ed.), *Reformed Theology in Contemporary Perspective* (Edinburgh: Rutherford House, 2006), p. 131. McCormack also argues (p. 130) that Calvin's doctrine is not decisively controlled by Christology: 'What was in the beginning with God was the decree, not Jesus Christ.' Calvin never personalizes the decree in this way, but, in any case, the antithesis is unfair. To say that the decree was with God in the beginning would simply be to say that the decree is eternal; and that is synonymous with saying that God never was without loving us. The fact that the Logos was with God in the beginning is decisive for the decree in the sense that the Logos, with the Father and the Holy Spirit, is the electing God; and that means that there can be nothing in the decree which contradicts what God is in Christ. The issue, however, is whether the decree of the triune God, which has the full consent of the Logos/Son, is one in which God is committed to ensuring that all human beings (Barth's 'man') come to obtain the grace of Christ. Does the Logos never pass by? In the great judgment scene of Matt. 25:31–46, it is precisely the incarnate Logos who has a different attitude to the sheep and to the goats.

53. No-one has stated this more eloquently than Barth himself: 'What kind of a God is it who in any sense of the term has to be gracious, whose grace is not his own most personal and free good pleasure?' (*CD* II/2, p. 19).

to the eternal will of God.[54] But among the data with which Christian theology has to reckon is the fact that there are those whose names are not written
in the Lamb's Book of Life (Rev. 20:15), and it is here that Barth, who so often
reminds us of the limitations of our knowledge, has to join us in being silent:
'But who are you, O man, to talk back to God?' (Rom. 9:20). In the last analysis, the astonished beneficiary of grace can say only it 'pleased' God! (Gal.
1:15). And whatever Barth has done, he has not resolved the issues raised by
the Remonstrants in 1610. He has bypassed them, and appropriated their terminology for another, entirely different, discourse.

There is, of course, a *via media* between Barth's willingness to proceed *on the
basis* of Scripture and the extreme Puritanical view that theology can build only
on the *express words* of Scripture: the doctrine of *good and necessary consequence*, as
set forth in, for example, the Westminster Confession (1.6). Assuming the perfection of Scripture as the rule of faith, this doctrine lays down that since the
Bible contains the whole counsel of God, all we need to know for the life of
faith 'is either expressly set down in Scripture, or *by good and necessary consequence
may be deduced from scripture*'. This is a perfectly legitimate application of apostolic authority. Using it, we can establish, for example, the doctrine of the
Trinity and (if we are paedo-baptists) the practice of infant baptism. It is also
entirely possible, in at least partial reliance on this principle, to take theology
where it has never gone before, to open up new discourses, and even to challenge the whole history of dogma on such issues as divine impassibility. But
we cannot use it to establish such dogmas as purgatory or the immaculate con-

---

54. A. I. C. Heron misrepresents the position of the Westminster Confession when
   he writes, 'According to the Confession, God in his free and eternal counsel has
   predestined some men to everlasting life, some to everlasting death' (*A Century
   of Protestant Theology* [Guildford: Lutterworth, 1980], p. 89). The Confession (3.3)
   deliberately refrains from applying the term 'predestinated' to the non-elect, and
   states instead, 'By the decree of God, for the manifestation of his glory, some men
   and angels are predestinated unto everlasting life, and others foreordained to
   everlasting death.' This is part of an overall concern to avoid conveying the
   impression of a symmetrical double predestination. Heron is also on debateable
   ground when he writes that 'This theology drew an outer and an inner circle, and
   located Christ in the inner one; the circle of sin and judgement stood quite
   independently of him' (*Century of Protestant Theology*, p. 89). Christ, the eternal Son
   and pre-incarnate Logos, is a party to preterition as he is to election. However,
   in relation to both the Father and the Son (and the Holy Spirit) preterition/
   reprobation is a 'strange' work (Isa. 28:21).

ception of the virgin, because the operative phrase is, 'by *good and necessary* consequence'. Nor can we use it to establish such doctrines as the *fallenness* of Christ's humanity, because such language points to corruption and depravity of nature, and thus contradicts the New Testament portrayal of Jesus as 'a lamb without blemish or defect' (1 Pet. 1:19).[55] Nor, again, can we use it to establish Barth's idea of election, because there is already a biblical discourse on this subject, a discourse from which the doctrine of a universal election allied to a universal reprobation certainly does not follow 'by good and necessary consequence'. On the contrary, Barth's doctrine on this issue lies unconformably across the biblical strata.

Ultimate criterion

What is clear is that in his critique of the church's proclamation Barth operates with some ultimate criterion by which he judges the church's creeds and doctors, and even Scripture itself. Is it possible to identify this criterion: or, alternatively, to identify the 'single truth' from which other truths are to be born?[56]

The answer is that the church's proclamation must be judged by the church's essence, and that essence is Jesus Christ.[57] The precise issue here is what has been referred to as Barth's Christocentrism or Christomonism,[58] and, of course, Christian faith will always warm to the claim that Christ must be the focal point and the test of everything: our doctrine of God (he is his form, image and glory), of creation (all things were made by him), of providence (which works to conform us to the image of the Son), of election (we are elect

---

55. Barth, of course, believes firmly in the sinlessness of Jesus (*CD* I/2, p. 152). The question is how we can maintain simultaneously that he was 'sinless' and that he was 'fallen'.

56. Cf. *CD* I/1, p. 484, where Barth contends that in Scripture 'we have to do with a single witness, i.e., a witness which points in a single direction and attests a single truth'.

57. Ibid., p. 3.

58. Alasdair Heron describes Barth's 'absolute, thoroughgoing christocentrism' as 'the most characteristic and distinctive feature of Barth's whole approach to theology': 'Barth, unlike Brunner and unlike Calvin, too, insisted in his mature work on unfolding every aspect of Christian faith in the light of Jesus Christ, and only in that light' (*Century of Protestant Theology*, p. 88).

in Christ), of redemption (we are redeemed by Christ) and of glorification (to be with Christ, which is far better). This is what Richard Muller calls *soterio-logical* Christocentrism, and it clearly implies that all saving knowledge is knowledge of God in Christ; or, conversely, that faith has Christ for its object.[59]

What Barth has in mind, however, is something different. His Christocentrism is located in the area of epistemology. Christ is the 'principle of knowledge' (*principium cognoscendi theologiae*).

One aspect of this for Barth is that only in Christ is God known. This is simply not true, at least not in the sense that prior to the incarnation or apart from the New Testament the human race has no knowledge of God. The Torah clearly gave knowledge of God, as Christ himself attests; and, despite Barth's objections to natural theology, there is clearly a revelation of God through the made things (Rom. 1:20), an unquenchable light in everyone who comes into the world (John 1:9), an awareness of deity in every heart and a seed of religion in every soul.[60] That is why God's anger may still justifiably fall even where Christ is not known (Rom. 1:20). It is true, of course, that neither of these avenues to the knowledge of God is independent of Christ. The principle that no-one knows the Father except the Son and those to whom the Son chooses to reveal him (Matt. 11:27) is unconditionally valid. Creation is revelatory only because it takes place in and through the Logos, the Son of God, and, equally, it was the Spirit of Christ who spoke through the prophets (1 Pet. 1:11). But it still remains that there can be a knowledge of God and of his law (Rom. 2:14) where Jesus as such has never been heard of.

It is also clear that in adopting this approach Barth is departing from *church* dogmatics and distancing himself from the Fathers, the Scholastics and the seventeenth-century dogmaticians (Reformed, Lutheran and Roman Catholic). Indeed, the roots of Barth's approach in this connection are with the liberalism on which he had turned his back, and he himself appears to admit as much. While at Marburg, he was an ardent student of Hermann's, and never entirely repudiated him. He later wrote, 'I soaked Hermann in through all my pores.'[61] More formally, he recalled, in the same context,

---

59. See R. A. Muller, 'A Note on "Christocentrism" and the Imprudent Use of Such Terminology', *WTJ* 68 (2006), pp. 253–260.

60. Calvin, *Institutes* 1.3.1; 1.4.1.

61. Busch, *Karl Barth*, p. 45. J. G. Machen also attended Hermann's lectures at Marburg, and was similarly impressed: 'I should say that the first time I heard Hermann may almost be described as an epoch in my life. Such an overpowering personality I think I almost never before encountered – overpowering in the sincerity of

'Although Hermann was surrounded by so much Kant and Schleiermacher, the decisive thing for him was the christocentric impulse, and I learned that from him.' The uncritical adulation did not survive. Barth may have persevered with Hermann's 'Christocentric impulse', but he did not persevere with Hermann's Christ, whom he came to see as the product of 'a romantic anti-intellectualism, individualism and a craze for truthfulness'. Yet, although Barth chose the Christ of orthodoxy as against the Christ of Hermann (who deplored Chalcedon and the Athanasian Creed), he appears, nevertheless, to have continued to believe in the possibility of unmediated access to *his* Christ as surely as Hermann believed in unmediated access to his; and in both cases this Christ stood as the *principle of knowledge* above the contradictions of historical dogmatics; above, indeed, the contradictions of Scripture itself.

Here Barth is clearly departing from *church* dogmatics. As Muller points out:

> It was never argued by any of the older Reformed theologians that direct encounter with Christ somehow mediated knowledge of God: their assumption was that the knowledge of God as Redeemer, grounded in and focused on Christ, was to be found in Scripture. Scripture, not Christ, was understood as the source or *principium* of knowledge of God.[62]

The fundamental issue here (and the decisive reason why we cannot appeal over Scripture to Christ) is that we have we no knowledge of Christ apart from Scripture. Even supposing him to be the *principium* (beginning) of our knowledge of God, we would need yet another *principium* for the knowledge of Christ; and that *principium* could be none other than holy Scripture. This alone can serve as what Barth called, in another connection, the *concrete authority* for theology:[63] not the church, not even Christ, but

---

religious devotion . . . It is inspiring to see a man so completely centred in Christ, even though some people might wonder how he reaches this result and still holds the views he does about the accounts of Christ in the New Testament' (N. B. Stonehouse, *J. Gresham Machen: A Biographical Memoir*, 3rd ed. [Edinburgh: Banner of Truth Trust, 1987], pp. 106–107). Machen's mature assessment of Hermann's theology is contained in *Christianity and Liberalism* (New York: Macmillan, 1929), though he does not mention Hermann by name.

62. 'Note on "Christocentrism"', p. 257.

63. In the chapter 'Church and Theology', in *Theology and Church: Shorter Writings 1920–1928*, trans. L. Pettibone Smith (London: SCM, 1962), pp. 288–298.

Scripture. The eternal, pre-incarnate Logos is as inaccessible as the eternal Father and the Holy Spirit, and can be known only through the word of Scripture, in which he accommodates himself to our capacities. Similarly, we know the historical Jesus only from the Gospels. These Gospels, like the earthly Christ himself, can be spat upon and crucified, not least by historical criticism. But we cannot remove them to a safe place. They must stand their ground. Nor can we protect the Jesus of the Gospels by dehistoricizing him and removing him into some sphere of supra-history. In the incarnation he takes a history as well as a nature, and he leaves his footprints in the sand. Equally, we have access to the risen, regnant Christ only through Scripture: that apostolic tradition, which has its source in himself, and which alone provides a foundation upon which he can build his church.

Barth often warned of the danger of creating a God behind and above his revelation, a God other than Jesus.[64] This was the great service, he would insist, rendered by the *homoousion*. The One who comes to us in Christ is *vere Deus*, the whole truth about God. By the same token, however, there can be no other Christ behind and above the Scriptures, no word behind the written word, casting the church into doubt, enveloping her in a cloud of uncertainty and raising the possibility that the Christ of Scripture is not the real Christ, or the final Christ. It may indeed be true that we see through a glass, only darkly. But what we see dimly is nevertheless the Eternal Light. Barth himself once remarked:

> A fundamental cause of the weakness of our present-day theology is the fact that when we pursue theology we have no church behind us which has the courage to say to us unambiguously that, so far as we talk together, this and this is dogma in the highest *concreteness*.[65]

The point is well put. A far greater cause of weakness, however, is that we no longer have behind us a Bible that says to us unambiguously, 'Thus says the Lord!' That Bible itself proclaims categorically the centrality of Christ, but it never volunteers to submit itself to him as the judge of its content. Instead, Scripture is his (and his Father's) witness to himself. It has, as the apostle Paul says of himself, the Spirit of God (1 Cor. 7:40).

---

64. See e.g. *CD* II/2, p. 115: 'In no depth of the Godhead shall we encounter any other but Him.'

65. *Theology and Church*, p. 290.

Christological concentration

It is a happy circumstance that it was in his Christology that Barth walked closest with orthodoxy, and praise for his magisterial contributions in this field should be in all the churches. It is noteworthy, too, that it was his very 'Christological concentration' that drove him to *church* dogmatics in the first place. He found it impossible to pursue this concentration in the company of his original mentors, Kant, Schleiermacher and Harnack, because the primary impulse behind their thought lay not in Christianity and its concerns, but in philosophy and its concerns. He could pursue the 'Christological concentration' only in the company of the Fathers, the Scholastics and the Reformers. Yet his predominant attitude to the church and its dogmas remained 'critical'. Is this a reflection of the fact that his first overwhelming intellectual experience was his immersion in the critiques of Kant?[66] To the end of his life, Barth was pursuing the Kantian question 'How do we know?', and his answer certainly was not 'We know because it is propounded in church dogmatics.'[67] On the contrary, his use of the said dogmatics was highly selective. He certainly would not have been intimidated, as was Placaeus, by the finding of the Twenty-Eighth Synod of the Gallican Church, which interdicted him and his fellow professors from teaching anything contrary to 'the common received doctrine of the Protestant churches'. When it came to the crunch, the Synod of Dort carried no more weight with Barth than the Council of Trent (perhaps, indeed, less).

What this means for us is that we must use Barth as selectively as he used

---

66. Barth recalled in later life that 'The first book which really moved me as a student was Kant's *Critique of Practical Reason*' (Busch, *Karl Barth*, p. 34), and by the time he went to Marburg he had 'worked through the whole of Kant'. In terms of his self-understanding, Barth's view was that he had cast off the influence of Kant as surely as he had that of Schleiermacher, Harnack and Hermann. It is arguable, however, that he remained under the influence of all four, and that his breach with Kant and nineteenth-century theology was nothing like as radical as he himself thought. See R. A. Muller, 'Karl Barth and the Path of Theology into the Twentieth Century', *WTJ* 51 (1989), pp. 25–50.
67. Muller's remark ('Path of Theology', p. 39) that Barth 'understood dogmatics, in the tradition of Schleiermacher, as the exposition of the church's faith' is inapposite. Barth's focus was not on the church's faith, but on the church's proclamation; and his concern was not to expound it, but to test it; and to practise theology, not in submission to it, but in dialogue with it.

church dogmatics. We approach him in the spirit of *critique*, testing *his* language about God and checking *his* proclamation in the light of Christianity's own, given, canon. Where we find it enriching our understanding of the church's dogmas, we shall rejoice. Where we find it in accord with them, we shall be encouraged, but not complacent. And where we find it diverging from them, we shall be alert, and perhaps suspicious. But whatever our assessment, our criterion shall not be Fathers or Schoolmen, creeds or Reformers, great Doctors or general councils. Nor shall it be 'the essence of Christianity' or the 'Christological concentration', as if Christ stood over and above the Scriptures ceaselessly warning against the dangers of bibliolatry. Our criterion, the Supreme Judge of both church dogmatics and Karl Barth, must be those very Scriptures, in which Christ speaks and of which he said, 'Scripture cannot be broken' (John 10:35).

Conclusion

There is one further point that should give us pause. For all Barth's concern to practise theology 'in the sphere of the church', he spent his entire professional career in the academy, not the church, serving successively in the universities of Göttingen, Münster, Bonn and Basle. Yet, in view of the intimate link between church and state in both Germany and Switzerland, the ecclesiastical influence was never very far away. In Britain at that same time theologians operated in even closer affiliation to the church, whether in the divinity faculties of the ancient universities or in the many colleges established by the Free Churches. The radical voices that sometimes sounded forth from these institutions raised eyebrows precisely because they were the voices of Christian clergy.

Since the 1960s this situation has changed dramatically. Higher education has become thoroughly secularized. Theology has given way to 'Religious Studies', the courses are no longer taught by clergy, and the programmes are no longer designed as vocational training for the Christian ministry. Religious Studies has the same status in universities as 'Religious and Moral Education' has in schools, and must be taught within the same framework of secular presuppositions and secular criteria.

There can be no objection to this in principle. Religion and theology have a legitimate place alongside the other disciplines in the academic curriculum. But is this their *only* place? What about *church* dogmatics: theology 'in the sphere of the church'? Or are we to concede that even Christian theology must be free from church control?

Athanasius and Augustine, Anselm and Aquinas, Luther and Calvin, Hodge and Barth were all *church* theologians. Can a full-blooded Christian theology now be practised anywhere else?

12. A STONY JAR: THE LEGACY OF KARL BARTH FOR EVANGELICAL THEOLOGY

Michael S. Horton

In *A Month of Sundays*, John Updike's main character is a Presbyterian minister who inherited from his father (also a minister) a fondness for Karl Barth. Weaving together allusions to the heavy wood furniture in the church – pulpit, table, font, and pews – and the timber in the father's voice, Updike's own religious views are pretty clear. The novelist may not be able to swallow the full-strength orthodoxy of Old Princeton (see his *In the Beauty of the Lilies*), but he loathes liberalism for its effete, sentimental, and dishonest ways. 'Mop up spilt religion!', he says. 'Let us have the truth in stony jars, or not at all.'

I know the voice Updike had in mind. Reared in conservative evangelicalism, for which I remain indebted in many respects, I nevertheless became dissatisfied with pietism: both for its style and substance. For a host of reasons, Barth's voice was different: far from sentimental, yet always full of grace. For all my remaining differences with Barth, his voice is still seductive at least in part because he started with God – a great God, under whose criticism everybody stood. At a time when evangelicalism's cultural captivity threatens to keep the church from being a witness to that truth, it only makes sense that Barth's work will continue to strike home. His famous No's and Yes's break up the backroom conferences where alliances have been signed with other covenant lords. Emphasizing God's sovereignty and grace is never popular, of course, but disrupting the powers and authorities in heavenly places is exactly what the church's commission entails. At the same time, Barth radically challenged and reformulated crucial Reformed doctrines. Before outlining those differences, some mention should be made of Barth's reception.

Barth's reception in evangelical circles

The initial reception of Barth in conservative evangelical and Reformed circles varied somewhat. Cornelius Van Til's *Christianity and Barthianism* in 1962 had a profound impact on wider appraisals in American evangelicalism.[1] However, it also exhibits critical weaknesses. Tragically, Van Til's legitimate insights – especially into the impact of Barth's refusal to think in terms of 'before' and 'after' in God's reconciling activity – seem sometimes to be obscured by sweeping generalizations and even caricatures of Barth's own stated positions. Although Van Til frequently cited G. C. Berkouwer's criticisms of Barth, the Amsterdam theologian distanced himself from the earlier analyses of Van Til and offered his own, more generous and careful critique in *The Triumph of Grace in the Theology of Karl Barth*.[2]

American evangelicalism has never had a consensus about whether to embrace or resist Barth. For some, perhaps following Van Til's critique (without also sharing his more nuanced comments especially at the beginning of that work), Barth has been treated as little more than another Protestant liberal. Charles C. Ryrie called Barthianism a 'theological hoax', liberalism cloaked in orthodox terminology.[3]

Of course, Barth himself had enough self-awareness to recognize that he was still in some sense 'a child of the nineteenth century', and more recent interpreters (especially Bruce McCormack and John Webster) have done a terrific job of placing him in his context, recognizing his debt to the legacy against which he revolted.[4] However, familiarity with Barth's writings at first hand challenges attempts to dismiss him as just another 'liberal'. His assault

---

1. Phillipsburg, N. J.: Presbyterian & Reformed, 1962. Prior to *Christianity and Barthianism*, Van Til treated Barth and Brunner in *The New Modernism* (Phillipsburg, N. J.: Presbyterian & Reformed, 1946).
2. Grand Rapids: Eerdmans, 1956.
3. *Neo-Orthodoxy* (Chicago: Moody, 1956), p. 62.
4. For Barth's admission of this point, see K. Barth, *Letters: 1961–1968*, trans. G. W. Bromiley (Grand Rapids: Eerdmans, 1981), p. 101. For analysis, see esp. B. L. McCormack, *Karl Barth's Critically-Realistic Dialectical Theology: Its Genesis and Development 1909–1936* (Oxford: Clarendon, 1995).

against trying to assimilate the gospel to the categories of modern thought, his resolute defence of a high doctrine of God, human sinfulness, the person and work of Christ, and the monergistic activity of the triune God in electing, redeeming, justifying, sanctifying and glorifying sinners, dominate Barth's horizon from the second edition of his *Epistle to the Romans* to the last fragment of the unfinished *Church Dogmatics*. He had a higher appreciation for the ecumenical creeds and the Reformation legacy than many who claim to belong to that tradition today.[5] And in comparison with the vast majority of liberal and evangelical trends, he sparked a revolution that is not without its blessings even to churches that find themselves largely critical of his system. John Webster correctly speaks of how radically 'Barth revised the whole shape of the theological enterprise', at least in its dominant schools of the day: 'no longer concerned with universal reason, morals or experience, the theologian is set firmly within the church, alongside the preacher who has been disturbed by the imperious summons to pass on in human words the *Deus dixit* of revelation'.[6]

However, Barth not only altered the theological landscape of neo-Protestantism; he radically revised evangelical and Reformed doctrine at points critical to the faith and practice of the church. Given his sweeping revisions of the doctrines of election, Scripture, and baptism, for example, one can only be astonished at Bernard Ramm's claim that 'Barth's theology is a restatement of Reformed theology written in the aftermath of the Enlightenment, but not capitulating to it.'[7] James Daane, Paul Jewett and Donald Bloesch have sought to harmonize Barth with the best of conservative evangelicalism, with varying degrees of success. Indeed, one wonders whether Barth's legacy would be anywhere near its current strength apart from its appropriation by Anglo-American evangelicalism in the second half of the twentieth century to the present. One hopes that we now have enough historical distance to listen attentively and critically to this revolutionary thinker beyond lionizing or demonizing him.

---

5. In addition to his commentary on the Heidelberg Catechism and other occasional articles, the best place to find a sustained treatment of the Reformed confessions is in K. Barth, *The Theology of the Reformed Confessions 1923*, Columbia Series in Reformed Theology, trans. D. L. Guder and J. J. Guder (Louisville: Westminster John Knox, 2002).

6. *Barth* (London: Continuum, 2000), p. 41.

7. *After Fundamentalism: The Future of Evangelical Theology* (San Francisco: Harper & Row, 1983), p. 14.

Evaluating Barth's theological revisions

Unlike many theologians, Barth was not interested in revising and reforming as an end in itself, like so many contemporary fads. It was always revision in view of a centre: the triune God who is God without us and yet has chosen to be God for and with us. However, I shall offer a brief analysis of some areas where Barth's system requires continued critique from confessional Reformed and evangelical quarters. Since it is impossible to appreciate either the merits or deficiencies of Barth's legacy apart from reckoning with his fundamental presuppositions, I shall begin there and try to show how they are reflected in his material conclusions.

Barth's ontology

It is hardly controversial to suggest that the *analogia entis* (analogy of being) is the chief antagonist in the story of Barth's revolutionary enterprise. Any point of contact between God and humanity other than Jesus Christ is strictly excluded. Identifying God's revelation with creaturely history and nature led inexorably to the paganization of the medieval church, neo-Protestantism and the Evangelical Church by the 'German Christian' movement. In reaction, Barth drew Kierkegaard's 'infinite, qualitative distinction between God and humanity' in thick, dark lines. Although Reformed and Lutheran orthodoxy had also emphasized this distinction (and nobody more resolutely in twentieth-century conservative circles than Van Til), Barth was more radical in his conclusions. His ontology, which affected every dogmatic locus, can be briefly summarized by reference to two main themes.

First, there is his diastisis between eternity and time. Not only creatively exploiting, Barth seems to me to be still under the thrall of the Platonist/Kantian ambit when he speaks so often of 'so-called history' (*Historie*) as the mere 'shadow' cast by the eternal (primal) history of the 'turn in heaven' (*Geschichte*, or, as he calls it, *Urgeschichte*). As Bruce McCormack points out, Barth's famous analogy of the tangent 'means that the new world touches the old world at a single point, without extension along the line of historical time'.[8] 'It is clear what Barth wanted to achieve with this dialectical relating of 'real history' and 'so-called history', McCormack adds. 'He wanted to put the movement and action of God in history beyond the reach of historical investigation.'[9] It is important to remind ourselves of the alternative in Barth's day: higher-critical quests

---

8. *Critically Realistic*, p. 253.
9. Ibid., p. 146.

for the 'historical Jesus' that ended up denying the Christ proclaimed by the apostles and confessed in the creeds in favour of some slender historical connection to the past. By the time of Wilhelm Herrmann, Barth's mentor, this thread had been reduced to the 'personality' of Jesus. It is no wonder that Barth reacted so strongly against the attempt to assimilate the person of Christ to a history that had been 'reconstructed' on presuppositions of unbelief.

So Barth employed Kierkegaard as well as the neo-Kantianism in which he had been trained in an effort to overcome the Kantian legacy.[10] In my view, this effort had mixed results. Although he highlighted the importance of eschatology (as a corollary of his emphasis on God's action over against human experience, reason, morality and evolving religious consciousness), Kierkegaard's concept of the 'eternal moment' penetrating history in punctiliar events with no extension in time could not provide sufficient resources for relating eschatology to history. By contrast, I would argue, the New Testament's categories, instead of 'so-called history' (temporal-linear) and 'real history' (eternal-vertical), are 'this age' (reality under sin and death) and 'the age to come' (the same reality under righteousness and life). Basically, adopting many of the presuppositions of modernity, he is finally less successful in refuting it. With Kant and Lessing, not to mention the more radical neo-Kantians at Marburg (Carnap and Natorp), Barth seems implicitly to accept the dualism between fact and value, phenomena and noumena, reason and faith, history and revelation.

Because of this ontological premise, Barth can only see Adam as Christ's shadow and the history of creation and redemption as a contradiction in terms. Creatures are not only distinguished from the Creator; the ontological status of the former is rendered questionable. Indeed, there is 'the curse that is laid upon [humanity's] mere createdness'.[11] In fact, Barth complained that the emphasis in Reformed orthodoxy on the outworking of eternal election in temporal stages and covenants in history was 'a fatal historical moment' in the tradition's development, paving the way for the assimilation of Revelation (Christ) to liberal historicism.[12] He definitely interprets the development of

---

10. Even here, it should be noted, Barth's appreciation for Kierkegaard was shared by his liberal mentor, Wilhelm Herrmann.

11. *The Epistle to the Romans*, trans. E. C. Hoskyns (London: Oxford University Press, 1933), p. 369.

12. *GD* 27.III, cited by D. L. Migliore, 'Karl Barth's First Lectures in Dogmatics: Unterricht in der christlichen Religion', in K. Barth, *The Göttingen Dogmatics: Instruction in the Christian Religion*, vol. 1, trans. G. W. Bromiley, ed. H. Reiffen (Grand Rapids: Eerdmans, 1991), p. xxxviii.

covenant theology in the Reformed tradition as a dogmatician rather than as a historical theologian. Cocceius, for example, 'earned the dubious credit for having introduced the idea of a temporal history of salvation into theology'.[13] Eternity and history, God and humanity, grace and nature stand in a fundamental diastisis for Barth.

McCormack points out that Barth often works with two types of dialectic: a Kierkegaardian one in which opposites stand in an irresolvable tension and a Hegelian one in which one partner in the pair is assimilated to the other in a higher synthesis.[14] In fact, McCormack observes that the Adam–Christ dialectic falls on the Hegelian side.[15] We shall see how these two rather different versions of dialectical thinking play out in Barth's revisions below.

Hans Urs von Balthasar spoke of Barth as evidencing 'a dynamic and actualist theopanism, which we define as a monism of beginning and end (protology and eschatology)', drawing on Idealist categories.[16] 'Too much in Barth gives the impression that nothing much really happens in his theology of event and history, because everything has already happened in eternity.'[17] The effect of this dialectic is that the historicity and reality of both nature and history are rendered questionable. Only God and divine action are accorded this unqualified ontological weight.

Not surprisingly, then, Barth has been challenged by a wide spectrum of theologians for having a weak doctrine of creation (especially anthropology). It may be that this dialectic accounts for Barth's account of creation and fall to the category of saga. In any case, he is wary of any notion of 'before' and 'after' in relation to the cross and resurrection: so thoroughly is history assimilated to eternity. Revelation, for Barth, occurs in an 'eternal Moment' with no extension in time, which 'God gives simultaneously to his Biblical witnesses and to those who accept their witness'.[18] This is Kierkegaard's notion of

---

13. *Theology of the Reformed Confessions*, p. 134. As usual in his treatment of this trajectory, Barth's narrative moves from the redemptive-historical approach of the federal theologians to the historicizing of Schleiermacher and Protestant liberalism (pp. 135–140).

14. *Critically Realistic*, pp. 266–272.

15. Ibid., pp. 266–269.

16. *The Theology of Karl Barth: Exposition and Interpretation*, trans. E. T. Oakes (San Francisco: Ignatius, 1992), p. 94.

17. Ibid., p. 371.

18. *The Word of God and the Word of Man*, trans. D. Horton (New York: Harpers, 1957), p. 244.

'contemporeneity', which Barth held consistently from the first edition of *Romans*.

Whatever credit Barth may give to modern criticism, it is important for evangelicals to recognize that his reticence to identify God and God's self-revelation with history and its successive unfolding in events extended in linear time is motivated by this ontology and not by any attachment to liberal theology or the critical method as such. More often than not, in fact, such moves are made in sharp reaction against what Barth perceives as the presuppositions of neo-Protestantism: especially the various quests for the 'historical Jesus' that led inevitably to a denial of the Christ of creedal faith.

Second, Barth's ontology is grounded in an actualist account of the God–world relation. Barth advances a radical notion of God's being-in-act that acknowledges revelation and reconciliation (which are the same thing) only in terms of indirect encounter. God and revelation (which in its primary objectivity simply *is* Jesus Christ) never intersect with nature and history, but such events graze creaturely reality and leave behind an effect – much as a bomb leaves a crater. Thus, revelation (which is always Christ himself) can never be directly identified with anything creaturely. It is always an act, an event in which eternity disrupts history without being directly discernable within it. I would suggest that the 'critical' side of Barth's thought emphasizes the inability of human thought and language to correspond to God's being and action leading to *equivocity*, while the 'realist' side underscores God's ability in grace to create a *univocal* identity between the Word-event and reality. Barth's very modern epistemology (knowledge as mastery and control over the object) drives both the equivocal human and the univocal divine moves, so that he can even say that in the miraculous event of revelation we 'master' God.[19]

Barth's actualistic emphasis undercuts the various attempts to offer mediations between Creator and creature other than Christ. Therefore, Barth is at his best in my view when he is counteracting the neo-Hegelian tendency to synthesize the Creator and the creature, Christ and his work and the church and its work. However, in the process he seems to rebound from monism into the arms of a dualism that does not allow any direct identification of revelation with creaturely reality.

Again, the missing element here is *analogy*. Analogy would suggest an ongoing relationship between God and the created order, rather than sudden irruptions from above. As a result, Barth's crucial claim that in self-revelation

---

19. See e.g. *CD* II/1, pp. 182, 189, 194, 202. I am grateful to my student Brannan Ellis for pointing out some of these references. Cf. G. Hunsinger, *Disruptive Grace: Studies in the Theology of Karl Barth* (Grand Rapids: Eerdmans, 2002), pp. 312–313.

God is wholly revealed and wholly concealed would have to be revised: God is partially hidden and partially revealed, both in general and special revelation. It seems that the consequence of rejecting analogy is an actualist ontology that simultaneously tends towards univocity ('wholly revealed') and equivocity ('wholly hidden'). A rationalist (univocal) to irrationalist (equivocal) dialectic appears to be the epistemological corollary of his actualist ontology.

As George Hunsinger emphasizes, Barth's actualism is inseparable from his basic commitment to the sovereignty of God and his grace.[20] Therefore, he could simultaneously affirm the epistemological critique of Kant and the Marburg neo-Kantians without surrendering to their scepticism, since God had revealed himself – not only beyond but against all human capacities or incapacities. Not even faith was central for Barth, as it had been in pietism and liberalism. Rather, God's act of reconciliation was the focal point, with faith and obedience as effects rather than causes. Balthasar pointed out:

> Like Calvin and unlike Luther, Barth turned away from the disposition of faith and focused on its content. Indeed Barth writes well because he strictly adheres to theological objectivism ('Faith lives from its object') and because he so sharply veered from the liberal Protestantism of Schleiermacher. This is why he is so readable and why we need not fear mushy piety or empty pastoral edification from him. The subject matter does its own edifying, builds its own edifice.[21]

Similar verdicts can rarely be rendered concerning much of contemporary theological reflection, much less preaching – in evangelical as well as mainline circles. Yet the motifs in Barth that yield some of the most profound insights also provoke some of the most severe criticisms.

Epistemology: Barth's theology of revelation

Theologies that emphasize the dialectic of time and eternity or matter and spirit over that of sin and grace and 'this age' under sin and 'the age to come' under righteousness and life have difficulty affirming how the 'Wholly Other' can actually be known and experienced by embodied and temporal creatures. Finitude is easily confused with an inherent deficiency; nature rather than the

---

20. *How to Read Karl Barth: The Shape of His Theology* (New York: Oxford University Press, 1991), pp. 30–31. G. C. Berkouwer (discussed below) perceived the same motive in his *The Triumph of Grace in the Theology of Karl Barth*, trans. H. R. Boer (Grand Rapids: Eerdmans, 1956).

21. *Theology of Karl Barth*, p. 25.

corruption of nature by sin can be regarded as the main obstacle to the crea-ture's relationship with God. While sharply critical of mysticism, especially of any human attempt to scale the heavenly ladder to possess God, Barth's the-ology of revelation in some respects derives from the same antithesis of time and eternity, matter and spirit that we find in the Platonist heritage, Christian or otherwise. A radical scepticism grounded in hyper-transcendence (equivo-city) is merely the foil for an equally radical certainty grounded in a direct and immediate act of divine self-revelation (univocity).

For Barth, knowing God involves not only a different *object* than knowing one's spouse; it is a qualitatively different *kind of knowing*. This is not the same as saying, with the Protestant scholastics, that God's knowledge as well as God's being is qualitatively (and not just quantitatively) different from that of creatures. As God is 'beyond being' for Plotinus, or 'wholly other' for Barth, there are no natural human capacities for knowing God. To suggest otherwise would lead in the direction of Pelagianism or at least semi-Pelagianism (as in Karl Rahner). However, I suggest that both Barth (in denying any natural capacity) and Rahner (affirming it) fail to distinguish natural and moral capacities. Reformed ortho-doxy asserted that the *natural* capacity for God remains intact even after the fall; what humankind has lost is its *moral* capacity for God. Nothing has been lost that makes humans truly human; rather, their whole being has become captive to sin. Consequently, grace renews and liberates nature to fulfil its ordained ends.

There is no such distinction between natural and moral inability in Barth, however. Thus, total depravity can easily be confused with the natural condi-tion of human beings as such. In the event of revelation, God must not only overcome our moral turpitude, but our natural finitude. God's self-revelation itself creates these capacities *ex nihilo*. This self-revelation does not correspond even analogically to anything else we know or experience. 'God and His Word are not given to us in the same way as natural and historical entities . . . But there is no human knowing that corresponds to this divine telling . . . In this divine telling knowledge of God and His Word is actualized with the God with us.'[22] The utterly surprising *content* of the gospel that sinful humanity could not have predicted, prepared for or mastered leads Barth to the further, more radical, claim that the *form* in which it comes is incommensurable with our ordinary natural capacities. Thus, the event of revelation, beyond opening eyes blinded by sin and ears deaf to God's voice, creates its own eyes and ears in the event of its occurrence. Grace does not so much restore nature as replace it.

If a naturalistic Protestantism had reduced 'God' to the evolution of nature

---

22. *CD* I/1, p. 132.

and history, Barth had trouble thinking that something could be called God's Word in an unqualified sense that was simultaneously a thoroughly human Word. God does not work through water, bread and wine: calling these 'means of grace' he regarded as reprehensible.[23] We may work through such things by way of response to God's grace, but creaturely mediation becomes particularly questionable in his treatment of the sacraments. We recognize this problem, for example, when Barth sharply separates the sign (water baptism) from the signified (Spirit baptism): a point I shall elaborate below.

T. F. Torrance also speaks of human knowledge of God as 'mystical' and 'intuitive'.[24] This revelation cannot be specified linguistically or logically, but we do meet Christ through it, according to Torrance. The Barthian school, it seems, reflects a reluctance to identify God's Word with material mediation – both in its doctrine of Scripture and, at least for Barth, in relation to the sacraments. In this respect, it continues the modern (indeed, Western) legacy of scepticism regarding the sign-signified relation – in other words, mediation. Alongside a 'Plotinian' hyper-transcendence one discerns a nominalistic hyper-immanence. This relates to the point I made above, namely that in Barth's dialectic thinking, hyper-transcendence (the critical side of his thought) and hyper-immanence (the realist side) coexist in tension. In the first mode, he embraces something close to *equivocity*, and in the second, *univocity*, while I have suggested above (in line with Protestant orthodoxy) that our knowledge of God is *analogical* all the way down. Instead of an *analogical* ('is' and 'is not') relationship between God and humanity, which affirms God's infinite transcendence (i.e. difference) without denying revealed similarities, Barth follows the *dialectical* thinking of univocity that defines God in opposition to finite reality.

Kant, of course, brought this conundrum to its logical conclusion, but Schleiermacher sought to get around it by appealing to the community's experience. Barth heroically broke from that position, yet it is difficult to resist the impression that revelation still occupies the sphere of the irrational. His actualism is at least in part the residue of nominalism's emphasis on the will. Even the union of the Logos with humanity in Christ's person is determined in every moment *by an act of will*.[25] In fact, Barth himself makes this connection:

---

23. *CD* IV/4, pp. 105, 129–130 etc. Titled *The Christian Life*, this volume is a fragment Barth developed and published as part of his unfinished dogmatics. Cf. *CD* IV/3.2, pp. 756, 783, 790, 843–901.

24. *God and Rationality* (Oxford: Oxford University Press, 1971), pp. 45, 137–138, 155–156, 185.

25. P. L. Metzger, *The Word of Christ and the World of Culture: Sacred and Secular Through the*

Again it is quite impossible that there should be a direct identity between the human word of Holy Scripture and the Word of God, and therefore between the creaturely reality in itself and as such and the reality of God the Creator . . . This is not the case even in the person of Christ where the identity between God and man, in all the originality and indissolubility in which it confronts us, is an assumed identity, one specially willed, created, and effected by God, and to that extent indirect, i.e., resting neither in the essence of God nor in that of man, but in the decision and act of God to man. When we necessarily allow for inherent differences, it is exactly the same with the unity of the divine and human word in Scripture.[26]

As with anyone's doctrine of revelation and Scripture, Barth's doctrine of God and the God–world relationship (and not any particular theory he may have inherited from liberalism) is the underlying rationale that critics often overlook. By God's decision, these human words become the Word of God. Scripture 'too can and must – not as though it were Jesus Christ, but in the same serious sense as Jesus Christ – be called the Word of God: the Word of God in the sign of the word of man, if we are going to put it accurately'.[27] Christ's humanity is 'the first and original sign', followed in order of dignity by

---

Footnote 25 (*continued*)

Theology of Karl Barth (Grand Rapids: Eerdmans, 2003), p. 50, drawing on Bruce McCormack's *Critically Realistic*, p. 365. To McCormack's helpful distinction between Barth's 'Kierkegaardian' and 'Hegelian' dialectics, I would humbly suggest another: *sub contrario* (under the form of its opposite). Like Luther and Kierkegaard, Barth emphasizes that God reveals himself not only by accommodating to our weakness (Calvin's emphasis), but in the form of the opposite. We look for God in majestic glory, where God in fact is found in the cross and suffering. Eberhard Jüngel emphasizes this perhaps more than Barth, but seems to have derived it as much from Barth as from his own Lutheran heritage. Jüngel writes e.g., 'If in this history [between God humanity] God is already with humanity, then for its part humanity must already be with God.' Especially in Jüngel, the voluntarism is marked: the only thing that distinguishes God from creation is his freedom to will to be whatever he will be (*God's Being Is in Becoming* [Edinburgh: T. & T. Clark, 2001], p. 96, 45–46, 89). 'From the very beginning it is true that Jesus is victor' (p. 94). See also John Webster's careful analysis of Jüngel's Christology in *Word and Church: Essays in Christian Dogmatics* (Edinburgh: Continuum, 2001), ch. 5.

26. *CD* I/2, p. 499.

27. Ibid., p. 500.

Scripture and preaching.[28] Barth's doctrine of revelation cannot be either appreciated or criticized by trying to locate him on the spectrum from liberal to orthodox. It is a specific ontology (yielding a specific account of the sign–signified relationship) that generates Barth's doctrine of the Word.

Barth's actualism, which so dominates his ontology, cannot be explained simply by the genealogy of voluntarism. Nevertheless, the comparison is instructive. Severing the link between sign and signified, the late-medieval thinker William of Ockham could only conclude that faith was an act of assent to the authority of the Bible and the church – an irrational leap that had no particular bearing on any observable connection between faith and reason, truth and evidence. While reason and sense-experience were sufficient by themselves for the study of particulars (such as natural science), faith was blind submission. When you put this nominalistic emphasis on the separation between sign and signified, faith and reason, intellect and will, discovery and submission to authority together with an emphasis on the *natural* rather than simply *moral* incapacity of nature to receive revelation through historical, intellectual, linguistic and cultural mediation, Barth's overall strategy of overcoming modernity seems less successful than it may at first appear.

In arguing that Scripture becomes the Word of God where and when God chooses, Barth was not saying (as is often suggested by some Barthians and anti-Barthians alike) that it becomes something other than what it is intrinsically. To understand what Barth means in these instances, we have to appreciate the philosophical presuppositions already summarized above. Revelation, in his view, is always an event, never an artefact that could be possessed – not even the Bible. 'We cannot have revelation "in itself".'[29] Scripture 'is a witness to God's revelation, but that does not mean that God's revelation is now before us in any kind of divine revealedness. The Bible is not a book of oracles; it is not an instrument of direct revelation.'[30] While Barth spoke eloquently and forcefully of the Bible as the primary *witness to* revelation, he was wary of considering it a *means of* revelation. Otherwise, he thought, revelation would become a given, a possessed object rather than a subject – namely, God's self-revelation.

Where the Reformed tradition has affirmed the union of sign and the signified in preaching and sacrament, 'Zwinglian' views tend to sever that connection, reducing the sign to a merely human act of testimony or witness. If some conservative accounts come too close to identifying Scripture with God's essence in

28. Ibid.
29. Ibid., p. 492.
30. Ibid., p. 507.

a Protestant variation on transubstantiation, Barth's view seems to render Scripture (like the sacraments) capable merely of offering a human witness.

In other words, Barth's theocentrism is not theocentric enough: 'indirect revelation' means that in Scripture, preaching and sacrament, it is not *God* who comes to us through human messengers who speak *his* Word, but human witnesses who come to us as reflectors but not actually bearers of that Word. This should in no way be confused with a 'symbolic' view of the human word. Barth is quite explicit in this respect: 'Speaking is not a "symbol" (as P. Tillich . . . thinks).'[31] Nor does he suggest that revelation occurs apart from natural, historical events – as even the incarnation attests.[32] Nevertheless, 'It implies first of all the spiritual nature of the Word of God as distinct from naturalness, corporeality, or any physical event.'[33] If we want to understand the background of Barth's doctrine of revelation, we should read Zwingli as well as Herrmann and Kierkegaard. He even speaks of 'the Word of God [in] an upper and lower aspect'.[34] In my view, this dualistic way of speaking about signs and the signified is the bane of so much historical reflection on the God–world relation and mediation.

Barth's sharp distinction between revelation and Scripture is also motivated by his view that revelation *is* reconciliation. Through the primary witness of the prophets and apostles to Christ, the Word himself (Christ) is God's revelation and reconciliation. 'Scripture is (now) recognized as the Word of God (by faith) by the fact that it is the Word of God,' and so has authority over the church.[35] When Scripture becomes the Word of God, it is only becoming what it already is, but it does not become the Word of God in any particular case for any particular person unless God wills. Again, we encounter the confusion of inspiration then and there with illumination here and now. If he separates too much the sign and signified, he collapses any distinction between revelation and illumination. To be the subject of revelation is to be 'saved'. Barth explicitly states that Scripture 'does not become God's Word because we accord it faith, but of course, because it *becomes* revelation for us'.[36] Its being is in act. Just as the Logos

---

31. *CD* I/1, p. 132.

32. Ibid., p. 133.

33. Ibid.

34. Ibid.

35. G. G. Bolich, *Karl Barth and Evangelicalism* (Downers Grove: IVP, 1980), pp. 196–197.

36. *CD* I/1, pp. 123–124; cf. J. D. Morrison, 'Barth, Barthians and Evangelicals: Reassessing the Question of the Relation of Holy Scripture and the Word of God', *TrinJ* NS 25 (2004), pp. 187–213.

sustains the union with humanity in Jesus Christ by a moment-by-moment decision, the coincidence of the Word of God with Scripture and preaching is
always an event of divine decision. 'God's word is identical with God himself'.[37]

Here again, an important ontological distinction is collapsed: God's self-
revelation is simply identified with God's eternal essence. If one were to follow
Barth in this conflation, of course one could never say that the Bible is the
Word of God without further ado. With good reason we do not offer our
worship to a book. Therefore, Barth's conclusion is not motivated by a low
view of Scripture but by an ontology of revelation that cannot allow for anything human to be anything more than a witness to revelation rather than revelation itself. In 'Nestorian' fashion, the Word of God is over here and the
words of human witnesses over there. That the latter coincide indirectly with
the former is always the result of a new decision on God's part, a new event
of willed action. To be sure, a functionalist or instrumentalist view of inspiration must take a step beyond Barth, but it is already possible when Barth
refuses to identify the divine Word with human words in a direct sense.

Furthermore, the humanity of Scripture means for Barth not only the
capacity for errors, but the recognition 'that in the Bible it may be a matter of
simply believing the Word of God, even though it meets us, not in the form
of what we call history, but in the form of what we think must be called saga
or legend'.[38] In fact, 'the vulnerability of the Bible, i.e., its capacity for error,
also extends to its religious or theological content'.[39] Once again, he adds in
that passage, this is a necessary presupposition of the claim that Scripture is
truly a *human* witness. Again, the Kierkegaardian dialectic of time and eternity
is apparent when Barth writes:

> What matters it whether figures like Abraham and Moses are products of later myth-
> making – believe it who can! There were once, a few centuries earlier or later, men
> who lived by faith like Abraham, who were strangers in the promised land like Isaac
> and Jacob, who declared plainly that they were seeking a country, who like Moses
> endured as seeing him who is invisible. There were once men who dared.[40]

In other words, the actual history is not really decisive: it is the eternal truth
of that to which they gave witness. The temporal events in history are

37. *CD* I/1, p. 304.
38. *CD* I/2, p. 509.
39. Ibid., pp. 509–510.
40. *Word of God*, p. 65.

simply manifestations of what has decisively taken place already in eternity.

> We may believe what we can and will concerning the something which encouraged
> them to dare, which moved these seers and hearers, but the movement itself into
> which they all, the named, the unnamed, and the pseudonymous, were drawn, we can
> no more deny than we can deny the rotation of the stellar firmament around an
> unknown central sun.

They are all signs pointing away from themselves.[41] It is 'not history but truth'
that is at issue in revelation.[42] 'Biblical history in the Old and New Testament
is not really history at all, but seen from above is a series of free divine acts and
seen from below a series of fruitless attempts to undertake something in itself
impossible.'[43]

Especially given the dominant approach of the history-of-religions school,
Barth's dialectical view of history is a bracing challenge to recognize that salvation is a miracle and cannot be explained according to immanent laws and
processes. Nevertheless, it does not take seriously enough the inextricable connection that the Bible makes between divine, eschatological, vertical acts and
their horizontal extension within history. Eschatology is always on the verge
of swallowing history in Barth's system. Despite his repeated criticisms of
Bultmann, Barth does not quite escape the lure of his mentors (especially
Herrmann):

> However it may be with the historical Jesus, it is certain that Jesus the Christ, the Son
> of the living God, belongs neither to history nor to psychology; for what is historical
> and psychological is as such corruptible. The resurrection of Christ, or his second
> coming, *which is the same thing*, is not a historical event.[44]

Again, it is important to recognize that by 'not a historical event' Barth is not
suggesting that the resurrection did not occur in history. Rather, he is denying
that it belongs to history; in other words, that it can be explained by historical
investigation. It happened in history but is not of history. His comparative lack
of concentration on history allows him to collapse the resurrection and the
second coming into one and the same event. 'The dawn of the new time, of the

---

41. Ibid.
42. Ibid., p. 66.
43. Ibid., p. 72.
44. Ibid., p. 90 (emphasis added).

sovereignty of him which is and was and which is to come – this is the meaning of Easter.'[45] Again, Barth helpfully reminds us of the significance of eschatology, but it seems to swallow rather than determine the direction of history itself.

At the same time, Barth can speak of the Bible as the Word of God by virtue of the fact that it can become the occasion for the event of revelation. We can speak of verbal inspiration perhaps, but not of a verbally inspired book (i.e. inspiredness).[46] Barth interprets the Reformers as teaching that it is the content of Scripture that constitutes its authority as the Word of God.[47] The post-Reformation theologians, however, surrendered God's sovereignty in his Word over the Bible, he charges, reducing inspiration to a visible, recognizable property inhering in a book: a species of natural theology.[48] Ironically, this led to the opposite intention: a reduction of the Bible to a natural book whose historical details could be discerned by anyone.

The Enlightenment, understandably, followed through on this presupposition, but with opposite conclusions. 'And again there is no point in joining the wolves of the 18th and 19th centuries and attacking the 17th-century doctrine of inspiration because of its pointed supranaturalism. We must attack it rather because its supranaturalism is not radical enough.' By positing an errorless Bible (as the Church Fathers also tended to do), Protestant orthodoxy made God's Word something that could be possessed, 'eliminating the perception that its actualization can only be its own decision and act'. 'Therefore,' Barth adds, 'we have to resist and reject the 17th-century doctrine of inspiration as false doctrine.'[49] Like many modern theologians, Barth seems to have gleaned his interpretation of the Protestant orthodox doctrine of Scripture from scattered quotations rather than from a close study of the sources. While I do not have the space to offer a rebuttal, Barth's dubious attempt to separate the Reformers from their heirs on this point – a commonplace in contemporary debates – is based in large part on the misunderstanding that Protestant orthodoxy identified verbal inspiration with a theory of dictation.[50]

---

45. Ibid.
46. *CD* I/2, p. 518.
47. Ibid., pp. 520–521.
48. Ibid., pp. 522–523.
49. Ibid., p. 525.
50. Among the many secondary sources that could be cited on this point, the most incisive and well supported is R. A. Muller, *Post-Reformation Reformed Dogmatics: The Rise and Development of Reformed Orthodoxy, ca. 1520 to ca. 1725*, vol. 2: *Holy Scripture, the Cognitive Foundation of Theology*, 2nd ed. (Grand Rapids: Baker Academic, 2003).

Protestant orthodoxy, with a docetic view of the Word and Enlightenment liberalism, with its 'Ebionite' understanding, were simply two sides of the same coin in Barth's view: treating the Bible as a book whose nature could be discerned apart from its content.[51] The only way around this impasse is to acknowledge that to speak of the Word of God 'is not to contemplate a state or a fact but to watch an event, and an event which is relevant to us, an event which is an act of God, an act of God which rests on a free decision'.[52] The Word of God is always a new event, a new work of God, not something that belongs to history.[53] The miracle is that God's Word is in fact spoken even in and through the erring words of sinful creatures who are nevertheless elected, called, justified and sanctified by God.[54] 'If therefore we are serious about the fact that this miracle is an event, we cannot regard the presence of God's Word in the Bible as an attribute inhering once and for all in this book as such and what we see before us of books and chapters and verses.'[55]

In my view, Barth's treatment retrieves an important Reformed emphasis on the sacramental Word – that is, the Word as an event here and now in which the Spirit presents Christ externally while illuminating us inwardly to receive him. Nevertheless, he does not do adequate justice to the ontological status of the canon as the product of a process of divine inspiration. Again, this is not the result of 'a weak view of Scripture' – as if this doctrine were an isolated island – but of an actualist ontology that leads to a doctrine of revelation that is, in my view at least, more realist (univocalist) *and* more idealist or critical (equivocalist) than it should be. Not even Scripture gives us access to God's archetypal knowledge, but rather accommodated, analogical, ectypal discourse. Yet that finite, creaturely, mediated knowledge can be identified with God's very self-revelation. Therefore, whatever its deficiencies, Barth's doctrine of Scripture is not driven by the principal presuppositions of liberalism. Although he accepts certain higher-critical conclusions that evangelicals would find unacceptable, the underlying assumptions are if anything practically hyper-Calvinistic. His emphasis on the sovereignty, transcendence and wholly otherness of God, not any celebration of humanity, is the principal motive. The analogical ontology and epistemology that Barth resisted was affirmed not only by patristic and medieval theologicans, but was accepted by

---

51. *CD* I/2, p. 526.
52. Ibid., p. 527.
53. Ibid., p. 528.
54. Ibid., p. 530.
55. Ibid.

Protestant orthodoxy. These successors of the Reformers agreed that creation participates analogically in God, and that our creaturely knowledge of God therefore consists of similarities with greater dissimilarities. God is not a being among beings, but the source of all being. Therefore, God and the world cannot be placed under a common category of 'being', with God on one end and the world on the other.

In my estimation, this analogical approach keeps us from yielding to the swinging pendulum of irrationalism (the scepticism of equivocity) and rationalism (univocity). Revelation is accommodated discourse, even 'baby-talk' in which God 'must descend far beneath his loftiness', as Calvin puts it.[56] For Barth, by contrast, there is a fundamental diastisis between the secular word that Scripture is as witness and the majestic Word-event that occurs in and through it. In short, for Calvin, revelation is never as lofty (univocal) as it is in Barth's Word-event nor as humble (equivocal) as it is in Barth's concept of Scripture's secularity. Not even in revelation, according to Calvin, does the believer 'attain to [God's] exalted state', but one does receive truth 'accommodated to our capacity so that we may understand it'.[57]

Given the presuppositions we have explored, Barth not only wants to affirm God's freedom from creation (including the human means of revelation) on the grounds of divine sovereignty; he also wants to avoid a static view of revelation. The same concern can be found, for example, in Otto Weber.[58] This is an important concern, shared by orthodox Reformed theologians, who have emphasized that the Bible is not a book of timeless doctrinal and ethical instruction, but an unfolding drama of redemption. However, here is the crucial difference: where Reformed thinkers like Geerhardus Vos see the dynamic aspect in *historical* terms, Barth sees it in *existential* terms. Wary of reducing revelation to historical progress (as in Protestant liberalism), Barth was suspicious of classic covenant theology for this very reason, as noted above.

The question is whether his tendency to assimilate history to eternity keeps him from this same weakness. Classic Reformed theology locates the dynamism of revelation in both its historical and existential aspects: it moves dynamically through the history of redemption and it is also 'living and active'

---

56. *Institutes of the Christian Religion*, trans. F. L. Battles, ed. J. T. McNeill (Philadelphia: Westminster, 1960), 1.13.1.

57. Ibid., 1.17.13.

58. *Foundations of Dogmatics*, trans. D. L. Guder (Grand Rapids: Eerdmans, 1981), vol. 1, pp. 78–181.

in judging and justifying the ungodly. However, Barth's wariness of the historical dynamism restricts him to the existential aspect.

An analogical approach reminds us that while all of our language – including the Bible's language – falls short of God's majesty (foreclosing univocity), God has accommodated himself to our meager capacity by using it (foreclosing equivocity). Through revelation, we see God 'through a glass darkly', not 'face to face'. Yet analogical revelation is true revelation. Since God selects the appropriate analogies, we are not left to choose our own expressions of pious experience, which would indeed be a revelation of our own psyches rather than of God. It is worth noting that conservative evangelicalism (at least as represented by Carl Henry) has been as resistant as Barth to the doctrine of analogy, as if it were a halfway house to equivocity and therefore epistemological scepticism.[59] Therefore, the criticisms offered here have wider relevance.

I can conclude only that while much of what Barth says concerning God's self-revelation in Christ, Scripture and preaching represents a robust challenge for the church to become once again a hearing church of the speaking God, erasure of important distinctions in classic Reformed theology introduces confusion rather than clarification. That further reflection on the meaning of revelation is required I do not doubt, and Barth raises important issues that should not be ignored. Nevertheless, at the end of the day, a doctrine of Scripture adequate to the Bible's own claims for itself has not yet been offered by Barth or his students. Even as sympathetic an interpreter as David Kelsey has concluded, 'There is a convergence of critical judgment from otherwise different theological perspectives that the allegedly "biblical" doctrines of "revelation" developed in the neo-orthodox era were conceptually incoherent.'[60]

Barth's doctrine of election

Barth's tendencies towards universalism were motivated neither by a Platonist myth of return (Origen's *apokatastasis* [restoration]) nor by liberal optimism, but by a doctrine of grace that I can only characterize once more as 'hyper-Calvinistic'. In traditional Reformed theology, there has been a running debate between 'supralapsarians' and 'infralapsarians'. The former have held that God's decree of election and reprobation was logically prior to his decree

---

59. See the interaction with Carl Henry on this point in my *Covenant and Eschatology: The Divine Drama* (Louisville: Westminster John Knox, 2002), pp. 189–191.

60. *The Uses of Scripture in Recent Theology* (Philadelphia: Fortress, 1975), p. 209.

to create and permit the fall, while the latter treat election and reprobation as logically dependent on the others.

What was at stake in this discussion was whether God's election was made with a view to humanity as created or humanity as fallen. If the former (the supralapsarian view), could election be seen as an act of divine grace: electing a redeemed people out of a race of fallen humanity? Furthermore, does not the supralapsarian position make Calvinism more vulnerable to the charge that God is the author of sin? In the infralapsarian view, there are clear differences between God's action in election and reprobation. Since the elect are chosen out of a race of condemned humanity, those who are lost are simply not included in God's election. They have only themselves to blame, whereas the elect have only God to thank. Supralapsarians, however, were concerned that if God's election took the fall into account, God's sovereignty in salvation and judgment would be compromised. The standard Reformed and Presbyterian confessions explicitly or implicitly endorsed infralapsarian, although supralapsarianism was never explicitly rejected as beyond the pale.

Although such distinctions seem at first blush to lend credibility to the caricatures of Protestant scholasticism, Barth saw the importance of the debate and sided resolutely with the supralapsarians. However, once again Barth radically revised the classical position by means of his dialectic method. First of all, he rejected any notion of a hidden divine will that did not correspond to God's action in Jesus Christ. Starting from the (dubious) premise that Christ's person and work reveal God's universal electing and saving will, he did away entirely with the Augustinian consensus that God had chosen some rather than all for salvation. Second, Barth made Christ rather than individuals the direct subject of election and reprobation. This move, I would argue, is the motivation for his recurring tendency to simply collapse anthropology into Christology. From all eternity, Christ is elected by the Father to be both the reprobate and the elect Son.

Combining these two moves, then, all of humanity is elect and reprobate in Christ. From the human perspective, determined by the conditions and possibilities of human existence, the race is reprobate, but from the divine perspective, determined by grace, all people are elect. Furthermore, this election is made without any reference to the fallen human condition.

> Now, this secret [of double predestination] concerns not this or that man, but all men. By it men are not divided, but united. In its presence they all stand on one line – for Jacob is always Esau also, and in the eternal 'Moment' of revelation Esau is also Jacob. When the Reformers applied the doctrine of election and rejection (Predestination) to the psychological unity of this or that individual, and when they

referred quantitatively to the 'elect' and the 'damned,' they were, as we can now see, speaking mythologically.[61]

After all, Barth continues, 'how indeed can the temporal, observable, psychologically visible individual be at all capable of eternal election or rejection?'

> The individual is not more than the stage upon which election and rejection take place in the freedom of men, that is to say, in the freedom of the individual who rests in God and is moved by Him – the stage can surely bear no further weight! We know already what this duality in God means. We know that it involves no equilibrium, but that it is the eternal victory of election over rejection, of love over hate, of life over death.[62]

Berkouwer justifiably concluded that 'Barth's revised supralapsarianism blocks the way to ascribing *decisive* significance to history.'[63] There is no historical transition from wrath to grace in Barth's theology.[64]

Barth's doctrine of election can be interpreted as a modern attempt at a satisfying theodicy, which has always been a lure of speculation. Despite his criticism of making God's Word captive to philosophy, Barth is a remarkably speculative theologian at many points. I realize that this seems counter-intuitive, especially with respect to a theologian who was so manifestly opposed to all human attempts to domesticate God's transcendence. Nevertheless, what other conclusion can there be when the New Testament texts confirm in even darker lines the prophetic anticipation of a final separation of humanity into 'saved' and 'damned'? Barth resolves this mystery of God's transcendent judgment by rendering God's ways opaque and satisfactory to human judgment.[65]

For all the talk of God's self-revelation in hiddenness, God's inner being really is univocally and exhaustively manifested in revelation. There can be no distinction between God's hidden and revealed will. '*This* No is really Yes. *This*

---

61. Barth, *Romans*, p. 347.

62. Ibid.

63. *Triumph of Grace*, p. 256. Van Til offered the same criticism throughout *Christianity and Barthianism*, but Berkouwer's analysis is more careful and compelling. According to E. Busch, *Karl Barth: His Life from Letters and Autobiographical Texts*, trans. J. Bowden (Philadelphia: Fortress, 1976), Barth said that Berkouwer's criticisms gave him 'a great deal to think about because of its acute analysis and the questions it raised' (p. 381).

64. Ibid., pp. 255–258.

65. *CD* II/1, pp. 319–320.

judgment is grace. *This* condemnation is forgiveness. *This* death is life. *This* hell is heaven. *This* fearful God is a loving father who takes the prodigal in his arms.'[66]

> There is no certainty of election today which may not become a sense of reprobation tomorrow, and, similarly, no sense of reprobation which may not become a certainty of election. The only eternal election is God's: the dispositions of history and of the individual mind are secondary and temporal.[67]

Here dialectic appears to surrender entirely to contradiction. Or rather, the Kierkegaardian dialectic (unresolved tension) surrenders to Hegelian dialectic (sublation of the 'lower' judgment into the 'higher' justification). Reprobation and election, of course, are a strict opposition or diastisis (a Kierkegaardian dialectic), while Adam and his race are assimilated to Christ in a higher synthesis (the Hegelian dialectic).

This novel doctrine of predestination not only affects Barth's treatment of election and salvation, but grounds much of his theology. Thus, Barth counsels, 'Our task is to interpret the Yes and the No and the No by the Yes without delaying more than a moment in either a fixed Yes or a fixed No.'[68] However, this dialectical rule does not work in reverse, since, as we have seen in his previous statement, No is Yes, judgment is grace. At the end of the day, Barth signalled the now widespread view that Scripture simply does not reveal the future destiny of those who have rejected Christ. Yet as Paul Louis Metzger points out, 'Bromiley replies that contrary to Barth's stance, most exegetes maintain that Scripture is anything but agnostic about the matter in question.'[69]

A sympathetic Roman Catholic interpreter, Hans Urs von Balthasar, confided, 'Barth's doctrine of election, this brilliant overthrow of Calvin, attracted me powerfully and lastingly; it converged with Origen's views and thus also with Adrienne's theology of Holy Saturday.'[70] While Barth's 'universalism' is very different from Origen's for a number of reasons, it is just as speculative and rationalistic. Since it cannot be justified on exegetical grounds, the only basis for Barth's defense of a dialectical doctrine of election is the constellation of presuppositions drawn from the philosophical-theological views I have

66. *Word of God*, p. 120.

67. Ibid., p. 59.

68. Ibid., p. 207.

69. *Word of Christ*, p. 97, referring to G. W. Bromiley, *Introduction to the Theology of Karl Barth* (Edinburgh: T. & T. Clark; Grand Rapids: Eerdmans, 1979), p. 248.

70. *Unser Auftrag*, p. 85, cited by E. T. Oakes, *Pattern of Redemption: The Theology of Hans Urs von Balthasar* (New York: Continuum, 1997), p. 306, n. 10.

described. It is the result of his movement from a Kierkegaardian diastisis to a Hegelian synthesis. My purpose here is not to offer an exegetical rebuttal, but to point up the fundamental differences between Barth's doctrine of election and that of Augustinian and evangelical theology, and especially to point out how his conclusions arise from the ontological presuppositions I have surveyed.

Grounded in his doctrine of election, reconciliation is simply the outworking of this eternal decree. Eschatology and history need each other, but this is another place where the dialectic surrenders to a synthesis, assimilating the latter to the former. Revelation *is* reconciliation. Furthermore, 'Adam' and 'Christ' do not really refer to two individuals, each representing two different groups of humanity and in neither case is there a historical unfolding of God's eschatological purposes. 'Adam' represents a movement from an original relation of divine grace and human obedience to rebellion, whereas Jesus Christ brings about, as McCormack describes, 'a return to the "Origin" (reconciliation). These two movements are not to be conceived of as sequential, but rather as parallel and simultaneous.'[71] At least to that extent, Barth's doctrine of election may be more like Origen's doctrine of restoration than I suggested above.

Basically, there are two moves here – both of them mistaken in my view. The first is to assimilate the linear-historical development of God's covenantal relationship with humanity to eschatology. The second is to assimilate history to a certain type of eschatology that, precisely because it is divorced from history, misses the dynamic future-orientation of the Adamic trial. Adam was not simply created in order to remain obedient, but with a task to complete, a commission to bring the whole earth under the lordship of the triune God. At the end of that road was the *consummation* – following the Creator-God from the 'six days' labour to the 'seventh day' of everlasting rest. When this scheme is forgotten (as it always is whenever eternity swallows time), the goal of redemption becomes essentially a return to the place of origin rather than a crossing beyond anything humanity has known in Adamic history. 'Paradise Regained' is different from the consummation, which can only be characterized as 'Paradise Transcended'. In other words, his eschatology is not eschatological *enough*.

So, on one hand, Barth's eschatology swallows history, yet for that very reason tends to be far less eschatological than the New Testament suggests. As Geerhardus Vos argued, biblical eschatology connects the vertical vector of eternity to the linear vector of time like a triangle. However, in Barth's case (as in countless other theologies), the latter is simply absorbed by the former (in Barth's more Hegelian moments) or set in opposition (in his more Kierkegaardian moments).

---

71. *Critically Realistic*, p. 147.

Ecclesiology

The Kierkegaardian diastasis is especially evident in Barth's ecclesiology, most notably, his treatment of the sacraments. He says some marvellous things about the church not being an extension of Christ's person and work, a caution that contemporary theologies desperately need to hear. Nevertheless, once again, whatever God does is an event, not a thing extended in time. Therefore, the empirical church is, for Barth, not only different from Christ and the gospel, but will be finally absent in the consummation. The 'kingdom of God' (apocalyptic and eschatological) is not only distinguished but is set over against the visible church (historical and transient). The church's activity 'is related to the Gospel only in so far as it is no more than a crater formed by the explosion of a shell and seeks to be no more than a void in which the Gospel reveals itself'.[72] The church's words and actions 'by their negation are sign-posts to the Holy One', never sacred themselves.[73]

In fact, Barth refers to the Church of Esau and the Church of Jacob – not as two discrete entities, but as observable and hidden, respectively. Once again, where the Reformers insisted that the church was partly hidden and partly visible in this age, Barth identifies the visible church with the Church of Esau 'where no miracle occurs, and where, consequently, men are exposed as liars, precisely when they hear and speak about God'.[74]

God's work and the church's work stand in a fundamental and unresolved opposition (Kierkegaard's dialectic). Even less than the Bible and preaching can human actions of baptizing and administering bread and wine be identified with God's work. They can only be acts of human witness, obedience and testimony to that which God has done apart from these instruments. Explicitly adopting Zwingli's approach over Calvin's and the Reformed tradition generally, Barth actually goes beyond the Zurich Reformer, denying that sacraments are 'means of grace'. Once again, all of this revision is related to an inadequate ontology that does not allow for a real union of the Creator and the creature, eternity and time, spirit and flesh. The sacraments are the purely human work of liturgical obedience.[75] Thus, baptism and the Supper cannot be conceived as sacraments or means of grace in any sense, Barth insists. In fact, there is the sharpest contrast between Christ: 'He is He, and His work is

---

72. *Romans*, p. 36.

73. Ibid.

74. Ibid., p. 341.

75. *CD* IV/4; cf. *CD* IV/3.2, pp. 756, 783, 790, 843–901.

76. *CD* IV/4, p. 88 (emphasis added).

His work, *standing over against all Christian action*, including Christian faith and Christian baptism.'[76] Accordingly, baptism is in danger of being reduced to a purely human work alongside other pious actions of believers.

After challenging the confessional Reformed interpretation along with Lutheran and Roman Catholic views, Barth argues that these actions of the church are not 'mysteries' or 'means of grace'. 'This consensus needs to be demythologised. We oppose it.'[77] He recognizes that Zwingli's separation of the sign from the thing signified was rejected by all of the Reformed confessions, even by the one drafted by his successor, Heinrich Bullinger: 'a backward step . . . in the direction of Calvin's sacramentalism'.[78] Barth accepts the designation 'Neo-Zwinglian' for his approach, although he denies that Zwingli is its source and suggests that the Zurich Reformer did not go far enough, since he still held to infant baptism.[79]

At the heart of his difficulties is the notion of a sacramental union – in other words, that creaturely actions can be means through which God communicates saving benefits. Obviously, such metaphysical presuppositions make it difficult from the outset to affirm a robust notion of mediation that Barth would not regard as surrendering finally to neo-Protestantism's identification of God and the world. Actualism looks a lot like occasionalism when revelation is treated merely as an event – and one in which all creaturely possibilities are suspended, set aside or overcome.[80]

For neither Zwingli's nor Barth's preaching was regarded as incapable of mediating grace. George Hunsinger attributes much of this difference not to Zwingli but to Barth's own dialectical Christology: 'Karl Barth is probably the first theologian in the history of Christian doctrine who alternates back and forth, deliberately, between an "Alexandrian" and an "Antiochian" idiom.'[81] At the same time, Hunsinger presses Barth on his reticence to identify the sacraments as a means of grace by appealing to his own doctrine of the Word of God:

> Barth famously rejected applying the term 'sacrament' to baptism and the Eucharist on the grounds that Jesus Christ himself is the only true sacrament. (He preferred to see them as 'means of gratitude' rather than as 'means of grace'). Yet Barth's logic

---

77. Ibid., p. 105; cf. p. 102.
78. Ibid., p. 130.
79. Ibid., pp. 129–130.
80. See D. Allen, 'A Tale of Two Roads: Homiletics and Biblical Authority', *JETS* 43.3 (Sept. 2000), esp. p. 492; cf. *CD* 1/1, p. 127.
81. *Disruptive Grace*, p. 135.

here seems strangely inconsistent with other positions that he takes. For although Jesus Christ is also the one Word of God, that does not prevent Barth from presenting Holy Scripture and biblical preaching as secondary forms of God's Word . . . I can see no reason why he could not have coordinated baptism and the Lord's Supper with preaching, and the idea of the church as sacrament with Scripture as the written Word. Jesus Christ would have remained the one true sacrament in the strict and proper sense even as he remained the one true Word of God.[82]

Whatever is said about the relation of the Word and words can be applied to the sacramental relation in baptism and the Supper as well.

Again, Barth's ontological assumptions are in play. The God–world relation is conceived as diastasis – a distinction that is always on the verge of breaking the sign–signified connection in a nominalist direction. This is a primary reason why the Word of God written and proclaimed cannot be identified directly with revelation and why the church and sacraments can only be witnesses to rather than also bearers of the realities of the age to come. The analogical link expressed when Reformed theology affirms with other traditions the 'sacramental union' between sign and signified is what is at stake here. As Calvin frequently pointed out, we hear *God* speaking whenever *Scripture* is read or proclaimed and we see *God's* pledge ratified towards us and our children through the *words and actions of the minister* in baptism, and towards us in the Supper. Such human offices are not mere occasions for the Spirit's sovereign work, but the means through which the Spirit ordinarily accomplishes that work.

Related to Barth's emphasis on God's radical freedom and transcendence is his somewhat peculiar formulation of the anhypostatic–enhypostatic Christology he attributes to his reading of the Reformed scholastics.[83] More a 'Word–flesh' (Alexandrian) than 'Word–man' (Antiochene) Christology (to borrow J. N. D. Kelly's categories), Barth's formulation is formally orthodox,

---

82. Ibid., pp. 275–276.

83. See F. LeRon Shults, 'A Dubious Christological Formula: From Leontius of Byzantium to Karl Barth', *TS* 57 (Sept. 1996), pp. 431–446; U. M. Lang, '*Anhypostasos-Enhypostasos*', *JTS* 49.2 (Oct. 1998), p. 630. Shults points out that the formula arises with Barth, not with patristic or Protestant scholastic sources. The Reformed scholastics certainly did affirm the traditional consensus, hardly peculiar to them, that Christ's humanity existed only as it was assumed by the Logos. However, they did not appeal to it as part of a veiling–unveiling dialectic and were suspicious, as Calvin was, of Apollinarian tendencies to undervalue the role of the humanity in securing redemption.

but, like Athanasius, he easily drifts in an Apollinarian direction.[84] This is because of his particular construction of the veiling–unveiling dialectic, according to which the subject is God and the veil is Jesus. As in the Alexandrian school, there seems to be a docetizing tendency, which, when taken to its ultimate extreme (monophysitism), absorbs the human into the divine (since the human qua human is incapable of directly revealing the Infinite, not just comprehending the Infinite). 'Because He is the Son of God, it is only as such that He is real man,' says Barth.[85] But can his unique humanity – not only human nature as such, but the life and ministry of this particular person – be so slighted? Is this not to assimilate the humanity to the deity?

Again, the critical question is whether an event of revelation and redemption can be fully attributed *to God* yet *through creaturely mediation*. At the same time, as Metzger points out, drawing on Bruce McCormack, Barth goes further in an Antiochene direction than the Reformed when he argues that 'the divine Word wills moment by moment to take the human nature to himself in his incarnation'.[86] Here an extreme voluntarism meets an equally radical actualism that, it may be said, is overly suspicious of the identification of the divine and human even when the relation is established from above.

Moving beyond Barth through Barth

If we have trouble with Barth – and I think we still should – it is not because of the *voice*; it must be something else. The *voice* is that of the

---

84. I have been chastened in my criticism of Barth's Christology by George Hunsinger's superb analysis of his dialectical treatment in *Disruptive Grace*. Since we cannot speak simultaneously of Christ's deity and humanity, it is easy to sound quasi-docetic at one point and quasi-Arian at another (along with Alexandrian and Antiochene extremes). Only when taken as a whole, especially with Barth's strong affirmations of Chalcedonian maxims, can we keep from one-sided interpretations of Barth drawn from isolated passages. While chastened, I remain convinced that the drift of Barth's Christology so emphasizes the deity of Christ that the salvific significance of his humanity is not given sufficient scope. For more on this, see my *Lord and Servant: A Covenant Christology* (Louisville: Westminster John Knox, 2005), ch. 6.

85. *CD* III/2, p. 70.

86. *Word of Christ*, p. 50, drawing on McCormack, *Critically Realistic*, p. 365.

prophets and apostles, the martyrs and Reformers. While much of American evangelicalism is intoxicated with human beings and a theology of glory, this voice was that of a witness pointing away not only from himself but from human possibilities – even the church – to the God who reveals and saves. For all of his acknowledged echoes of nineteenth-century neo-Protestantism, the rediscovery of God and God's grace was nothing short of epochal.

In my view, contrasts between liberal and conservative, modern and post-modern, even 'Barthian' and 'orthodox' never get us very far. While these impressive labels with their equally impressive histories and serious impact still bear some validity, I am more interested in being a Christian in a manner consistent with the ecumenical creeds and Reformed confessions. We have all known a lot of conservative preaching that seems to have missed the point: namely, Christ placarded before starving souls in his saving office, and a flattering of humanity in its presumed autonomy rather than giving God all of the glory. Barth actually did pretty well at countering the ever-attractive heresy of Pelagianism. To the extent that Barth proclaimed that message, he should be appreciated and honoured; to the extent that he departed from it or insufficiently abandoned modern presuppositions, he should be both heard and critiqued.

The question, of course, is from what standpoint such criticism can be justified. While Scripture alone possesses the intrinsic authority that renders it absolutely normative, the ecumenical creeds and Reformed confessions provide the abiding definition of what it means to confess the Christian faith in a Reformed manner. Even in more conservative circles, the label 'Reformed' has become elastic. It has increasingly come to be defined no longer by the specific content that its adherents confess, but by certain doctrines or emphases that individuals or coalitions find congenial. The question is not whether Barth was Reformed by self-identification or church membership, but whether his dogmatics can be adequately described as such. It is not arrogant to define Reformed faith and practice by its own confession; what is arrogant is allowing any one of us to raise ourselves above the community and define it according to our own lights. It is a church, with its public and corporate confession of the Christian faith, not a school, with its attachment to major figures and their body of work, that should define our consensus.

When it comes to the question of what can be considered authentically 'evangelical', the issue is far more complicated. Doubtless, Barth's own definition would be more restrictive than many that have been proposed in recent years. Stanley Grenz, for example, has argued that evangelical identity is defined by piety rather than by creeds and confessions.[87] In fact, his description of the role of Scripture and doctrine in Christian faith and practice is, to my mind at least, indistinguishable from what George Lindbeck identifies as the 'experiential-expressivist' perspective. As I have argued elsewhere, I think that it is difficult to challenge this sort of definition, given the historical fact that evangelicalism is composed of a variety of tributaries.[88]

Although the Reformation stream has carved deep canyons, Anglo-American evangelicalism is shaped at least as much (perhaps more) by the currents of pietism as by post-Reformation orthodoxy, and revivalism has to a large extent eroded much of the Reformers' legacy. In comparison to Charles Finney's legacy, Barth's is positively healthy. 'There must be some meaning in the fact that the same front which Zwingli and Calvin presented to Catholicism was defended by the fathers of Dort against the Arminians one hundred years later,' Barth wrote. 'But where today will not the careful observer find Arminian teachings taken for granted?' Yet if one finds affinity with such presuppositions, one must ask 'by what right and to what end we wish to take sides as Reformed churchmen against the Pope'.[89] Furthermore, he and his heirs can be regarded as allies in the struggle to define the church and its mission in relation to the gospel rather than worldly fads. In view of what passes for 'evangelical' today, perhaps the real question is not whether Barth is worthy of being included but whether he would want to be included in such a movement.

Since there is no official consensus of evangelical teaching, I cannot appeal to anything more decisive than an impression gained by some representative statements of evangelical organizations and committees that suggest an attempt among some leaders at least to define the movement by a commitment to historic Christianity, a high view of Christ and Scripture, salvation by grace alone, the necessity of the new birth, and the bodily return of Christ.

On all of these points, surely Barth scores high marks – again, higher than some evangelical thinkers, pastors and movements claiming our attention today. In recent years, evangelicals have increasingly moved, at least in practice, away from the authority of Scripture in favour of what Barth would have called a 'natural theology', where the human sciences, marketing philosophies,

---

87. *Revisioning Evangelical Theology: A Fresh Agenda for the 21st Century* (Downers Grove: IVP, 1993). Clark Pinnock, Roger Olson and John Franke, to name just a few, have pursued similar trajectories.

88. M. S. Horton, 'Is Evangelicalism Reformed?', *Christian Scholar's Review* 31.2 (winter 2001), with a response by Roger Olson, pp. 131–168.

89. *Word of God*, p. 253.

political ideologies and cultural myths are often treated as revelations alongside Jesus Christ as God's living Word. Where Barth excoriated Paul Tillich's
method of correlation, 'post-conservative' evangelicals treat culture as a
source of theology.[90] John Franke, for example, appeals to Barth as a chief
model for the future of Reformed theology, yet seems at least as intrigued by
Tillich.[91] That which is central in Barth's dogmatics – namely, the sheer objectivity of Christ's completed work – is pushed into the background in Franke's
account of the relation between the gospel and culture. The task of theology
is not so much to hear again the gospel as a disruptive speech that comes to
the ungodly in every age from 'outside us' (*extra nos*), but is to facilitate a conversation between gospel and culture that is 'incarnational'. As Laura Smit
reminds us concerning Calvin's view, 'all of our knowledge of God is mediated, [but] he believes that it is mediated, not by our cultural context, but *to* our
context by God himself'.[92]

While Franke offers some sound criticisms of correlationism (*à la* Tillich,
Kaufman and Tracy) and 'translation' (as in evangelical missiologies of con-
textualization), 'taken together they point the way forward'.[93] He adds:

> Neither gospel nor culture can function as the primary entity in the conversation
> between the two in light of their interpretive and constructed nature; we must
> recognize that theology emerges through an ongoing conversation involving both
> gospel and culture.[94]

It was just such statements at which Barth shuddered in horror.

Barth signals the non-foundationalist agenda and is therefore the obvious

---

90. E.g. Stanley Grenz suggests in *Revisioning Evangelical Theology*, 'The appeal to Bible
    and culture in the completion of the theological task is, of course, not unique to
    evangelical methodology. In fact, perhaps the most erudite twentieth-century
    articulation of this approach is the well-known method of correlation proposed by
    Paul Tillich.' He adds the growing popularity of the 'Wesleyan quadrilateral', with
    its four sources (*Scripture, reason, experience* and *tradition*), as evidence of the triumph
    of spirituality over theology (especially as the latter is defined by the Princeton
    theology) (pp. 90–91).
91. *The Character of Theology* (Grand Rapids: Baker Academic, 2005), p. 103.
92. 'The Depth Behind Things', in J. K. A. Smith (ed.), *Radical Orthodoxy and the
    Reformed Tradition* (Grand Rapids: Baker Academic, 2005), p. 209.
93. *Character of Theology*, p. 103.
94. Ibid.

candidate as a resource against modernity. Nevertheless, unlike the essay, to which I refer below, by an explicit Barthian (George Hunsinger), Franke has not a single reference to Kuyper or Bavinck in this entire volume of theological method. The same is true of the earlier book co-authored with Stanley Grenz, *Beyond Foundationalism*.[95] Why do Barthians like George Hunsinger and John Webster seem more appreciative of the resources of Reformed orthodoxy for giving a confident witness to Christ in a postmodern context?

As Barth began to prepare his Göttingen lectures, he expressed wonder at how his training could have skipped over the rich heritage of Protestant orthodoxy. Neo-Protestantism (i.e. liberalism) sought to 'push through' this period in ever-new proposals that were really little more than 'a new mixture of Enlightenment and Pietism'. However, Barth realized:

> Success can come only if we have previously learned to read the Reformers as the Church's teachers and, with them, Scripture as the document for the Church's existence and nature, and therefrom to ask what Church science might be. That precisely may be learned, nay must be, from the early Orthodox men.[96]

He cautioned his students:

> Even though you may later decide to go along with the great Schleiermachian revolution which characterizes almost all modern dogmatics, my urgent recommendation is that you should know what you are doing when you take this course, having first learned and considered the unreconstructed dogmatics of the older writers.[97]

By his own recollection, exposure to the Reformed scholastics gave Barth resources for reconceiving theology in a manner that transcended 'the clear nonsense: Schleiermacher and everything that creeps and flies after him'.[98] He lamented, 'The fact that an introduction to dogmatics is generally regarded as necessary, at times in the form of a so-called philosophy of religion, is a symptom that we do not live in a classical age of theology.'[99]

---

95. Louisville: Westminster John Knox, 2001.
96. Foreword to Heinrich Heppe's *Reformed Dogmatics: Set out and Illustrated from the Sources*, ed. and trans. G. T. Thomson, rev. E. Bizer (London: George Allen & Unwin, 1950), pp. vi–vii.
97. *GD*, p. 21.
98. Letter to Brunner, 26 January 1924, cited by McCormack, *Critically Realistic*, p. 332.
99. *GD*, p. 18.

In my estimation, *God, Revelation and Authority*, Carl F. H. Henry's *magnum opus*,[100] while in some ways offering a closer reading of Barth's total corpus on areas related to biblical authority, offered an alternative model that is also unsatisfying at least to those of us who hold to the traditional Protestant distinction between archetypal and ectypal knowledge and refuse to reduce the concept of truth to propositional statements without remainder. At present, evangelical theology seems to be forced to choose between Carl Henry and Karl Barth, and a growing number of younger evangelical theologians and pastors are attracted to the latter, as 'post-liberal' mainliners and 'post-conservative evangelicals' meet in the middle. What is missing, in my estimation, is any critical engagement with the classic Reformed tradition even among evangelicals (conservative or progressive) who would identify themselves as Reformed. A notable exception comes from the Barthian side in a chapter by George Hunsinger titled, 'What Can Evangelicals and Postliberals Learn from Each Other?'[101]

Although Henry's constructions are too indebted to modernity, Hunsinger points out, 'other and very different formulations of Henry's concerns have standing within the evangelical community, formulations that uphold a strong doctrine of "inerrancy" without Henry's modernist excesses'. He adds:

> In particular I will suggest that the views of Abraham Kuyper and Herman Bavinck offer a greater possibility for fruitful evangelical dialogue with postliberalism than the

---

100. Paternoster: Carlisle, 1999 (6 vols.).

101. *Disruptive Grace*, pp. 338–360; previously published in T. R. Phillips and D. L. Ockholm (eds.), *The Nature of Confession* (Downers Grove: IVP, 1996), pp. 134–150. In another chapter in *Disruptive Grace*, Hunsinger cites Barth to this effect: '"Through God's revelation" we become "participants" in this occurrence (II/1, p. 49), receiving and having a part in God's eternal self-knowledge (II/1, p. 68). For as "God gives himself to us to be known in the truth of his self-knowledge" (II/1, p. 53), we receive a share in the truth of his knowledge of himself' (II/1, p. 51).' It is, however, 'indirect', since it is mediated through Christ (*Disruptive Grace*, pp. 170–171). Even granting Barth's veiling–unveiling dialectic, such quotes would seem to suggest a univocal view, although Hunsinger claims that Barth is more nearly identified with an analogical perspective. I would argue that even in our union with Christ, we do not share in God's self-knowledge. It is not simply the means (direct/indirect), but the content, that is in view in these distinctions. This is not to deny that what Christ mediates is real knowledge, but that it is and always remains analogical and ectypal.

tendency represented by Carl Henry. (And in order not to make things too easy for myself, I will follow not the interpretation of Kuyper and Bavinck advanced by Jack Rogers and Donald McKim, but instead that of Richard B. Gaffin, Jr., of Westminster Theological Seminary, who subjects the Rogers-McKim interpretation to a full-fledged revision and critique.)[102]

Hunsinger grants that 'in general the account of scriptural unity, authority, and inspiration among many postliberals is, to say the least, fairly thin and unsatisfying so far'.[103] While Henry was motivated by a univocal view of truth reduced to propositional assertions 'that can be known in a value-neutral way apart from any self-involving perspective or propositions', there is, Hunsinger points out, another evangelical tradition with roots in Reformed orthodoxy.[104]

This first area of proximity to post-liberalism is Kuyper's view that 'the unity of Scripture is the presupposition of a faithful reading of Scripture, not a logical inference independent of faith'.[105] Second, the unity of Scripture for Kuyper and Bavinck is viewed not as a 'rational unity', as in Henry, but as a Christocentric unity.[106] Thus, with Henry's approach, the propositional content is divorced from the personal encounter with Christ, whereas the two are held together in Kuyper and Bavinck.[107] Third, in terms of factuality, there is interesting convergence:

> For both theologians, according to Richard Gaffin, 'the biblical records are impressionistic; that is, they are not marked by notarial precision or blue-print, architectural exactness.' They do not intend to convey 'historical, chronological, geographical data . . . in themselves'; rather, what they intend to attest is 'the truth poured out on us in Christ.'[108]

Fourth, while they held to inerrancy even on historical details, 'They both felt, writes Gaffin, that "pushing infallibility into the limelight is intellectualism" of the kind "that began with the rationalists".'[109]

---

102. Ibid., p. 340.
103. Ibid., pp. 340–341.
104. Ibid.
105. Ibid., p. 355.
106. Ibid.
107. Ibid., p. 356.
108. Ibid.
109. Ibid., pp. 356–357.

According to Calvin, we discern in Scripture a pattern – he refers to the 'screen image of those features most useful for the understanding of Christ'.[110]

> What I wish to suggest, therefore, about what evangelicals might learn from postliberals is simply this. Although on these matters they may not wish to go as far as theologians like Frei and Lindbeck, they should at least be prepared to go as far as theologians like Calvin, Kuyper, and Bavinck. Freed from the encumbrances of excessive modernity, the real conversation could then begin.[111]

Hunsinger judges that finally Yale post-liberalism's 'cultural-linguistic pragmatism', attractive to many post-conservative evangelicals, 'is not so much "postliberal" as "neoliberal," since pragmatism has always been a routine liberal option'.[112] Here we encounter a Barthian encouraging evangelicals to look more to Calvin, Bavinck and Westminster than to Frei and Lindbeck. An evangelicalism that is faithful to the Reformation *solae*, centring on Christ's saving work *extra nos*, can provide a rich source for renewing the church.[113] When it comes to Kuyper and Bavinck as well as the Yale post-liberals, 'The rejection of univocity separates them from someone like Henry, just as the affirmation of adequate and reliable reference separates them from modern skeptics.'[114]

Conclusion

Witness, testimony and martyrdom are not generated by a method of correlation. Theology as the product of a Spirit-led conversation between Scripture and culture, with both as media of evangelical revelation, has been tried and tried again. Schleiermacher, Ritschl, Harnack and Herrmann are some of the greatest examples of what can be done in this ambit. No-one will persecute a church for witnessing to its own self-understanding, its own religious consciousness or its own communal language and practices. The world will have no trouble allowing that various communities find meaning, identity, hope, inspiration and therapeutic well-being in different forms of life. Christians

---

110. Ibid.
111. Ibid., pp. 357–358.
112. *Disruptive Grace*, p. 11.
113. Ibid., pp. 358–359.
114. Ibid., p. 360.

have always encountered difficulty not when they are trying to show the relevance and situatedness of their claims within their time and place, but when they make public, universal claims about the nature of reality itself. This encounter has always produced a clash as much as a conversation.

Whatever its deficiencies with respect to its own doctrine of Scripture, Barth's project at least represents a Copernican revolution in the history of modern theology on just this very point: opposing the anthropocentrism of neo-Protestantism with a thoroughgoing theocentrism that threw the light once again on divine initiative. God not only determines the answers, but the questions. We have every reason to challenge Barth's doctrine of the Word of God, but when it comes to the source of theology, we are at one: Scripture, and not the church or the culture, is the *norma normans non normata* (the norm that norms, but is not itelf normed).

Drawing on the heritage of pietism, Stanley Grenz and others who defend a post-conservative evangelicalism often exhibit a more Schleiermachian than Barthian view of Scripture and doctrine. Where Barth spoke forthrightly about sin and grace, evangelical theology and preaching now tends to speak in terms of dysfunction and recovery, extending Christ's mission by 'incarnating' his love and transforming life. Barth was convinced that human beings could not contribute to their own redemption and that nothing short of a sovereign act of divine mercy was required. By contrast, evangelicalism is increasingly swamped by a practical Pelagianism that justifies Bonhoeffer's appraisal that American Christianity is 'Protestantism without the Reformation'. Today, a growing number of evangelical theologians share the older liberalism's discomfort with the doctrine of Christ's substitutionary atonement, while George Hunsinger, Donald Bloesch, William Placher, George Lindbeck and other students and admirers of Barth defend it.

Some evangelicals today display a greater openness to other religions as sources of redemptive revelation, viewing the gospel in terms of following Christ's example (which of course has its parallels in other religions and religious figures or moral distinction). Whatever we may make of Barth's 'optimistic' tendencies towards universalism, they are grounded in his view of divine election and grace, with Christ alone as the basis. In other words, the monergism of Reformation Christianity has Barth for its courageous defender, in contrast to the synergistic soteriologies that have always flourished in American evangelicalism. In the land of 'Protestantism without the Reformation', Barth is a refreshing voice indeed. I join the gallery of admirers especially when the alternatives are liberalism or fundamentalism, both movements having more in common with each other (namely, the pietistic heritage) than either has with Reformation Christianity. Confessional

Reformed Christians can learn a lot from Barth and his heirs. However, I remain convinced that *where these roads diverge*, the latter represents a declension rather than a renewal of the great Reformation legacy. Barth remains an important figure to be reckoned with, neither to be lightly dismissed nor to be uncritically embraced. For good and for ill, his voice is still very much with us.

SELECT BIBLIOGRAPHY OF KARL BARTH'S WORKS

BARTH, K., 'The Authority and Significance of the Bible: Twelve Theses' (1947), in idem, *God Here and Now*, trans. P. M. van Buren (London: Routledge, 1964), pp. 55–74.

—, 'Biblical Questions, Insights, and Vistas' (1920), in idem, *The Word of God and the Word of Man*, trans. D. Horton (New York: Harpers, 1957), pp. 51–96.

—, *Christ and Adam: Man and Humanity in Romans 5*, trans. T. A. Smail (New York: Collier; Edinburgh: Oliver & Boyd, 1965).

—, 'The Christian Understanding of Revelation' (1948), in idem, *Against the Stream: Shorter Post-War Writings 1946–52*, trans. S. Godman, ed. R. G. Smith (London: SCM, 1954), pp. 203–240.

—, *Christliche Dogmatik im Entwurf* (Munich: C. Kaiser, 1927).

—, *Das christlichen Leben. Die kirchliche Dogmatik IV.4: Fragmente aus dem Nachlass Vorlesungen 1959–1961*, ed. H.-A. Drewes and E. Jüngel (Zurich: Theologischer Verlag, 1976).

—, 'Church and Theology' (1925), in idem, *Theology and Church: Shorter Writings 1920–1928*, trans. L. Pettibone Smith (London: SCM, 1962), pp. 286–306.

—, *Church Dogmatics*, ed. G. W. Bromiley and T. F. Torrance (Edinburgh: T. & T. Clark, 1956–75).

—, *Credo*, trans. P. Jundt and J. Jundt (Paris: Je Sers, 1936).

—, 'The Doctrinal Task of the Reformed Churches' (1923), in idem, *The Word of God and the Word of Man*, trans. D. Horton (New York: Harpers, 1957), pp. 218–271.

—, *Dogmatics in Outline*, trans. G. T. Thomson (London: SCM, 1949).

—, *Einführung in die evangelische Theologie*, 3rd ed. (Zurich: Theologischer Verlag, 1985).

—, *The Epistle to the Romans*, trans. E. C. Hoskyns (London: Oxford University Press, 1933).

—, *Evangelical Theology: An Introduction*, trans. G. Foley (Edinburgh: T. & T. Clark, 1963).

—, 'Foreword', in H. Heppe, *Reformed Dogmatics: Set out and Illustrated from the Sources*, trans. G. T. Thomson, ed. E. Bizer (London: George Allen & Unwin, 1950), pp. vi–vii.

—, 'Foreword to the English Edition', in O. Weber, *Karl Barth's Church Dogmatics: An Introductory Report on Volumes I:1 to III:4*, trans. A. C. Cochrane (London: Lutterworth, 1953).

—, *God, Grace and Gospel*, trans. J. S. McNab (Edinburgh: Oliver & Boyd, 1959).

—, *The Göttingen Dogmatics: Instruction in the Christian Religion*, vol. 1, trans. G. W. Bromiley, ed. H. Reiffen (Grand Rapids: Eerdmans, 1991).

—, *The Humanity of God*, trans. T. Wieser and J. N. Thomas (Richmond, Va.: John Knox, 1960).

—, *Die kirchliche Dogmatik* (Munich: C. Kaiser, 1932; Zurich: Evangelischer Verlag, 1938–67).

—, *The Knowledge of God and the Service of God according to the Teaching of the Reformation*, trans. J. L. M. Haire and I. Henderson (London: Hodder & Stoughton, 1938).

—, *Letters: 1961–1968*, trans. G. W. Bromiley (Grand Rapids: Eerdmans, 1981).

—, '*Parergon*: Karl Barth über sich selbst', *EvT* 8 (Dec. 1948), pp. 268–282.

—, 'The Principles of Dogmatics according to Wilhelm Herrmann' (1925), in idem, *Theology and Church: Shorter Writings 1920–1928*, trans. L. Pettibone Smith (London: SCM, 1962), pp. 238–271.

—, *Protestant Theology in the Nineteenth Century: Its Background and History*, trans. B. Cozens and J. Bowden, new ed. (London: SCM, 2001).

—, 'Revelation' (1934), in idem, *God in Action: Theological Addresses*, trans. E. G. Homrighausen and K. J. Ernst (Edinburgh: T. & T. Clark, 1937), pp. 3–19.

—, 'The Strange New World within the Bible' (1916), in idem, *The Word of God and the Word of Man*, trans. D. Horton (New York: Harpers, 1957), pp. 28–50.

—, 'A Thank-You and a Bow – Kiekegaard's Reveille: Speech on Being Awarded the Sonning Prize (1963)', in M. Rumscheidt (ed.), *Fragments Grave and Gray*, trans. E. Mosbacher (London: Collins, 1971), pp. 95–101.

—, *Die Theologie Zwinglis, 1922/1923: Vorlesung, Göttingen, Wintersemester 1922/1923*, ed. M. Freudenberg (Zurich: Theologischer Verlag, 2004).

—, *The Theology of John Calvin*, trans. G. W. Bromiley (Grand Rapids: Eerdmans, 1995).

—, *The Theology of Schleiermacher: Lectures at Göttingen, Winter Semester of 1923/24*, trans. G. W. Bromiley, ed. D. Ritschl (Grand Rapids: Eerdmans, 1982).

—, *The Theology of the Reformed Confessions, 1923*, Columbia Series in Reformed Theology, trans. D. L. Guder and J. J. Guder (Louisville: Westminster John Knox, 2002).

—, *Unterricht in der christlichen Religion*, vol. 1: *Prolegomena, 1924*, ed. H. Reiffen (Zurich: Theologischer Verlag, 1985).

—, *Unterricht in der christlichen Religion*, vol. 2: *Die Lehre von Gott / Die Lehre vom Menschen, 1924/25*, ed. H. Stoevesandt (Zurich: Theologischer Verlag, 1990).

—, *The Word of God and the Word of Man*, trans. D. Horton (New York: Harpers, 1957).

—, *Das Wort Gottes und die Theologie* (Munich: C. Kaiser, 1925).

BARTH, K., and THURNEYSEN, E., *Karl Barth–Eduard Thurneysen Briefwechsel*, vol. 2: *1921–1930* (Zurich: Theologischer Verlag, 1974).

—, *Revolutionary Theology in the Making: Barth–Thurneysen Correspondence, 1914–25*, trans. J. D. Smart (London: Epworth, 1964).

INDEX OF NAMES

INDEX OF SUBJECTS

INDEX OF BIBLICAL REFERENCES

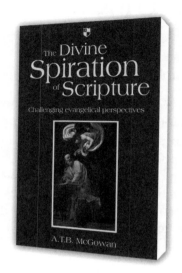

Panentheism

John W. Cooper

Panentheism (literally, 'all is in God') has experienced a renaissance, especially among contemporary thinkers who study the intersection of science and religion. This ground-breaking book surveys its development and proliferation, and offers a defence of classical theism.

Along the way, Cooper examines the panentheism of contemporary thinkers such as Jürgen Moltmann, Wolfhart Pannenberg, Philip Clayton and John Polkinghorne. Furthermore, he discusses how panentheism has influenced liberation, feminist and ecological theologies. The discussion also examines the so-called open view of God to consider whether this view is panentheistic.

Cooper's aim throughout is to provide a fair, 'accurate, and empathetic overview of panentheism that is helpful for all readers, including panentheists'.

'This is a groundbreaking attempt to demonstrate the philosophical background of much modern Christian theology, to identify its "natural religion". Written with the utmost clarity and with quiet passion, it greatly helps to sharpen the differences between classical Christian theism and other views. Though dissenting from panentheism and from the theologies it fosters, John Cooper nevertheless writes with courtesy and good sense, letting the record speak for itself. The book is a model of lucidity and fair-mindedness.'

Paul Helm

Paperback 368 pages
ISBN: 978-1-84474-174-8

Available from your local Christian bookshop
or via our website at **www.ivpbooks.com**